Loving God

❦

WORSHIP AS A LIFESTYLE SERIES - VOLUME 1

APOSTLE LINDA MAHONEY

First Edition
Copyright 2016, Linda Mahoney
Connect u 2 Christ Ministries
PO Box 513, Kingston Springs, TN 37082
(615) 952-4162
WWW.CONNECT2CHRIST.COM

All rights reserved.
This book is protected under the copyright laws of the United States of America. No portion of it may be reprinted or copied, in part or in whole, without written consent of the publisher.

ISBN-13: 978-0-9791327-4-2
ISBN-10: 0-9791327-4-6

☙ All Scripture references
are from the King James Version of the Bible
☙ All Hebrew and Greek reference numbers and definitions
are from the Strong's Concordance.
☙ Excerpts of English definitions
are from the resources of Dictionary.com
☙ The names of satan and lucifer are not capitalized; he is not worthy of any respect, so I refuse to give it to him.

Dedication

First of all, I dedicate this book to my LORD and King, Jesus Christ, whom I have purposed to love and serve with all my heart, soul, mind and strength. It's by His gentle and persistent leading that He guides me, step by step, into my God ordained destiny. His tender loving kindness, mercy and grace make it possible for me to become the person He has called me to be. We're enjoying this journey of life together: He leads, and I follow; He teaches, and I listen; He commands, and I obey; He sends, and I go. My greatest goal in life is to exalt His name, so that I can bring glory and honor to Him.

Secondly, I dedicate this book to the most awesome man I've ever known — my beloved husband, Apostle Ore' Mahoney. You are my greatest source of earthly encouragement. You are the love of my life, my ministry partner and my greatest supporter. You continue to cheer me on, through the struggles and into victory. I couldn't have asked for a better man. Sweetheart, thank you for all you do, all you are and all you mean to me. You are a precious gift from the LORD, and I love you with all my heart.

Special Acknowledgments

☙❧

This book, <u>Loving God (Volume 1, Worship as a Lifestyle Series)</u>, has been a major undertaking. I could not have accomplished this work without the help of three very special women of God. With a grateful heart of love and appreciation, I acknowledge Minister Dashan Hungate, Pastor Cheryl Womack and Dr. Peggy Enochs for their amazing friendship and for helping to bring this work to completion.

Minister Dashan, thank you for the countless hours of reading, editing and formatting required for the completion of this book. Thank you for the days we've spent perched on your couch (in the mist of babies, oatmeal and Veggie Tales), inching our way through this manuscript, writing and rewriting over and over again. Your patient love, encouragement, guidance and insight has encouraged my heart and made this book possible. I couldn't have done it without you.

Pastor Cheryl and Dr. Peggy, I'm so grateful for the impact you've had in my life. You've both challenged and mentored me in so many awesome ways. Thank you for your part in the proof reading and editing process of this book. I truly appreciate your sacrifice of love, and I thank God for both of you.

☙❧

Books by Apostle Linda Mahoney

❧❦

Theology of Dance:
A Study in the Old and New Testaments

❧❦

The Priesthood & The Garments:
A Biblical Study with Spiritual Significance for Everyday Living

❧❦

Biblical Forms of Worship:
Finding Freedom to Passionately Worship God in Spirit & in Truth

Contents in Brief

Dedication 3
Special Acknowledgments 5
Books by Apostle Linda Mahoney 6
Contents in Brief 7
Table of Contents 9
Introduction 17

PART 1: LOVING GOD WITH ALL YOUR HEART
    Chapter 1 – The Love Motivation 21
    Chapter 2 – Religion versus Relationship 37
    Chapter 3 – Family Idols and Heart Attitudes 49
    Chapter 4 – The 'Whole Heart' Worshipper 63
    Chapter 5 – The 'Perfect Heart' Worshipper 105
    Summary of Loving God With All Your Heart 251

PART 2: LOVING GOD WITH ALL YOUR SOUL
    Chapter 6 – The Soul Defined, The Breath of God 253
    Chapter 7 – Seven Manifestations of the Soul 261
    Chapter 8 – The Thirsty Soul 305
    Summary of Loving God With All Your Soul 347

PART 3: LOVING GOD WITH ALL YOUR MIND
    Chapter 9 – The Battle for the Mind 349
    Chapter 10 – The Spiritual Mind 387
    Chapter 11 – The Fearlessly Sound Mind 403
    Chapter 12 – Trusting God & Overcoming Fear 435
    Summary of Loving God With All Your Mind 463

PART 4: LOVING GOD WITH ALL YOUR MIGHT & STRENGTH
    Chapter 13 – Zealous Love 465
    Chapter 14 – The Righteous Might of a King 491
    Summary of Loving God with All Your Might and Strength 523

PART 5: LOVING GOD IN ALL YOU DO
    Chapter 15 – Living Life in Christ: What's it Look Like? 525
    Chapter 16 – Loving God Through Service 555
    Chapter 17 – Love God through Self Denial 579
    Chapter 18 – The Restorative Vision of God 597
    Chapter 19 – Loving God = Living Beyond Religion 619
    Summary of Loving God In All You Do 631
    FINAL WORDS FROM THE APOSTLE 635

TABLE OF CONTENTS

DEDICATION 3
SPECIAL ACKNOWLEDGMENTS 5
BOOKS BY APOSTLE LINDA MAHONEY 6
CONTENTS IN BRIEF 7
TABLE OF CONTENTS 9
INTRODUCTION 17

PART 1: LOVING GOD WITH ALL YOUR HEART
Chapter 1 – The Love Motivation 21
   OLD TESTAMENT 23
     Fear God, Walk in His Ways and Serve Him 24
     Listen Attentively and Seek Him 26
     Freely Obey His Word 29
   NEW TESTAMENT 30
     Love the LORD thy God 32
     Love God With All Thy Heart 33
    Love God, Love Your Neighbor 33
Chapter 2 – Religion versus Relationship 37
   Prove Your Love 38
   Obedient Relationship = Blessing 40
   The Word = Blessing 43
   Repentance = Blessing 44
   Grace for Spiritual Babes 46
Chapter 3 – Family Idols and Heart Attitudes 49
   Case Study 1 – Saul 50
   Case Study 2 – Michal 53
     Background on Michal 57
   Lessons Learned 58
   The King of Our Hearts 60
Chapter 4 – The 'Whole Heart' Worshipper 63
   Celebrates the Works of the LORD 63
     Yâdâh ~ Extend Your Hands as Thanks and Praise 65
   Worships in the Assembly & the Congregation 66
   Keeps and Seeks 69
     Keeps 69
     Seeks 70

Pursues the LORD 71
Seeks Understanding 76
Moves in the Opposite Spirit 78
   Know Who Your Enemy Really Is 79
   Know Who You Are in Christ 80
   A Personal Testimony 82
   Focus on His Word & Witness 90
Is Unashamed 91
   Yâdâh ~ Throw a Stone in Praise 92
   The Character and Nature of the Lord 94
   Be Free, Not Bound 96
Finds God's Peace and Rest 99

Chapter 5 – The 'Perfect Heart' Worshipper 105
Sees the Strength of the LORD 105
   Lean not to Thine Own Understanding 107
   Beware of Lust, Consider God's Kingdom Purpose 108
   Be Fit, Not Fat / Carry Your Cross 112
   Sacrifice the Fat, Submit Your Life 116
   Avoid Distraction, Stay Focused 124
   Serve the LORD, Not Your 'Self' 130
   Be Perfect with the LORD 132
Gives the Word of God Top Priority 138
Stays in Position 141
Declares Righteous Judgment 145
Yearns for God 147
   A Froward Heart Shall Depart 152
   Take a Personal Inventory 157
Receives Favor and Long Life 159
Will Not Compromise 162
   Knowing and Serving the LORD 170
   A Willing Mind 173
   Seeking Him 178
   His Place, Our Heart and Repentance 179
   The Inner Man, The Inward Parts — Our Heart 181
   Loving, Enraptured Transportation 185
   Belief Systems 186
   A New Spirit of Worship 191

Take Heed: Be Strong and Do It 195
Leading Well 198
Rejects Trouble (Ignorance, Disobedience & Dishonor) 200
The Truth Stands 201
Strongholds are a Choice 203
When You Should Know Better… 207
Please The LORD 212
Enjoy Pure Celebration 221
   Recognize Deception & Forsake Idolatry 224
   Know & Celebrate the Truth 225
   Choose Truth Over Tradition 226
   Conquer Compromise 230
Remains Pure from Sexual Sin 234
   What's in a Name? 236
   Walk Faithfully: Mortify Your Members 242
SUMMARY OF LOVING GOD WITH ALL YOUR HEART 251

PART 2: LOVING GOD WITH ALL YOUR SOUL

Chapter 6 – The Soul Defined, The Breath of God 253
   Have Breath? Praise the LORD!! 255
Chapter 7 – Seven Manifestations of the Soul 261
   1 — The Revived Heart & Soul 261
   2 — The Cleaving Soul 263
   3 — The Boasting Soul 265
      Manifests Hope, Encouragement & Unity 268
      Manifests Faith over Fear 270
   4 — The Joyful Soul 273
      Manifests Christ — Salvation & Righteousness 275
   5 — The Hopeful Soul 278
   6 — The Satisfied Soul 282
      Manifests Wholeness, Health & Integrity 283
      Manifests Wholeness, Health & Prosperity 290
      Health Starts in the Heart 292
   7 — The Redeemed Soul 298
Chapter 8 – The Thirsty Soul 305
   Manifests a Deep Desire 306
   Water In The Wilderness 308
   Lessons in the Wilderness 311

Christ in the Wilderness 314
Motivations & Expectations in the Wilderness 316
Rivers, Fountains, Pools & Springs – Oh My! 319
Rivers in the High Places 323
Fountains in the Valleys 324
Still Waters — Pools in the Wilderness 325
Springs in the Dry Land.. 326
Living Waters — Eternal & Refreshing 331
Fountains of Supply, Salvation & His Presence................. 331
The LORD's River of Reflection & Light 333
The Tree of Life, Eternal Life & the Bride of Christ............ 339
The Leaves of the Tree & the Taking of the Water 344
SUMMARY OF LOVING GOD WITH ALL YOUR SOUL... 347

PART 3: LOVING GOD WITH ALL YOUR MIND

Chapter 9 – The Battle for the Mind 349
Walk... 352
War 353
Cast down 356
Bring Into Captivity 358
Gird Up Your Sober Mind 359
Help in the Midst of the Storm 362
When All Seems Lost 363
Put Your Armor On! 367
1 — Belt of Truth.. 369
2 — Breastplate of Righteousness... 371
3 — Gospel of Peace... 372
4 — Shield of Faith... 374
5 — Helmet of Salvation.. 376
Eyes.. 377
Ears 379
Mouth 380
6 — The Sword of the Spirit 382
7 — Prayer... 384

Chapter 10 – The Spiritual Mind 387
The Renewed Mind 389
Renewal Brings Transformation 391
Renewal Brings Obedience 393

Think On These Things 395
   1 — True 396
   2 — Honest 397
   3 — Just..397
   4 — Pure...398
   5 — Lovely 399
   6 — Good Report 399
   7 — Virtue..400
   8 — Praise..401

Chapter 11 – The Fearlessly Sound Mind 403
   The Spirit of Fear 404
   The Spirit of Power, Love and a Sound Mind 407
   God's Perfect Love 409
Don't Believe the Lies! 412
   The First Lie..412
   The Father of Lies 416
   Motive for The Lie 420
   The Influence and Effects of The Lie..............................424
Love God & Put The Devil Under Foot! 429

Chapter 12 – Trusting God & Overcoming Fear....................... 435
   Fear vs. Faith..435
   1 — Mary (Luke 1:26-38) 437
      God's Grace, Favor & Holy Ghost Power.........................438
      God's Call, Our Response..440
      Be Courageous...443
   2 — The Shepherds (Luke 2:4-20). 445
      Desire to Participate in Miracles!....................................447
   3 — Jairus (Luke 8:41-42, 49-56) 449
      Receive a Supernatural Infusion of Faith.......................450
   4 — An Angel & Two Women (Matthew 28:1-8)...........452
      Love & Relationship Rise Above Fear 454
   5 — Paul 455
      Walk in Boldness with Our Helper 456
   6 — Jesus..457
      Pray to be Strengthened...457
      Pray to Persevere 458
      Pray to Endure & Obey 460

SUMMARY OF LOVING GOD WITH ALL YOUR MIND 463
PART 4: LOVING GOD WITH ALL YOUR MIGHT & STRENGTH
Chapter 13 – Zealous Love 465
    Fan the Flame 471
    Dancing Mightily Before The LORD 472
    An Overcomer's Love 475
    An Overcomer's Identity 480
    Requirements of Love 483
        Love has a Purpose — Life! 485
Chapter 14 – The Righteous Might of a King 491
    Leading Well 492
    Temple Cleansing 495
    Have We Let Perversion In? 497
        Religion versus True Christianity 498
        Compromising? Repent! 503
        Stand Strong! 506
        Protect the Helpless 511
    The Next Phase of Cleansing 512
        Breaking Down Corruption 514
        Burning Up Convenience 515
        Restoring Worship 517
SUMMARY OF LOVING GOD WITH ALL YOUR MIGHT AND STRENGTH 523
PART 5: LOVING GOD IN ALL YOU DO
Chapter 15 – Living Life in Christ: What's it Look Like? 525
    Humble Servanthood 527
    Labor & Rest 528
    Meekness & Exaltation 532
    As a Little Child 534
    Staying in Position 536
    Focus — Ministering to Others 537
    The Mind of Christ in You 541
    Be Like Christ 545
    Abide in Him 551
Chapter 16 – Loving God Through Service 555
    Doing Good to Others 558
    Supporting and Assisting Others 560
    Consideration of Others 564

  Food Preferences 565
  All to the Glory of God 568
  Heartily, In the Name of the LORD 574
Chapter 17 – Love God through Self Denial............................. **579**
  Not My Will 580
  Submission Exemplified 584
  See, Hear, Speak & Do 587
  Expect and Respond to Persecution 590
  Follow God's Direction...593
Chapter 18 – The Restorative Vision of God............................. **597**
  Know Your Earthly Ministry, Become His Vessel 600
  Lovers of God Walk in Love 602
  Lovers of God Cease from Sin 605
  Crucified, Risen & Filled — Victory! 606
  We Have a Covenant Mind 609
  A Covenant of Love 614
Chapter 19 – Loving God = Living Beyond Religion.................. **619**
  Living Beyond Self 624
  Living in His Kingdom 627
SUMMARY OF LOVING GOD IN ALL YOU DO..631
FINAL WORDS FROM THE APOSTLE **635**

INTRODUCTION

The purpose of this book, <u>Loving God</u>, is to discover what it means to truly love the LORD. While this topic may seem self-explanatory, these lessons on loving God with all your heart, soul, mind and strength, contain considerable detail. For this reason, it is strongly recommended that you take your time reading and studying the material. Give yourself permission to take it slow and really meditate on these lessons from the Word of God. Allow the LORD's Holy Spirit to teach you extensive personal applications about what you read.

This book will encourage you to intentionally develop and deepen a personal relationship with your Creator. As you discover the wonder of who He truly is, you will also better understand His great love for you. Your relationship with Him will become richer, more profound and increasingly intimate, as you learn how to love Him with your entire being, as well as worship Him with complete adoration and abandonment. Really, regardless of where you currently are in your relationship with the LORD, this study will challenge you to ascend to the next level of intimacy with the LORD of Glory!

The LORD God Almighty is the only source of life, and from Him, all creation was spoken forth. He is eternal; He has always been and always will be. In Heaven, God is known as the Father. He is the completely righteous and holy Judge; the Supreme Authority and Ruler of all things. In the New Testament, He manifested as the Son of God, in the physical personage of Jesus Christ; He became the Word of God made flesh. He is the King of kings and LORD of lords. Today, He is physically present in the earth as the Holy Spirit, through which He reveals His power and presence, in and through the lives of His worshippers. Without a doubt, He still speaks to us. May you have an ear to hear what our living, everlasting, righteous and holy Creator, who wields the power to save, has to say to you in this day and hour.

Be prepared — this book will expose and deal with the deceptions that hinder us from relentlessly pursuing the heart of God. Sadly, we live in a world today where (even in Christian churches) man-made religious traditions, customs and rituals have replaced biblical truth in what is referred to as "worship." Those who undermine biblical truths, whether intentionally or not, dismiss the Lord and exalt themselves. They also set themselves up to be ruled by the ambitions of demonic influence. Of course, true believers never aim to do this, but deception is deviously tricky. This book will be an alarming wake-up call for those who are unaware of their sin. If this is you, I implore you to repent. Repentance is essential and mandatory, if you're to overcome deception and live as a true lover and worshipper of God!

As a final preface, it may be helpful to acquaint readers with my use of the Old and New Testaments of the Holy Bible. Many of the core scriptures referenced in this teaching are from the Old Testament, which required strict obedience to the Law of God. However, as New Testament believers, we're not required to live under the old Law. Through the work of Jesus Christ, who fulfilled all the Law and the prophets, we now live under grace and walk in the law of love (Matthew 22:35-40; Romans 13:10). Nevertheless, the beauty of God's grace cannot be fully understood without knowing the truth of His Law. The Law of God is the foundation and foreshadowing of New Testament truth revealed.

Therefore, my purpose in sharing the Old Testament references is to reveal the heart of God and the fact that He's always wanted a love relationship with His people. God established His heart's desire in the Old Testament. In the New Testament, Jesus — the Son of God and Son of man — became our example of the Father's will fulfilled. He demonstrated how to walk in a love relationship with the Father in Heaven. May you embrace the journey of love that God has ordained for you, and may you dwell in His eternal presence.

Apostle Linda Mahoney

Part 1
Loving God with All Your Heart

ᷡ Chapter 1 ᷤ

THE LOVE MOTIVATION

The LORD God Almighty, Creator of Heaven and Earth, is a Lover! The object of His great love and affection is mankind. We were created to experience a mutually loving relationship with this passionate God. As a result, our lives are to exude worship. Giving Him praise, honor and glory is a reflection of this intimate love. It's important to understand that our worship expression isn't just an external exercise or ritualistic function. Our worship must begin in and radiate from the heart; it must be motivated by love.

When God gave the Ten Commandments to Moses and the children of Israel, the first thing He said was, "Thou shalt have no other gods before me..." This command implies that the people had issues with 'other gods' in their lives. Otherwise, the LORD would not have given them such a commandment. As an extension of this first commandment, the people were also warned to make no graven images of

Part 1 • *Loving God* with All Your Heart

anything in heaven or earth for the purpose of worship. They were not to bow down before or serve such images or idols (Exodus 20:3-5). The children of Israel lived as slaves in the land of for Egypt 400 years. While in captivity they had been exposed to all manner of idolatrous practices. God knew their hearts had been influenced by idolatry; therefore, they needed such a commandment.

Man was created to seek and serve God. Every true purpose in life can only be found in Him. When people forget or ignore Almighty God — the one who formed them, the Creator who breathed His life and purpose into them — then they cannot know His destiny for them. Without acknowledging God and embracing His original intent, they will choose to go their own rebellious way and, by default, fall into idolatry.

While idolatry may or may not be connected with a physical or tangible idol, the seed of idolatry always begins in the imagination of misinformed human reasoning and pride. There, it sprouts into a false identity, which influences a person to practice self-exaltation. A person does this as they mentally fabricate and value images, ideals and characteristics that oppose God's Word. By practicing self-exaltation, a person creates a fantasy god in their own likeness. Once created, that person will cause their self-made godhood to comfortably conform and subordinately comply with their own human thought processes. So, basically, a person can imagine that their personal values (or lack thereof) will determine why and how they live. This is how a person becomes their own idol — a god of their own making.

However, we cannot define God by our natural, human reasoning or by how we would do things, if we were in charge of the universe. God has already defined Himself in His Word, and He has declared how our relationship with Him should be. Any other standard (other than what God has established) leads to deception, sin and rebellion.

OLD TESTAMENT

The following Old Testament scriptures were directed toward the nation of Israel (aka. the Jewish nation). In these verses, we see that God's heart desire is to have a faithful love relationship with His people. Today, in the Spirit of the Word, His people include all those who choose to love, trust, obey and serve Him through a faith-based relationship in Jesus Christ, His Son.

It's important to understand that the LORD does not desire a limited portion of who we are or what we possess. He wants 100% of all we are and all we possess. He wants our total, fervent dedication, as we see in the following scripture references:

Part 1 • *Loving God* with All Your Heart

***Deuteronomy 6:5** And thou shalt love the LORD thy God with all thine heart, and with all thy soul, and with all thy might.*

In this verse, according to the Strong's Concordance, the word **love** *(H157)* means *to have affection* for and *love* as a close *friend*. The word **heart** *(H3824/H3820)* refers to *the heart (as the interior organ)*. It's also used figuratively to represent *the feelings, the will and even the intellect; likewise,* the heart represents *the center of anything*. It's evident that God has consistently desired an affectionate, completely transparent love relationship with His children. Again, it all begins in the heart, the center of our being. In like manner: If one loves the LORD with all their heart, then loving Him with all one's soul and might will follow closely behind.

FEAR GOD, WALK IN HIS WAYS AND SERVE HIM

We (like the children of Israel) are to love God in such a way that we choose to reverence, honor and obey Him as an act of affectionate worship according to:

***Deuteronomy 10:12** And now, Israel, what doth the LORD thy God require of thee, but to fear the LORD thy God, to walk in all his ways, and to love him, and to serve the LORD thy God with all thy heart and with all thy soul.*

Notice, this verse is not a suggestion, but a demanded requirement! By definition, to **fear** *(H3372)* the LORD is to have godly *fear*, *to morally revere* and *reverence* Him. This is demonstrated through showing great regard, respect, veneration and awe.

To **walk** *(H3212)* in the **ways** *(H1870/H1869)* of the LORD is to figuratively *carry, bear, bring, follow, grow, prosper, march* with and *pursue* the LORD; adapting ourselves to His *mode of action*. Our conversations, lifestyles, customs and mannerisms come into alignment with His guidance, according to the *course of life* He has ordained for us. In other words, to walk in the ways of the LORD is to earnestly and enthusiastically submit to and obey His Word.

Love *(H157)* (also as mentioned in Deuteronomy 6:5), means to have *affection* and to love the LORD as a close friend. As we love Him, we see His goodness and are willingly compelled to **serve** *(H5647)* Him. To serve the LORD is to work with Him as a worshiping, servant *laborer*.

Loving and serving the LORD is not an isolated or peripheral ritual we perform. It's an act of love that flows from deep within the heart and soul. Therefore, we delight to give godly fear, honor and reverence to the LORD. We take pleasure in submitting to His Word and ways. We passionately express our love and affection for Him as our cherished friend. We willingly give ourselves to work with Him; fulfilling the desire of Heaven in Earth. It's our eternal blessing to be able to worship Him.

Part 1 • *Loving God* with All Your Heart

LISTEN ATTENTIVELY AND SEEK HIM

When the children of Israel were coming out of Egyptian bondage and preparing to enter into the land of Canaan, the LORD promised to pour out His provision and blessings upon them. However, His promise was conditional. As our next scripture portion explains, the children of Israel were to love and serve the LORD with all their heart and soul:

<u>Deuteronomy 11:13-17</u> And it shall come to pass, if ye shall hearken diligently unto my commandments which I command you this day, to love the LORD your God, and to serve him with all your heart and with all your soul, ¹⁴That I will give you the rain of your land in his due season, the first rain and the latter rain, that thou mayest gather in thy corn, and thy wine, and thine oil. ¹⁵And I will send grass in thy fields for thy cattle, that thou mayest eat and be full. ¹⁶Take heed to yourselves, that your heart be not deceived, and ye turn aside, and serve other gods, and worship them; ¹⁷And then the LORD'S wrath be kindled against you, and he shut up the heaven, that there be no rain, and that the land yield not her fruit; and lest ye perish quickly from off the good land which the LORD giveth you.

Notice in verse 13, the blessings of abundance, provision and great harvests were directly related to hearkening diligently — giving heed and attention to the commandments of God. To willingly keep the commands of God is evidence of loving and serving Him. While this evidence demonstrates the desire to remain in right relationship with Him, it is also the catalyst for receiving the blessings of God.

In verses 16 and 17, the LORD warned His people to take heed to themselves, so their hearts would not be deceived into worshiping other gods. To take *heed (H8104)* is *to hedge about as with thorns; that is,* to *guard, protect* and *attend to.* If we do not take heed to ourselves — guarding, protecting and attending to God's Word in our lives — then we will be deceived.

To be *deceived (H6601)* means to be mentally and morally *open,* to be *simple* (ignorant, foolish, or gullible) and/or deluded (easily misled in thought or judgment). When it comes to the Word of God, we're not to be mentally or morally open. We're not to be receptive to different opinions and ideas that are not in agreement with God's standard of righteousness. When we take heed to ourselves, we're bringing all thoughts and actions into agreement with the authority of God's Word.

Do you see the progression to deception in the text? First of all, for a person to be deceived, they will reject or ignore the truth of God's Word. Then, by default, they will automatically believe a lie. Once they believe a lie, their mindset becomes distorted. Distortion warps the mind, twists the understanding

Part 1 • *Loving God* with All Your Heart

and perception, and causes one to turn aside from that which is right. A person who turns from what's right is drawn into evil and will rebel against the LORD. Rebellion causes the heart to revolt and break away from God's authority, creating a spiritual mutiny and a mental turning away. Those who do such things have fallen into idolatry, because they have forsaken the LORD to pursue and serve other things.

Deception is the devil's tool bag. It is filled with allurements, flatteries, enticements and folly. His tools of deception become tentacles of destruction to ensnare and destroy the lives of those who refuse to hedge up, guard and protect the sanctity of their relationship with the LORD. Those who willingly participate in the deception of idolatry kindle the wrath of God and cause their own lives and blessings to be cut off.

In Deuteronomy 11:13-17, the LORD was speaking to a nation — His people, Israel. Nations (and individuals) who love and serve God and honor His Word will be blessed, but those who forsake Him will experience His judgments. If debilitating lack is a continual state of existence, this is an indicator that something is out of order. Yet, even those who have turned from the LORD can return to Him. If they will repent of their sins, hear His voice and obey His Word, He will have compassion on them and restore them (Deuteronomy

30:1-5). As part of that restoration, the LORD will circumcise their hearts:

***Deuteronomy 30:6** And the LORD thy God will circumcise thine heart, and the heart of thy seed, to love the LORD thy God with all thine heart, and with all thy soul, that thou mayest live.*

For God to *circumcise* (H4135) a heart is to *curtail, reduce* or *diminish* the flesh mindset; to *destroy* all that's not needful, productive or life giving. Every human being needs spiritual heart surgery. Repentance is the required prerequisite for the heart of man to be fixed. The repentant heart experiences the mercy of God, as He tenderly cuts away sinful and selfish tendencies. Heart circumcision (or lack of it) will affect the generations that follow.

FREELY OBEY HIS WORD

Part of loving God with all our hearts, is to trust that He has given us His Word as the standard for our lives. Its instructions are the keys that unlock the potential for us to live victorious, righteous, holy lives. The scriptures give us insight as to what the LORD expects of us. We see evidence of this in:

***Joshua 22:5** But take diligent heed to do the commandment and the law, which Moses the servant of the LORD charged you, to love the LORD your God, and to walk in all his ways, and to keep his commandments, and to cleave unto* *him, and to serve him with all your heart and with all your soul.*

The purpose in selecting this verse is not to bring anyone under the heavy yoke of the Old Testament Law of God. Rather, it is chosen as an encouragement to diligently accept the charge we have been given. May we freely enjoin ourselves to the appointed will of the LORD! If we love Him, we'll not need to be constrained to obey His Word, because it will be our heart's desire. We'll not need to be forced to walk in His ways, because we'll take great pleasure in the journey of getting to know Him. We'll not be drawn away by the distractions of life, because we'll closely follow and pursue the LORD. As we worship and serve Him, we'll choose to abide in His presence, because He has captivated our hearts. Loving God is our simple expression of gratitude for who He is and all He's done for us. It's all about having a personal and cherished relationship with Him.

NEW TESTAMENT

As stated previously, the Old Testament records Father God's desire for a love relationship with the nation of Israel. In the New Testament, we see His desire for a love relationship with all people of all nations. Jesus came to Earth in order to reveal the Father's heart to mankind. He said in:

Matthew 22:37 Thou shalt love the Lord thy God with all thy heart, and with all thy soul, and with all thy mind.

Again, we see that the LORD is after the heart, soul and mind of man. He wants our entire being to be a love offering to Him. Our number one purpose in life is to love God. We see this in:

Mark 12:30 And thou shalt love the Lord thy God with all thy heart, and with all thy soul, and with all thy mind, and with all thy strength: this [is] the first commandment.

Jesus said that loving the LORD thy God is the first and greatest commandment. If we choose to obey this commandment, then love will motivate us to obey the rest of God's Word. Loving obedience to Him keeps our heart, mind and soul free from the idolatrous worship of other gods.

On the other hand, if we refuse to obey this first commandment, then we'll not obey any other command the Father has given. We cannot love and serve God and our own selfish, rebellious desires at the same time. Loving God and the idolatry of self-worship do not go together. We cannot serve both; we must choose one or the other. Love and obedience demonstrate our commitment and willingness to walk in covenant with our God. Disobedience demonstrates a heart and soul that has placed its affections somewhere else and, thereby, has fallen into some form of idolatry.

LOVE THE LORD THY GOD

So, exactly what does it mean to "love the Lord thy God with all thy heart"? Thayer's Lexicon (1889), states that loving God "involves the idea of affectionate reverence, prompt obedience, [and] grateful recognition of benefits received." Now, let's examine Matthew 22:37 and Mark 12:30 more closely. In both verses, we're commanded to **love the LORD thy God.** This word **love** (G25) means *to love (in a social or moral sense)*. In other words, we love God because it's the right thing to do.

Notice, the LORD is referred to as **thy God.** The word **thy** (H4675) is defined as *of thee;* it speaks of being associated with, belonging to and being possessed by the LORD. It also indicates that we've made a choice to surrender. Thereby, we enter into union through a submitted relationship with Him. Because He is our God, we intentionally choose to love and worship Him, as an act of adoration. When we claim God as our own, we're saying:

- We've made a decision to love Him.
- We belong to Him and He belongs to us.
- We allow Him to possess us, having full reign in our lives.

Love God With All Thy Heart

The next part of the text says to love the LORD thy God with *all thy heart*. The word *all (G3650)* means *whole and complete*. Remember, the word *thy* represents union, possession and relationship. The word *heart (G2588)*, figuratively, means the *thoughts or feelings (mind)* and, by analogy, *the middle*. It speaks of the center of one's being — the origin from which thoughts or feelings proceed. When we consider these definitions we understand that we're to completely and wholly love the LORD with every feeling and thought we possess — from the innermost core of our being.

Love God, Love Your Neighbor

Our love for the LORD (or lack of it) will affect how we treat and respond to others. When we love the LORD, we'll choose to live and associate with those around us in a way that brings honor to our God. As a result, we'll extend His love to them through our actions. If we do not love the LORD, then we'll not live in a way that honors Him. Nor will we be able to respond to others with His love. We cannot give that which we have rejected or do not possess. It's only as we become a recipient of God's love that we're empowered to share it with others. This correlation is found in:

<u>Luke 10:27</u> And he answering said, Thou shalt love the Lord thy God with all thy heart, and with all thy soul, and with all thy strength, and with all thy mind; and thy neighbour as thyself.

Part 1 • *Loving God* with All Your Heart

And he said unto him, Thou hast answered right: this do, and thou shalt live.

When we love the LORD, we become a conduit of His love for others. We reach out to them desiring that they would know and intimately experience Him. Love motivates us to share the truth of God's Word, show them the importance of repentance and lead them to salvation in Christ. Our intention is to draw them into the Kingdom of God. If we love our neighbors as ourselves we'll not sin against them. We'll not cause harm or take advantage of them. Rather, we'll seek to encourage and strengthen them in the LORD, always having their best interest at heart.

Once more, when we look at Matthew 22:37, Mark 12:30 and Luke 10:27, we see that we're to love the LORD with all our heart, soul, mind and strength. As a demonstration of our love, we're to:

- Have affection for Him
- Fear (morally reverence) Him
- Walk in His ways
- Serve Him
- Listen attentively
- Seek Him
- Freely obey His Word
- Cleave unto Him
- As an extension of our love for the LORD, we're to love others as ourselves

In so doing, we're fulfilling the first and greatest commandment. Everything else in life is determined by how well we live out this most important, primary command of the LORD.

Furthermore, our love and worship of the LORD reflects the condition of our hearts. If the heart is pure and right, then our worship will be pure and right. If the heart is messed up and tainted, then our worship will be messed up and tainted. Those who are true lovers of God will be caught up in the passionate pursuit of His heart. Those who possess the heart of God choose lifestyles that exhibit His endearing love, including the expression of unrestrained worship; love and worship flow from the core of their existence.

CHAPTER 2
RELIGION VERSUS RELATIONSHIP

In Matthew 15:6-9, Jesus said of the Pharisees that, by their traditions, they made the commandments of God of none effect or useless. He called them hypocrites! They said all the right religious words with their mouths. They gave the illusion that they were drawing close to the LORD, but in reality, their hearts were far from Him. This is not what the LORD wants from His people. Just because a person has been taught a set of religious beliefs and/or traditions does not mean they have received truth. Nor does it indicate they're in right standing with God. Just because someone has a religious experience, doesn't mean they're engaged in a love relationship with the God who created them. The Pharisees had a religion that had a form of godliness, but it denied the power thereof (2 Timothy 3:5). Jesus said their worship was vain.

True worship is a relational experience between mankind and the one true and living God. Our worship expression is to be a demonstration of our intimate and beautifully passionate love for Him. It's to be a time of basking in His presence and glory, as we offer all that we are and all that we have to Him. When we worship, we're acknowledging that God is superior and we are submissively subordinate to Him.

Part 1 • *Loving God* with All Your Heart

True worship is also a lifestyle of love in motion! We declare that He is LORD in every area of our lives; there's nothing hidden or kept back from Him. He has ultimate authority and the final say in every matter; we don't move without His blessing. Our love for the LORD (or lack of it) will be evident in the manner with which we consistently live our lives.

PROVE YOUR LOVE

We're commanded to love the LORD with our total being and every ounce of life and energy that we possess. This is not a suggestion! It's a command; a law; a statute of the LORD. We're commanded to *love the Lord thy God* with everything we've got (Matthew 22:37; Mark 12:30; Luke 10:27)! This word *love (G25)*, as mentioned before, means *to love in* both *a social and moral sense.* It involves an obvious demonstration of obedience, along with emotional affection, gratefulness and reverence to the LORD for benefits received.

To love the LORD (in *a social sense)* doesn't mean we live our lives as if we're members of a social club — coming, going and doing as we please. Rather, we're to be devoted to the LORD and continually seek to cultivate our personal relationship with Him. To love Him (in *a moral sense),* is to love Him according to the truth and principles of His Word. Thereby, distinguishing between good and evil and allowing His righteous ways to govern our lives. By loving the LORD this way (Romans 12:1-2), we become internally transformed and visibly sanctified. Truly mature worshippers will do whatever is necessary to obey the LORD. They'll bring glory and honor to Him, even if it means personal sacrifice or the loss of possessions. In fact, according to Jesus, love is measured by obedience:

John 14:15 *If you love me, keep my commandments.*

Thus, our love and obedience toward the LORD (or lack of it), is a reflection of our moral fiber and true spiritual condition. We're not able to keep the commandments of God, apart from surrendering our lives to Him. But we can't surrender our lives to Him, unless we're willing to repent of our own sinful ways, and enter into a salvation relationship with the LORD. Joyful obedience (motivated by love) is a form of worship. But a form of worship without a love relationship is worthless and empty.

There's nothing we can do to make God love us more than He already does. We do not have to earn His love and approval. Jesus Christ, through His death, burial and resurrection already did that for us. If we believe that Jesus Christ, the Son of God, died in our place and paid the penalty for our sins; if we confess and repent of our sins; if we ask the Father in Heaven to cleanse us of all unrighteousness, through the blood of Jesus; and if we truly mean it deep in our hearts and boldly confess our faith concerning these things, then we qualify to receive salvation (Romans 10:9-11, 13; 1 John 1:9). We cannot earn our salvation through obedience, but salvation is verified and proven through obedience. Salvation is a gift; it cannot be earned, bought or sold. It is freely given and must be freely received.

When we receive the gift of salvation, we are born again by the Spirit of God (John 3:3-7, 16-18). We become a new creature; old things are passed away and all things become new (2 Corinthians 5:17-21). Our righteousness is found in Christ (Romans 3:22-26, 10:4; Philippians 3:8-9). In Him, we are changed and transformed (2 Corinthians 3:18; Romans 12:2). He delivers us from the darkness of our sinful past and we become the children of light (Colossians 1:12-14; Ephesians 5:8). We are loved, forgiven, approved and in right standing with Father God, through faith in Christ (Philippians 3:9).

While obedience is evidence that we have received salvation, it's but a small expression of appreciation to the LORD for His redemptive sacrifice. Remember, in obedience to the Father, Jesus laid down His life to have a relationship with us. Should we not lay down our lives in obedience to His Word, as a demonstration of our thankfulness for all He has done on our behalf? What evidence of love does your level of obedience prove?

OBEDIENT RELATIONSHIP = BLESSING

As we experience the blessing of God, we begin to understand the wonder of His deep love for us. An awakening begins to take place in the depths of our being. We're stirred with the desire for greater intimacy with Him. The joy of experiencing God draws us into a sweet, passionate pursuit for more of His presence. We're consumed with a glorious, magnificent obsession for our King and Heavenly Bridegroom. We realize there's no greater blessing than knowing Him! He is the reward of the relationship! Remember, in relation to obedience, Jesus said:

<u>John 14:15</u> *If you love me, keep my commandments.*

The word *if (G1437)* is *a conditional participle* denoting *indefiniteness or uncertainty* based on our choices. It's not enough to just speak of our love. Our lifestyle must reflect it. To *keep (G5083)* the *commandments (G1785/ G1781)* of the LORD means *to guard from loss or injury by keeping an eye on* His *authoritative prescription.* For something to be *authoritative* means it has been recognized or accepted as being true and reliable. A *prescription* is a written directive or decree given by a physician, so that a person can receive what is needed to facilitate healing. Thus, we can receive God's reliable prescriptions and healing, if we choose to obey His Word.

Jesus was (and is) the Great Physician. His words contain the remedy for every sickness and disease of the body, soul and spirit. In Him, each of us can find spiritual, emotional, mental, volitional and physical hope and healing for every condition. Truly, He is the cure for every wound, every sorrow, every sickness

Part 1 • *Loving God* with All Your Heart

and disease, every abuse, every broken heart and every disappointment we may face in life.

But, if we hope to obtain the cure, we must be willing to follow His authoritative prescription as found in His Word. Psalm 107:20 says, **"He sent His Word, and healed them and delivered (H4422) them from their destruction (H7825)."** We have access to the written Word of God; we have Jesus, the Word of God made flesh; we have the Spirit of God who brings His Word to our remembrance (John 14:26). As we combine the promises of God with faith and obedience, we prepare ourselves to receive the manifestation of complete wholeness from the LORD. Within the Word of God, there's power to mend everything that has been damaged or broken in our lives.

Sometimes, if I have a wounded or chaffed place on my skin, I will apply oil to help bring healing and comfort. The Word of God acts in much the same way. Like oil on the skin, the healing power and anointing in the Word of God calms the rough places in our lives. His Word operates like a healing balm to bring revelation, truth, repentance, deliverance, health, restoration, salvation and peace into our lives (Jeremiah 8:22; Matthew 9:12-13; Mark 2:17; Luke 5:31).

What's more, when we are saturated in the truth of God's Word, His anointing delivers us from every *pitfall*. In Psalm 107:20, to be delivered means to be made *smooth* and implies that we *escape (as if by slipperiness)*. Accordingly, the LORD's anointing makes us slippery in the spirit, so the enemy has no grip or control to maneuver us into his snares. Again, mixed with faith and obedience, the personal application of God's authoritative prescription preserves, saves and protects us from the grasp of the enemy and delivers us from destruction. Obedience brings forth a life of blessing!

THE WORD = BLESSING

Jesus, the Word of God made flesh, is grace and truth personified (John 1:14). He brought the will of the Heavenly Father to mankind, in a way that could be easily understood and received. Through the Word and will of God, He demonstrated the Father's mercy, healing, deliverance, salvation and miracle working power. Every word He spoke and everything He did was (and is) motivated by and graciously wrapped in love.

Through our love relationship with Him, He desires that we partake of and enjoy the benefits and blessings of His peace and restoration. This relationship is a precious gift to be highly respected, treasured and guarded. If we allow the cares of life to choke out the Word of God, we might become ripe pickings for the temptations of the enemy. He'll waste no time at all, as he seeks to pluck us from the peace and presence of the LORD and lead us astray. Just because we're saved and redeemed doesn't mean we're immune to sin. Salvation means that the price of sin has been paid, and we're free to walk in the overcoming power of our redemption.

As our love for the LORD grows, we desire to fill our hearts with the beautiful truths and treasures of God's Word. From these priceless promises and jewels of the Kingdom, we form our values, opinions and the basis for our actions. We choose to live our lives as a reflection of His grace, love, mercy and character, which He's perfecting in us (Romans 13:10). This does not mean we'll never fail. Rather, it means that our true heart's desire is to please the LORD above all else. This is the heart of the true worshipper, and this is the blessed life.

Repentance = Blessing

Even as believers, we can still choose to reject the Word of the LORD, go our own way, and do our own thing. We do have a free will. But consider this: If we choose to depart from the LORD, then in that moment, we're choosing to love sin more than we love God. We're rejecting truth and choosing to be led into deception. The god of self has been erected upon the heart's throne, as we bow down to an idol of our own making. It is just that simple.

The choices we make do affect our relationship with the LORD. As believers we have two choices concerning the Word of God. Either we'll choose to hear and obey, or we'll choose to reject His Word and sin. Regardless of how the carnal mind may try to justify disobedience, God's Word still sets the standard. We read in:

James 4:17 Therefore to him that knoweth to do good, and doeth it not, to him it is sin.

It is important to understand that, when we make a decision, the condition of our soul and spirit are also revealed in the final outcome. Our spirit may discern what is right, but if our soul (mind, will and emotions) disagrees with our spirit, then an inner conflict arises. If the sinful mindset of the flesh nature is allowed to prevail in the soul, sin will be the end result.

As we consider the decision making process, we must realize that the consequences of wrong choices could be life altering and/or disastrous. Certainly, if we choose to sin, consequences will follow. We will be held accountable for every wrong thought we willingly choose to entertain; every wrong word we speak and every wrong action we carry out. The only solution for sin is repentance. In the Greek, to **repent** *(G3338/G3340)* is to *regret* one's sinful actions and attitudes, and turn from them. Repentance causes one to *think differently* and *reconsider* their prior thoughts and actions. This results in a change of mind and a return to the LORD and His ways. We have a beautiful promise in:

1 John 1:9 *If we confess our sins, he is faithful and just to forgive us our sins, and to cleanse us from all unrighteousness.*

Repentance is the key to restoration. When we ***confess*** *(G3670/G3674/G3056)* our sins to God, we're choosing to *acknowledge* our wrong doing, turn from it, and come back into the blessing of our *covenant* relationship with Him (Romans 2:4).

GRACE FOR SPIRITUAL BABES

As we close out this chapter on religion versus relationship, let me say something in reference to newly born spiritual babes and obedience. These babes are precious, new souls; they are just coming into the Kingdom of God. A new believer in Christ must have time to grow in their relationship with the LORD.

A natural baby must be taught and nurtured as it learns how to eat, drink, smile, laugh, respond to family members and observe his/her surroundings. Babies must develop the ability to hear, speak, scoot, crawl, sit up, walk and eventually, run and play. Good parents will display much love, patience and encouragement to help their new baby grow and mature properly.

Likewise, spiritual babes must be taught God's truth, as they feast on His life-giving Word. As they learn and grow, they become His disciples and adapt to their new life in the Kingdom of God. Every fellowship of believers should operate with compassion and consideration toward those who are new to the faith.

As babes grow (whether naturally or spiritually), there are learning experiences and mistakes along the way. Just as good parents lovingly and patiently instruct their children in the right way to go, the LORD will also instruct His children. If they fail or make a mistake, it does not mean they have lost their salvation. It simply means they have an opportunity to experience a life lesson that will cultivate wisdom and maturity into their understanding and character.

Spiritual babes should never be discouraged with threats of hell, fire and damnation if/when they mess up. Babies simply make messes in the learning process. They should be taken under the wing of a godly mentor to be trained, encouraged and strengthened in the things of God. Those who are more mature should, by example, teach the younger ones how to love and serve the LORD. It's important to take a babe's hand and run with them in the race that is set before them, at least until they are strong enough to run on their own. There should be an abundance of grace to cover the baby blunders of new babes in Christ.

The heart of the Heavenly Father lovingly dotes over His children, but He also expects them to mature. Growth, discipleship, study, training, understanding and operating in the principles of God are a natural part of living a healthy spiritual life. However, I want to make one further comment. If the "babe" is twenty years old in the LORD and is still not showing any signs of maturity, there's something terribly wrong.

All believers in Christ are expected to obey the Word of God. We're to understand and walk in biblical truth. Stunted spiritual growth in a believer's life is a sign of disorder. Fruit from such disorder is neglect of God's Word, disobedience and outright rebellion — including an arrogant failure to forsake sin. If this be the case, vigilant self-examination (2 Corinthians 13:5) along with strong counsel and steady accountability would be advisable (Matthew 18:15-17; 2 Thessalonians 3:14-15).

As spiritual babes, we speak, understand and think like children. But, in due time, we must grow up and put away childish things (1 Corinthians 13:11). The time comes when we must rise up and walk in spiritual maturity, so we can enter into the fullness of our God ordained destiny.

CHAPTER 3

FAMILY IDOLS AND HEART ATTITUDES

Idolatry has to do with people's heart attitudes toward Father God — the only Creator. Don't be deceived into thinking that false gods and demon worship are reserved only for people groups who run naked through jungles. This is simply not the case. Personally, I have been in various jungle villages where I've had the privilege of meeting many precious brothers and sisters in Christ. Likewise, I've also met those who were obviously tormented by the demons of their false worship, in what would be considered civilized nations. Whether a nation is well-developed (or not) is irrelevant.

Furthermore, false worship doesn't always have an external or physical, touchable statue or graven image connected with it. In fact, idolatry is an internal issue working within the soul. If we have spiritual eyes to see, we'll clearly discern how idolatry and heathenism run rampant in the earth today. The father of lies, satan, is the perpetrator of all idolatry. So, it's demonic at its very root, and it always begins with tolerating or believing a lie. A lie is any thought contrary to the Word of God. Eventually, those who consistently choose to embrace a lie (whether knowingly or not), will experience the twisting and perverting of their minds. Their perspective becomes warped as their thoughts turn to patterns of stubbornness, rebellion, witchcraft, iniquity and idolatry. Let's be clear, idolatry always begins with compromise, because when truth is rejected, lies automatically take root. The reality is: If we fail to love the LORD as we should, then we can (and surely will) fall into idolatry.

Mankind is created/designed to believe in something and someone. When we reject the truth of that someone — the God who created us — then we can't believe in the 'something' He has intended for us. This is why we cannot allow the enemy to exploit our trust.

When satan's seeds of deception and idolatry are sown into an unregenerate soul, they will bring forth the fruit of corruption. To make matters worse, if not dealt with, the lies of the enemy can become a generational issue — a wicked family inheritance passed down through belief systems, traditions or social mores. Unfortunately, there are many people who flounder in this enslaving, double-dealing spiritual condition today and, thereby, imprison their own destinies. Remarkably, this is not a new swindle; even biblical royalty has been manipulated by the wiles of the enemy.

CASE STUDY 1 – SAUL

Before Saul was anointed to be King over all Israel, he was humble and small in his own eyes. But during his reign, he became a proud and arrogant King. He no longer saw himself as being dependent upon the LORD, and he began to disobey His Word. In response to Saul's disobedience, the LORD spoke a very strong rebuke, through the Prophet Samuel in:

<u>1Samuel 15:23</u> For rebellion is as the sin of witchcraft, and stubbornness is as iniquity and idolatry. Because thou hast rejected the word of the LORD, he hath also rejected thee from being king.

Saul disregarded the Word of the LORD, because he chose to believe a lie. The lie deceived Saul and convinced him that it was okay to allow his human reasoning to overrule the commands and wisdom of God. In effect, Saul dethroned God from His rightful place in his heart, and made himself to be the supreme ruler of his life. Stubbornly rejecting the will of the LORD, he sought to fulfill his own rebellious agendas. Saul's *rebellion (H4805/H4784)* was birthed out of *bitterness* and pride, which took over and ruled the throne of his heart.

Through the Prophet Samuel, the LORD makes it perfectly clear that rebellion, *witchcraft (H7081)* and *divination* are offensive to Him. He'll have nothing to do with it! Besides, to rebel against the LORD is to submit to satan! To submit to satan is to step into his character. To step into his character is to step into witchcraft. Saul experienced this truth personally.

While King Saul and his armies were in battle, he sought the LORD'S counsel about what to do, but he received no response. At that point, he should have repented for the wrong he'd committed. Sadly, his rebellion led him straight into witchcraft, as he turned to the witch of Endor for counsel instead.

King Saul's rebellion was evidence of his hardened heart toward the LORD. He turned from seeking the direction of God and, as an alternative, sought the direction of devils! As a result, within twenty-four hours of his encounter with the witch of Endor, Saul lost it all. The armies of Israel were defeated; he lost his kingdom; his three sons died prematurely in battle by the hand of the Philistines; and King Saul was also killed (1 Samuel 28, 31). Rebellion, defiance and resistance against the authority of the LORD brought serious consequences to Saul and his lineage.

Continuing on with 1 Samuel 15:23, we read that "**stubbornness (H6484)** is as **iniquity (H205)** and **idolatry (H8655/H7495)**." By definition, this means that those with a stubborn, rebellious heart will become *dull* in their understanding of what's right. With great exertion, they'll continually press and insist upon their own way. They'll *pant* with exhaustion, in the effort to carry out their *wickedness*, mischief and unrighteousness.

Stubborn people are obstinate, arrogant and immoveable. They are set in their ways and will not listen to reason or the opinions of others. They have exalted their own will to the place of highest priority. Therefore, stubbornness is directly attached to the iniquity and idolatry of self-worship. If not repented of, stubbornness can bring trouble, affliction, distress, mourning and even death.

CASE STUDY 2 – MICHAL

In the Hebrew, one of the words for an *image* (H8655/H7495) of idolatry is ***teraphim (ter-aw-feme')***. This was *a family idol* or household god; teraphim were created to represent former ancestors. It was believed that the idols brought healing and prosperity to the family.

There's an example of a teraphim or family idol being used in 1 Samuel 19:11-16. In this passage, King Saul was pursuing David to try to kill him. Saul's daughter, Michal (who was also David's wife), helped him to escape. After David fled, she put an *image* (teraphim) in the bed with a pillow of goat's hair. When Saul sent guards to seize David, Michal (hoping to deter them from their mission) told them he was sick. This deceptive ploy temporarily diverted the guards from their assignment, and they returned to King Saul without further investigation. It wasn't until the second time Saul sent his guards to apprehend David that they learned of Michal's scheming.

Consider this question: If David was a man of God, how did the teraphim get into his house? Most likely it was a family idol from the house of Saul, or perhaps it belonged to one of the servants. It's possible that Michal may have brought it into their home after she and David were married. Scripture doesn't tell us where the idol came from, but one thing was for sure; Michal had easy access to it. This lets us know that, to some degree, idolatry had infiltrated (and been given a place in) Saul's household.

Putting the idol in the bed to impersonate David was a shrewd and slick maneuver. It bought him some time, so he could escape the murderous intentions of King Saul. However, the effects of idolatry and compromised religion would later cause conflict in the lives of David and Michal.

Based on scripture alone, we don't fully know the spiritual upbringing of Michal. While her father was chosen by the LORD to be the first King of Israel, this does not guarantee that he was faithful to teach and train his children in the ways of the LORD. In fact, Saul's probable neglect was indicated in Michal's attitude toward King David when he brought up the Ark of the Covenant from the house of Obededom to the Tabernacle of David.

King David had assembled a great procession of the Priests, Levites, singers, musicians, door keepers, the elders of Israel and the captains of thousands to celebrate in the relocation of the Ark of the Covenant. For David and all of Israel, this was a great and notable day. After all, the Ark of God's presence was now in the city of Jerusalem, where it rightfully belonged. The people celebrated with King David and filled the city with rejoicing, dancing, music and shouting. The procession stopped as the people gathered at the tent King David had prepared for the Ark. In the midst of great joy, sacrifices and peace offerings were offered up to the LORD. After the Ark was in its rightful place, the King made sure all things pertaining to its care were in proper order. Then, he blessed the LORD and the people of Israel, as he concluded the festivities.

David's wife, Michal, did not support or participate in the procession of praise. She watched from a distance, and chose not to enter into the joy of the LORD. As the Ark of the Covenant was carried into Jerusalem, the City of David, Michal observed her kingly husband dancing and playing before the LORD. David danced with all his might, and she ***despised*** *(H959)* him in her heart (1 Chronicles 15:29). By definition, this means she *disesteemed* him and held him in low regard. She disdained him, as if he were not worthy of her favorable response. She looked down on him with contempt, dishonor and disgrace. She scorned and rejected her husband, as if he were a vile, depraved and offensively despicable, disgusting person. This is how she viewed her worshipping husband and King. This also demonstrated her disregard for the God whom he worshipped. When David returned home to bless his own household, Michal, who had been watching him from the window, went out to meet him and scathingly mocked his extravagant worship:

<u>2 Samuel 6:20-22</u> Then David returned to bless his household. And Michal the daughter of Saul came

out to meet David, and said, How glorious was the king of Israel to day, who uncovered himself to day in the eyes of the handmaids of his servants, as one of the vain fellows shamelessly uncovereth himself! [21] *And David said unto Michal, It was before the LORD, which chose me before thy father, and before all his house, to appoint me ruler over the people of the LORD, over Israel: therefore will I play before the LORD.* [22] *And I will yet be more vile than thus, and will be base in mine own sight: and of the maidservants which thou hast spoken of, of them shall I be had in honour.* [23] *Therefore Michal the daughter of Saul had no child unto the day of her death.*

Obviously, David and Michal were not on the same spiritual wave length. David pursued the LORD with his whole heart, while Michal ridiculed her husband's actions. Confidently, he wasn't concerned with her criticisms and refused to be dissuaded. David would not allow his royal position to make him so proud and dignified that he could not praise, worship and celebrate his God. In response to Michal's comments, he declared that he would become even more vile and base in his worship. David was willing to be demeaned, pressed down and humbled, so that his God would be exalted. He determined that, if his own wife of royalty would not honor him, then he would be content to celebrate the LORD with the handmaidens of servitude.

Michal was not in union with her husband. Therefore, all she could see was what she didn't like about him. Like her father, King Saul, she had risen up against the anointed of the LORD. Consequently, for the rest of her life, no child came forth from her womb (1 Chronicles 15-16; 2 Samuel 6).

BACKGROUND ON MICHAL
It's important to understand a bit about the life of Michal, since this may provide insight concerning her actions. She was one of the daughters of King Saul. Her father was jealous of David, because the people loved him, publically honored him and celebrated his battle victories against the Philistines. Saul's pride and envy became the catalyst for planning the demise of David. Therefore, Saul used Michal as the enticement for David's destruction.

In a deceitful plot to get rid of David, Saul made an agreement with him: If David would kill 100 Philistines and present their foreskins as the booty of war, in lieu of a marriage dowry, Saul would give Michal to him in marriage. The King's intent was that David would be killed in battle, but that didn't happen. When David and his men returned from the battle, he presented 200 foreskins to the king and claimed Michal as his bride (1 Samuel 18:20-28).

In the beginning of their relationship, Michal truly loved David and desired to be his wife, but Saul's spiteful meddling would bring division between them.

While David was in the wilderness of Paran, King Saul took Michal and gave her to another man by the name of Phaltiel (1 Samuel 25:44). But at the death of Saul, David commanded Abner (the leader of Saul's armies) to retrieve Michal from Phaltiel and return her to him as his wife. Phaltiel apparently loved Michal, because he followed behind her weeping as she was being reclaimed (2 Samuel 3:13-16). Michal may have fallen in love with Phaltiel, but when David demanded that she be returned, she had no say in the matter. This may explain some of her bitterness toward David. In reality, it was Michal's father that sinned against her and used her as a pawn for his own agendas; but her heart had turned from David, and he became the object of her scorn.

Their relationship went downhill from there, and there's no record that Michal and David had any children together. It may be that the LORD closed her womb when she came against the anointed of the LORD, or perhaps their relationship became so alienated and estranged, it was devoid of intimacy. Regardless of the reasons why Michal didn't conceive, there was no opportunity for her hostile attitude to be passed on to future generations.

LESSONS LEARNED

There are two powerful lessons in these biblical accounts of Saul, David and Michal. First, we must understand that disobedience (including, but not limited to: rebellion, witchcraft, stubbornness, iniquity, idolatry and bitterness) is not an option for those who love the LORD. Such things pollute the heart, wreck the soul, distort the mind and steal the strength — altogether, our essence of life. How can we love the LORD with all our heart, soul, mind and strength, if the ravages of sin have eaten us alive?

Let me give a warning for those who may be tempted to compromise with sin. We need to understand that if we choose to do what we want to do, instead of what God has called us to do, then we have moved into a state of rebellion and witchcraft. If we elevate ourselves above the Word of God, then we've joined ourselves to the enemy of God and taken on a demonically inspired mindset. If this happens, it means we've rejected the LORD and exalted our self as the god we choose to serve. This is self-worship, and it's rooted in pride, stubbornness and iniquity. If not dealt with, this idolatry will pave the way for demonic torment to manifest.

Personally, I choose not to give the enemy any inroads into my life. I'm persuaded that it's far better to fervently love the LORD and enjoy the blessings of God upon my life, than to be possessed or oppressed by devils, robbed of my destiny and die before my time. As I judiciously aim to obey His commands, I'm also serious and vigilant to seek the LORD for His protection; I know what's at stake.

Secondly, if we're going to worship and celebrate the LORD in a biblical manner (in a way that will bring great honor and joy to the heart of God), we must realize that there are people who will not understand our joyful abandonment in praise. They may reject the LORD and those who celebrate Him. This may result from their own blind ignorance, the bitterness of life's events, or their rebellion against God. They may watch from a distance and voice their cruel criticisms, seeking to discredit us and the God we serve.

We cannot be responsible for how other people react to our praise and worship, but we are responsible for how we respond to them. We must be careful not to allow their wrong or religious attitudes to rob us of our joyful intimacy with the LORD. The only thing we need to concern ourselves with is making sure that the LORD is pleased with how we behave before Him. If the LORD is pleased, then the opinions of men have no power against us.

THE KING OF OUR HEARTS

The LORD should be able to find a position in our hearts where He can set up His kingdom and freely rule and reign in our lives. Jesus said, *"...the kingdom of God is within you"* (Luke 17:21). We understand that every kingdom has a king, and he is to rule the realm in which his kingdom exists; it is so with God's Kingdom as well. Our hearts are to be the holy places wherein the LORD dwells. We're to give Him access to our whole heart and completely yield ourselves to Him.

If we hold anything back from the LORD, then that thing (which we have sought to set aside for ourselves, to the exclusion of His sovereign rule) has taken control and begun to rule over us. It has become an idol, a false god. If this happens, our hearts are not completely or wholly given over to the lordship of our King. We have usurped the authority of His rule in our lives.

Relative to our study so far, if we're to love the LORD our God with all our heart, then we must seek the LORD to help us:

- Rid ourselves of all forms of idolatry, whether inwardly or outwardly.
- Allow no temptation to come between us and our relationship with the LORD.
- Choose to honor Him by obeying His Word above all things, as an act of ardent love (not hollow ritual).
- Allow Him to have preeminent and supreme rule in every area of our lives, as we give Him the gift of a worshipping heart.

May you always love the Lord thy God with all thy heart.

CHAPTER 4

THE 'WHOLE HEART' WORSHIPPER

While preparing this _Loving God_ teaching, the LORD directed me to study scriptures relating to the "whole heart" and the "perfect heart." So, we're going to go deeper into our journey of loving God, as we see how these scriptures apply to us. Our objective is to gain a richer understanding of how the LORD wants us to seek His heart and lovingly respond to Him.

To fulfill the command of the LORD, to love Him with **all** *(G3650)* thy heart, is to love Him with a *whole and complete* heart. You may recall that this word **heart** *(H3824/H3820)* figuratively refers to the *center of the feelings, the will and the intellect.* When we love the LORD completely — with a whole heart — we're inviting Him into everything that pertains to whom we are. As we search the scriptures, we'll discover that the **whole heart** is also linked to different expressions of praise and worship. Our focus is to note the characteristics and actions of a whole hearted lover of God within this context.

CELEBRATES THE WORKS OF THE LORD

When we love somebody, we speak openly of them. We celebrate who they are and what they've done for us. We're delighted to share the details of their sweetness and the significance of our interactions. If human relationships can be this wonderful, how

Part 1 • *Loving God* with All Your Heart

much more should we speak of and celebrate the LORD? After all, He loves us and does more for us than any other person! The psalmist, King David, was a whole hearted lover of God, and he declared his praise to the LORD in:

<u>Psalm 9:1</u> *I will praise thee, O LORD, with my whole heart; I will show forth all thy marvelous works.*

First, it's important to notice the phrase "*I will*" in this verse. When a person says *"I will"* do something they're making a conscious, determined decision to perform a specific, deliberate act. With this in mind, read the verse again.

David emphatically declared words of thanksgiving and praise, after the LORD vindicated him and destroyed his enemies (Psalm 9:3-6). As he gave thanks, David was clear that he desired to praise the LORD completely — with all his thoughts, feelings and actions. This included the exhilarating celebration and proclamations of the specific details and victorious deeds that the LORD had performed.

When it comes to personally applying this scripture amidst life circumstances, we may not always feel like praising the LORD or declaring His works. However, having lackluster or uninspiring thoughts and emotions simply presents opportunities for us to rise above the reasoning of our limited understanding. Regardless of our circumstance or countenance, we can (and should)

CHAPTER 4 • THE 'WHOLE HEART' WORSHIPPER

make the choice to celebrate our God, and give Him the glory due His name (1 Chronicles 16:29; Psalm 29:2, 96:8).

Truly, loving the LORD through our praise expression has absolutely nothing to do with how we feel physically, emotionally, mentally or spiritually. If you don't know how to do this, read Psalm 9:1 once more, but this time, read it from the perspective that David may have actually been in the midst of a difficult situation. If read from this angle, instead of a declaration of thanksgiving, he sounds as though he is encouraging or reminding himself to praise the LORD and show forth His marvelous works. If he was sad or depressed and feeling emotionally off track or disengaged from the Father, he would be calling himself back into mental or emotional alignment with his God. When we are challenged, that's when we must choose to reach toward a new level of faith and trust in the LORD, God Almighty. Reverently, this is who we serve. The fact that we have breath in our lungs is reason enough to praise Him. So, expressing praise and worship to God only has to do with how great He is, all by Himself.

YÂDÂH ~ EXTEND YOUR HANDS AS THANKS AND PRAISE
When we celebrate the LORD with our whole heart, our bodies will also automatically respond. In Psalm 9:1, **praise (H3034/H3027)** translates as the Hebrew word **yâdâh (yaw-daw')**, which means to offer up thanksgiving and *worship* to the LORD with open, *extended hands, held out* in *reverence*. The *open*

hand indicates *power, means and direction.* When we open our hands to the LORD and release all we have and all we are to Him, then He bestows upon us that which He holds in His hands. Our own power, means and direction are limited, but His are limitless. The exchange is definitely to our advantage. Praise will cause the blessing of God to flow into our hands.

When we **show** *(H5608)* forth the **marvelous works** *(H6381)* of the LORD with our praise, we're declaring, *inscribing,* creating and *recounting* a detailed *record (a tally)* of His great accomplishments. His works are miraculously *distinguished* above all the works of men. They reflect the *wonderful, great* and (seemingly) *difficult* things that He has so effortlessly performed. As we raise our hearts and hands to the LORD in *celebration* of who He is, we're also proclaiming His complete perfection in every circumstance.

Worships in the Assembly & the Congregation

The whole hearted lover of God will openly and publically praise the LORD, as we see in:

<u>**Psalm 111:1**</u> ***Praise ye the LORD. I will praise the LORD with my whole heart, in the assembly of the upright, and in the congregation.***

In this scripture, the word **praise** is mentioned twice. The first word for praise is the Hebrew word **halal (haw-lal')** *(H1984),* which means *to shine,* to make a *clear* sound in which we *boast, make a show, rave* and *celebrate* our covenant relationship with the LORD. *Hälal* engages our entire spirit, soul and body with the LORD, and our praise becomes a beautifully, orchestrated demonstration of what's in our hearts. In this verse, the second word for ***praise*** is translated ***yädäh***. As already mentioned, this refers to the lifting up of open hands in thanksgiving, reverence and worship to God. When we enter into ***whole heart*** expressions of praise, our hands, voice and entire being are very much engaged.

To praise the LORD with one's ***whole (H3605/H3634), heart (H3824/H3823/H3820)***, is to do so with a perfect or *complete* heart, which has become an inner sanctuary for the LORD. It's a heart that's tender, full of courage and understanding. It's a heart that is able to *transport love.*

This whole, complete, perfect, courageous heart of love is to be demonstrated ***in the assembly of the upright and in the congregation.*** The ***assembly (H5475/H3245)*** of the ***upright (H3477/H3474)*** specifies a *company of people* who are *in close deliberation* and *intimate* relationship. They've been made *straight*, just and *right*eous before the LORD. There's no crookedness, perversion or divisions among them, because the assembly of the upright receives counsel from the Word of God. Whole hearted, upright worshippers won't allow schisms to rise up in their midst. Rather, they'll choose to quickly settle disputes and make things right. Therefore, their relationships with one another are *pleasant and prosperous* in the LORD.

Part 1 • *Loving God* with All Your Heart

The word **congregation** *(H5712/H5707)* could imply a different kind of *assembly*. Generally, it means *a family or crowd*. The Hebrew words linked with it also indicate an established *concourse* (gathering); *fixture*; *witness, testimony* or *recorder*. The congregation can be a mixture of those who love the LORD and those who do not know Him. Just because a person enters a church building and sits in the congregation, does not mean they're a part of the assembly of the upright. The mature disciple of Christ understands that it's possible for people to 'go to church' and not yet 'be the Church.' Nevertheless, the whole hearted worshipper will praise the LORD with the same fervor, regardless of who is or isn't in the congregation.

As followers of Christ, we're exhorted to provoke one another unto love and good works, as well as to not forsake the assembling of ourselves together (Hebrews 10:24-25). We're to be in consistent fellowship with other believers. In this way, we're encouraged and strengthened in the LORD. Whole hearted worshippers are devoted to God and, ultimately, accountable to Him, but they're also accountable to (and for) their brothers and sisters in Christ.

The integrity of our praise and worship (both in and outside the church walls) reflects our relationship with the LORD. We're to live a lifestyle of worship that influences everything we think, say and do. This mature lifestyle is also evidenced in our personal human relationships. A truly passionate heart of love for the LORD will overflow and positively affect the lives of others. However, if we choose to mistreat our fellow man, then we're not living in the integrity of who we say we are. If this happens, it's time for a heart check. If the heart isn't right toward others, nor will it be right toward the LORD. If this isn't dealt with, then our praise and worship becomes tainted and displeasing to the LORD.

KEEPS AND SEEKS
If we want to experience the blessings of God in our lives, we must have a heart that's willing to keep and seek. Since blessing is directly related to a lifestyle of worship and obedience, each person must make a decision to willingly submit to the will of the LORD.

***Psalm 119:2** Blessed are they that keep his testimonies, and that seek him with the whole heart.*

KEEPS
To **keep** *(H5341)* the **testimonies** *(H5713/H5707/ H5749)* of the LORD is to *obey, guard, protect, maintain, record, duplicate and testify* to the truth of His Word. Those who keep His testimonies are a **blessed** *(H835/H833)* and happy people. They accept God's Word as the final authority and standard for godliness, and allow Him to instruct them in every area of their lives.

Part 1 • *Loving God* with All Your Heart

The testimonies of the LORD impact the behavior and lifestyle of believers. They influence how we think, what we say and do, where we go, who we spend time with and how we make decisions. The visible manifestation of our choices gives witness to the condition of our hearts. As we obey the LORD, a restored, healed, overcoming, joy-filled life will be the manifest evidence of His blessing upon us.

SEEKS

To **seek** *(H1875)* after the LORD means to care for Him, and therefore, we choose to *follow* (*pursue* and *search*) after Him. We make *frequent* efforts to spend time with Him and *ask* Him questions. But more than anything else, to **seek Him with the whole heart**, means to *worship* Him.

The most prominent Hebrew word in reference to worship is **shâchâh** *(H7812)*. By definition, **shâchâh** is a worship expression of humility. It means that we *depress* ourselves to a lower position before the LORD. It also means to *prostrate* one's self *in homage to royalty or God*. In the Old Testament, besides being translated as the English word 'worship,' shâchâh is also translated as: bow down, crouch, fall down (flat), humbly beseech, make to stoop, as well as give reverence and obeisance (showing deep respect or deferential courtesy, as a subordinate to a superior). How often do you see this type of worship in your local church? How often do you engage in this type of worship in your personal time with the LORD? It's important to note that this depressing of self and prostrate positioning must first happen in the attitude of the heart (the center of our being) and soul (the emotions, mind and will), before it will manifest in our physical posturing.

To **seek** (*follow, pursue and search after*) the LORD with the **whole heart** (and to keep his testimonies) requires humility. Therefore, the proud person will never truly seek the LORD, because to be a God seeker requires one to be God-focused, not self-focused. God seekers understand and acknowledge the superiority, authority and highly exalted position of the LORD God Almighty. They joyfully and humbly lay prostrate before Him, in complete submission. The proud refuse to willingly bow before the LORD, physically or mentally. Their arrogance robs them of the blessings of God. But those who seek the LORD with their whole heart will experience the fullness of His blessings.

PURSUES THE LORD

King David was a passionate worshipper. He was a man after God's own heart. His greatest desire was that nothing would come between him and his relationship with the LORD. David's pursuit was God!

***Psalm 119:10** With my whole heart have I sought thee: O let me not wander from thy commandments.*

Part 1 • *Loving God* with All Your Heart

David was one who truly **sought** *(H1875)* the LORD. This means that he *followed after, searched for* and *pursued* the LORD *frequently* in worship. Often, we think of the act of prayer as the main practice by which we seek the LORD. But we need to understand physical worship as an expression of faith that touches the heart of God as well. The end result may even be the same — that we would enter into His presence and experience the delights of His glory, honor, strength and gladness (1 Chronicles 16:27-28). Whatever the method, the worshipper who seeks the LORD invests time, energy and resources to pursue and cultivate a passionate, intimate relationship with Him.

If we're in pursuit of God, we'll have no time or desire to wander away from Him. David had no desire to let his heart **wander** *(H7686)* from the **commandments** *(H4687)* of the LORD. Within the Word of God we find wisdom, direction and protection, because it contains the *divine* precepts and Laws of the Kingdom of Heaven. Therefore, if we honor the Word of God, then we're honoring Him. When we honor the LORD with our whole heart, we'll not crave the deceptive and temporal delights of sin. Instead, we'll choose to boldly stand against the wickedness and temptations of immoral behavior.

Out of love for the LORD, we'll refuse to be lulled into the intoxicating and deadly lusts of the fleshly nature.

Does this mean we will never be tempted? Of course not! But we have the power to determine the outcome of temptation based on how we deal with it. As we obey the commandments of the LORD, we'll automatically reject the influence of anything that's contrary to the ways of God.

There were times when David was tempted and fell into sin. He loved God with great intensity, but he still struggled with the fears, doubts and lustful failures of his humanity. The reality is that, before David could fall into sin, he had to make a choice to go against the Word and ways of the LORD. If David had remained in an attitude of worship, he would not have made such dreadful decisions. David was quick to repent of his weaknesses when the LORD corrected him, but unfortunately, there were times when he (and those around him) still suffered the consequences of his sin.

The solution to overcoming sin is to seek the LORD and continually remain in His presence through an attitude of worship. We cannot worship the LORD and willfully sin at the same time. The opposite is true as well; we cannot be in sin and live a lifestyle of worship.

Life doesn't just happen to us. Most of the time, we make our own decisions as to how we'll live and whom we'll serve. If we choose to serve the LORD, then we must give Him our whole heart. If we hold anything back from Him, then we're not allowing Him to reign supreme in our lives. If we've not yielded the full possession of ourselves to the LORD, then we'll not be able to fully possess all He has for us.

As long as a part of self is on the throne of our lives, then we've created space for the idols of our own will. This causes a divided heart, a double mindset and a spiritually split personality. A divided heart and double-mindedness will cause a person to entertain and rationalize temptation. Rationalization then becomes the catalyst that ushers in sin and spiritual conflict; causing a war between the will of God and the will of the lustful flesh. The devil and our flesh nature can only rule over us if we give into temptation.

We overcome temptation when we submit ourselves to God and resist the devil. When we submit to the LORD and exalt Him as our supreme ruler, the devil is forced to flee (James 4:7). He can no longer stand to be in our company! Our willing praise and worship are to be the expression of our love; a submissive demonstration that He is worthy of His kingly position in our lives.

If we're seeking, pursuing and worshipping the LORD, then we'll experience Him at a more intimate level. It's in the intimate presence of the LORD that we begin to comprehend His great love, mercy, kindness, favor and faithfulness. He has set His loving desire toward us. This should persuade us to obey His Word and not wander into sin. When we reject sin and seek God, then our lives become a proclamation of whom we truly love and serve. Sin can no longer rule over the heart of the committed worshipper.

Understand this: Whoever or whatever we seek will become that which rules over us. If we seek a relationship with the LORD, we'll experience His joyful, supernatural reign in our lives. However, if we seek a relationship with other things, such as money, fame, wrong relationships, lusts or any other distraction that would lead us into sin, then our lives will bear the painful evidence of our choices. We cannot serve two masters, for we will hate one and love the other, or we will hold to one and despise the other (Matthew 6:24; Luke 16:13). We cannot move in two different directions at the same time. Again, it's all about the choices we make, and our choices are motivated by the condition of our hearts.

We must take personal responsibility for our decisions. Every choice produces either the fruit of blessing or corruption. Those who choose to sin cannot blame others for the consequences they suffer. Their suffering was the fruit born from the seeds of their disobedience. If we see the corrupt fruit of sin in our lives, there are steps we must take to rectify the situation:
- Don't blame others for your actions.
- Take responsibility for your sin.
- Repent of all wrong doing.

Part 1 • *Loving God* with All Your Heart

- Reject, renounce and tear down every enemy stronghold you've allowed to be erected in your life.
- Ask the LORD for His forgiveness.
- Receive the cleansing power of His blood.
- Be reconciled into a close, loving fellowship with Him.
- Serve God and purpose in your heart to sin no more.

We don't have to carry the sins of yesterday into today or the future. That's the beauty of the LORD'S forgiveness. If we fully repent of going our own way, the LORD will cleanse and restore us. He will reconcile us to Himself and re-establish our relationship with Him. He's after our whole heart. He wants pure, unadulterated love from His people and He'll not settle for anything less. Take a moment right now and consider the LORD'S amazing, everlasting love. Remember, His mercies are new every morning. Now, praise Him and give thanks for all He has done! (1 Chronicles 16:34; Lamentations 3:22-23)

SEEKS UNDERSTANDING

"Whole heart" worshippers seek to please the LORD through understanding His ways. Therefore, they make it their priority to study, examine, observe and meditate on His Word. In so doing, they receive understanding. We see such seeking in:

***Psalm 119:34** Give me understanding, and I shall keep thy law; yea, I shall observe it with my whole heart.*

To be given **understanding** *(H995)* means to receive the ability *to separate mentally (or distinguish)* the difference between truth and error, in the light of God's Word. This spiritual discernment gives proper perspective to every situation of life. The **whole heart** worshipper also desires to **observe** the precepts of the LORD. Interestingly, this does not mean to just obey; to **observe** *(H8104)* means to *guard, protect* and *attend to* His Word in such a way as to *hedge it about (as with thorns).*

When God's truth is applied to our lives, deception is ripped away, and we're freed from the bondage and lies of the enemy. Once we're free, the Word of God works not only in our spirits, but it also begins to manifest in our thinking processes and actions. The reality of God's Word operating in our lives, is evidenced through our changed hearts and renewed minds.

Get this into your spirit: Believers are the epistles of Christ (2 Corinthians 3:2-3). We carry a message of God's love, grace and truth within our lives. We're to become the Word of God personified — a powerful, visual, living, breathing, walking, talking example of the character and nature of Christ — as we're transformed into His image and likeness.

MOVES IN THE OPPOSITE SPIRIT

As we become more like Christ, there will be those who will misunderstand us. They may think we're different or strange. They may even seek to attack, ridicule and slander our good name or character. As followers and lovers of God, we have a responsibility to show them an opposite spirit. It's true that these people operate either in ignorance or under deliberate malice; but whichever it is, we're to operate in wisdom and under the control and direction of the Holy Spirit. Regardless of who or what we encounter, we're to keep our hearts focused on the truths of God. In reference to being falsely accused, King David said in:

***Psalm 119:69** The proud have forged a lie against me: but I will keep thy precepts with my whole heart.*

Whether they realize it or not, those who have the audacity to hurl derision and insults, operate as the **proud** (H2086/H2102) or *arrogant* who are deceived. They are also presumptuous and *insolent*; they may even *seethe* over their accusations. While people who live this way, definitely, walk in the darkness of hatred and corruption, they're blind to the flaws of their own perception, character and spiritual condition. Therefore, they ridicule and look down on others who they don't identify with, especially the righteous. As followers of Christ, it's our responsibility to pray for their salvation and deliverance, because the proud are like puppets tied to the whims of the enemy.

KNOW WHO YOUR ENEMY REALLY IS

Before his rebellion, satan was known as lucifer; he held the position of being the anointed, covering cherub upon the holy mountain of God in Heaven. He was to cover, guard and protect the throne of God. Yet, his pride stirred him to exalt himself against the LORD. This caused his downfall and complete humiliation. In an instant, satan lost his ministry, was thrown out of the presence of the LORD and fell as lightening from Heaven (Ezekiel 28:13-19; Luke 10:18).

This was the first recorded confrontation between good and evil, and it happened in the heavenly realms. Just as satan sought to exalt himself against God, he now seeks to lift himself up against God's people, as the accuser of the brethren (Revelation 12:10). But just as God cast satan — the devil — out of His presence, we can do the same in the name, power and authority of Jesus (Luke 10:19; Mark 16:17).

While it is most important to understand who our true enemy is, let's also be clear about the people he uses. These people may not realize they're in cahoots with satan, but by aligning themselves with his behaviors, they're guilty, nonetheless. They become instruments of wickedness, as they aim fiery darts of cruel words against the righteous. Knowingly or unknowingly, these accusers become accessory mouthpieces of the devil and take on his attributes. In fact, they operate in the same pride, rebellion and wickedness as the master of iniquity they serve. Literally, these minions imitate the one they allow to control their lives, and as he is, the underlings of satan are already defeated. Those who trust in the LORD shouldn't be intimidated by them.

Know Who You Are in Christ

Regardless of the lies others may speak against us, we must know who we are in Christ. The lies of the enemy are powerless, if we refuse to give them place in our lives. Psalm 119:69 says **the proud forged (H2950) a lie (H8267/H8266)**. In the Hebrew, this means they sought to *cheat* and bring failure to the righteous, by applying lies that would *stick on* the accused *as a patch*. A patch is used to try to mend or hide something that is torn or broken. Lies are spoken to hide or distract from the truth of a given situation. From this analogy, we need to remember that a sticky patch of lies from the accuser will not adhere to anyone that is anointed with the oil of the Holy Spirit and living according to the Word of God. If you know who you are in Christ, and you walk in your authority, the words of the enemy are defeated before they can even reach your ears. The lies of the proud can have no power to wound us, unless we allow them to do so.

When the enemy speaks lies against you or brings up your forgiven past, rejoice! We already know that satan is a liar and he hates the truth (John 8:44). He's the enemy of God and God's people. If satan has to concoct fictitious lies to try to make you look bad, if he has to pull up your past sins (which have already been washed away by the blood of Jesus), this means he's desperate! That rat has run out of evidence, and he can't find any recent, nasty morsels of sin and condemnation to hurl against you. Never allow his accusations to scare, unnerve or discourage you. Know that you're no longer who you used to be; you've become a new creature in Christ!

Think about this: If the enemy accuses you of your past, he's trying to attach something to you that no longer exists. This antagonist desires to manifest a figment of his own imagination in your life, and he's watching to see if you'll swallow the bait! If the LORD has cleansed the sins of your past, then they are no more. Therefore, no weapon of the enemy formed against you will prosper, and every tongue he tries to lift up against you in judgment, you will condemn. This is your heritage as a righteous saint of the LORD (Isaiah 54:17)! You have the power to silence the enemy.

The LORD has redeemed everything about you — the good, the bad and the ugly. If you allow Him, He'll use it for your good and His glory. He will use your redeemed life and victorious testimony as a weapon to continually defend you and restrain satan. The

Part 1 • *Loving God* with All Your Heart

enemy is already defeated; take advantage of him! Expose his deceptive viciousness and assault his tactics with the truth of God's Word!

A PERSONAL TESTIMONY

Let me share a personal story about when the devil tried to put a sticky patch of condemnation on me. This happened through a family member who had forged lies against me. Our relationship was such that, no matter what I did, this person was never satisfied with my performance. They suffered from a negative mindset and had the tendency to reject most positive input in any given situation. Therefore, instead of speaking words of life, encouragement and blessing, their words were usually very negative, judgmental, discouraging and self-focused. Regardless of what the enemy tried to do (thru this person in my life), the LORD (in His great grace and mercy) extended His love and encouragement to me, changing my life forever.

At fourteen years of age, I came to know Christ as my LORD and Savior. I repented of my sins and put my trust in Him for salvation. There was an immediate change in my life. I was freed from tormenting fear and experienced a great manifestation of joy! However, I wasn't raised in a Christian environment. I'd never read the bible and wasn't trained in godly thoughts or behaviors. I had many things to learn and struggled to understand the scriptures. Though I attended church, I lacked solid godly leadership in my personal life.

In my late teens and early twenties, I didn't always make the best of choices. Even so, God's grace covered me. I began to learn and grow as the Holy Spirit taught me. It was a slow process, but in time, I began to understand the ways of the LORD and He delivered me from many of the snares of the enemy. I loved the LORD, but my life was a work in progress. I still had issues and broken places in my life, and I needed to allow the LORD to deal with them.

When I was twenty-one years old, I was engaged to be married. A month before the wedding my fiancé and I suffered a moral failure and chose to have premarital sex. Not long after our immorality, I began feeling ill. Several weeks after the wedding I still wasn't' feeling well. In my naivety, I thought I had the flu. Almost two months later, I learned that I was pregnant.

Shortly after the wedding, the family member of this story asked if I was pregnant, and I said "no." At the time of the questioning, I didn't know I was pregnant yet. Then she asked me if I'd had sex before I was married and I, again, said "no." The first lie was spoken ignorantly, from a lack of knowledge. The second lie was spoken blatantly, from fear.

I'd been caught. I was ashamed and embarrassed by the questions, because I feared what others would think and say about me. I knew that having sex before marriage was wrong when I did it; there was no excuse. That's why I lied. Although I tried to cover my sin, the LORD knew all the truth of the matter, and he began to convict me of immorality and lying.

After feeling ill for several weeks, I was advised to take a pregnancy test, which of course, was positive. Now, I was in a mess. I had lied and it was only a matter of time before the truth would be known. I knew I had to deal with it, but I delayed. A couple of weeks later, I began to spot and bleed. At that time the LORD spoke very clearly to me and said, "You lied about your sin, and if you do not repent and get it right, you will lose this child." The Word of the LORD was very strong in my spirit. I had set myself up for disaster. I knew that if I did not confess the truth of what I had done, I would reap the reward of my own doing.

With great remorse in my heart, I repented before the LORD and asked His forgiveness. Once things were restored in my relationship with Him, I went to see the family member I had lied to. Again, I confessed my sin and apologized. I asked forgiveness for lying to them and for disappointing them by my actions. They said they forgave me and it seemed that we were restored. I went on with my life of raising a family and serving the LORD.

In my early thirties, I began full-time ministry. I enrolled in various schools of ministry training, and was ordained and licensed as a Minister of the Gospel. I travelled domestically and in foreign mission fields. The LORD blessed me to be able to minister the Word of God in twelve different nations. I was enjoying the sweet goodness and tender mercies of the LORD.

I still had a relationship with my mentioned family member and loved her. I wanted her to know the joy, forgiveness and freedom that I had experienced in Christ. I reached out to her with love in various ways. But when it came to the gospel, she would only allow me to share with her to a certain point, and then she would cut off the conversation. Though I felt the rejection, I continued to move forward into my God ordained destiny.

After walking with the LORD for more than thirty years, I was still reaching out to this same family member and trying to include her in my life. However, she became combative in her attitude and was very difficult to deal with. This person (I would find out many years later) was bearing grudges against me, because I had given my life to Christ and left Roman Catholicism — the family religion. My decision had greatly offended her and had become the root of what would be a forty year division in our relationship. I have come to understand that, those who have never truly known, understood or embraced the amazing grace and complete forgiveness of the LORD, will not know how to extend it.

In my late forties, there was a major shift in my life. My first husband of twenty-five years died suddenly. This was a very devastating time, but I continued to serve the LORD and found my comfort and contentment in Him. I didn't know if I would ever marry again, but it really didn't matter to me, because I found great joy in my Heavenly King and Bridegroom, Jesus.

Nevertheless, in the LORD'S amazing plan and tender mercies toward me, He brought a wonderful man of God into my life. We courted for two years and knew we were destined to be married. I was entering into a new season of love and wanted to share my joy with my family members, including the one in this story. I thought they would be happy for me and rejoice in the fact that I had found love again. Some did share our joy, but some did not.

The problem (from their perspective) was that I was a 50 year old white woman who was planning to become the wife of a younger black man! When my intended and I gave no place to the unholy idols of family pride and prejudice, foolish attitudes began to manifest in some of the family members. True to form, my aforementioned family member began to bitterly unleash a tsunami of what she perceived to be all my lifelong short comings, including the fact that I was considering a cross-cultural marriage.

False accusations began to spew forth against myself and my future husband. A campaign from hell had risen up to try to stop me from moving into my ordained destiny. It was as if I was being falsely judged as unworthy of experiencing the wonderful blessings of God in my life. This was one of the most painful and devastating storms I'd ever experienced. During that time, my heart was breaking, but I heard the Holy Spirit speak very clearly to me. He said, "The accuser of the brethren!" The Word of the LORD caused me to realize that the stabbing words weren't originating from the mouths of those speaking, but from the demonic influence that was operating through them.

Many times, people don't realize when they've joined themselves to satan's agenda. They don't know they've been manipulated into assisting him in his role as the accuser of the brethren. The devil doesn't usually show up and say, "Okay, this is the plan: Today I'm going to use you to tear down and accuse _____ (fill in the blank). I'll use your voice, your fears, your pride and the lies you've believed for my purposes. I'll take advantage of your doubts, unbelief and ignorance, to humiliate, discourage, embarrass, harass and shame them. You will use your mouth to assault their character, strip them of their worth and thwart them from fulfilling their destiny! I will use you to destroy them, just because I can!" No!! That's not how the devil usually works; he's not that obvious. This sly infiltrator comes with

Part 1 • *Loving God* with All Your Heart

subtlety and gains access through the natural reasoning of the carnal mind. This is how those who are not submitted to Christ become the devil's pawn to destroy others.

In the midst of the attack and in my sorrow, I found my anchor of hope in my God! I knew He loved me, regardless of what others said or did against me. Ultimately, the devil was using others to try and keep me from the plan and purposes of God for my life.

The experience also caused my fiancé to rise up as my protector. That night we established firm boundaries concerning family members. We would no longer tolerate ungodly or devilish behavior manifesting through human participants. From that time forward, there would be no negative or ungodly input spoken in our presence; we wouldn't allow it.

Through it all, I learned some very important lessons, and I desire to share them:
1. There will be those who do not understand or appreciate what God is doing in our lives.
2. We must learn to discern between those who are for us and those who are against us.
3. Choose friends and relationships carefully.
4. Use discernment to know who can and cannot be trusted; don't share everything with everybody.
5. Don't tolerate the false accusations of the devil or allow him to mock who you are in Christ!

6. Don't let anyone or anything steal your God ordained destiny!
7. Understand that, in some relationships, there comes a time when you just have to let people go. You forgive them; commit them to the LORD; pray for them and go do what the LORD has called you to do.

On October 30, 2010, I married my blessed man of God, and it's been one of the best life decisions I've ever made. My sweet husband and I are enjoying life, love and ministry together in the LORD. We've refused to allow the accuser of the brethren to steal what God had ordained for us! Having shared all this, I want to encourage you with one final thought:

> Although the proud may forge lies against us, if we will keep our hearts focused on the Word of God and what He says about us, we will enjoy the blessings of God, regardless of what others may say or do.

For instance, the person I've referred to throughout this story has since passed away. Sixteen months before she died, she received a diagnosis of terminal lung cancer. Sadly, the loving relationship I desired to have with her, never really came to pass. Despite that, the fear of her impending death began to work humility and godly fear into her heart. She did, eventually, trust Christ as her Savior. Thus, my most pressing prayer for this one I love was answered. For this, I give God praise!

Part 1 • *Loving God* with All Your Heart

FOCUS ON HIS WORD & WITNESS

Through my life experiences — both the good and the bad — I've learned some powerful lessons. My conclusion is that, regardless of what's going on around us, we must focus on the LORD and pursue Him with a passionate heart of love. Also, if we're to fulfill our divine purposes in Him, we cannot allow ourselves to stagnate in the miry distractions of life or be squelched by the opinions of men.

No matter what comes our way, we're to **keep** *(H5341)* our focus on the **precepts** *(H6490)* of the LORD (Psalm 119:69). This means we're to *guard, protect, maintain* and *obey* the LORD'S *appointed mandates.* A mandate is a command or authorization to act in a particular way on a public issue. God's mandates are issued from the throne of Heaven to His representatives in the earth, and we're to carry them out for the entire world to see.

God has purposeful mandates for His Body of believers, both corporately and individually. As citizens of the Kingdom of God, we're to fully submit to the holy desires of our King. In keeping with the precepts of our God, we reject and expose all lying schemes of the devil and give him no place of rest.

God, in His wisdom, even uses the pain of our past failures to help fulfill our heavenly mandates. Our failures become the catalysts of vital life lessons. They help us understand the ways of God, the consequences of sin and the grace of His forgiveness and mercy. Repentance, deliverance and submission to the LORD qualify us to share with others what the LORD has done in our lives. Our greatest areas of struggle, if submitted to the LORD, will usually become our most powerful areas of ministry.

What ministry mandate has the LORD assigned to you?

What past failures has He used to prepare you for your Kingdom assignment?

Are you fulfilling your assignment?
If not, why?

Is Unashamed

The shameless worshipper is delivered from the slavery and disgrace of their past. They walk in freedom and understand that Christ has redeemed and cleansed them of their sins. They're no longer the person they used to be. Therefore, they can boldly praise Him with their whole heart!

***Psalm 138:1** I will praise thee with my whole heart: before the gods will I sing praise unto thee.*

In this verse, the two words for *praise* are translated from two different Hebrew words. The first is *yâdâh (yaw-daw')* *(H3034/H3027)* and the second is *zâmar (zaw-mar')* *(H2167/H2168)*. By definition, this scripture means that the **whole heart** worshipper praises and *celebrates* the LORD with *open hands, extended* in

Part 1 • *Loving God* with All Your Heart

reverence and thanksgiving, as well as with *singing and music*. When we lift our hands in praise we're, figuratively, exchanging what we're holding for what the LORD desires to impart to us. We're surrendering and releasing our own agendas, in pursuit of seeking and fulfilling the will and desires of the LORD.

YÂDÂH ~ THROW A STONE IN PRAISE
The second definition of the Hebrew word *yâdâh* means to physically *throw (a stone or arrow) at or away*. What does it mean to throw a stone in praise? We see an example of this in 1 Samuel 17 when David, an unashamed worshipper of God, uses a stone to destroy an enemy.

Before David became King of Israel, he was a shepherd boy. He had three older brothers (Eliab, Abinadab and Shammah) who were soldiers in the armies of Israel. They were supposed to be fighting the Philistines, but instead they were in a standoff. Both armies were decked in battle array; Israel was encamped in the valley of Elah and the Philistines were encamped in Shochah. And there was a valley between them. David's father, Jesse, wanted to know how his older sons were doing, so He commanded David to take parched corn, loaves of bread and cheese to his brothers and to report back with news of the battle.

Upon arrival, David realized there was no battle taking place. Instead, the Philistine champion (the giant, Goliath)

Chapter 4 • The 'Whole Heart' Worshipper

was reproaching Israel and defying the armies of the living God. Goliath's hostile words struck paralyzing fear in the ranks of the Israeli armies.

Once David saw what was going on, he knew that with God's help, he could knock the life out of that big mouthed giant. Everyone else was not convinced. David's older brothers had even questioned his integrity and doubted his motives in coming to the camp. Goliath, the Philistine giant, also mocked him. But David intended to bring glory to the LORD and put a stop to the taunting accusations of this heathen Philistine. He intended to kill the giant and cut off his head!

David was a worshipper; he knew that his God would help him take down the enemy. Armed with only his staff, a slingshot, five smooth stones and his faith in God, David went after the giant — the enemy of God's people. David pulled one stone from his shepherd's bag, put it in his sling, whirled it over his head and sent it flying. One propelled stone delivered a death blow straight into the forehead of that uncircumcised Philistine. Since David had no sword of his own, he took Goliath's and cut off the giant's head! The same weapon that Goliath intended to use against David became the weapon of his own destruction!

David's bold faith encouraged the armies of Israel. His attitude and actions also struck fear in the hearts of the Philistine soldiers. When Israel pursued the Philistines in battle, the enemy army was scattered and suffered many casualties.

Our praise can have the same powerful effect. If we will shamelessly walk in faith and boldly declare that our God is strong and mighty, then He will do great and marvelous things in and through us! The Almighty already has victory over every scheme of satan. As we serve the LORD, our enemies are scattered and El Shaddai is glorified!

What are you sending forth in your praise?

THE CHARACTER AND NATURE OF THE LORD

In relation to **yâdâh** being associated with praise and the throwing of a stone, let's look at how stones are literally and symbolically connected with the works, character and nature of God. A stone became <u>a place of rest</u> for Jacob's head and <u>a marker</u> for <u>the house of God</u> (Genesis 28:18); <u>protection</u> over water wells where the sheep came to drink (Genesis 29:2-3) and a <u>witness of covenant</u> (Genesis 31:44-46). Jacob's son, Joseph, was referred to as the <u>stone of Israel who preserved nations</u> during the 7 year famine (Genesis 49:22-24). A sharp stone was used for <u>covenant circumcision</u> for the son of Moses (Exodus 4:25). A stone became a place of rest and <u>help in the battle</u> (Exodus 17:12). Stones were used for the building of <u>altars</u> (Exodus 20:25). Precious stones were set into the <u>priestly</u> ephod and breastplate (Exodus 25:7). The

Chapter 4 • The 'Whole Heart' Worshipper

Ten Commandments were inscribed in stone (Exodus 31:18; Deuteronomy 9:10). Stones were used to carry out the death penalty in the punishment of sin, thereby putting the offender and the opportunity for his crime to be recommitted to death (Leviticus 20:2, 20:27, 24:14, 16). David used a stone to slay the giant Goliath, who mocked God and ridiculed the people of God (1 Samuel 17:50). Stones were also used to repair the breeches in the house of the LORD (2 Kings 12:12). Arrows, which could have been made of stone, refer to a weapon of deliverance in the hand of the LORD (2 Kings 13:17; Psalms 64:7; Zechariah 9:14). Jesus is referred to as the stone of stumbling; a rock of offense; the precious cornerstone; the stone the builders rejected and the head of the corner (Isaiah 8:14, 28:16; Matthew 21:42-44; Mark 12:10; 1 Peter 2:8). A stone was placed over the entrance of Jesus tomb, and that same stone was supernaturally rolled away (Matthew 27:60, 66; Mark 16:4). The LORD appears as jasper and sardine stones upon the throne (Revelation 4:3). Also, the Bride of Christ, the New Jerusalem, the dwelling place of God among His people are described as a Jasper stone, clear as crystal (Revelation 21:9-11).

Do you see where I'm going with this? All of these references represent the character and nature of the LORD. I challenge you to reread them. We need to realize that Jesus is our rest, our protection and the shepherd of His flock. He is our covenant maker and the one who preserves us in hard times. He cuts away our flesh nature and writes His law in our hearts. He's with us in the battle and is a very present help in trouble.

Jesus met us at the altar of the cross to become the sacrifice for our sins. He took our punishment and died in our place; but death could not hold him, and the stone on the tomb could not stop Him. Though He was rejected as the cornerstone of truth, He was (and is) the standard by which the household of God is built up. Through Christ, the breeches between man and God have been repaired. He shines forth in glory upon the throne and is coming for a Bride that reflects His radiant beauty. He is our Mighty God and He has delivered us from all the enemy's snares.

When we raise our hands and hearts to the LORD, we're acknowledging all He is and all He has done for us. We're openly declaring that He is worthy of our praise and that He is the one and only, true and living God. We're shamelessly demonstrating through our praise that there is none like Him. We're offering all we have, and all we are, to Him. Our confessions of praise and lifestyle of worship become strong weapons of warfare, to cast down the powers, principalities, rulers of darkness and spiritual wickedness in high places.

BE FREE, NOT BOUND

Jesus came to set the captives free. Everything He's done for mankind has been so that we could have a relationship with Him. He wants us to experience His

CHAPTER 4 • THE 'WHOLE HEART' WORSHIPPER

peace, life, freedom and joy without shame. He desires that we know Him as our Creator, Savior, healer, deliverer, strength, lover and friend.

As we continue our study on *yâdâh* the third definition has to do with the *wringing of the hands and bemoaning*. In the spiritual realm, when we use our hands to praise the LORD, I believe demonic forces become distressed and filled with grief. So consider this, we can praise the LORD and cause the enemy to become distraught or we can refuse to give Him our praise, and we can become the ones who are wringing our hands and moaning in distress. So, either we choose to make devils uncomfortable or they will make us uncomfortable. Praise (or the lack of it) — this is the determining factor.

In reference to Psalm 138:1, the second word for praise is *zâmar (H2167/H2168)*. It means to *touch or strike a musical instrument with the fingers* and *to play upon it* and *make music*. It also means to *celebrate in song and music*. Elsewhere in scripture, *zâmar* means to give and sing forth praise and psalms. Remember, one of the definitions of *yâdâh* is to throw. Now we see that two of the definitions of *zâmar* are to touch and to strike. Praise is a spiritual weapon. Even the motion of playing the instruments is symbolic of buffeting the enemy (Psalm 149)! Anointed music will shift the spiritual atmosphere and devils cannot remain where the presence of God is allowed to manifest (1 Samuel 16:23).

Another reference for *zâmar* may also identify with *trimming* (a vine, as in pruning). This speaks of a separation between that which is beneficial and that which hinders proper spiritual growth and fruitfulness. When our heart is right, the power of praise and worship will sever the bondage of the enemy, allowing us to enter into our full level of productivity and fruitfulness in the LORD.

Referring again, to Psalm 138:1, to praise the LORD *before* (H5048) the *gods* (H430) means to boldly exalt Him in *front* of, *over* and/or *against* any earthly authority or spiritual force other than the true and living God. This includes *magistrates*, rulers, angels, devils, false gods and/or idols. If we're to live a life of bold, unashamed worship before our God and freely celebrate Him, we must cut away anything and everything that hinders us from doing so. Whether those hindrances have to do with the fear of man, governments, perceived circumstances, demonic influences or our own contrary thoughts and actions, we need to praise and worship God and prefer Him above everything else. All other so called *gods* must be made to bow in subjection before to Him! This is unashamed, righteously audacious praise!

CHAPTER 4 • THE 'WHOLE HEART' WORSHIPPER

FINDS GOD'S PEACE AND REST

As we walk through this journey called life, the LORD desires for mankind to be in a personal, interactive relationship with Him. However, it must happen based on His terms, not ours. Let's see what the LORD said concerning King Asa and the tribes of Judah and Benjamin through the prophet Azariah in:

<u>2 Chronicles 15:1-2</u> The LORD is with you, while ye be with Him; and if ye seek Him, He will be found of you; but if ye forsake Him, He will forsake you."

The history behind this scripture is that King Asa and the tribes of Judah and Benjamin had become slack in their relationship with the LORD and had fallen into idolatry. In fact, there was no functioning priest or law. As a result, the presence of God was absent from the nation, and there was great turmoil and unrest with no peace to be found. The LORD brought adversity upon them, because of their idolatrous abominations. The corrupt fruit of their idolatry manifested, as nations and cities were destroyed. In His immeasurable grace, the LORD used this strife to turn their hearts back to Him.

In 2 Chronicles 15:3-6, once His people turned from their own ways and sought the LORD again, He allowed Himself to be ***found*** *(H4672)*. This meant that He *met* with his people and made His *presence* known. He delivered and encircled them with His peace and rest, demonstrating that He was all they needed. Notice, the

Part 1 • *Loving God* with All Your Heart

presence, peace and rest of the LORD did not manifest, until the people made Him their number one priority.

As far as the LORD is concerned, nothing has changed today. He is still looking for a covenant people that will treasure and honor Him, above all else. When He sees them, He will manifest His glorious presence and provide His peace and rest.

Looking again at 2 Chronicles 15, we see that after the people repented, King Asa found hope in the words of Azariah and the prophecy of Obed:

<u>2 Chronicles 15:7</u> Be ye strong therefore, and let not your hands be weak for your work shall be rewarded.

When Asa heard these words, he took courage because he knew the LORD was with him. He removed the abominable idols out of all the land of Judah and Benjamin, as well as the cities of Ephraim, Manasseh and Simeon. After the land was cleansed and the people repented, there was a great sacrifice of 700 oxen and 7000 sheep offered to the LORD.

The people entered into covenant with the LORD and promised to seek Him with all their hearts and with all their souls. This covenant was made with much fervor; a decree was even made that whoever would not seek the LORD would be put to death (2 Chronicles 15:8-13). In 2 Chronicles 15:14-19, the people *sware* (H7650) unto the LORD with a loud voice. This means they *declared 7 times* that they would seek the LORD with all their hearts, souls and desires. They declared this, in an exceedingly great manner with all their might, confirming and making the covenant *complete*.

The people fully honored and magnified the LORD with shouting, music and much rejoicing. Because the people repented and swore with a covenant commitment to fervently seek the LORD, He allowed Himself to be found of them. When we truly fall in love with Him and Him alone, then all He has is already ours.

I sense a prompting of the Holy Spirit to clarify something. If we only come to the LORD when we need Him to deliver us from the consequences of our own unrepentant sin and foolishness or when we need provision, then I think it's safe to say that we should not expect very much. Relationship with God requires more than just our grocery list of wants and desires. We must realize that He is our greatest need and our most prized possession. He's more than enough to meet every need. When we make a **whole heart** commitment to Him, He promises and delights in an intimate relationship with us.

Scripture says that King Asa's heart was perfect toward the LORD all his days. He loved the LORD so much that he even removed his idolatrous mother from being queen and destroyed and burned her idol. He also restored the house of the LORD. As a result, King Asa (and the people of his kingdom) had no more war until after the 35th year of His reign (2 Chronicles 15:16-19).

In summary, the people had rebelled and committed spiritual adultery against the LORD. This brought suffering upon them. Although they were His people, they had loved and served other gods — gods conceived in their imaginations and created by their own hands. They turned from the LORD and, by default, abandoned their blessings; they ran full speed into their own destruction. Only when they forsook their sin and idolatry; returned back to the true and living God; and worshipped Him — only then — did He move on their behalf to deliver them from their enemies and bring restoration.

Likewise today, as God's people (those who are called by His name), if we will humble ourselves, pray and seek His face, He will respond. If we will repent of our wicked ways, destroy our idols and turn back to the LORD with a covenant commitment, He will hear our cry, forgive us and heal our land (2 Chronicles 7:14). He will restore lives, strengthen nations and give us peace and rest. He will free us from our oppressors, and we'll know the fullness and joy of His salvation. Changing a nation begins in the hearts of God's people.

As we have studied in this chapter, I hope and pray that every believer would worship the LORD with their whole heart, both publicly and personally. Let us celebrate His works, and reverence Him in the assembly and the congregation. May every follower of Christ seek and keep His Word; pursue Him; search for understanding and follow the leading of His Holy Spirit. Let us be completely unashamed, as we freely and powerfully represent Him, and find our rest in God's peace.

The priceless treasures of restoration, strength, discernment, joy and salvation make up a fruitful harvest for those who choose to worship and serve the LORD whole heartedly. The hearts of such worshippers are wholly captivated with the passion of knowing the magnificence of God and pleasing Him. Knowing God intimately brings such wonderful fulfillment! Once you've encountered Him, no one and nothing else will truly satisfy.

CHAPTER 5

THE 'PERFECT HEART' WORSHIPPER

In the first four chapters of this book, we've studied what it means to love God and to do so with our whole heart. Our devotion to the LORD must be our primary motivation for seeking, serving and obeying Him. As we submit every area of our lives to Him, our hearts are perfected in love, and we're free to affectionately pursue Him. This brings joy to the Father's heart and releases that same joy into our lives.

Apart from the LORD, we do not have the power to change our own hearts. Only the LORD can create a *perfect heart.* He creates this masterpiece within those who yield their lives to Him. Let's also look at the character traits and benefits of loving the LORD with a *perfect heart.*

SEES THE STRENGTH OF THE LORD

Let's again consider King Asa and the people of Judah. They made a covenant agreement with the LORD in 2 Chronicles 15. As long as they honored their covenant and trusted the LORD, they lived in peace and prosperity. They were free from the conflicts of war and harassment from their enemies. Proverbs 16:7 tells us that when a man's ways please the LORD, He makes even his enemies to be at peace with him.

However, in the thirty-sixth year of King Asa's reign in Judah, King Baasha (of Israel) came against him and built (fortified) the city of Ramah. He did this to prevent interaction between the kingdom of Israel and the kingdom of Judah. King Baasha feared that his subjects would join themselves to the house of David in Judah.

Ramah was a city that belonged to the tribe of Benjamin and it was located between the two kingdoms of Israel and Judah. When King Baasha fortified the city of Ramah, it most likely blocked the road which led to Jerusalem, the capital city of Judah. Therefore, nobody (including merchants) could communicate or travel from Israel to Judah or vice versa, unless they had the approval of King Baasha. This caused war between these two kings (1 Kings 15:16).

Unfortunately, King Asa took matters into his own hands and did not seek the counsel of the LORD, concerning the situation. He took gold and silver from his own household and from the treasury of the house of the LORD. He used it to bribe and persuade King Benhadad (of Syria) to break his covenant (league) with King Baasha (of Israel). Therefore, King Benhadad formed a new covenant with King Asa and sent his armies against Israel. He made war in the cities of Ijon, Dan, Abelmaim and Naphtali. When King Baasha (of Israel) heard of it, he stopped building the city of Ramah. Then, Asa took all Judah and carried away the stones and timbers of Ramah (2 Chronicles 16:1-6).

CHAPTER 5 • THE 'PERFECT HEART' WORSHIPPER

LEAN NOT TO THINE OWN UNDERSTANDING

King Asa was a good king. He wanted to bring deliverance to Judah, but in this instance, instead of seeking the wisdom of the LORD, he leaned to his own natural wisdom and human reasoning. He chose to put his trust in the strength of men, instead of in the strength of God. This displeased the LORD.

The prophet Hanani came to Judah to remind King Asa of previous victories when enemies had risen up against Judah and were defeated. As King Asa had relied on the LORD, supernatural intervention took place. God Almighty fought for Judah and faithfully delivered the king's enemies into his hand (2 Chronicles 16:7-8). However, Asa did not seek the LORD concerning King Baasha. For this reason, the Prophet declared in:

***2 Chronicles 16:9** For the eyes of the LORD run to and fro throughout the whole earth, to show himself strong in the behalf of them whose heart is perfect toward him. Herein thou hast done foolishly: therefore from henceforth thou shalt have wars.*

Though King Asa, historically, did what was right in the eyes of the LORD (1 Kings 15:11), his heart did not remain perfect toward the LORD in his dealings with King Baasha. Therefore, he did foolishly. Though the LORD wanted to show His strength to King Asa and the people of Judah, they missed that supernatural opportunity when the king leaned to his own understanding. This could have been avoided if he had taken heed to:

> **Proverbs 3:5-6** *Trust in the LORD with all thine heart; and lean not unto thine own understanding. ⁶In all thy ways acknowledge Him and He shall direct thy paths.*

God's Word is the standard and final authority for our lives. If we know the Word of God, we'll be able to clearly discern His voice. If we can discern His voice, we'll be able to make wise decisions.

To **lean** *(H8172)* to one's own understanding is to rely on and seek to *support one's self* based on one's own knowledge, apart from the knowledge and wisdom of God and His Word. Remember, if something leans in the wrong direction far enough, it (and anything attached to it) will eventually fall. When we trust in the LORD, He will give us solid direction in every area of life and we will not fall nor fail. Through King Asa's example, we learn how foolish it is to put trust in men to provide protection and deliverance, instead of consulting the LORD.

BEWARE OF LUST, CONSIDER GOD'S KINGDOM PURPOSE
According to 2 Chronicles 16:9, failure to seek the LORD is one characteristic of foolishness. In this case, it resulted in wars. **Wars** *(H4421)* are generally defined as *the engagement of fighting a battle* or *warfare*. Human reasoning, without the wisdom of God, is also a

leading instigator of war. In addition, the New Testament reveals root causes of war in:

James 4:1-3 From whence come wars and fightings among you? come they not hence, even of your lusts that war in your members? ²Ye lust, and have not: ye kill, and desire to have, and cannot obtain: ye fight and war, yet ye have not, because ye ask not. ³Ye ask, and receive not, because ye ask amiss, that ye may consume it upon your lusts.

Notice, the root causes of wars and fighting are directly connected to the fulfilling of one's own selfish lusts. **Lusts** *(G2237)* are defined as those things which bring forth sensual *delight* and stir up *desire*. Lusts can also be defined as passionate or overmastering, uncontrolled or illicit sexual desires, appetites and cravings. Lust causes a person to become self-focused — to have a mental and physical preoccupation with whatever brings a high degree of personal and/or perverted pleasure. Lust is like a beast in hot pursuit, chasing after the object it desires to devour. It's the picture of a wild animal, breathing hard, panting and exerting all its energy to obtain what it wants.

To clarify, I'm not saying that it's wrong to desire good things. The Heavenly Father is pleased and delighted to bless those who truly love Him. Prosperity and increase are included in the blessing of being a child of God. But we're not to allow our desires to control us or lead us away from the LORD and what He's intended for us; if this happens, desire has deviated into lust.

Those driven by lust have a longing to fulfill the overindulgent, forbidden pleasures and desires of their flesh. When lusts and desires are entertained and pursued, they cause people to behave foolishly. Prohibited sensual delights and illicit appetites feed the carnality of the fleshly, worldly mindset and the five senses. Immorality, lewdness, deception, immodesty, perversion, addictions, materialism, excessiveness and a lack of restraint give evidence of lusts that have been conceived and nurtured in the mind and made manifest in the flesh. For those who misbehave in such a foolish manner, the lust that feeds upon the desire of their flesh will, ultimately, consume them. And those consumed by their lust will fight to get what was never intended for them, even to the point of killing one another.

Referring back to 2 Chronicles 16:9, the Prophet declared that King Asa would have *wars*. Why? Well, lust and pride are at the root of every war. In his efforts (likely fueled by fear, greed and pride) to preserve his nation, King Asa took possession of what belonged to the Lord and gave it to an enemy. He also carried away the stones and timbers of Ramah that did not belong to him. Lust activates those overtaken by it to pursue what does not legally belong to them, or it wrongfully denies that which rightly belongs to others. This usually leads to fighting, civil uprisings or declarations of war. Whether it is people, governments or nations who are seeking to fulfill their lusts, their motivation is always selfishness and their methods usually require taking from others to fulfill their own ambitions.

We see unfortunate situations like this throughout the world every day. Nations trust in their own strength, ability and understanding. They rise up against one another, fighting for what they desire to possess or destroy. In their lust to rule, one way or another, destruction is usually the end result. Those who are ruled by the lusts of their flesh do not have a perfect heart toward the LORD.

Those who possess a perfect heart toward the LORD will not be led by their fleshly desires. Rather, they will allow the Spirit of God to direct and lead them in the decisions of life. They will intelligently think through and diligently consider the end results and welfare of those who will be influenced by their decisions and actions.

A perfect heart understands that the blessings we receive and enjoy are given by the hand of the LORD. Every blessing has a kingdom purpose. Therefore, we have no right to be selfish with what we possess. We're to hold our blessings lightly, in an open hand, in case the LORD has need of them.

Part 1 • *Loving God* with All Your Heart

When King Asa faced conflict with King Baasha of Israel he should have humbled himself by confessing his own agendas and fears to the Lord, as he sought Him for counsel. Instead, he leaned to his own understanding and did foolishly in the eyes of the LORD. Remember, decisions made and actions taken based only on one's limited understanding equals foolishness! When situations come our way, we need to stop and carefully consider the direction we will take. Those who are wise will honor the LORD and avoid needless trouble by seeking His counsel first.

BE FIT, NOT FAT / CARRY YOUR CROSS
Going deeper into our study of 2 Chronicles 16:9, let's see what it meant when the Prophet said that King Asa had done foolishly. The Hebrew word for *foolishly* (H5528/H3688) is defined as being *silly* (playing or becoming the fool). Another Hebrew definition means *to be fat*. Now, if you are a few pounds overweight, take authority over your thoughts right now. Don't get offended or let the devil run his mouth in your ears. Stay with me, and let's see how this applies in the Spirit.

Let's consider both the natural and spiritual effects of being *fat* in reference to foolishness. First of all, to be physically fat is defined as having too much flabby, loose, limp body tissue. Comparatively, spiritual flabbiness represents a lack of strength, determination and vision for one's life. In addition, it represents a lack of personal restraint, self-control and a failure to submit to God's righteous standard of modest, moral behavior. Moreover, excessive spiritual fat represents a lack of firmness, substance, vitality, force, energy, conviction and godly character.

Those who say they love the LORD and are called by His name, yet allow their flesh nature to control them, are exhibiting the fat of foolishness in their lives. They have not established biblical standards or morals. They lack the needed godly conviction, determination, vision, strength or personal restraint. They're not reflecting the character and nature of Christ, because they have either ignored or rejected the wisdom and instruction of God's Word. Therefore, they lack proper discernment and the ability to perceive their compromised state of existence. Their flesh nature (faulty reasoning, lustful thoughts and actions) conflicts and wars against the Spirit of God (Galatians 5:16-17). Prioritizing their own ways, these people compromise what they know to be true, so they can do what they want. This is foolishness in eyes of the LORD, and He is not pleased with it.

Furthermore, toxins are stored in the fat of the flesh. If we love the LORD and declare that we belong to Him, then we cannot allow ourselves to become spiritually, emotionally, mentally or volitionally toxic. We cannot allow our soul to become polluted through ungodliness. If there's any mess (uncleanness, pride, idolatry, rebellion, stubbornness, iniquity, immorality, selfishness, lust, fear, doubt, unbelief or any other sin) in our lives, we need to repent and ask the LORD to purge us of all unrighteousness. The power of Jesus' blood washes and cleanses away all filthiness of the flesh (Psalm 51:7, 79:9; 1 Corinthians 6:9-11).

We avoid spiritual flabbiness by exercising (practicing and training) ourselves in godliness, holiness and devotion to the LORD (1 Timothy 4:7-8). We need to come into His presence spiritually naked, open and honest — withholding nothing, as we lay our lives down in submission before Him. We are exhorted in:

<u>**Hebrews 12:1**</u> *Wherefore seeing we also are compassed about with so great a cloud of witnesses, let us lay aside every weight, and the sin which doth so easily beset us, and let us run with patience that race that is set before us.*

In this verse, **weight** (G3591/G43) is defined as *a mass (as bending or bulging by its load)*, a *burden* and/or *hindrance*. Excessive **weight** will cause us to *bend* and *ache* under the heaviness of it. In this context, weight is not specifically referring to the physical poundage of a person. Although if there are issues going on in your life that trigger overindulgence, you will need to take a closer look at what the LORD is saying to you. Weight is referring to the things that we have picked up along the way that we were never intended to carry, and it is directly related to sin.

Sin (G266/G264) is defined as *offence, to miss the mark (and so not share in the prize); that is, to err and sin morally.* The weight of sin hinders us from running the race of victory, which the LORD has set before us. If we're carrying burdens we were never meant to carry, and harboring past hurts in our hearts; if we're allowing our walk with God to be hindered through sin and offences; if we're missing the mark of who God has called us to be, then we have allowed ourselves to be distracted from our God ordained kingdom purpose. To choose sin and self-will over obedience to the LORD is to live foolishly. We're to cast the weight of these things aside, repent and triumphantly run the race that has been set before us. We're to cast off everything that hinders us from fulfilling our destiny.

The only weight we're to carry is the weight of the cross. Jesus said, "*If any man will come after me, let him deny himself, and take up his cross, and follow me*" (Matthew 16:24, Mark 8:34, 10:21). The cross is a symbol of death. We must die to self (and everything we think we want in life) if we're to follow the LORD.

Death must come before true life can be revealed. When we die to our personal agendas — casting off the weights of our flesh nature — and submit to the will of the LORD, we are conformed into His image and likeness. Our lives and hearts are transformed, as we take on the holy, righteous, spiritual DNA of our

Part 1 • *Loving God* with All Your Heart

Heavenly Father. We walk in resurrection power as the LORD becomes the manifest reality of our lives.

SACRIFICE THE FAT, SUBMIT YOUR LIFE

From another viewpoint, let's continue to deal with how King Asa did **foolishly** before the LORD and that one of the definitions pertaining to this means *to be fat*. Consider that the priests in the Old Testament offered animal sacrifices before the LORD, to cover the sins of the people. This was done in a very particular manner, for a very special reason.

Every part of the sacrifice was consecrated for God's divine purpose. The blood of the sacrificial animal was poured out as an act of God's mercy to cover the sins of the people. The kidneys, a portion of the liver and all the fat were burned upon the altar with fire. The people were not allowed to partake of it. It was to be offered up as a sweet smelling savor, a fragrance of worship and obedience to the LORD.

Before the sacrifice could be offered up as a burnt offering before the LORD, every part of the animal had to be examined. The priest inspected it to be sure there were no blemishes, deformities, diseases, broken bones or imperfections. If the animal was found to be perfect, it was accepted, slain and cut open. The inside of the animal was closely examined (including its organs and muscles), and the blood was sprinkled upon the altar and at the door of the tabernacle.

Chapter 5 • The 'Perfect Heart' Worshipper

Every part of the sacrifice had to be perfect, because it was holy to the LORD.

All the fat (along with the kidneys and part of the liver) was removed from the inside of the sacrificial animal. The fat was offered on the altar and burnt with fire as part of the sin and peace offerings. The burning fat was offered up as a sweet smelling savor before the LORD. This part of the sacrifice belonged to Him, and He commanded the people not to eat the fat or the blood (Exodus 29:13, 22; Leviticus 1:5, 3:3-5, 4:8-19, 7:23-25, 8:25, 9-11, 14-15, 17:6, 26, 31; 1 Samuel 2:15-16).

Now, why would the LORD want the fat, the kidneys and the liver? In part, maybe it's because the animal fat and filter organs contain toxins and, likely, parasites. Certain parasites are organisms that feed off another life form, sucking the nutrients out of its host. Toxins are the poisons produced by organisms; they create an environment for diseases to manifest. If toxins or parasites infiltrate the body, then injury, destruction and death could soon follow. Anytime they are given a place to thrive, they will compromise or attack the flesh in which they're embedded. The Lord desired to spare His people from any potential physical harm, and it was His good pleasure to do so.

Spiritually, the Old Testament is a shadow or natural example of what the Lord does today. In order to demonstrate how He would receive unto Himself and consume every damaging force from our lives —

whether natural or spiritual — the LORD required the fat of the sacrifice. The fragrance of our obedient submission and deliverance is a sweet smelling savor to Him.

From this correlation, we can also discern a warning. If we partake of spiritual and soulful things not intended for us, we open the door of our lives to trouble. Mental toxins and spiritual parasites would have opportunity to enter in through deception and disobedience. Thereby, they'd suck the life, hope, joy and peace of God out of their host. The body and soul of the unregenerate man becomes a contaminated, noxious environment with the potential of breeding demonic activity. Devils will seek to influence the mind and/or entrench themselves in the body and soul of those who are not submitted to the LORD.

Some of this was evident, when King Asa failed to seek the LORD and the counsel of His Word, because his perspective was distorted. Therefore, he made foolish decisions, which put him into an unholy alliance with an enemy of the people of God. The parasitic fat (of fear, doubt, unbelief, pride, uncertainty, wrong perspective, etc.) of King Asa's foolishness should have been offered up to the LORD in prayer. He should have sacrificed his concerns and human reasoning (which caused a spiritual blindness to the purposes and intentions of God), upon the altar of faith, to be consumed by the holy fire and presence of God. But instead, he fed upon it. Asa's consumption (instead of sacrifice) of his limited human reasoning allowed mental toxins and spiritual parasites to enter into his decision making processes. If he had sought the LORD this would not have happened.

Furthermore, there is insight we can discern specifically in reference to the kidneys and liver, which the LORD also required to be burned in the fire. These organs were created to be the filtering systems of the body. The kidneys remove waste from the blood, balance body fluids and form urine that will be excreted from the body through the bladder. The liver detoxifies and removes harmful elements from the body. It aids in digestion and makes proteins, which promote the clotting of blood for the healing of wounds. Likewise, when the truth of God's Word is active in our spirit, it cleanses our soul, renews our mind, brings unity into the body of Christ (the Church), restores balance, gets rid of what's no longer needed and brings forth healing. Figuratively speaking, these organs represent the function of the Word of God in our lives.

If we forget God's Word, then we've stepped out of the way of life and into the way of death — out of the way of godly wisdom and into foolish ignorance. We can't take this lightly. The continued neglect of our covenant gives opportunity for unclean and destructive spirits of the enemy to gain access to our lives. We can't afford to forget God's Word.

Jesus is the personification of God's Word. He was offered up as the covenant Lamb of God and became a sweet smelling sacrifice. In Christ, we receive the merciful, cleansing power of His precious blood. In Him, we find our life. As we confess to Him the harmful, toxic, polluted, hindering, unhealthy things of our lives and invite the purifying fire of God to burn them out of us, we allow the LORD to consume us with His love. This is how the fat of our foolishness is put to death — in sacrifice.

The Word and promises of our God will protect and keep us through every detail of our lives. We should consistently invite the LORD to help us develop and maintain a perfect heart toward Him. Through His Word, as He sets us in perfect order, our lives will become a pleasant offering and a sweet smelling savor to Him.

While foolishness is the way to death for the spirit and soul, holy sacrifice always demands death to the flesh. Without death, there is no sacrifice; and without sacrifice, there is no death. Just as the sacrificial animals were slain to cover the sins of God's people, even so, Jesus Christ, the Son of God, was offered up as the sacrificial Lamb for the sin of mankind. Like the animal sacrifices, He was examined and judged. The sacrificial animals were never beaten, but Jesus was mocked, ridiculed, whipped, beaten, bruised, abused, pierced and, ultimately, crucified. His flesh was ripped open, his blood poured forth, and He died. We read the prophetic words of Isaiah concerning the death of the Messiah in:

<u>Isaiah 53:3-7</u> He [Jesus] is despised and rejected of men; a man of sorrows, and acquainted with grief: and we hid as it were our faces from him; he was despised, and we esteemed him not. ⁴Surely he hath borne our griefs, and carried our sorrows: yet we did esteem him stricken, smitten of God, and afflicted. ⁵But he was wounded for our transgressions, he was bruised for our iniquities: the chastisement of our peace was upon him; and with his stripes we are healed. ⁶All we like sheep have gone astray; we have turned every one to his own way; and the LORD hath laid on him the iniquity of us all. ⁷He was oppressed, and he was afflicted, yet he opened not his mouth: he is brought as a lamb to the slaughter, and as a sheep before her shearers is dumb, so he openeth not his mouth.

Before Jesus began His public ministry He was baptized by the prophet John. John was the forerunner of Christ; he was the voice of one crying in the wilderness to prepare the way of the LORD (Matthew 3:3; Mark 1:3; Luke 3:4; John 1:23). As Jesus arose from the waters of baptism, the Spirit of God descended on Him like a dove. In that moment, the Father declared from Heaven, "**This is my beloved Son, in whom I am well pleased**" (Matthew 3:13-17, 17:5; Mark 1:11; also 2 Peter 1:17). Shortly thereafter, John was put in prison, and Jesus began preaching the gospel of the kingdom of God (Mark 6:17; Luke 16:16).

The people were drawn to Christ's kingdom message of repentance, deliverance, healing, grace, forgiveness, freedom and power (Isaiah 61:1; Luke 4:18-19). But the chief priest and scribes (the Jewish religious leaders) envied Him and feared the people. When they couldn't stop Jesus' message and ministry, they sought to kill Him (Matthew 27:18; Mark 15:10; Luke 22:2). He didn't fit their preconceived ideas about who the Messiah was or how He would deliver Israel from her enemies and rule His kingdom.

The religious leaders had Jesus arrested. He was brought before Pontius Pilate and falsely accused of perverting the nation, forbidding the people to pay tribute to Caesar and declaring Himself to be a King. But when Pilate questioned Jesus, he found no fault in Him. So, Pilate sent Him to King Herod. Then, the religious leaders also accused Jesus before the king. When King Herod questioned Jesus, he found no fault in Him and sent Him back to Pilate. Pilate examined Jesus again and found no fault in Him that was worthy of death. So, Pilate sought to release Him, but the chief priest and scribes stirred up the people to cry out for

Chapter 5 • The 'Perfect Heart' Worshipper

the crucifixion of Jesus. Jesus was examined 3 times and, every time, it was declared that He had no fault within Him (John 19:4, 6; Luke 23:14-15, 22). Jesus was the spotless, innocent Passover lamb — the perfect, holy and blameless sacrifice (Luke 22:1-2). When Pilate couldn't suffice the people to release Jesus, he gave the order for the Lamb of God to be put to death (Luke 23:1-25).

Jesus chose to obey the will of the Heavenly Father: He revealed the Father's heart of love and called mankind to repentance; He fulfilled all the Old Testament prophecies concerning the events of His conception, birth, life, death, burial and resurrection; He spoke God's truth and confirmed it with signs, wonders and miracles; then Christ, the Lamb of God, fulfilled His ministry and willingly laid down His life for all peoples, nations and tribes. Jesus came to earth on a mission of reconciliation. Christ's love for the Father and His people caused Him to offer up His holy and acceptable sacrifice of obedience. Every follower in Christ is called to do the same according to:

***Romans 12:1** I beseech you therefore, brethren, by the mercies of God, that ye present your bodies a living sacrifice, holy, acceptable unto God, which is your reasonable service.*

Like Christ, we're to yield our lives to God as a **holy** *(G40), blameless, sacred, pure* and *consecrated* sacrifice. We're to present our **bodies** *(G4983/G4982)* as whole offerings, consumed by the fire of God's presence. As we submit every fiber of our being to God's divine purpose, we come into full agreement with His will for our lives. We become an acceptable and well pleasing love offering — the sacrifice God desires. Thus, our fragrance of worship becomes a sweet smelling savor before the LORD. This is what it means to love the LORD with all your heart, all your soul, all your mind and all your strength.

Avoid Distraction, Stay Focused

By definition, to be distracted means to be in a state of mental distress and derangement. The results of derangement are disorder and confusion. People in this condition are likely to make unwise, irrational and foolish decisions. If we're to gain victory over perplexing circumstances and not do foolishly, there are four things we must do instead. They are:

— 1 —

No matter what's going on, stay focused on the LORD, not the distractions of the enemy.

If we're to function with a godly mentality, then we must bring our thoughts into obedient alignment with God's Word (2 Corinthians 10:5). As we do this, our minds truly become sound, peaceful and pure. We'll not be controlled by emotion or distracted by any situation (Isaiah 26:3; 2 Timothy 1:7). This is how God's wisdom, power and truth will prevail over any temptation to be foolish.

Even as we seek the LORD and hear His voice, He will never speak anything contrary to the truth of His Word. When God speaks, what we hear in our spirits will always, always, always be in agreement with His Word. No exceptions! If we hear something contrary to the Word of God, then it's not God speaking. Stay focused on His Word!

— 2 —
Let God counsel you through His Word;
then act accordingly.

In the midst of difficult circumstances, sometimes, our thoughts and feelings tend to play a major role in determining our actions. Our own natural reasoning can become our worst distraction. Therefore, we must bring our minds into submission to the Holy Spirit and yield to His guidance. When the thoughts of our minds are in alignment with the Word of God, then the Holy Spirit will keep our emotions in check. When our thoughts and emotions are under God's control, our actions will also be in agreement with His plans for our lives. God is bigger than all that troubles us, so we all need godly counsel and wisdom operating in our lives. We cannot allow our human reasoning, emotions, circumstances, fears, doubts, unbelief, sinful motives or insecurities to rule over us.

So, how do we align our minds with God's Word? 1) We read it. 2) We study and meditate on it. 3) We counsel with God about it. Keeping His Word before us, we humbly ask for His wisdom concerning any challenges, or lack of understanding we may have. We're to become so thoroughly acquainted with God's Word that we can recall it at any moment and effectively apply it to any situation, in a way that glorifies Him.

Let's be clear, merely giving mental assent to the validity of God's Word is not good enough. It must be applied to every area of our lives, if we're to live in victory. Information without application equals vain and unproductive ignorance! People get into trouble when they do not properly respect the LORD or when they fail to honor and appropriate His Word.

The deep issues of the heart, the thoughts of the mind, the emotions of the soul and actions of the body are intricately woven together. If the heart (the center of one's being) is messed up, this will affect the condition of the mind. If the mind is messed up, thoughts become irrational and can cause broken emotions. Wounded emotions become the catalyst that ignites irresponsible behavior. It's a destructive chain reaction, causing negative ripple effects throughout the entirety of one's being and disrupting every area of life. Even so, the LORD desires to bring peace, healing and restoration to our spirit, soul and body. When the heart is free of bondage and the mind is renewed by the Word of God, the soul is made healthy and the body responds in proper order and harmony with the plan of God.

Since it all starts in the sanctuary of our hearts, how do we get our hearts right? This question is why this book has been written, so keep reading! As followers of Christ (operating in our renewed minds), we're to understand that our bodies are the temple of His Holy Spirit (and our actions represent Him). We've been bought with a price — the blood of Jesus. Our spirit, soul and body do not belong to us personally. They belong to God, and we're to use them to glorify Him (1 Corinthians 6:19-20, 7:23)! When we allow the LORD to create a perfect heart within us, the beauty of that perfection spreads into all areas of our lives.

Rest assured that, if we have already trusted in the Lord for salvation, we are already newly created in Him (2 Corinthians 5:17). By no means does our salvation depend on what we do; it's all about what Christ has done. We are called righteous, because He is. However, salvation and sanctification are not the same. Salvation through Christ is the redemption key that opens the door to relationship with Almighty God; sanctification is allowing His purity and holiness to operate in our lives. For the purposes of this section in the book, being sure to submit all personal agendas and motives to the LORD, as well as recognizing and declaring that He is greater than any circumstance, reveals that we desire for God's will to be manifest above all.

Part 1 • *Loving God* with All Your Heart

We also do not have the right to allow ourselves (or anybody else, including the enemy) to mistreat that which belongs to God. Therefore, we'll not use, abuse or neglect our bodies in any way that dishonors the LORD. Nor will we participate in any lustful and/or sinful activities. When we live as God intended, we show honor and respect to Him and ourselves. Don't allow the enemy to twist your perspective; his evil intentions are to persuade you to forfeit what the LORD has placed in your care.

— 3 —
Know that the LORD will be your help
in time of trouble.

The Lord is mighty in battle (Psalm 24:8)! He is our protection and strength (Psalm 27:5, 37:39)! Don't be distracted by the troubles of life; they can blind you from the truth and the greater purposes of God. Allow Him to show Himself strong in every situation.

King Asa was motivated by fear, personal ambition and his own twisted perspective. He was very short sighted in his decision to allow an enemy to possess the treasures of God. His decision did not bring strength and safety to the situation. Instead, it brought the exact opposite — war!

Remember, if there's war or entanglement with an enemy, then controlling lust, pride and/or fear is the root cause of the matter (James 4:1-3). Don't be overtaken. Those who allow fear, lust, wrong emotions, hurts and disappointments to rule in their hearts will lose their proper perspective.

— 4 —
Remember that our God is faithful to direct, protect, provide, deliver, save, heal and prosper us in every circumstance of life.

If we, as the people of God, have hearts that are perfect toward the LORD, then He will show Himself strong on our behalf (2 Chronicles 16:9). As we remain diligently faithful and trust in Him, He will empower us to do and receive whatever is necessary in any given situation. It is His strength that ensures our victory.

To continue to walk in victory, we must not create or allow conditions which would give the enemy license to build his strongholds of destruction in our lives (2 Corinthians 10:4-5; Ephesians 4:23-27). We cannot allow our minds to be polluted with the filthy ways and ungodly philosophies of this world (1 Timothy 1:4-6; 2 Timothy 1:13-14). Nor can we afford to flirt with, entertain or allow our souls to feed upon or be consumed with wickedness (Psalm 101:3).

Instead, we must choose to renew our minds through the Word of God, and put on the righteousness and holiness of God through faith in Christ (Ephesians 4:23; Romans 3:22; Ephesians 4:24). If we do these things, the LORD will surely give us every victory!

Part 1 • *Loving God* with All Your Heart

SERVE THE LORD, NOT YOUR 'SELF'
How we live is determined by who we serve, because who we serve influences how we think and do. There are only two choices. Either we will serve the LORD or we will serve self. But here's the deal: those who serve self are actually serving satan, because they've chosen to live their lives apart from the influence of God. If we're driven, controlled or motivated by anything other than the counsel of God for our lives, we'll find ourselves in situations the LORD never intended for us to experience.

There's no middle ground and no grey areas. Either we choose to be a citizen of the Kingdom of God, or we'll be controlled by the powers of darkness. Our master of choice profoundly impacts our lives and our eternal destinies. A life choice to serve and trust in the LORD will always lead to blessing and eternal life. In the end, serving and trusting in self (or any other false god) will lead to disappointment and eternal separation from God.

When King Asa failed to seek the LORD in his time of trouble, he made decisions that were not his to make. He took the choice treasures from the house of the LORD, which did not belong to him, and used them to bribe a heathen king into forming a military alliance against his enemy. Asa thought this would be beneficial for him and his kingdom, but instead, it was detrimental. Hanani, the prophet of God, rebuked the

King for his foolishness and warned him that he would have wars because of it. Yet, Asa refused to humble himself and repent. Instead, he threw the man of God into prison and oppressed some of the people. Three years later, he was afflicted with a disease in his feet. Yet, even then, when the disease was exceedingly great, he would not seek the LORD; he only consulted with the physicians. After three years of suffering, King Asa died in the forty-first year of his reign (2 Chronicles 16:9-10, 12-13).

Like King Asa, those who fail to trust in the LORD will take on an "I'll do what's best for me" mentality. When this happens, they become self-focused instead of God-focused. Once their focus is on self, they'll rationalize and make excuses for the misuse or abuse of what the LORD has entrusted to them. It's important to understand that a self-focused heart is filled with pride, lust, rebellion, idolatry, iniquity and stubbornness. Consequently, the person who chooses to remain in this condition prefers to be a slave to sin and will be controlled by their own evil passions. If not dealt with, natural consequences and demonic forces will cause the life of such a one to careen out of control and into destruction. The only way out of impending disaster is through godly sorrow, true repentance and submission to the LORD.

Each one of us makes our own choice as to whom we will serve. We cannot serve 'self' and the LORD at the same time. Those who serve themselves will do so to their own detriment. They've aligned themselves with satan and will never experience the full potential or blessing of God's plan for their lives. Please understand, alignment with the devil is as simple as just doing our own will, instead of the will of the Heavenly Father.

Instead of becoming self-absorbed, allow your 'self' to be absorbed and engaged with the awesomeness of God. Everything you need is found in Him; be fascinated by how He cares for you. Realize that the LORD has already given you the treasures, anointing, calling, purpose and wealth you need to fulfill His destiny for your life. When we willingly choose to love and serve the LORD, we'll experience the amazing blessing of intimately knowing Him. Remember, we become like that which we pursue, and we will experience the blessing or cursing of the master we choose to serve. So, the question is:

What do you pursue and who do you serve?

BE PERFECT WITH THE LORD

In relation to having a perfect heart, many times people will make excuses for their moral failures. Instead of taking responsibility for their actions, they'll say, "Well nobody's perfect!" or "I'm only human!" Yes, in our own strength, we are imperfect humans, but this does not release us from God's expectations for us. We're commanded to be perfect, as we see in:

Chapter 5 • The 'Perfect Heart' Worshipper

Deuteronomy 18:13 *Thou shalt be perfect with the LORD thy God.*

So how can imperfect human beings be **perfect with the LORD?** First of all, we must understand the definition of **perfect** *(H8549)*. It means to be *entirely of integrity and truth*. Elsewhere in scripture, this word is also translated: to be without blemish or spot, to be undefiled, upright and completely whole.

Also, notice that the scripture says we're to be perfect **with** the LORD thy God. This tells us that, without the LORD, we can never be perfect. It also tells us we're not expected to perfect ourselves through our own strength. Perfection is a work of God, and it takes place **with** God. He is accompanying us and teaching us how to walk in His expected perfection. Remember, He does not require anything of us, unless He has made a way for the requirement to be properly met. Whatever God requires is possible with Him.

Of course, the manifestation of perfection may not be immediately visible in our lives; perfection is a work in progress. When we're adopted into the family of God (through faith in Christ Jesus), we become heirs of God and inherit the righteousness of Christ (Galatians 4:7; Hebrews 11:7). As sons of God, we receive new spiritual DNA; what is in the Father is passed down to His children. Thus, our perfection is directly connected to God revealing His character and nature to us, and our allowing Him to display it through us. As we grow in the things of God, we also grow into the image and likeness that He has always intended for us.

Because the LORD created us to have His character and nature, we're to look, talk, think and act like Him. When people look at us, they should see a resemblance with the Heavenly Father in every way. Remember, we'll never be perfect in our own strength, but in the strength of our God, all things are possible.

Referring again to 2 Chronicles 16:9, notice that the Prophet declares that the eyes of the LORD, literally, **run to and fro (H7751) throughout the whole earth.** This means His gaze is *traveling* — looking, searching, patrolling, scouting, watching and waiting — for people and nations to turn their hearts toward Him. Indeed, the eyes of the LORD are eagerly roving and surveying for potential opportunities in which He can demonstrate His strength, on the behalf of those whose hearts are perfect toward Him.

The **eyes** *(H5869)* of the LORD are defined as being like a *fountain (as the eye of the landscape)*. The Hebrew word for eye is *'ayin*. Elsewhere in scripture, this word is also translated as: His countenance, His face, His favor, His presence and His regard. The LORD is looking for those with a perfect heart, because He wants to personally reveal Himself to them. His presence will spring forth in their lives like a refreshing fountain of favor.

Chapter 5 • The 'Perfect Heart' Worshipper

The word *perfect* (H8003/H7999), in the context of 2 Chronicles 16:9, is defined as *complete* and *especially friendly*. It comes from another Hebrew word meaning *to be safe (in mind, body or estate)* and *to reciprocate*. It's also translated as: full, just, made ready, peaceable, quiet, perfected and whole. God is looking for a heart that is friendly and peaceable toward Him. He longs for a people whose hearts are completely given over to Him — hearts that are able to reciprocate (give and receive) His love. It's this type of heart that will experience the powerful presence of God. The LORD also reciprocates His perfect hearted lovers with an abundance of His grace upon their lives.

While this kind of relating is satisfying and wondrous, such interpersonal wealth also results in practical outcomes. For instance, since they have experienced forgiveness from the LORD, those with a perfect heart are willing to extend forgiveness to others. They refuse to harbor judgments, bitterness, anger, fear, pride or hatred against others. They willingly seek to make amends and set things right for any wrongs committed. They're willing to make restitution and seek restoration, whenever possible and wherever necessary. All these characteristics are evidence that the perfect hearted person trusts in the LORD and is wholly submitted to Him. They have learned to love and please Him with the totality of their hearts, even as He has loved and extended His pleasure toward them. Such rich communion affects a worshipper's heart attitude, and their attitude affects their decisions and conduct. Ultimately, it will profoundly influence how they achieve their destiny.

Because the LORD highly regards those who have a perfect heart toward Him, He extends His provision to them. He makes His presence known and causes them to walk and dwell in His safety and protection. Not only do these blessings apply to the individual person, but they apply to all their estate and possessions too. As part of the LORD's favor, He also watches over and protects their legal right to possess what He has given them.

Without question, the strength of the LORD is a tangible blessing. When the LORD shows Himself **strong** (H2388), He joins Himself to the perfect hearted. He huddles in tight, *fastening* and *binding* His presence upon His true worshippers. Those of us who belong to the LORD have experienced the manifestation of his strength, as He becomes our *cure*, our *help*, our *courage* and our *restraint*.

We serve Almighty God and in Him we are strong! As we seek the LORD, He is faithful to remind us that we need the counsel of His Word. It is by His counsel that He empowers us to obey Him. Through obedience, He helps us overcome the enticements of this world and focus on His Kingdom purposes. Truly, the LORD is our mighty conqueror and He prevails on our behalf!

There is no way our hearts can be perfected without the holy, supernatural manifestation of God working within us. The LORD gives us the direction and vision we need for our lives and the ability to walk it out in humility. He gives us godly wisdom, knowledge and understanding, faith, courage and freedom from sin. He teaches us to receive and hold our blessings with an open hand. He adorns us with self-discipline, modesty and purity. He leads us to a place of death to self and provides overcoming strength to take up our cross, follow Him and walk in His resurrection power. He commands us to sacrifice the foolishness, selfishness and hindering distractions that would keep us from loving, following and serving Him. Our God, in His tender mercies and loving kindness, challenges us to believe that we can be perfect in and with Him. Every point given, demonstrates the LORD'S continual faithfulness in our lives and His determination to lead us into spiritual maturity in Him.

To summarize, God's strength brings restoration and wholeness to us. The reality is that we all need spiritual heart surgery. In those who choose to yield their lives to Him, a **perfect heart** is a masterpiece created by the grace and tender mercies of the LORD.

So, are you one of those with a perfect heart, to whom the LORD can show Himself strong?

Is He searching the whole earth for you?

GIVES THE WORD OF GOD TOP PRIORITY

So, the LORD requires His people to have a perfect heart. He desires a heart of integrity; a heart that meets His standard of holiness; a heart that is completely yielded to Him; a heart that honors Him and conforms to the truth of His Word. The LORD is looking for a heart that will choose to continually walk in His ways.

<u>1 Kings 8:61</u> Let your heart therefore be perfect with the LORD our God, to walk in His statutes, and to keep His commandments, as at this day.

When we *let* our hearts do something, we're allowing and/or causing it to do what we desire. Therefore, we are personally responsible for the attitudes and condition of our hearts. If our hearts are not perfect toward the LORD, it's because we have a different agenda than what He has prescribed. We have usurped His rightful position and authority in our lives, thereby, creating an imperfect heart. It's time to put an end to the debate of who's really in charge of our lives.

It's our responsibility to decisively bring our hearts into submission to the Word of God. Those who struggle to do this need to genuinely pray, asking God for the desire to submit their hearts to Him and to reveal anything that's keeping them from doing so. In the process, the LORD will likely reveal unholy motives and seditious agendas to the one struggling. These sins need to be confessed and repented of, in order for all hindrance to be removed. Such deliverance is His good pleasure (Philippians 2:13)! Furthermore, let's be reminded of the words of Jesus:

<u>John 14:14</u> *If ye love me, keep my commandments.*

The first word in this scripture is the word *if*, which infers that there is a condition to the verse. We cannot just say, "Oh yes, I love the LORD!" and then turn around and live our lives in any lackadaisical way we please. Those who love the LORD are to exhibit a godly standard in how they conduct their lives. That godly standard is not based on what individuals think to be acceptable to the LORD. It's not based on what society considers acceptable. That standard is based solely on the truth of God's Word. If we do not adhere to the standard of His Word, then we do not love Him. It really is that simple.

If we truly know the LORD and love Him, then our greatest pleasure and number one priority will be to learn of Him. Through joyful obedience, we will seek to honor Him in all we do. If we believe He loves us, then we should also know that anything He would ask or require of us would have great blessing and kingdom purpose attached to it. We choose to obey the LORD as a demonstration of our love for Him. We must not allow ourselves to be self-deceived; thinking we know the LORD when we really don't. God's Word provides a test, whereby, we can check our own heart condition:

Part 1 • *Loving God* with All Your Heart

***1 John 2:3-6** And hereby we do know that we know him, if we keep his commandments. ⁴He that saith, I know him, and keepeth not his commandments, is a liar, and the truth is not in him. ⁵But whoso keepeth his word, in him verily is the love of God perfected: hereby know we that we are in him. ⁶He that saith he abideth in him ought himself also so to walk, even as he walked.*

The Apostle John is not playing around. Not only did Jesus declare that, if we love Him, we will keep His commandments, but now we see that our obedience is the evidence that we really do *know* Him. The Greek definitions of the New Testament teach us that to *keep (G5083)* the *commandments (G1785/G1781/G1722/G5056)* of the LORD means to *keep an eye on* His Word and *guard* it. We're to take it into our protective *custody* and *watch* that it's properly carried out. We're to hold fast to it, and *maintain* its proper operation in our lives. We recognize and adhere to the Word of God as the *fixed* standard and the *authoritative prescriptions* that are to be applied in every situation.

Our obedience (motivated by love), is confirmation that we know the LORD and belong to Him. To *know (G1097)* the LORD means that we have intimate and friendly knowledge of Him. We have come to understand Him — that is, His nature and, especially, His holy will and affection for the sanctification and redemption of men through Christ (Source: <u>Thayer's Lexicon</u>, 1889).

This kind of knowledge and understanding happens only through relationship. That is, through a personal and cherished familiarity with His Word, dwelling in His presence, yielding to His Holy Spirit and seeing Him move in our lives. As we allow Him to sow His living truth into us, we become one with Him, and our flesh begins to manifest what we've received from Him. In this way, as we manifest His living truth, the Word becomes flesh in us.

How well do you truly know and love the LORD?

Are you spending time with Him before you expect to receive from Him?

Is His Word becoming flesh in you?

What is your lifestyle reflecting?

STAYS IN POSITION

Those who have a perfect heart toward the LORD are able to discern what He's doing in the earth and in their personal lives. They understand their assigned position in the Kingdom of God, and they know how to **keep rank** in the army of the LORD. We see an example of this in the life of David. After King Saul died, the mighty men of war came from all the twelve tribes of Israel to join themselves to David. It was God's timing for the political shift of national leadership to take place, and David was crowned King over all the people of Israel (1 Chronicles 11 and 12). In complete unity and oneness

Part 1 • *Loving God* with All Your Heart

of heart, the warriors positioned themselves to support David as their king:

<u>1 Chronicles 12:38</u> *All these men of war, that could keep rank, came with a perfect heart to Hebron, to make David king over all Israel: and all the rest also of Israel were of one heart to make David king.*

Notice, these were men of war! They were accustomed to being engaged in battle and they knew how to keep rank. They understood the importance of being under proper authority. They also knew that the LORD had ordained David as the next King. Therefore, with a perfect heart, they ushered David into his kingship over all Israel.

The men who joined themselves to David were skilled. They had a warrior mentality and were equipped to overcome and destroy their enemies. Figuratively speaking, they would even *feed on* and *consume* their enemies. Essentially, in their minds, personal defeat was not an option. Although they were fearsome warriors, these men came to David with a **perfect** *(H8003)* heart — in a *friendly,* peaceable and quiet manner — to fulfill the will of the LORD.

To **keep** *(H5737)* **rank** *(H4634/H4633)* is a military phrase. It means to mentally and physically *arrange* and set in order for *military array*. Those who **keep rank** create a unified military force; they're on a mission to create or restore order. They obediently serve and support their commanding officers. They understand the vision and purpose of the battle, as well as the vital role of each warrior. They're mighty in their cause, because they've emptied themselves of their own personal agendas for the greater good of their comrades. This was the mindset of those who joined David's army.

The term *military array* refers to being clothed in ornamented garments with decorative adornments. The adornments are the embellishments that reflect special accomplishments or heroic acts in battle. Such decorations would only be presented to those who fully submitted to their leaders, remained in their assigned positions and completed their required tasks.

In every military situation, order and obedience is required. Those who refuse to obey the orders of their commanding officers could find themselves facing a court-martial! Renegades would not be allowed to endanger the safety and well-being of their fellow comrades and officers. For battles to be won, unity is required. Those who rebel against authority will never become qualified leaders. Every potential leader must first learn that before they can be in authority, they must be under proper authority.

Those in positions of authority are not to flaunt their power for their own agendas. Rather, they're required by God to carry a mantle of great responsibility, for the safety and well-being of those they lead. Leadership must view those who serve under them as vital members of their success team; realizing that each person is valuable and fulfills an essential role and purpose. For this reason, those in authority cannot afford the false luxury of indulging in any rebellious, stubborn, self-centered, prideful or abusive actions or attitudes. Such misbehavior would destroy their team and endanger the success of their intended and shared destiny.

Likewise, every person (whether in or under authority), has an assigned, God-ordained position to fulfill in life. Each position has related responsibilities which are vital in the process of bringing an assignment to a successful conclusion. Unity is required from all those involved, and each person must do their part. When proper order is established, every person becomes accountable and answers to someone of higher rank in the chain of command. The Highest Commander-in-Chief is God Himself, and ultimately, all tribes, tongues and nations will answer to His sovereignty.

Levels of authority exist in both the natural and the spiritual realms. In the Kingdom of God, the LORD requires His spiritual warriors to keep rank, submit to His godly leadership, stay in proper position, and accomplish the mission tasks that have been assigned to them. As King of all creation, the LORD God Almighty issues our marching orders through

His Word. We're to serve willingly and obediently as we carry out His commands, under the direction and leadership of His Holy Spirit.

The importance of staying properly submitted to God's authority can't be emphasized enough. As perfect hearted servants in the LORD'S army, we must uncover, expose, empty out and lay aside every personal ambition or agenda that is not in agreement with His will. We must view every selfish, ungodly or demonically rooted hindrance as a disruption and diversion from our kingdom purpose and destiny. Our hearts (and all motivations therein) are to radically reflect valiant, passionate worship for the One we say we love. Our fervent enthusiasm and holy zeal for our King must rival and surpass all other desires. This is a picture of the perfect heart; it is found in every surrendered lover of God. As we close this section on the perfect heart, here are some personal questions you must consider:

> Are you in your God ordained position?
>
> Are you properly submitted to God's authority?
>
> Are you fulfilling your kingdom responsibilities?

DECLARES RIGHTEOUS JUDGMENT

Those who fear the LORD and judge righteously also demonstrate a perfect heart. In 2 Chronicles 19:5-10 King Jehoshaphat had set up judges in the land of

Part 1 • *Loving God* with All Your Heart

Judah and in the city of Jerusalem to declare verdicts concerning the conflicts and controversies of the people. These judges were warned to **take heed** as to how they judged the people. The LORD required that they specifically and impartially render the judgments and verdicts of God's divine law — not just what the people wanted. These judges were required by the LORD to operate in integrity. They were not allowed to take gifts or bribes from (or on behalf of) those who would be judged of them.

The judges were commanded to fear the LORD and not waver from the truth of His Word, for He was with them. They were public leaders, and they were to deal with people **faithfully** *(H530/H529/H539)*. This means they were to make decisions which brought *security, moral fidelity,* stability and truth to the people. They were to establish themselves as *trustworthy* in order *to build up* and *support* the people in a manner that was in their best interest before God. These leaders were to have the heart of fathers caring for their children. Therefore, there was to be no iniquity, distortion, wickedness or perversion in their judgments.

In the same way, when our hearts are perfect toward the LORD, we'll love him, fear Him, uphold His Word and make righteous judgments in the affairs of life. We'll live our lives in a way which demonstrates that the Word of God is our final authority and measure of righteousness. Remember, we're Ambassadors to the nations for the Kingdom of Heaven (2 Corinthians 5:20). He is the KING of kings and the LORD of lords, and we're to be reflections of the King we serve. As God's spokesmen in the earth, we're to declare His name, His authority, His words and His ways. Hence, we proclaim the will of our Heavenly King in the courts of this world.

With God's Word as our standard, we have the authority to stand against every form of corruption or evil compromise. The perfect heart never considers the option of selfish gain at the expense of others. If we live in truth and godliness, then we have the authority to preach and minister to others. Our judgments are to be based on what is pleasing and reverential in the sight of the LORD. These standards raise a question that must be considered:

Are you declaring the righteous and uncompromising truths of the Word of God?

YEARNS FOR GOD

The perfect heart yearns for the presence of God; it takes delight in singing of His **mercy *(H2617)*** and ***judgment (H4941)*** as well. The songs that flow from our hearts are to testify of His *kindness, reproof, beauty,* favor and good deeds. The harmonies and melodies of our lives are to be in tune with His *formal decrees* and *divine law.* We may not have what some would call a 'good singing voice,' but when we live in an upright manner, our lives create a beautiful symphony that declares the truth and goodness of our God. This is the way of the perfect heart. We see this in:

Psalm 101:1-4 *I will sing of mercy and judgment: unto thee, O LORD, will I sing. ²I will behave myself wisely in a perfect way. O when wilt thou come unto me? I will walk within my house with a perfect heart. ³I will set no wicked thing before mine eyes: I hate the work of them that turn aside; it shall not cleave to me. ⁴A froward heart shall depart from me: I will not know a wicked person.*

The psalmist, David, was a worshipper who took great delight in expressing his thoughts to the LORD through the writing and singing of songs. He understood the mercy and judgment of the LORD, and he desired to have a perfect heart. In verse 1 of our text, the word **sing** *(H7891)* refers to *the idea of strolling minstrelsy.* As David sang to the LORD, sharing the intimate places of his heart, he also walked with the LORD.

In verse 2, David declared that he would behave himself wisely, in a perfect way. To **behave wisely** *(H7919)* is to act *circumspect* (to be watchful, cautious, prudent) and *intelligently* consider how to bring about success in the management of one's affairs. The **perfect** *(H8549)* **way** *(H1870)* speaks of *a course of life or mode of action* (conversation and/or custom), which demonstrates *complete integrity* (truthfulness, sincerity and uprightness). These are the consistent behavior patterns of those who walk with the LORD.

Chapter 5 • The 'Perfect Heart' Worshipper

David yearned to abide in the presence of the LORD, as he asked, *"O when wilt thou come unto me?"* As David waited for the LORD'S response, he brought his heart and actions into agreement with the Word of God. In so doing, he created a spiritual atmosphere, which drew the presence of the LORD to him.

As David continued to seek the LORD, he declared, *"I will walk within my house with a perfect heart."* This word **house** *(H1004)* spoke not only of the physical structure where he lived, but it also represented his children and *family* members. It was David's desire to not only honor the LORD, but to be a godly example to those of his household and lineage. It's in the privacy of the home, behind closed doors, that our true character is revealed. What we partake of, when we think no one is looking or listening, greatly reveals the condition of our hearts and the truth of who we serve. Privacy creates an atmosphere that reveals the secrets of the heart, whether good or evil.

In verse 3 of Psalm 101, David declared that he would set no **wicked** *(H1100/H1097/H1086)* thing before his eyes. This means he did not regard or give a place of position to anything that was *unprofitable, worthless, destructive,* evil or ungodly. He did not waste his time by allowing that which represented *failure, decay* or corruption into his life. David also hated the **work** *(H6213)* of those who turned **aside** *(H7750)* from the LORD and His ways. He is referring to those who became *derelict* by their *idolatrous practices*. He refused to allow their wickedness to **cleave** *(H1692), cling or adhere* to him. He would not join himself to, pursue after, or be overtaken by wicked people or things.

In verse 4, David declares that a ***froward heart*** would depart from him, and that he would not know a wicked person. A ***froward*** *(H6141/H6140)* heart operates from a mindset that is *distorted, crooked, perverse* and *false*. It's full of treachery, betrayal and dishonesty, and it's disobedient to the Word of God. It joins itself to the evils of sin and becomes twisted, *knotted* and tied up in wickedness. But David was a man after God's heart, and his desire was that any false mindset or inappropriate thoughts and feelings would depart from him. In this context, to ***depart*** *(H5493)* means *to turn off*. Elsewhere in scripture, this word translates as: decline, leave undone, pluck away, revolt against, and withdraw from. David must have known there were displeasing issues in his heart that needed to be dealt with and removed. Since his greatest desire was to please and honor the LORD, there were some things that could no longer be a part of his life.

As we grow in the LORD, there comes a time when we must depart from and *turn off* certain attitudes and actions. Thereby, leaving, declining from and undoing anything that would separate us from the presence of the LORD. We're to revolt against wrong beliefs and withdraw from ungodly behaviors. These decisions are necessary requirements, if we're to walk in maturity and obedience, in our personal relationships with the LORD.

Many times, we're also required to withdraw from those who will not walk in unity with the things of God. In fact, one of the most decisive things a person can do is choose with whom they will and will not associate. It matters who your friends are, because they have an impact on your life. Therefore, choose carefully. People of like heart and mind tend to group together.

For instance, in verse 4, David associates a froward heart with knowing a wicked person. To **know** *(H3045)* a **wicked** *(H7451/H7489)* person means to *observe* and receive *instruction* from those who are *bad, evil* and immoral. The wicked have no regard or respect for what's right, as they *spoil,* shatter and break in pieces the lives of others. Through their wickedness, they cause adversity and destruction to themselves and those associated with them. Those who love the LORD are not to learn their ways. Therefore, either lead them to Christ, or separate from them. In their current state of existence, the wicked are good for nothing.

Those who desire to remain in the continual close company of the wicked have an insidious appetite for evil. Their common ground of depravity and immorality is the enticing bond that holds their relationship together. If you find yourself in this situation, beware! Sin is already crouching at the door of your heart and preparing to enter in. Those who choose to associate in close relationship with the wicked also tend to be tolerant of their ways and will, eventually, take on their behavior patterns. Through wicked relationships ***froward*** hearts are cultivated (1 Corinthians 15:33).

A FROWARD HEART SHALL DEPART
The life choices we make are directly related to the spiritual condition of our hearts. Each of us must choose whether we desire a perfect or wicked heart. It's one way or the other; we can't have it both ways. Also, we cannot blame anybody else for our own heart condition. Regardless of what others may think, say or do against us, we are still responsible to be the keeper of our own heart. For that reason, we're held accountable before God for its condition and content. David could only choose to have a ***perfect heart***, because he chose to reject a froward heart. The phrase ***froward heart*** is stated two other times in scripture:

<u>**Proverbs 11:20-21**</u> ***They that are of a froward heart are abomination to the LORD: but such as are upright in their way are his delight. ²¹Though hand join in hand, the wicked shall not be unpunished: but the seed of the righteous shall be delivered.***

A froward heart is an ***abomination*** (H8441/H8581) to the LORD. This means He is morally *disgusted* by it and finds it *abhorrent, loathsome,* hostile, repulsive and hateful. He finds it to be *detestable,* for it is set upon its own *idolatrous* ways.

In contrast, those who choose to live with an **upright** *(H8549)* heart, operate with *integrity, truth* and sincerity. They are led by the Spirit of God and exemplify godly morality. They lift up the standards of the LORD and are His **delight** *(H7522/H7521)*. This means He finds them to be acceptable and well *pleasing,* and He extends his favor and pleasure toward them. It's easy to see that those with a froward heart are diametrically opposed to those of an upright heart and vice versa; they are polar opposites and do not coexist well together.

Continuing in Proverbs 11:21, let's consider the phrase **though hand join in hand**, which can mean "through all ages and generations" (Source: Gesenius' Lexicon, 1857). The wicked may think they stand in strong unity. They may imagine that their ongoing generations of corruption will hold power against the righteous. They may assume their power can't be broken, as they stand hand in hand. Even so, the LORD will surely punish them as He renders His righteous judgments upon them. Regardless of what the wicked think, they'll not be able to stand against the holy, righteous God or His people.

The LORD not only punishes the wicked, but He also causes the seed of the righteous to be **delivered** *(H4422)*. This means He makes things to be *smooth,* which implies *escape* (as if by *slipperiness*). It also means to *release or rescue; specifically, to bring forth young.* The word *slipperiness* makes me think of oil, because it causes things to move easily, swiftly and smoothly.

Part 1 • *Loving God* with All Your Heart

Comparably, the oil of joy and the power of God are resident within every follower of Christ, since the anointing of the Holy Spirit resides within each believer (Isaiah 61:1-3; Luke 10:19). Those who love and worship the LORD with an upright heart (walking in obedience to Him), will not find themselves left to the hand of their enemies. The wicked (including humans and devils) will never be able to hold, handle, restrain or overcome the anointed, Word focused, Holy Spirit led people of God.

The LORD always takes care of His people! Even if our enemies threaten us with persecution or death, the LORD is with us. For the sold out, born-again believer, death is just the doorway into God's eternal joy and presence. Because we trust in Him, He is faithful to deliver and release us from every snare and tactic of the enemy. We've been set free through the blood of Jesus, the truth of His Word and the power of His Spirit working within us! Therefore, we will stand boldly for Christ and will not submit to wicked men or devils!! In our final verse pertaining to a froward heart, we see it's also associated with a perverse tongue:

<u>Proverbs 17:20</u> *He that hath a froward heart findeth no good: and he that hath a perverse tongue falleth into mischief.*

For the froward heart to find no **good** (H2896) means it will not perceive, grab a hold of or acquire anything that is cheerful, beautiful, gracious, joyful, kind, loving, pleasant, prosperous, precious or *well* favored. The froward heart is pessimistic in nature. It expects or creates the worst scenarios in every given situation.

A *perverse* (H2015) tongue is one that uses language to speak evil, to accuse, slander and babble on with foolishness. It implies an effort to *change, overturn* or *pervert* others. It literally means *to turn about or over*. Basically, those with a perverse tongue create a diversion; they mislead and misguide with the intent to overthrow. For a perverse tongue to fall into *mischief (H7451/H7489)* means it participates in what is *morally evil*. Instead of the tongue being used to bring forth life, hope, truth and blessing, it's used to bring forth adversity, affliction, calamity, distress, grief, hurt, harm, displeasure, misery and sadness. The perverse tongue is filled with wretchedness.

A froward heart finds no good, and a perverse tongue falls into mischief. The contents of the froward heart will manifest through the perverse tongue, and it will create a rebellious pit of iniquity where devils are pleased to dwell. Therefore, when a perverted tongue spews out the contents of a forward heart, it is operating under a demonic influence. Hence, it becomes a weapon of wickedness used to break down, demoralize (morally pollute and/or corrupt), defile, impair and degrade people, while mentally seducing and abusing them.

Scripture tells us that out of the abundance of the heart (be it good or evil), the mouth speaks; death and life are in the power of the tongue (Luke 6:45; Proverbs

Part 1 • *Loving God* with All Your Heart

18:21). We see this truth in Matthew 12:22-34; Jesus rebuked the Pharisees for their religious unbelief, when they accused Him of casting out devils by Beelzebub – the prince of the devils. They were so proud that, in their pompous arrogance, they couldn't see the truth of who Jesus really was. These spiritual leaders, who should have recognized their Messiah, were saying that Jesus — the Christ, the Son of the living God — was of the devil! The cutting words that flowed from the lips of the Pharisees revealed the ignorance and corruption of their hearts, as they blasphemed the LORD of Glory.

Jesus knew what was in the heart of every Pharisee. Thus, the LORD called them into accountability. He told them to examine the fruit of their lives, and either make the tree and its fruit good or corrupt. They couldn't have it both ways. Jesus knew where they stood, but He wanted them to discover and discern the condition of their own hearts. Jesus revealed the truth concerning their attitudes in:

<u>Matthew 12:34</u> *O generation of vipers, how can ye, being evil, speak good things? For out of the abundance of the heart the mouth speaketh.*

These religious leaders had evil hearts and wicked mouths. In their viperous mentality they were incapable of speaking anything good. If this were not true, the LORD would not have called them a generation of vipers (venomous snakes)! They were masquerading as if they were godly, but the fruit of wickedness flowed abundantly from their lips. Their corrupt hearts were exposed. Religious facades and pious rhetoric could no longer hide the truth of who they were.

As with the Pharisees, the LORD sees all that's in our hearts. We cannot hide in the shadows of religious ignorance and a holier than thou attitude. We are accountable for every idle word that comes out of our mouths (Matthew 12:36).

TAKE A PERSONAL INVENTORY
We do not want to be like the hypocritical Pharisees, but many in the church today desperately need to determine what's really in their hearts. Occasionally, we all need to stop and take a mental and verbal inventory. For example, we must discern what's flowing from our hearts, across our tongues and out of our mouths. Are we speaking forth words of life or death? Are we speaking the things of the Kingdom of God or the things of the world?

If the mouth is releasing words that are ungodly, hateful, angry, destructive, distasteful, disrespectful, dishonest, distorted and lewd, then spiritually, the speaker has a severely corrupt heart condition. This fatal condition works death from the inside out, as perverse lips spew the poison of the heart with projectile force. On the other hand, if the words coming out of the mouth are godly, truthful, loving, kind, encouraging, hope-filled and life-giving, then

Part 1 • *Loving God* with All Your Heart

this is evidence that the heart is submitted to the LORD and is being directed by His Holy Spirit. Our words reveal who we truly serve and what we believe.

Loving the LORD with a perfect heart requires that we conform to His commands for our lives. In brief, though we have previously expounded on the following standards, they bear repeating. If we love the LORD with a perfect heart, we will:

- Refuse to partake in any form of wickedness.
- Reject ungodly entertainment and instruction.
- Run from sin (including secret lust), whether in reality or fantasy.
- Shun the idolatrous ways of the world.
- Avoid close friendship with those who push away or debase and adulterate the things of God.
- Remove anything, everything and anybody who tries to turn us away from our God.
- Set ourselves apart for Him

Those with a perfect heart love the LORD and honor His holy Word. They delight to obey Him — choosing to do what's right and opposing all that's wrong. They endeavor to behave in a godly manner at all times — reflecting the character of Christ's name. This is the way of the perfect heart.

If our true desire is to have a perfect heart before the LORD, He will extend His mercy and grace to help us. He knows we cannot accomplish such a task on our own, because a perfect heart is a supernatural work of God (Ezekiel 36:26-27). If you are yearning for the LORD to perform such a work in you, please consider and seek Him concerning the following questions:

- Are you behaving wisely? If not, are you willing to change your behavior?
- Are you guarding your heart against evil?
- What is your spiritual heart condition?
- What's coming out of your mouth?
- Is there any area of your life that is compromised?
- Are there any areas of your heart that are distorted, false, crooked or perverse?
- Are there things tucked away in the hidden places of your character that need to be exposed, changed or done away with?
- Are there secret sins that you know you need to repent of? If so, take the time to do that now.

RECEIVES FAVOR AND LONG LIFE

Those with a perfect heart will find great grace and favor in the LORD. The condition and integrity of our hearts can, literally, add years to our lives. We have an example of this in the biblical account of King

Part 1 • *Loving God* with All Your Heart

Hezekiah. We read the words of the LORD (spoken by the Prophet Isaiah) and King Hezekiah's response in:

<u>Isaiah 38:1-5</u> *In those days was Hezekiah sick unto death. And Isaiah the prophet the son of Amoz came unto him, and said unto him, Thus saith the LORD, Set thine house in order: for thou shalt die, and not live. ²Then Hezekiah turned his face toward the wall, and prayed unto the LORD, ³And said, Remember now, O LORD, I beseech thee, how I have walked before thee in truth and with a perfect heart, and have done that which is good in thy sight. And Hezekiah wept sore. ⁴Then came the word of the LORD to Isaiah, saying, ⁵Go, and say to Hezekiah, Thus saith the LORD, the God of David thy father, I have heard thy prayer, I have seen thy tears: behold, I will add unto thy days fifteen years* (also 2 Kings 20:1-6).

Hezekiah was a righteous King who sought to please the LORD and do what was right in His sight. This created a favorable history with the LORD that would allow the king to appeal the timing of his death. After receiving the words of the prophet, Hezekiah reminded the LORD of how he had **walked** *(H1980/H3212)* before Him in **truth** *(H571)* with a perfect heart. This means that throughout his life he presented himself in a *trustworthy* manner before the face of the LORD; he built and established a *stable* and faithful relationship with Him. Although Hezekiah struggled with the words of the prophet, He understood that his peace would only be found in his God whom he loved and served. Therefore, in his time of need, the King turned his face toward the wall and **wept** *(H1058/H1065)* **sore** *(H1419)*; bemoaning, lamenting and *greatly* mourning before the LORD.

It's interesting that the name **Hezekiah** *(H2396/H2388)* means to be *strengthened of Jah*. It's from a word that implies he was strengthened (received *courage* and the *cure*) through the action of *binding to* and *fastening upon* the LORD. Indeed, the King turned his back to the world, looked at the insurmountable wall of pronounced death that was before him, and in this position, he poured out his heart to the LORD. As a result of his prayer, the LORD told the Prophet Isaiah to go back and tell Hezekiah that He had heard the king's prayer, seen the king's tears and promised to add 15 years to the king's life (Isaiah 38:4-5). It was the character of Hezekiah and his love relationship with the LORD that caused his life to be extended.

Even in the face of death, those who walk before the LORD with a perfect heart, have access to receive what they need from Him. Faithfulness and loving obedience are a heavenly currency we can draw upon, in times of need. God gives honor to those who honor Him; His ears and heart are open to those whose ears and hearts are open to Him.

Part 1 • *Loving God* with All Your Heart

WILL NOT COMPROMISE

In the case of King Hezekiah, his perfect heart exhibited a lifestyle of trustworthiness and integrity before the LORD. He established a standard that would not compromise or negotiate with anything that displeased the LORD. King David, like King Hezekiah, also understood the importance of having a perfect heart. But he learned it through a very difficult life lesson.

King David had sent his armies out to fight the Ammonites, but he remained in Jerusalem. In the evening, he walked on the roof of his house, and from his vantage point, he could see a beautiful woman washing herself. David enquired of her and learned that she was Bathsheba — the wife of Uriah the Hittite, one of David's soldiers. Knowing full well that he had no right to her, he sent for her, slept with her and sent her home again (2 Samuel 11:1-4).

David committed adultery with Bathsheba and she conceived his child. When she told David that she was pregnant, he contrived a plan to cover his sin. He sent for Uriah to come home from the battlefield and encouraged him to go home to his wife. But Uriah was a man of honor and principle. He refused to enjoy the pleasures of his wife, while his comrades were engaged in battle (2 Samuel 11:5-13). So, David sent Uriah back to the battlefield with a letter to General Joab. Within the instructions of that letter, Joab was ordered to put Uriah in the hottest part of the battle, and then pull back from him, so he would be killed. In an effort to cover his deliberate sin of adultery with Bathsheba, David sinned again by treacherously plotting the unjust death of her husband (2 Samuel 11:14-17).

After Uriah's death, King David married Bathsheba, but the LORD was greatly displeased (2 Samuel 11:27). Consequently, the LORD sent Nathan the prophet, to uncover and openly expose David's sin. Once exposed, David came to a place of full repentance before the LORD, but the first born child of that adulterous union died (2 Samuel 12:1-23).

Scripture records the account of David's repentance in Psalm 51. In the first five verses, he acknowledged and took full responsibility for his sin. He offered no excuses for his selfish lust, pride, deception and murderous ways. He recognized that his sin was against the LORD and his judgment was justified. When he neglected God's truth and wisdom in his time of temptation, David allowed sin to reign in his heart. He contritely reveals his need for the integrity of the LORD in:

***Psalm 51:6** Behold, thou desirest truth in the inward parts: and in the hidden part thou shalt make me to know wisdom.*

First, we must ask, what does it mean to say that the LORD **desirest** *(H2654)* **truth** *(H571/H539)* in the inward parts? Well, the word **truth** in this verse is defined as *stability; to build up or support, foster* and *to be firm*. **Truth** is the foundation upon which *trustworthiness, faithfulness* and that which is *certain* and *right* is established. Also, the word **desirest** means *to incline to*; it implies *to bend* and, figuratively, *to be pleased with*. God is pleased when we morally, mentally and spiritually, incline or bend ourselves in the right direction toward Him. In fact, He looks for the evidence of His truth and the characteristics of His trustworthiness, His faithfulness, His righteousness and His stability in the innermost parts of our being.

Furthermore, everything about God's Word is truth! He's pleased when we build our lives upon His Word, because He desires the wisdom of His truth to dwell within us. Besides, He is truth personified and He delights to see Himself in us (Deuteronomy 32:4; Psalms 31:5, 86:15; John 14:6).

Second, let's see what it means to **know wisdom in the hidden part**. Using the Strong's Concordance, we find that to **know** *(H3045)* **wisdom** *(H2451/H2449)* means to *see, recognize* and *carefully observe* by godly *instruction* (and, if need be, by *punishment)* how to deal wisely and skillfully in a situation. This is especially true concerning one's own *thoughts, words and actions*. Godly wisdom equips us to properly discern the underlying causes, consequences and solutions of a given situation. Thereby empowering us to make sound decisions, walk in truth and live in freedom.

Chapter 5 • The 'Perfect Heart' Worshipper

In David's adulterous condition and irresponsibility as king, he acted foolishly. Although he tried to conceal his sin, he was caught and disciplined by the LORD through the prophet Nathan. The profound reality and consequences of David's wickedness brutally invaded his understanding. He knew he would have no peace, assurance or pleasing fellowship with the LORD, if he did not fully repent of his sins. If he had 'known wisdom' he would have understood how to properly handle temptation; he would have avoided sin and the shameful predicament in which he found himself.

The word **hidden** (H5640) means *to stop up; figuratively, to keep secret;* and it implies a need *to repair.* Initially, David tried to keep his treacherous secrets hidden. The clutter of compromise, selfishness and uncontrolled passion, stopped up and shut down his fellowship with the LORD. Remember, it wasn't until the prophet Nathan openly exposed and rebuked him that David admitted to the evil he had committed. Because of David's position in the nation, his sin had far reaching effects. For this reason, God brought judgment upon his household. David knew that, if this breach was to be repaired, full repentance of the hidden and broken parts of his life was required. In the following verses, we see the heart cry of David regarding his need to make things right with the LORD:

<u>**Psalm 51:7-12**</u> <u>**Purge me**</u> *with hyssop, and I shall be clean:* <u>**wash me**</u>*, and I shall be whiter than*

Part 1 • *Loving God* with All Your Heart

snow. ⁸Make me to hear joy and gladness; that the bones which thou hast broken may rejoice. ⁹Hide thy face from my sins, and blot out all mine iniquities. ¹⁰Create in me a clean heart, O God; and renew a right spirit within me. ¹¹Cast me not away from thy presence; and take not thy holy spirit from me. ¹²Restore unto me the joy of thy salvation; and uphold me with thy free spirit.

This Psalm expresses the depths of David's desire to be forgiven, restored and freed from the weight of his transgressions. He knew he was to blame for what had taken place. In his soul, he knew He was guilty, morally evil and filthy before the LORD. Sin had stolen his joy and brought him to a place of being **broken** *(H1794)*, causing him *to physically and mentally collapse.* He was ashamed before God and desperately wanted to be cleansed and purified of the harm he had caused. He asked the LORD to purge him and create a **clean** *(H2889/H2891), innocent, pure, holy, unadulterated, uncontaminated* heart within him.

David also asked the LORD to **renew** *(H2318)* a **right** *(H3559)* spirit within him. He wanted his spirit — his life — to be *rebuilt*, repaired and *fixed*. He wanted to be perfect and upright. He desired to live a life of faithfulness before the LORD, but he knew his sin would cause him to be cast out and separated from the **presence** *(H6440/H6437)* of God. To not be able to seek God's *face* and favor was not a peaceful

CHAPTER 5 • THE 'PERFECT HEART' WORSHIPPER

option for this man of God. He didn't want to suffer the loss of the *sacred* presence and influence of God's Holy Spirit from his life. Therefore, true repentance was his only real option.

After David repented, he asked the LORD to restore unto him the joy of His salvation. In this verse, *joy (H8342/H7797)* is defined as *cheerfulness; specifically, welcome;* and *to be bright.* The joy of God's salvation refers to His miracle of welcoming us into right relationship with Himself. Hallelujah! For those whose hearts are perfect toward Him, our God is the God of restoration!

Now, let's consider the word **restore** *(H7725/H7619/H7617/H410),* which refers to the *strength* of *the Almighty* to *return* (or turn us back) to Him. Let's remember that we have no power to restore ourselves; it is the LORD who restores. Our only role in being restored is to repent and receive. Once David repented with complete sincerity and surrender, the LORD circumcised every area of his heart and life. Only after repentance, did the LORD deliver David and cause him to recover from the ravages and torments of his sin.

A person can only experience the joy of **salvation** *(H3468/H3467)* when he or she realizes the root of their sinfulness. Because the flesh desires to have its own way and do its own thing, it operates in opposition to the Spirit of God and His Word. So, sin is rooted in corruption and disobedience, which is resident in the nature of the unregenerate man.

Without repentance and apart from God's power, sin and its consequences are inescapable. Restored joy only happens when the disobedient heart chooses to properly align itself with the Word of God and live accordingly. Such choices tug at the gracious and merciful heart of God, calling upon Him to save and *deliver*. He will put the repentant heart in a place of *safety* and bring it into *liberty* and *prosperity*.

I'm sure David also remembered how the LORD dealt with his predecessor — the erring King Saul — when the LORD rebuked him through the prophet Samuel (1 Samuel 15). Samuel declared to Saul, *"For rebellion is as the sin of witchcraft, and stubbornness is as iniquity and idolatry. Because thou hast rejected the word of the LORD, he hath also rejected thee from being king"* (1 Samuel 15:23). David did not want to find himself in the same situation.

David knew he was morally weak and needed the LORD to **uphold** (H5564) him. He needed to *take hold* of, *lean upon* and be *propped* up by the LORD. Only then, could he be established and sustained. Ultimately, David wanted his heart and life to be a sanctuary for the LORD — a place where His presence could dwell. Like David, if we're to be established in the LORD and experience the full joy of our salvation, we must allow the truth of God's Word to purge the inward parts of our hearts (Psalm 51:6-12).

After the death of David and Bathsheba's first son, David comforted Bathsheba and she conceived again. They named their second born son **Solomon** *(H8010)* which means *peace*. The prophet Nathan gave Solomon the name **Jedudiah** *(H3041)* which means *beloved of Jehovah* (2 Samuel 12:24-25). God, in His great mercy toward David, chose Solomon to build the temple of the LORD. Therefore, when the time came for David to step down from His role as King of Israel, he appointed his son Solomon to rule in his stead and to fulfill the plan of God.

Solomon was young, with a great destiny ahead of him. David had learned some things the hard way; hence, he sought to give wise counsel to his son. He knew that Solomon's level of dedication in his relationship with the LORD would affect every aspect of his reign as King. The effectiveness of Solomon's kingship and the decisions he made would have a huge impact on the people, the heart of the nation and David's royal descendants. David also knew that, if Solomon was to be successful, then he must have a perfect heart and a willing mind to obey the LORD:

<u>1 Chronicles 28:9-10</u> And thou, Solomon my son, know thou the God of thy father, and serve him with a perfect heart and with a willing mind: for the LORD searcheth all hearts, and understandeth

Part 1 • *Loving God* with All Your Heart

all the imaginations of the thoughts: if thou seek him, he will be found of thee; but if thou forsake him, he will cast thee off for ever. ¹⁰Take heed now; for the LORD hath chosen thee to build an house for the sanctuary: be strong, and do it.

KNOWING AND SERVING THE LORD

David counseled Solomon to **know and serve** the LORD. In this context, to **know** *(H3045)* the LORD means to *observe, recognize* and receive His *instructions* as one who learns of Him. To **serve** *(H5647)* the LORD means *to work* and implies becoming a *tiller, servant* and *slave*. This type of worshipper makes the LORD their first priority; everything else is secondary. Whatever the LORD desires is what the worshipper is willing to do or give to Him.

The kingly worshipper is chosen and anointed to be a servant and a husbandman — sowing the Word of God into the hearts of men, while joyfully working in the harvest fields of the LORD. This type of worshipper is motivated by a love which extends not only toward the LORD, but also to all those around them. Such worshippers allow the LORD to use them to heal the broken hearted, set the captives free, and open the prison doors to those that are bound (Isaiah 61).

Learning how to know and serve the LORD is an experiential skill that develops over time. It begins with a personal encounter with the living God. In love, He reaches out to us and reveals the need to repent of our sins. He extends His mercy, grace and forgiveness to us, as we accept the atoning work of Christ. As we enter into a close relationship with Christ, we become His disciple. As a disciple, we labor with Him and learn His ways. In the process, we discover His splendor and majesty. We begin to love Him more deeply, and our desire is stirred to experience more of His abiding presence and tender affections.

As we continue receiving from the LORD, He continues to pour the reality of who He is, into our hearts. Many times, in the midst of worship, the LORD speaks into our spirits and reveals His Word and will for our lives. It's up to us to receive and conceive the seed of that Word, and allow the LORD to grow it on the inside of us. This is how we demonstrate our trust and confidence in Him to bring it to pass. He becomes the very fulfillment of our greatest joy and destiny. He becomes everything we need!

As we abide in the LORD'S presence, intimate praise and worship should become as natural as breathing. Nobody will have to stir us up, because our joyful passion for the LORD will overtake our innermost being. He becomes the very essence and vitality of our expression and existence, and serving Him becomes our greatest delight!

Thank God — we have been called out of the darkness of sin and into the marvelous light of the LORD! The LORD has called and chosen every single believer to

Part 1 • *Loving God* with All Your Heart

hold a position of kingship and priesthood within His Kingdom. We're a chosen generation, a royal priesthood, a holy nation and a peculiar people. And, if God be for us, who can stand against us (Romans 8:31)? Therefore, our praise and lifestyle are to be the evidence that we're walking in the light of His truth (1 Peter 2:9; Revelation 1:6, 5:10).

We're to be a reflection of God's glory; carrying a mantle of His anointing upon our lives. So, when we step into a situation, spiritual darkness should flee and devils should be looking for an escape route. Our godly presence should also cause sinners to come under heavy conviction, and our lifestyle should stir a desire within them to know our God. We're not supposed to look or act, in spirit or character, like the people of this world. When people perceive the glory and anointing of the LORD upon us, they're observing the overflow of what has happened in our private time of intimate worship with Him.

King David was a worshipper; he not only desired for Solomon to intimately know and passionately serve the LORD for spiritual reasons, but he understood the practical necessity as well. The task that was set before Solomon was great. He could not accomplish it without the LORD.

David gave spiritual guidance and encouragement to Solomon; he also provided the pattern and needed materials for Solomon to be able to build the temple of the LORD (1 Chronicles 28:11-28). In a greater (yet similar) way, the LORD has also provided all that's needed for us to walk in our royal son-ship and authority to build up the Kingdom of God. We, like Solomon, are called and anointed for the task! If we will believe God, all things are possible. As a caring Father, the LORD will pour out His abundant provision (Matthew 19:26; Mark 9:23; Philippians 4:19).

Graciously, the LORD reveals His purpose for our existence and shows us who we are in Him, as He lovingly reveals the calling and anointing He has determined for our lives. To equip us for our destiny, the LORD has even blessed us with spiritual gifts. Passionately serving the LORD and fulfilling our kingdom destiny exemplifies a lifestyle of worship.

A WILLING MIND
David told his son, King Solomon, to not only know and serve the LORD with a perfect heart, but also with a willing mind. (1 Chronicles 28:9-10). A person with a *willing mind* (H2655/H2654) is one who is *inclined to bend* their thoughts, feelings, desires and decisions to fulfill the LORD'S purposes. A willing mind is a source of *pleasure* and refreshing to the LORD. When we please Him in this way, His favor and delight are our reward. As David exhorted Solomon, we must remember: If we're to fulfill our ordained life purpose, we must know and serve the LORD with a perfect heart and a willing mind.

Part 1 • *Loving God* with All Your Heart

Serving the LORD with a willing mind is a mutually satisfying experience of enjoyment between us and our Creator. Therefore, we cannot allow ourselves to merely fall into a state of dutiful busyness, religious obligation or dead ritual. This may be what some people are accustomed to; it may be what they've always done. It may be their personally preferred form of godliness, but that doesn't mean it's right or pleasing to the LORD. It may be tradition, but that doesn't mean it brings life. To serve the LORD with a willing mind is not about fulfilling our usual routine and functioning from a religiously stale mindset. It's about bending our routines, thoughts, desires and actions to serve the LORD in a way that brings pleasure to Him.

In the sweetness of knowing and serving the LORD, deeper levels of intimacy are developed. As we yield to Him, there's a reciprocal drawing together (James 4:8). In the sanctuary of secure relationship, He affirms who we are in Him and reveals Himself as the Beloved Bridegroom (Song of Solomon 1-8)! He knows the hidden secrets of our hearts and the fullness of our thoughts:

1 Chronicles 28:9 **_...the LORD searcheth all hearts, and understandeth all the imaginations of the thoughts..._**

The LORD pursues us in love, and all that has been concealed within us is opened and laid bare. He uncovers the veiled obscurities of our true self and reveals Himself. As the LORD searches our hearts, He fully **understands** *(H995)* and *mentally separates* all the *imaginations (H3336)*; the *forms, concepts* and details of every **thought** *(H4284/H2803)*. He meticulously examines the secret place of who we are and *distinguishes* every *intention, purpose, plan, plot* and piece of *advice* that we *contrive* and *weave* together.

The LORD is captivated by a heart that is focused on Him. He's looking for the perfected heart into which He can pour Himself. For this reason, it's important that we guard our hearts from anything that would pollute our relationship with the LORD. The Psalmist David knew this when he wrote:

<u>Psalm 66:18</u> If I regard iniquity in my heart, the LORD will not hear me.

To **regard** *(H7200)* **iniquity** *(H205)* in the **heart** *(H3820)* means to provide a place in the *center* of our being *(figuratively, our mind, will and emotions)*, where we *see*, approve of and enjoy experiences of *wickedness*. Such approval and enjoyment gives place to *idolatry, vanity, mischief, evil, sorrow* and *unrighteousness*. Simply put, iniquity just means doing things in our own sinful way.

Anytime we choose our own will and ways, instead of the will and ways of God, it's a personal affront to Him. If we're filled with our own will and ways, then we'll reject the will and ways of God. The heart that regards iniquity is captivated by its own foolishness and bound by its own *trouble*.

Part 1 • *Loving God* with All Your Heart

Those who deny the LORD of His rightful place in their lives have erected their own will upon the throne of their hearts and have displaced God. Beguiled by their own ways, they become cruel task masters of their own destruction. Instead of the authority and power of God, they've chosen the iniquity of self and have become slaves of their own idolatry. By preferring to serve a false god of their own making, they've rejected the LORD. For this reason, the LORD will not **hear** *(H8085)* those who permit iniquity to rule in their hearts. This means He will not consider, give ear to, pay *attention* to, or listen in any way. This is what happens, if we allow anything other than the power, presence and Word of God to have full reign in our lives. It's utterly and absolutely impossible to serve wickedness and righteousness simultaneously.

The LORD will not compromise His standards. He will not wink at sin. But He will honor those who willingly submit to Him. David gives us the prevention plan and the prescriptive cure for keeping iniquity out of our hearts in:

<u>Psalm 119:11</u> *Thy word have I hid (H6845) in mine heart, that I might not sin against thee.*

When we hide the Word of God in our hearts, we're creating a secret place where we can fortify ourselves by preserving, building up and, even, *hoarding* His commands and promises on the inside of us. When we honor God's Word, He activates and confirms His promises to us. He grants His protection, favor, wisdom, provision, healing, deliverance and discernment to us, in every situation. When sin and temptation come knocking at the door of our hearts and minds, we will recognize the deceptive schemes of the enemy; speak God's truth into the situation; provide the needed rebuke; and destroy the temptation of sin, rendering it completely ineffective.

The LORD sees and understands that which presses in upon us, distresses us, causes vexation and limits our understanding. Thankfully, sin cannot operate where God's holiness dwells. Knowing this, we can open our hearts and surrender all our human frailties to Him. If we do, our hearts will become His inner sanctuary — His holy place, where He will manifest His power, reveal the truth of His existence, and make His presence known in our lives.

If you're reading this book and you do not know the LORD, He still knows the condition of your heart. He still loves you and desires to make you His own. He sees every wounded and broken place. He sees every sorrow and disappointment. He wants to apply the soothing balm of His love, forgiveness and restoration to every part of who you are. Cry out to Him right now; repent of your sins; let Him draw you into His glorious presence; listen for His voice; He wants to speak to you. You're important to Him and He has an amazing destiny for you. Seek Him and He will answer.

Part 1 • *Loving God* with All Your Heart

When you choose Him with a willing mind, He will give you a clean, perfect, courageous, overcoming heart.

SEEKING HIM
The LORD is always looking for those who are on a quest to know and discover Him. In spite of our frailties and short comings, He recognizes the willing servant. He will always reach out to those who desire to have a perfect heart toward Him. After David told King Solomon to know and serve the LORD with a perfect heart and a willing mind, He continues to instruct his son in:

1 Chronicles 28:9 *...if thou seek him, he will be found of thee; but if thou forsake him, he will cast thee off for ever.*

Notice the first word in this portion of our scripture is *if* (H518). As emphasized earlier in this study, this word denotes a conditional situation which has requirements or demonstrates an uncertain possibility based on the actions of all parties involved. It tells us that, if we do this, God will do that. In other words, He watches our response to His Word and He responds accordingly. Another way to say the first part of 1 Chronicles 28:9 is, "...providing that you seek the LORD, He will allow Himself to be found by you..." It is up to us to make provision for the LORD to be welcomed in our midst.

To **seek** (H1875) the LORD means to *worship* Him, to care for Him, to *frequently ask* questions and inquire of Him; to *pursue, search* or *follow* after Him. Seeking the LORD is all about relationship. If we're willing to seek, then He's willing to manifest Himself to us.

This reminds me of when I was a child, and we would play the game 'hide and seek.' The object of the game was for everybody to hide, while one person (who was 'it') closed their eyes and counted to a designated number. Then the 'it' person would begin searching and seeking out those who were hiding. If those who were hidden were spotted, then they had to quickly run to the base where they would declare themselves safe — free from the risk of being tagged by the one who was seeking them. If the 'it' person caught someone that had been hiding, then they would good naturedly switch roles, and the game would go on. My point is this, the one who was seeking would never find the ones who were hiding, if they were not willing to search and pursue them.

When we pursue the LORD, He will always reveal Himself and let us get hold of Him. He will manifest His existence, joyfully taking hold of us and running with us into His glorious freedom. Seeking and worshiping the LORD becomes the prerequisite for any great work of God that takes place in our lives.

HIS PLACE, OUR HEART AND REPENTANCE

David knew that God would do a great work through his son, and that Solomon needed the wisdom of God to accomplish the task. So, David encouraged him to know and serve the LORD with a perfect heart and a willing mind, which also required that Solomon seek and pursue after the LORD. Indeed, David was right to set his son along this path; the task before him was arduous, meticulous and overwhelmingly important.

For seven years, Solomon built an extravagantly beautiful temple for the LORD. After its completion, he gathered all the leaders and elders of Israel together. The priests took up the Ark of the Covenant of the LORD from the tabernacle of David, and the Levites brought up the tabernacle of the congregation (and all the holy vessels that were in the tabernacle) to the temple of Solomon. Then, Solomon and all the congregation of Israel that were with him sacrificed innumerable animals to the LORD before the Ark (1 Kings 8:1-5). After the sacrifices were offered, the priests brought the Ark into 'His' place, according to:

<u>1 Kings 8:6</u> And the priests brought the Ark of the covenant of the LORD into His place, into the oracle of the house, the most holy place, even under the wings of the cherubims.

The word **priests** (H3548/H3547) speaks of those who *officiate* in the position and responsibility of divine *service*, by fulfilling their appointed religious functions and duties. These priests of the LORD carried the Ark — which represented the presence, power, glory and Word of God — upon their shoulders. Then, they brought it into the **oracle** (H1687) of the house, which was the *innermost part of the sanctuary,* the most holy place. It was the priest's responsibility to tend to the things of God and prepare a place for His presence to dwell.

Interestingly, the most used Hebrew word for **heart** *(H3820/H3824/H3823)* is defined as the *interior* and most enclosed part. This also refers to the inner man or the spirit of man, which dwells in the inward parts. True worship and the presence of God are no longer centered on the Ark — a wooden box overlaid with gold. Nor are they confined within the walls of temples made by the hands of men. Rather, the LORD (and all that the ark represented) has found *His place* in the *most holy (H6944/H6942) place* — the *sacred,* dedicated, hallowed sanctuary of hearts that have been *cleansed,* consecrated, purified and prepared to receive Him. The holy place, the sanctuary, the hidden man of the heart, the inward parts of us are to be places of truth — where Jesus sits upon His throne, finds His rest and rules supreme as KING and LORD. This is where we meet with Him, worship Him, commune with Him, consider His promises and invite His presence.

THE INNER MAN, THE INWARD PARTS — OUR HEART
Concerning our hearts, let's look at some other verses relating to the 'inner man' or 'inward parts.' These verses illustrate the consistency of the Word:

Jeremiah 31:33** But this shall be the covenant that I will make with the house of Israel; After those days, saith the LORD, <u>I will put my law in</u>

Part 1 • *Loving God* with All Your Heart

<u>*their inward parts, and write it in their hearts;*</u> *and will be their God, and they shall be my people.*

Through the original **covenant** (H1285/H1262/H1254) that the LORD established with Abraham and the house of Israel, He selected a people to call His own. Covenant was made in the midst of blood and the *cutting* of flesh through the act of circumcision (Genesis 17:12). The LORD has always desired that His people would treasure and hold His covenant in the center of their hearts — a place reserved as the dwelling place for His holiness.

When His holiness is present in our hearts, then the evidence of His covenant living in us is expressed and demonstrated through our lives (emotions, thoughts, words, deeds and actions). Consequently, it's in the spiritual heart attitude that we choose to submit to the LORD and cut away the sinful, fleshly nature of self. Even with the new covenant, the Apostle Paul addressed this:

<u>**Romans 2:29**</u> *But he is a Jew, which is one* <u>*inwardly;*</u> *and* <u>*circumcision is that of the heart, in the spirit*</u>*, and not in the letter; whose praise is not of men, but of God.*

Outward appearances and dutiful religious rituals cannot be substituted for one's heart being right toward the LORD. Natural circumcision will never change a heart, nor make a soul righteous before

God. It's the work of God's Spirit within our spirits that stirs up a holy hunger and righteous desire to live in pleasing obedience toward the LORD. Our obedience is our expression of love and gratitude for who He is and all He's done. As we join our hearts to the LORD, we willingly yield and submit to the cutting away of all that hinders us from sweet fellowship with Him. When we're circumcised in heart, our inward man finds joy and delights in the covenant of God.

***Romans 7:22** For I delight in the law of God after the inward man:*

To **delight** (G4913/H4862/H2237) in the **law** (G3551) of God after the **inward** (G2080/1519) man, means to *desire, rejoice* and take pleasure in the *prescriptive usage* of the Word of God. The phrase *prescriptive usage* implies that His Word is the cure — the prescription for every situation. When we accept and apply God's *principles,* instructions, rules and *regulations,* as found in His Word, we have positioned ourselves to receive His perspective and insight for all of life's encounters.

The LORD wants us to see things from His perspective. He desires the anointing of His Spirit, along with His power, salvation, healing, freedom, deliverance, wisdom, knowledge and purposes to be released and made manifest in our lives. He wants us to experience the riches of His glory as we see in:

Part 1 • *Loving God* with All Your Heart

Ephesians 3:16 *That he would grant you, according to the <u>riches</u> of <u>his glory</u>, to <u>be strengthened with might by his Spirit in the inner man</u>;*

Through Christ we're gifted with the **riches** *(G4149/ G4130), wealth, abundance* and *fullness* of God's glory. By His **Spirit** *(G4151/G4154), breath* and *mental disposition* working within us, we're **strengthened** *(G2901/G2900/G2904).* He *mightily empowers* our inner man with *great vigor, dominion* and *purpose*. As we experience and embrace the glory of God and submit to Him, we're radically changed. Day by day, our inner man is renewed, but our renewal is not just for our own personal benefit. We are to use what the LORD has given us to encourage and strengthen others (2 Corinthians 4:15-16).

When it comes to the inner man being renewed, we're not simply talking about being familiar with or conforming to "Christian culture." We're not talking about a veneered façade of knowing the right churchy things to say or do in a given situation. Submission to God is not a game of charades. Our relationship with the LORD is about what's on the inside. It's in the inward, hidden depths of our hearts that the Spirit of God wants to bring forth the beauty of who He's created us to be.

1 Peter 3:4 *But let it be the <u>hidden man of the heart</u>, in that which is not corruptible, even the* *ornament of a meek and quiet spirit, which is in the sight of God of great price.*

This scripture is in reference to a wife; her relationship with her husband; and how she can win him to faith in Christ by her lifestyle. Her adorning is not to focus just on her exterior appearance, but she's to have a beauty that shines from deep within. The phrase **hidden (G2927/G2928) man of the heart** in this verse speaks of the center or secret place of thoughts and feelings which are *concealed* deep within the *private* place of the heart. This place of the heart is to be a humble place of *undisturbed stillness* wherein the Prince of peace dwells.

LOVING, ENRAPTURED TRANSPORTATION
In this study of loving the LORD with all our hearts, I've found that one of the Hebrew definitions for the word **heart** *(H3820/H3824/H3823)* implies to *transport with love*. Some of the English definitions of the word transport are: to carry, to go from one place to another, to have a strong emotional effect upon, to enrapture and rapture. When we're connected to Christ and He finds His dwelling place in us, we find great fulfillment in Him. He transports us by His love, from one level of faith to another and from one level of glory to another. The graciously rich truths of His Word and the sweetness of His presence will stir up strong emotions of joy, excitement, expectancy, peace, love and acceptance as we are enraptured in His glory.

Though some people are not comfortable with what might be considered 'religious emotionalism,' the fact is, God created our emotions. When our hearts are in right standing with Him, our emotions are just a natural expression of pleasure in the amazing supernatural relationship that we share with Him. I believe the LORD is very pleased when we celebrate Him in this way.

BELIEF SYSTEMS

There are two groups of people in the earth and each has a belief system. There is the belief system of the lost and the belief system of the saved. Within the group of people that are lost, there are two groups — the religious and the non-religious.

The religious may have personal standards of self-righteousness by which they, apart from the holiness of God operating in their lives, seek to justify themselves. They may attend 'church' services, dutifully practicing their sanctimoniously devout rituals. However, because their manmade standards and rituals are not based on the truth of God's Word, their religion is dead and powerless. Therefore, they can find no genuine satisfaction, enduring peace or divine purpose in them. While they seek to make themselves feel better, their religious activity is a work of vanity. These are who I call the religiously lost.

The religiously lost have a belief system that is devoid of Christ and His salvation. Therefore, through their own works, they strive to be acceptably good enough, for whoever or whatever they perceive their god to be. Their belief system may have been passed down from one generation to the next. It may have been associated with their family name or culture. In reality though, their powerless, Christ-less religion is nothing more than an empty, shallow, external façade of lifeless formal procedures holding them in deceptive bondage.

Then there's the belief system of those who are saved through faith in Christ. These believers do not work to obtain their salvation; they just receive it as a gift from the God who died to save them. They've put their trust in Christ and are accepted as holy and righteous before the Father, because the blood of Christ has washed away all their sins. Therefore, they enjoy the freedom of a rich, loving relationship with the God who created them. The salvation of all true believers is based on Christ's work of redemption — His mercy, His grace and the truth of His Word — not on the efforts and good works performed by men.

As mentioned previously, in the Old Testament, God had a purpose for the Ark — that beautiful wooden box overlaid with gold. It contained His law, and it was accompanied by the present glory of God. Correspondingly, in the New Testament, Jesus (who was the Word of God made flesh) became the manifestation of the glory of God. The old religious ways were replaced by a new covenant, a new priesthood and a new type of man. Jesus, our High Priest, carried the Word of God on the inside of Him and demonstrated the glory and power of God. Likewise, as priests of the LORD, we're also to be manifest carriers of the Word, the glory and the power of God.

Unfortunately, there are some who are still stuck in the old religious ways of doing things. As with the law in the Ark, they are still striving to be good enough to earn God's favor, and trying to 'sacrifice' to earn their salvation. Symbolically, they carry an obsolete, superseded box of religion upon their shoulders. They try to bear up under the heaviness of all their religious rules and burdens. It may seem spiritual, but in reality, their belief system only makes their life miserably hard and heavy.

Those who become unsatisfied or disgruntled with their archaic religion may deal with it in very different ways. Some will mistake the counterfeit religion for real faith, but when they see it has no power, they reject it. As a result, they harden their hearts toward the LORD and walk away from Him altogether. Others may continue to ineffectively strive to meet all the religious requirements in relation to their belief system, simply hoping to be good enough for acceptance by a holy God. While still others, who don't feel they can live up to what they consider to be their spirituality, may just tuck that belief system (and whatever they perceive God to be) into their confining, restrictive, boring religious box and put it on a shelf, only to be pulled out in times of trial and difficulty. Instead of rejecting God, hoping against hope or playing games of fickleness, once anyone who has been duped by false religion realizes their plight, they need to call it what it is and repent from their sin.

Any belief system that's based on anything except the full truth of God's Word is just a religious lie. When a lie is embraced, deception is conceived, and it brings forth emptiness, confusion, discontentment, destruction, judgment and death. On the other hand, the belief system that is solely based on the truth of God's Word, will allow the believer to experience the life, grace, forgiveness, salvation, joy and peace of the LORD.

Before I knew Jesus as my LORD and Savior, I was involved in a lifeless, idolatrous belief system. I attended religious services and went through the motions, rituals and chants. After an hour of such nonsense, I went home and figured I'd performed my good deed for the week. I had put my time in, and therefore, God should look favorably upon me. Though I never really felt the assurance of that idea, I was still hoping I would be acceptable because, after all, I had done something for Him. I was hoping that, in the end, my good deeds would outweigh my bad deeds,

Part 1 • *Loving God* with All Your Heart

and then (maybe) this God I did not know would let me come and live in His Heaven.

My religion continually reminded me of my wretched sinfulness. The problem was that nobody could tell me how to rectify the situation. I was given all sorts of prayers to pray (before the idols) and penance to do, but I never felt better afterwards. I never found peace. Instead, I found myself trying to be good enough to earn my way into God's favor. Yet, in my own strength, I failed over and over again. I could not save myself and I was miserably tormented with fears of an eternity in hell.

I was so foolish and ignorant. I had religion, but no revelation of God's love for me. All I knew was the bondage that had been passed down to me, with all its hard laws and consequences. I had a faulty, idolatrous belief system, but I didn't know that God wanted to reveal Himself to me, personally. My Creator wanted to have an intimate, supernatural relationship with me, but I was too blind to see it.

Thankfully, the LORD was merciful to me. He looked beyond my ignorance. He saw that I was searching for Him and desired to know Him. I just didn't know how to make it happen. I didn't know the truth of who He was. I didn't know the Word of God, and I wasn't acquainted with true Christianity. In the LORD'S compassion, He slowly began moving me along a spiritual journey, leading me straight to His heart and into His arms of love.

A New Spirit of Worship

The ways of God are gracious. The ways of man (apart from God) are corrupt. The LORD originally gave the Law of the Ten Commandments to the nation of Israel (Exodus 20:3-17). God's Old Testament laws stated:

- Thou shalt have no other Gods before me.
- Thou shalt not make unto thee any graven image.
- Thou shalt not take the name of the LORD thy God in vain.
- Remember, the Sabbath day, to keep it holy.
- Honor thy father and thy mother.
- Thou shalt not kill.
- Thou shalt not commit adultery.
- Thou shalt not steal.
- Thou shalt not bear false witness against thy neighbor.
- Thou shalt not covet.

When He engraved the Ten Commandments in tablets of stone, the LORD demonstrated the condition of man's heart. These tablets were a visual picture of the resistant, hard, cold, stony, self-righteous heart of man. They were also a picture of the hardness of the Law — unchangeable and set in stone.

Part 1 • *Loving God* with All Your Heart

Words engraved in stone can never change the heart of man. These commandments, like a schoolmaster, point out mankind's inability to live holy lives. The sinful nature of man is embedded with the corruption of lawlessness. He's enslaved to sin and the Law of God magnifies the moral failures of humanity. Man, in his own strength, character and ability, cannot keep the Law of God. He'll never be good enough (through his own merits) to stand righteously before Holy God.

Christ's birth, life, death, resurrection and ascension redeemed, cleansed and justified mankind from all sin. He kept the law on our behalf and became our mediator, so that we can inherit the promises of God (Galatians 3:17- 29). Through faith in Christ, we are accepted before God.

Look at the Ten Commandments again; instead of seeing them as pointing out your failures, see them as promises. For instance, When God said, "Thou shalt have no other God's before me," don't see it as a hard rule of God making demands and placing limitations on you. Instead, see it as a promise that He will keep you free of the deception, bondage and idolatry of those things that would steal your life purpose and destiny. When He says, "Thou shalt not commit adultery," don't see it as being deprived of pleasure. Instead, see it as a promise that He will help you to be loving and faithful to your spouse. Do this with each of the commandments, and let the LORD speak His promises to your heart.

The heart of man can only be changed by the supernatural power of God. In the beginning, man was created perfectly, but he chose to rebel against the LORD and this caused him to fall into sin. The Prophet Ezekiel declared a wonderful promise of the LORD concerning His erring people:

<u>Ezekiel 11:18-20</u> And they shall come thither, and they shall take away all the detestable things thereof and all the abominations thereof from thence. ¹⁹And I will give them one heart, and I will put a new spirit within you; and I will take the stony heart out of their flesh, and will give them an heart of flesh: ²⁰That they may walk in my statutes, and keep mine ordinances, and do them: and they shall be my people, and I will be their God.

The LORD understands the ways of mankind. His desire has always been to have a people whose hearts belong to Him. For this reason, anybody who comes to Him in true repentance will receive the mercy of the LORD. He will extend His forgiveness, salvation and grace. He will give them everything they need to walk uprightly before Him. For those who surrender to the LORD, they will find that holy place in their hearts where God will dwell with them.

Part 1 • *Loving God* with All Your Heart

Remember, as previously mentioned in 1 Kings 8:6, the priests of the LORD brought the Ark *into His place . . . to the <u>most holy place.</u>* God still has a place that He longs to fill with the glory of Himself. Ultimately, that place is found in the soft, pliable, cleansed, holy hearts of those who choose to become His people.

The Word of God says that, after the Ark of the Covenant was set in *His place*, the priest came out of the holy place, and the cloud of God's weighty presence filled the house of the LORD. Everything was touched by His glory. God manifested and filled the whole house with Himself! It was not 'church' as usual. The priests were unable to stand and minister in God's presence; all they could do was lie on the floor and worship in reverential fear (1 Kings 8:10-11).

As mentioned in Chapter 4, the most used Hebrew word for the **worship** *(H7812)* of God is **shâchâh**. It means to *depress* (to press self down); that is, to *prostrate* oneself *in homage to royalty or God*. It is also translated as: to bow down, crouch, fall down (flat), to humbly beseech, to stoop, as well as give reverence and obeisance (showing deep respect or deferential courtesy, as a subordinate to a superior). In short, it is the positioning of oneself into a place of humility, while at the same time, exalting and giving great honor and glory to the LORD in reverential worship. If we want the glorious presence, power and anointing of God to manifest in our lives, we must give Him His proper place in our hearts and lives.

TAKE HEED: BE STRONG AND DO IT
After David exhorted Solomon to know and serve the LORD with a perfect heart and a willing mind, He gave a warning and mandate to the young king in:

<u>1 Chronicles 28:9-10</u> ...but if thou forsake him, he will cast thee off for ever. ¹⁰Take heed now; for the LORD hath chosen thee to build an house for the sanctuary: be strong, and do it.'

Solomon was in a position of great honor, to be chosen to build the house of the LORD. David warned Solomon to not *forsake (H5800), refuse, fail* or *permit* himself to be *loosened* from the LORD. Yet, Solomon still had to make his own personal decisions concerning the fulfillment of his destiny.

In the New Testament, Jesus promised that He would never leave nor forsake us (Hebrews 13:5). However, this does not mean that we will never leave or forsake Him. We must choose whom and what we will serve. If a person chooses to forsake the LORD, then they're putting themselves in a position of potentially being *cast off (H2186), pushed aside, rejected* or removed from His presence.

Just as Solomon had a God ordained destiny to build the Temple of the LORD, we have a God ordained destiny to build up the Kingdom of God in the earth. If we forsake the LORD and the destiny He has for us, we will miss our opportunity, and we'll be replaced by those who are willing to walk in obedience with His plan (Matthew 25:14-30). Submission and obedience are keys that unlock God's purposes in our lives. The work of God's Kingdom will never be stopped; it's just a matter of whether or not we're going to do our part.

In 1 Chronicles 28:10, in relation to Solomon building the house of the LORD, David commands him to **be strong, and do it!** There were no questions, no excuses, no arguments — just a mandate to fulfill the will of the LORD. Sometimes, the LORD gives us a kingdom assignment, and we don't have a clue as to how we're going to complete it. But if we'll make the decision to move forward in faith, He'll equip us with what's needed for the task. It takes strength of spirit and a persistent character to step out of our comfort zones and into the unknown with God. We, like Solomon, must make the decision to **be strong, and do it!** Let's expound upon this phrase:

First of all, let's look at the word **be**. The English definition of 'be' means: to exist or live, to take place, to occur, to occupy a place or position, to continue or remain as before, to belong or attend. The word **strong** (H2388) is defined in the Hebrew as *to fasten upon, to seize;* figuratively, to be *courageous;*

causatively, to *strengthen, cure, help repair, fortify, and to conquer*. In other verses, the word **strong** translates as: to encourage (self), to maintain, to become mighty and prevail, to be recovered, to be urgent, to behave oneself valiantly and to withstand. The word **and** is a connecting word. By its English definition, it relates to increase, addition, timing and repetition. The word **do**, by its English definition, means to perform an act, duty or role, to accomplish, finish, complete, to put forth, to bring about and execute a piece or amount of work. In the Old Testament, the word **do** *(âsâh - H6213)* also translates as: to advance, appoint, be busy, have charge of, commit, furnish, govern, be industrious, observe, be occupied, practice, be a warrior, a workman, and to yield. The English definition of the word **it** is connected to or in relation to something that is previously stated, understood, acted upon or mentioned. The power of words is truly amazing!

If we tie all these definitions together, to **be strong and do it** means we understand that our existence includes an assigned, ordained purpose. Therefore, we commit ourselves to function in our assigned place or position. We courageously and valiantly fasten ourselves upon God's divine purpose and destiny. God's purpose and passion upon our lives provides the motivation that empowers us to prevail in all the required duties of our calling. We, as mighty warriors, obediently submit and yield to the will of the Father.

Part 1 • *Loving God* with All Your Heart

We are faithfully committed to all that has been placed in our charge. Therefore, we will be strong and do whatever the LORD has required of us.

LEADING WELL

David well understood the purpose of God that Solomon was to fulfill. Thus, he poured his wisdom and resources into that great work with immense joy. As an act of worship, David gave the largest offering of his life. He understood that the task before Solomon was enormous and he needed all the help he could get. First Chronicles 29:2 says that David prepared for the house of the LORD with all his *might* (H3581). This means he gave abundantly of his wealth with great *vigor* and ability.

David loved God and wanted to see the temple — the house of the LORD — built. Therefore, he gave the pattern for the house of the LORD, as well as great quantities of gold, silver, brass, iron, wood, precious stones, gems and marble as an offering for the temple. He also provided for all the implements needed in the service of the LORD. As David gave, he also challenged others to consecrate their services and abilities to the LORD, in order to accomplish the building of the temple.

David understood that giving was a part of worship, and He was motivated by his love for God, as well as God's love for him. His perfect heart and willing mind to serve the LORD were demonstrated by his actions.

Without restraint, he abundantly poured out his costly possessions and lavished them upon the LORD. The King set such an extraordinary example — a pattern of worship — that the chiefs of the fathers, princes of the tribes, captains and rulers all followed David's example; they also offered willingly to the work of the LORD. As the leaders gave, the people rejoiced and were also inspired to give, according to:

<u>1 Chronicles 29:9</u> Then the people rejoiced, for that they offered willingly, because with perfect heart they offered willingly to the LORD: and David the king also rejoiced with great joy.

Notice, this perfect heart and willingness of mind became joyously contagious. David had commanded Solomon to have a perfect heart and a willing mind concerning the things of God, and he led by example. The leaders also followed David's example, and then that same perfect heart eventually manifested in the people who served the king. Together, they successfully accomplished the will of the LORD. David, with the power of godly influence, taught the people how to give; He gave as one king to another — lavishly.

Here's an important principle: People watch their leadership! Godly leaders lead well, when they lead by personal demonstration. Their commitment and willingness to serve the LORD will inspire and influence others to become involved in the work.

Part 1 • *Loving God* with All Your Heart

1 Chronicles 29:9 says the **people** *(H5971)* ***rejoiced*** *(H8055)*. This means the *congregation* brightened up and became joyful. It was offering time, and the people were celebrating. They, like David, demonstrated their love for the LORD by willingly presenting their gifts to Him. To offer ***willingly*** *(H5068)* means that the people freely and *voluntarily presented* their *spontaneous* offerings to the LORD, *like a soldier* would give his service (gun) to his military commander. Nobody had to push, prod, beg, manipulate or shame them. They gave from a willing, unselfish, perfect heart attitude.

The people gave with their whole heart, because they loved with their whole heart. They were in unity with their king and their God. When the people of God come into unity, the greatest tasks are made easy; many hands and hearts are joined together to accomplish the vision. Hallelujah!

REJECTS TROUBLE (IGNORANCE, DISOBEDIENCE & DISHONOR)

Earlier, we expounded on the Ark of the Covenant and how the cloud of God's glorious presence filled the temple of Solomon. We also mentioned that before the Ark was delivered to its proper place in the temple, it was located in the Tabernacle of David. But, many years before David took possession of the Ark, it had fallen into the hands of the heathen Philistines as the booty of war.

For years, the Philistines had feared the presence of the Ark on the battle field. However, after they had slain thousands of Israelites, they became emboldened. They encouraged and strengthened themselves in battle and captured the Ark. I wonder if they thought the God of Israel was impotent. I wonder if they assumed they had overpowered Him. Obviously, they had no idea what they were getting themselves into. They failed to diligently consider their fatal outcome when they took on the Ark — the representation of God's power, presence and holiness. Their ignorant arrogance became the bait of their own destruction.

THE TRUTH STANDS

After the Philistines captured the Ark of God and brought it from Ebenezer to Ashdod, they set it up next to their god Dagon, the fish god (1 Samuel 4:1-17, 5:1-2). During the night, the LORD caused the idol of Dagon to fall prostrate upon its face before the Ark (1 Samuel 5:3). The next morning the Philistines set the idol of their powerless god back up, and that night it fell upon its face again. When the idol fell the second time, its head and hands were severed and all that was left of Dagon was the stump or base of the idol (1 Samuel 5:4). Imagine that! The fish god — the thing the Philistines had created with their own hands and worshiped — was so powerless, it couldn't even hold itself up in the presence of God.

I can just see this happening in my mind. Their god, not only couldn't stand before the true and living God, it couldn't even pick itself up from the dust!!

Part 1 • *Loving God* with All Your Heart

Who would want to serve a god that couldn't even defend itself, stand on its own or pick itself up? How could such an impotent god do anything for those who claimed to believe in it? The LORD God Almighty made an absolute spectacle of this manmade god and disgraced its very existence.

This fish god couldn't lead, protect or provide for its followers. I believe, the first time that Dagon fell to the ground, the LORD was mocking their entire belief system. When the idol fell the second time, the LORD severed its head and hands and broke it into pieces. The head represents leadership — the ability to think and the capacity to see, hear, taste and smell (discern). The hands represent the ability to create, touch, work, help, guide and assist. This despicable fish god had no ability to think. It had no sensory perception. In its destruction, the LORD demonstrated the utter impotence and powerlessness of this so called god.

The Philistines, in putting the Ark next to their idol, had mixed their idolatry with the holy presence of God. They tried to unite that which was polluted and defiled, with that which was pure and sacred. But, their idolatry couldn't stand before the face or in the presence of God. The LORD would not tolerate such mockery! Anytime the lies of satan are flaunted against the truth of God, the lies will fall and the truth will stand.

Chapter 5 • The 'Perfect Heart' Worshipper

Strongholds are a Choice

The Philistines handled the ark and presence of God in a shameful manner. Therefore, His hand was heavy upon those who lived in Ashdod. He struck them with emerods throughout their coasts and destroyed them (1 Samuel 5:6-7). The English definition of the word *emerods* is piles. These are hemorrhoids or varicose veins of the rectum, which can cause a very swollen, painful and itchy condition. In the Hebrew, ***emerods** (H6076/H6075)* represent a *fort* or stronghold that is lifted up. Those Philistines had lifted themselves up against the LORD, so they were afflicted with emerods — painful strongholds planted and piled up in their backsides. Yikes! God certainly knows how to deal with His enemies!

These Philistines were from the city of **Ashdod** *(H795/H7703)*, which is defined as the *powerful ravager*. Elsewhere in scripture, it is translated as: destroyer, oppressor, robber and spoiler, and to utterly waste. This definition implies that those who lived in Ashdod were a people of great wickedness. Naturally, idolatry and wickedness are always found together. The name of their city also defines the nature of their religion. Anytime a false god is worshipped, it opens the opportunity for its followers to be ravaged, destroyed, oppressed, robbed, spoiled and utterly wasted.

If Dagon was supposed to be so mighty, why didn't this little fishy god rescue his followers, when the

God of Creation ravaged their city with plagues and judgment? The answer is simple; Dagon couldn't, help anybody, because he was only a lifeless, powerless, and worthless idol of vanity. He was nothing more than a satanic religious counterfeit — demonically conceived in the minds of deluded men. The fact that the Philistines were worshipping a fish god, instead of the true and living God of Heaven, truly put them in a position of oppression and destruction.

Clearly, the hemorrhoid laden people of Ashdod wanted the Ark removed from their city, so they decided to pass the trouble on to the Philistines in Gath (1 Samuel 5:8). Yes, basically, when the people of Ashdod experienced enough of the judgment of God, they passed it on to their relatives! Go figure! Ignorance knows no reasoning!

As the Ark arrived in the city of Gath, the hand of the LORD was also against that city. He struck the men with emerods in their secret parts and great destruction fell upon them (1 Samuel 5:9). For emerods to break out in their secret parts, meant that hemorrhoids erupted in the hidden, private places of their flesh. The strongholds of satan bring all sorts of misery, addictions, diseases, curses, physical, mental and emotional pain, distresses and destruction. How many people do you know that have satanic strongholds, secret sins and playgrounds of the enemy in the secret parts of who they are? Now, consider the following questions:

Are they serving gods of their own making?

How's that working for them?

Also, remember that the Hebrew representation of emerods is defined as a 'stronghold' that is lifted up! So, let's discuss exactly what a stronghold is. Our English word, stronghold, is defined as a fortress; a well-fortified place that serves as a center for militant groups or persons holding a controversial viewpoint. There are different types of strongholds in scripture. Though the enemy may seek to erect his wicked strongholds, the LORD is a stronghold of safety to those who trust in Him (Nahum 1:7).

Even a city (be it good or evil) can represent a stronghold. Babylon was a real city, but figuratively, it represents the world system, with its wicked ways and idolatry. The city of Babylon is referred to as the habitation of devils; the **hold** *(G5438)* (a caged, *guarded place* of imprisonment) of every foul spirit; and a cage of every unclean and hateful bird. Spiritual Babylon represents strongholds of the enemy — a place of whoredom, fornication, spiritual adultery (idolatry), perversion and the merchandising of the things of the flesh and the world (Revelation 18:2-3).

Those who play with sin are laying the ground work for satanic strongholds and bondage to be established in their souls and lives. Strongholds develop in the mind of a person when satan plants a seed of deception into their thoughts and they receive it. As the deception takes over the thought processes, one's perspective is damaged. When the perspective is damaged, the deep things of the soul become twisted, abnormal, perverted, sick, bitter and cruel. The condition of the soul will then affect the body in adverse ways causing weakness, disorders, sickness, disease and possibly death.

The way to avoid satanic strongholds is to make the LORD our stronghold. He is our place of salvation, peace, deliverance, safety, provision and protection. If we do this, then the enemy will not be able to get a foothold in our lives.

Of course, those who are already in the enemy's grasp can still choose the LORD as their stronghold; they can still be free. First, they must deal with the root(s) of any satanic strongholds by addressing the sin(s) that started it all. They must repent before the LORD, which means to change the mind concerning those things. With the change of mind comes a change of heart. The changed heart causes one's actions to be adjusted and altered. Altered actions will amend and transform one's life direction and freedom will come. But, it all starts with repentance from their initial sin(s).

Those who've repented and been delivered from satanic strongholds no longer desire to go their own way. They've rejected the lies of the devil and have submitted their heart, soul, mind and strength to the LORD. They've stopped chasing the things of the world and started pursuing the LORD, who has saved and delivered them.

WHEN YOU SHOULD KNOW BETTER...
Now, let's get back to the Philistines. We must understand that those who continue in their sin will continue in the curse of their idolatry, and they will pass it on to others. Such was the case with the Philistines. After the people of Ashdod experienced the judgment of God and were all messed up; and the secret parts of the men in Gath were all messed up; then, the men of Gath decided to pass the Ark, the judgments and the plague on to the people of Ekron (1 Samuel 5:10)! When the Ark arrived in Ekron, the people cried out in fear. They believed the LORD would destroy and afflict them with emerods, just as He did with the Philistines in the previous two cities.

It's interesting that the name of the city of **Gath** *(H1661/H1660)* means *a wine-press* or *vat for holding the grapes* to press them. When grapes are under pressure, they're crushed and what's on the inside is revealed. The name of the city **Ekron** *(H6138/6131)* means *eradication, to pluck up by the roots* and, figuratively, to *exterminate*.

Anytime people choose to serve a false god, whether a physical idol or in their minds, they're serving a destroyer. By nature of the destroyer they choose to submit to, they will be oppressed, spoiled, wasted, robbed and pressed beyond measure. If they don't repent, their ignorance and stubborn rebellion will be the source of their own eradication and extermination.

After seven months of desperation, the Philistines, the diviners (soothsayers) and the idolatrous priests knew they needed to return the Ark to Israel (1 Samuel 5:11, 6:1-2). Evidently, they were slow learners. Even so, it's amazing how the fear of God and His judgments can persuade people to change their perspectives. Through their painful and distressing encounter with the LORD, the Philistines learned that He was not a God to be trifled with. He wouldn't play games with them or tolerate being dishonored!

Obviously, the LORD did not tolerate the ignorance of the Philistines in the way they initially handled the Ark. They suffered greatly and many died, because they failed to recognize that the Ark was not just another idol made by the hands of men; it contained the presence of the Living God! After all they had been through, they were hoping to appease the LORD.

So, to be free of the torment (which they had brought upon themselves), the Philistines returned the Ark to Israel. As part of their preparations, they presented a trespass offering and gave glory to the God of Israel —

all this in hopes that He would remove His hand of judgment from them (1 Samuel 6:3-5, 6:17-18). Then, they made a new cart, put the Ark on it and attached the cart to two milk cows, which pulled the Ark of God (1 Samuel 6:7-12). But, through Moses, the LORD had given specific instruction as to how His Ark was to be carried, which was with staves upon the shoulders of the Levites (Deuteronomy 10:8; 1 Chronicles 15:15). The Philistines were likely ignorant of this command, but (perhaps, in their experiment with the unguided and unskilled cows, coupled with their renewed fear of Him, and considering they had no priests of the LORD to carry the Ark back to the people of Israel), it seems the LORD extended His mercy toward them. When the Ark was returned to Israel, it was brought to the field of Joshua, a Bethshemite of the city of Bethshemesh, and the people of God rejoiced. Then, the Levites took the Ark of the LORD off the cart. Using the wood from the cart and the cows that pulled it, the Levites offered burnt offerings and sacrifices to the LORD (1 Samuel 6:14-15).

For whatever reason, the men of Bethshemesh also looked into the Ark of the LORD. In so doing, they violated the parameters of God's Word; thus, they disobeyed and dishonored Him. Now, if the LORD would not tolerate the ignorant dishonor of the Philistines in handling what embodied His glory and presence, then He surely would not tolerate it among His own people. Therefore, the LORD struck down and killed fifty thousand seventy men, and the people lamented greatly (1 Samuel 6:19). One might wonder why they risked looking into the holy Ark of God at all? Perhaps it was ignorance, a lack of godly fear and reverence or sheer curiosity. Maybe they wanted to make sure everything was in order inside. After all, it had been in the hands of enemies. Whatever the reason, obviously, there was no excuse. When God's people desecrated the Ark of the Holy One, they lost their very lives; and this was not the last time this kind of violation and consequence would take place.

At any rate, because of God's wrath, the people of Bethshemesh sent messengers to Kirjathjearim, asking them to take the Ark. The men of that city did so and brought the Ark of God into the house of Abinadab. Eleazar, the son of Abinadab, was sanctified to guard and have charge over the Ark of the LORD. Although the Ark was settled for a season, for the Bethshemites, the cost of blatant disobedience to God's directives was overwhelmingly.

The scripture goes on to say that the Ark was at Kirjathjearim for 20 years, and the house of Israel was still lamenting after the LORD (1 Samuel 7:1-2). Then Samuel, the Prophet, declared that if they would return to the LORD with all their hearts and put away the strange gods and Ashtaroth from among them; if they would prepare their hearts for the LORD and serve Him only, then He would deliver them out of the hand

CHAPTER 5 • THE 'PERFECT HEART' WORSHIPPER

of the Philistines (1 Samuel 7:3). So Israel forsook their false gods and their idolatrous worship. Then, Samuel gathered the people to Mizpeh to pray for them, and they fasted and repented of their sin before the LORD (1 Samuel 7:4-6).

Mizpeh *(H4708/H4707/H6822)* is defined as a place in Palestine; a military *observatory,* a watch tower used to lean forward and to *peer* into the distance, to *observe* and *await.* Because the people had returned to the LORD and forsaken their wickedness, the LORD would fight for them. Israel would observe the works of the LORD, by seeing their enemies defeated before their eyes!

When the lords of the Philistines knew that Israel was gathered at Mizpeh, they began to go up against them. The children of Israel feared and cried to Samuel to intercede on their behalf. Therefore, Samuel offered a burnt offering before the LORD for the sins of the people and cried unto the LORD, and the LORD heard him. As the sweet savor of sacrifice ascended before the LORD, the Philistines drew near to battle against Israel. Yet, the LORD fought for Israel; He uproariously thundered upon the Philistines, and they were all defeated (1 Samuel 7:7-11).

Unlike the Bethshemites who sinned against the LORD and received His judgment, all of Israel repented. So, Israel received His forgiveness, mercy and deliverance. Then, the LORD gave them victory over their enemies with the sound of His thunder. Regardless of how the enemy tries to attack, the fragrance of worship from the hearts of the true lovers of God will cause Him to rise up and fight for those who belong to Him!

PLEASE THE LORD

Before we go on to our next portion of scripture, we must understand that the LORD is not pleased when people (either ignorantly or deliberately) violate His commands or compromisingly mix the lies of satan and the fleshly idolatrous ways of the world with the truth and holy ways of God. Anytime a lie is added to truth, the truth has been corrupted and it becomes a lie (Romans 1:18-32)! As lovers of God and priests of the LORD, we must learn to discern between the clean and the unclean, thereby separating the holy and the profane. We must make a separation between that which is pleasing to the LORD, and that which is unacceptable according to His Word (Ezekiel 44:23).

As shared in the previous section, both the Philistines and the men of Bethshemesh wrongfully and disrespectfully mishandled the Ark of God. They failed to reverence that which represented the power and presence of God. Whenever man, apart from the truth of God's Word, creates his own religious ideas about how he's to worship God, trouble and destruction are sure to follow. Therefore, many were afflicted and destroyed.

CHAPTER 5 • THE 'PERFECT HEART' WORSHIPPER

In the case of the Philistines, they eventually, responded by giving glory to the God of Israel; they provided a trespass offering and returned the Ark of the LORD to Israel on a cart. Although they were likely ignorant, this method of transporting the Ark was against God's law. For whatever reason, God did not penalize them for this infraction.

Upon the Ark's arrival, the Levites broke up the wood of the cart, used it to build a fire and sacrificed the cows that had pulled the cart. Both the cart and the cows represented the ignorant and carnal mindset concerning the things of God, including the religious works of unregenerate man. Symbolically, we can see that the vanity of man's reasoning, as well as his presumptuous works were destroyed in the fire of sacrifice.

Unfortunately, the men of Bethshemesh did not glean even a symbolic lesson from the heathen Philistines. Astonishingly, they committed their very own vain and presumptuous sin against the LORD, by looking into the Ark. When the LORD responded with His judgement, the people lamented, but they did not repent. Instead, they asked for the Ark of the LORD to be removed from them.

While both the Philistines and the Bethshemites provoked the LORD's judgement by disrespecting Him with their offensive religious practices, in the end, they had opposite responses. Being heathens, the Philistines would not be expected to repent. It was their sheer fear of the powerful judgement of God that made them want to appease Him. On the other hand, in the midst of grief and pride, the people of Bethshemesh preferred to be without the presence of the LORD than to please Him. Surely, if the LORD was willing to have mercy on the Philistines, He would have done the same, if not more, for the Bethshemites who were His people. Let's keep these responses in mind, as we consider how they apply to the church today.

In most churches today, there are still religious methods being used that are not in accordance with the Word of God; this is not pleasing to Him. As the people of God we're to have an understanding of what the LORD expects of us. This only comes with the study and application of His Word in our personal lives. The worshipper with a perfect heart seeks to know what pleases the LORD and does whatever is necessary to live accordingly.

Many times, I hear Christians justify their mixture of the holy and the unholy by saying, "Well, we'll redeem it for God!" In reality, the 'it' they refer to is usually an area of compromise in their lives. They're looking for a way to 'Christianize' a pagan custom or to validate their own fleshly desires. Therefore, they seek for a way to attach the name of the LORD to whatever it is they want to do. They rationalize that if they label their compromise with His name, then it becomes acceptable. In their deception, they feel justified in fulfilling their fleshly desires, even though they have no scriptural basis for their actions. If God Himself did not create, decree, establish or instruct a thing in the first place, why would we want to attach His name to it? Why would He want anything to do with it? The desire behind the justification has nothing to do with redemption or the glorification of God; it has to do with people loving the things of the world more than the things of God (1 John 2:15-16).

If God's people reject truth and embrace the lies, customs and compromise of the world, they are guilty of propagating a lie, misrepresenting Him and aligning themselves with satan. This is unacceptable behavior!! For those who have compromised, rejected, neglected or ignored the truth of God's Word, it's time to repent and turn from your wicked ways! To live according to the corrupt standards, traditions, practices and idolatrous beliefs of this world, is to live rebelliously against the LORD. God's people must forsake wickedness and lift up the standard of His truth! We must reject polluted social mores and political correctness, which are laden with the perversion of this wicked and adulterous generation. Jesus said, you shall know the truth, and the truth shall make you free (John 8:32). The ultimate truth is found in God's Word; and by His Word, we are sanctified for the purposes of God (John 17:17).

In relation to fulfilling the higher purposes of God, we must also understand that His Spirit is the source of truth and life, which leads each of us into our ordained destinies in Him. All that originates with Him is holy, righteous and good. However, all that is contrary to God's truth and life is instigated by the devil. He is a thief and his goals are to bring forth deception, destruction and death (John 10:10). For this reason, it's important to check the origin from which things spring forth. If the root of any tradition, practice, thought or deed is contrary to the truth of God's Word then it is evil; no matter how much we try to justify it, symbolize it or dress it up, it's still wicked and corrupt at the core, and it's not of God! Anything that's not in agreement with the truth of God's Word is a counterfeit from the enemy and must be rejected.

The LORD clearly says in His Word that His people are not to learn the ways of the heathen (Jeremiah 10:1-5). Let's look at a prime example of when the people of God did things in a heathen manner. Once again, it involved the Ark of the LORD. Pay attention to what happened when the glory and presence of God was mishandled in ignorant, neglectful disobedience:

<u>2 Samuel 6:1-8</u> Again, David gathered together all the chosen men of Israel, thirty thousand. ²And David arose, and went with all the people that were with him from Baale of Judah, to bring up from thence the ark of God, whose name is called by the name of the LORD of hosts that dwelleth between the cherubims. ³And <u>they set the ark of God upon a new cart,</u> and brought it out of the

house of Abinadab that was in Gibeah: and Uzzah and Ahio, the sons of Abinadab, drave the new cart. ⁴And they brought it out of the house of Abinadab which was at Gibeah, accompanying the ark of God: and Ahio went before the ark. ⁵And David and all the house of Israel played before the LORD on all manner of instruments made of fir wood, even on harps, and on psalteries, and on timbrels, and on cornets, and on cymbals. ⁶And when they came to Nachon's threshingfloor, Uzzah put forth his hand to the ark of God, and took hold of it; for the oxen shook it. ⁷And the anger of the LORD was kindled against Uzzah; and God smote him there for his error; and there he died by the ark of God. ⁸And David was displeased, because the LORD had made a breach upon Uzzah: and he called the name of the place Perezuzzah to this day (also see 1 Chronicles 13).

From the time that Samuel ruled as judge over Israel and throughout the forty year reign of King Saul, the Ark of God resided in the house of Abinadab. It wasn't until after Saul died and David became King of Israel that the Ark was removed from the house of Abinadab. With 30,000 chosen men of Israel, David sought to bring the Ark into the city of Jerusalem (1 Samuel 7; Acts 13:21).

In 2 Samuel 6:3, notice that instead of the Ark of God being carried on the shoulders of the Levite priests, as God commanded, they set the Ark on a new cart

Part 1 • *Loving God* with All Your Heart

as the Philistines did decades before (Deuteronomy 18:8; 1 Chronicles 15:15; 1 Samuel 6:7-8)! The Ark of God was never meant to be moved on a cart, but the Word of God had been neglected and the people of Israel had, inadvertently, either adopted the way of the heathen Philistines or leaned to their own understanding, as any heathen would have done. Whatever the case, in so doing, they disrespected the LORD, and trouble was soon to follow.

The great musical procession and celebration moved toward Jerusalem. As the great multitude came to Nachon's threshing floor, the oxen pulling the cart stumbled, and Uzzah reached out his hand to steady the Ark. However, his good intentions were faulty, because they were not in line with the Word of God. So, the LORD struck Uzzah down; he instantly died beside the Ark, because of his presumptuous error. David was displeased, because the LORD killed Uzzah, but David didn't realize that they all had disobeyed the Word of God, which led Uzzah to defile the Ark of God. In the mind of Uzzah, I'm sure he did not get up that morning with plans to blatantly disobey the LORD and drop dead, as a result of his actions. Due to neglect and ignorance, David, the priests and the people were caught up in their own zeal, but they forgot to honor the specific instructions of the LORD regarding how His Ark was to be moved. What should have been a day of great celebration became a day of immense sorrow, trouble and mourning.

As the LORD would have it, David did not remain fearful of Him, after His judgment against them. Instead, He continued to observe the Lord and gained understanding of their wrongdoing. 1 Chronicles 15 and 16 records the details of the day they got it right:

<u>1 Chronicles 15:13-15</u> For because ye did it not at the first, the LORD our God made a breach upon us, for that we sought him not after the due order. ¹⁴So the priests and the Levites sanctified themselves to bring up the ark of the LORD God of Israel. ¹⁵And the children of the Levites bare the ark of God upon their shoulders with the staves thereon, as Moses commanded according to the word of the LORD.

This is the example that the church of today needs to model. At the present time, we may not have a full understanding as to why the LORD commands us to worship Him in a particular way, but there is a reason to everything our God asks of us. The current state of affairs in the church is evidence that we have not fully sought Him concerning how we are to worship Him, and we need to get it right.

Have you ever wondered why the LORD commanded the Levites to carry the Ark upon their shoulders? Well, in the Old Testament, the priests were to walk with God and carry out His government among the people of Israel. They bore the power, presence and Word of God upon their shoulders, because the shoulders actually represent priestly responsibility and governmental authority. In fact, this lines up with a prophecy concerning Christ, our heavenly High Priest, bearing the government upon His shoulder:

Isaiah 9:6-7 *For unto us a child is born, unto us a son is given: and the government shall be upon his shoulder: and his name shall be called Wonderful, Counsellor, The mighty God, The everlasting Father, The Prince of Peace. ⁷Of the increase of his government and peace there shall be no end, upon the throne of David, and upon his kingdom, to order it, and to establish it with judgment and with justice from henceforth even for ever. The zeal of the LORD of hosts will perform this.*

Even as the Old Testament priests carried the presence and Word of God, Jesus was the manifested Word of God who carried the full power, anointing and glory of God in His human vessel. How marvelous it must have been to experience God in human flesh.

Jesus came the first time as Messiah, but when He returns the second time, He is coming as King of kings and LORD of lords. He will set up His kingdom, and we will experience the perfect reign of Christ throughout all the earth. All peoples, nations and tribes will be subject unto Him.

Until that day comes, being motivated out of pure love, New Testament believers are to already be submitted to His kingly lordship. As members of His royal priesthood, we're to proactively carry out the responsibility and authoritative government of God in the earth. Furthermore, we're to sing forth a song of glorious praise in the earth, as we're being trained to reign in the Kingdom of God (1 Peter 2:9) — these acts please God.

ENJOY PURE CELEBRATION
So how does the mixture of the holy things of God and the unholy things of the world, specifically, apply to us today? Well, have you considered some of the unbiblical traditions that are allowed in the church? Have you considered the heathen origins of most of our holidays? New Year's Day, Valentine's Day, Saint Patrick's Day, Easter, April Fool's Day, Halloween and Christmas are all rooted in paganism!

Many people in the church are ignorant concerning the occult connections with these so-called holidays, but each of them has Babylonian influences and/or idolatrous origins. Other church-goers seek to justify their participation in such celebrations, because they love the things of the world and have not renewed their minds in certain areas. Either way, they are not walking in truth.

If you want to find hidden treasures of truth, you must be willing to dig them out of God's Word. I will give you just one not-so-quick example of a holiday that the church tries to 'Christianize' — Easter. Many people believe that Easter is about the resurrection of

Christ. In truth, Easter and Christ's resurrection are two entirely different events.

The origin of Easter has its roots in the worship of a pagan fertility goddess. In the Holy Bible, this object of idolatrous worship is referred to as Astarte. She was revered as the female counterpart or wife of Baal (the supposed sun god). The name, Astarte, is identified in the definition of the word 'grove.' In context, let's look at this from the following verses:

Deuteronomy 16:21-22 Thou shalt not plant thee a grove of any trees near unto the altar of the LORD thy God, which thou shalt make thee. ²²Neither shalt thou set thee up any image; which the LORD thy God hateth.

In this reference, the LORD clearly states that no groves of trees were to be planted or idolatrous images erected, near the altars that were dedicated to Him. The LORD does not tolerate His altars being polluted with the presence of idols. His hatred against manmade idols and false gods is so fierce, that He will not receive the worship of His people when they mix it with the worship of other gods. He's zealous over us, and He refuses to share physical altars (or the altars of our hearts) with any other.

The word **grove** *(H842/H833/H6253),* translates as the Hebrew word ăsherāh or 'ăsheyrāh. By definition it means happy, asherah *(or* Astarte), *a Phoenician* *goddess; also an image of the same.* A grove was made up of trees and, many times, idolatrous practices and worship took place within the groves. The entire concept of worshiping in the groves of trees is directly tied to idolatry.

The primary root definition for *grove* means *to be straight, especially to be level, right* and *happy. Figuratively, to go forward, be honest* and *prosper.* However, in the context of this scripture, if we're to live lives that are straight, level, right, happy, honest, prosperous and moving forward into what the LORD has for us, there must be a separation from any and all false gods and idolatrous practices in our lives.

Based on Deuteronomy 16:21-22, *grove* is directly related to the worship of idols. The idol of the groves was known as Astarte. But who is Astarte? Well, the demonic spirit behind this idol has been worshipped as the goddess of fertility, fortune, perverted sexuality, war and animals. Depending on the culture of the different nations, Astarte was called by a variety of names, including but not limited to: Asthoreth, Asherah, Semiramus, Aphrodite, Venus, Diana, Ishtar, Kali, Ostara, Eostre, Demeter, Hathor, Tanit, Snake goddess and the Roman Catholic version of the Madonna (Mary). Regardless of the name used, she/it comes from the same demonic root of Baal worship.

Part 1 • *Loving God* with All Your Heart

Recognize Deception & Forsake Idolatry

Astarte was given a place of worship under the name 'Diana of the Ephesians' in Acts 19:24-35. The silversmiths of Ephesus used the worship of Diana as a source of great wealth. One particular silversmith by the name of Demetrius (and other craftsmen and workmen of like occupation) made shrines for Diana.

But then, the Apostle Paul came preaching the gospel. He persuaded many of the people that idols created by the hands of men, were not gods at all. As a result, purchases that facilitated idolatry began to dissipate and affect cash flow to the idol makers' moneybags. As Paul preached the truth of God's Word, the worshippers of Diana began to turn from their idolatry and to seek the LORD.

Therefore, Demetrius used fear and anger to stir up the craftsmen against Paul and caused a massive uproar in the city. They not only feared that they were in danger of unemployment, but also that the temple of their goddess would be despised and her grandeur would be destroyed. In protest, they cried out for two hours, "Great is Diana of the Ephesians!" This put the entire city in a state of confusion.

Stop and think! How much money is spent and made on pagan rooted holiday celebrations every year? What if people were to understand the spiritual connection and activities behind the tradition? Do you think there would be confusion? Do you think people would be set free from deception? Do you think the LORD would be pleased if His people forsook their idolatry?

Know & Celebrate the Truth

In relation to Astarte, Roman Catholicism embraces a person they call Mary, also known as the Madonna. They address her as Holy Mary, the Mother of God and the Queen of Heaven. But the Roman Catholic Mary is a remake of Astarte; she is not the Mary of scripture.

The Mary of scripture, who was betrothed to and married Joseph, did give birth to Jesus physically. But, Mary was not the genetic mother of God, because God has no genetic mother. God is a spirit and He is eternal; He's the Alpha and the Omega, the beginning and the end (Revelation 1:8, 11; 21:6; 22:13). There's nothing before or after Him. He is above all things; and by Him, all things consist (Colossians 1:17).

Mary is also not the Queen of Heaven. As a matter of fact, she is no queen at all!! The Queen of Heaven refers to another version of the false goddess, Astarte, and those who served her suffered the anger of the LORD (read Jeremiah 7:16-20 and 44:15-30)!

What does the Word actually say in respect to Mary? **"Blessed art thou among women, and blessed is the fruit of thy womb"** are the words of Elisabeth toward Mary, who she knew was pregnant with the Messiah.

In response, Mary worshipped the LORD and said, *"**For he hath regarded the low estate of his handmaiden: for, behold, from henceforth all generations shall call me blessed. For he that is mighty hath done to me great things; and holy is his name.**"* (Luke 1:39-49). These statements are in line with those of the angel who greeted her, *"**Hail, thou that art highly favoured, the Lord is with thee: blessed art thou among women.**"* (Luke 1:28). Let's be clear, Mary was blessed and had favor with the LORD; the Bible never refers to her as having supreme holiness, or being the Queen of Heaven or the Mother of God (even though she did give birth to Jesus).

The true Mary of scripture was no more holy than any true, dedicated follower and lover of Christ today. She loved the LORD and obediently submitted to His will. She was not a goddess and she was not sinless. She was a human vessel with a kingdom assignment to fulfill, and she served her LORD with humility.

Choose Truth Over Tradition

Now, let's look at the relationship between Astarte as Ishtar in the tradition of Easter eggs. This idol is symbolized as a bare breasted goddess of fertility. Legend has it that Ishtar was the reincarnation of Semiramus, the wife of Nimrod, who built the tower of Babel. The story goes: She fell from Jupiter in a large egg into the Euphrates River during the spring solstice. Then, after she hatched out of the egg, she proved that she was a goddess by, supposedly, turning a bird into an egg-laying rabbit (as a symbol of her power to abundantly reproduce). This is the origin of the traditions of eggs, bunnies and chicks at Easter time. I know, it's insanely ludicrous, but there's more.

As part of the worship ritual of Ishtar, her priests would commit fornication on her altars with virgins. Naturally, the women would conceive and deliver their babies. Then, three months later, these same babies were offered up as human sacrifices to Ishtar. After the babies were slaughtered, their blood was used to color bird eggs. These babies became an offering to the demonic spirits operating behind the lies of a false religion and a pagan fertility goddess.

The religious beliefs and rituals of the followers of Ishtar (the Easter goddess) included: worship of the sun and planets, reincarnation, idolatry, perversion, lust, incest, fornication, infanticide and, obviously, satanic deception. I repeat — the traditional and spiritual origins of Easter and the resurrection of Christ are not the same. The pagan origins of Easter are a hellish offshoot of Baal worship.

In contrast, the prophetic foretelling of God's plan of redemption is straight from heaven; it is also unique. The conception, birth, life, death and resurrection of Christ from the dead are the most significant events in history! They're the distinguishing marks of the Christian faith; there is no comparison. Without the resurrection of Christ, in particular, our faith would be powerless and vain. So, when we celebrate Jesus for what He has done, we should do so in a way that proclaims Him as He is — exceptional and matchless! In no way should celebrating the LORD share in the traditions, deceptions and foolishness of Ishtar.

Church of the living God, it's time to reject Ishtar! Let's rise up and be who God has called us to be! It's time to sever the wicked traditions of men from the righteousness and truth of the Kingdom of God!

Every year, I bristle at the fact that so many 'Christian' churches around the world celebrate the resurrection of Christ mingled with an Easter egg hunt! Hellooo?! Easter eggs, mythological fertility goddesses and devils have absolutely nothing in common with the resurrection of Christ! There is no spiritual value in mixing the two. All this does is cause confusion and feed fantasy. We're not to mix the reality of Christ with the perversion of false gods!

When I've approached church leadership on the matter, their justification is that we should meet those who are lost on a level they can understand. My questions for them: Why are heathen methods being used to tell people about Jesus? Why must people be appeased with bribes of tradition, especially when a tradition is demonically inspired? I grasp the principle of being relevant, but we can't build truth upon the foundation of a lie!!

Chapter 5 • The 'Perfect Heart' Worshipper

When churches use Easter egg hunts for evangelism, the message of the gospel is defiled and adulterated. Thus, people are deceived and demonic activity is released among those who participate. Be aware — this is an evil abomination in the sight of the LORD (Exodus 20:3; Leviticus 18:1-5; 20:7, 24, 26; Deuteronomy 6:5,14; 12:28-32; Proverbs 12:22; Joshua 24:15; 24:20; Mark 12:30; 1 Corinthians 10:14-22).

Let's look beyond the surface as to why so many church leaders boldly advocate using such methods of wicked foolishness. Why would they attempt to build their ministries this way? At best, I think church leaders permit Easter egg hunts, because they're ignorant about the origins of the holidays. At worst, church leaders are in a state of unholy compromise and/or rebellion to the Word of God. Compromise and rebellion happen when leaders know the truth, but they still have their own agendas, or they're seeking to be people pleasers, instead of God pleasers. In addition, there's no excuse for ignorance. Information and discernment are easily accessible for seekers of truth. The methods a leader chooses to use, certainly reveals the state of their mind and heart.

These root causes of disobedience are how church leaders justify using ungodly methods and the ways of the world to draw the lost into the church. Of course, by doing so, they compromise, contaminate and pervert the truth of God. This is a prime example of mixing the holy with the unholy, and God is not pleased!

Conquer Compromise

Referring back to Deuteronomy 16:22, the LORD said, **'Neither shalt thou set thee up any image; which the LORD thy God hateth.'** The word *image* (H4676/H5324) is defined as *something stationed; that is, a column or memorial stone; by analogy, an idol.* Therefore, an idol or image is something that has been created, exalted and set up by man.

Many times, the images of idolatry are hidden in the imaginations of one's thought life. These idolatrous thoughts, bow down to the mental images of one's own deception. When these deceptive thoughts are given preeminence, they become the root of error that will lead the heart into the rationalization of sin, false justification, idolatry and death.

So, how does this verse and definition of the word 'image' apply to the Church today? Well, what image is the church of Jesus Christ trying to represent? Are we trying to create an image that will be acceptable to the world by bringing the spiritual things of God down to the level of a carnal mindset or being 'politically correct' by never speaking against the sin and rebellion running rampant in our world, because we don't want to offend anybody?

If so, we've become compromised cowards! The devil uses compromise to strip the church of its power. The world doesn't need another powerless religion; it needs a supernatural encounter with the living God.

It's time to do a self-inventory. Please, ask yourself the following questions: Have you created an image of what you think the church should or shouldn't be? Can you tolerate celebrating overly sentimental traditions that are rooted in wickedness? Do you prefer a diluted version of the truth, so people (including yourself) can be at ease in a lifestyle of unrepentant sin? Are you content to allow people to continue in the lies and deceptions of satan, instead of telling them the truth? Are you at peace with multitudes of people slipping into hell every day, because they do not know Christ?

— OR —

Are you a holy, righteous and uncompromised vessel of God who's willing to be a voice in the earth for the Kingdom of God? Are you willing to love people enough to reach out to them with the truth, the whole truth and nothing but the truth? Obviously, these are forthright questions that require authentic answers. This line of questioning is necessary, because we cannot continue in compromise and expect to minister effectively. Let's search our hearts to know whether our faith is genuine (2 Corinthians 13:5-8; Jeremiah 17:9)

If we're creating another gospel and watering it down to the point that there's no godly sorrow or conviction, no need for repentance, no power in the blood and no deity in Christ; If we're trying to make the ungodly feel comfortable in their sin and telling them they don't have to change; if the ways of the sinner have become our ways, then we have lost sight of our purpose. If this be the case, then we're in rebellion against God and we are an idolatrous people! If we're being silenced into the darkness of ungodly compromise, then we are not declaring the light of God's truth! This must change!

It's time for the Church to grow up, train up and rise up! We cannot remain as spiritual babies. It's time to cut the umbilical cords that hold us to the unholy and immature things of the past. We cannot remain ignorant. We can no longer learn, teach, promote, practice or train ourselves (or others) in the ways of the heathen (Jeremiah 10:2)!! Rather, we must expose the lies of the devil, and teach people the truth of God, so they can be free! This is our calling!

Jesus was our example. He never mixed the holy with the unholy or the pure with the polluted. He preached the unadulterated Word of God — the truth, the whole truth and nothing but the truth — and He confirmed it with signs, wonders and miracles. As a result, multitudes were drawn into the Kingdom through faith in the atoning blood of Christ and by the glorious power of God. I repeat, when it came to ministering to people, Jesus never used heathen methods to teach about the Kingdom of God.

So, what does the church need in order to effectively minister and evangelize? What worked for Jesus, will work for us. If the power of God is operating in the church, and the glory of God is present, it will draw people like a spiritual magnet. There will be no need for worldly gimmicks, because the Spirit of God will call their names and they'll respond. The lost are not looking for religious, churchy games. They're looking for something relevant that will gloriously invade the cry of their hearts and change their lives forever. If we're to reach the lost, it must be done by the power of God's Spirit operating through human vessels that honor Him and declare His truth.

Traditional lies destroy lives. If you've never researched the pagan origins of your national holidays, I challenge you — in the name of the LORD — to do so. Search for the truth, so that you may be free from the empty delusions of this world. We are warned in:

***Colossians 2:8** Beware lest any man spoil you through philosophy and vain deceit, after the traditions of men, after the rudiments of the world, and not after Christ.*

Once you understand the truth, you must make a decision. Understanding that to compromise with a lie is an alignment with satan, what will you do with this knowledge? If we reject God's truth, whether knowingly or unknowingly, then we will automatically believe a lie. But, self-induced deception is the worst deception of all. If we knowingly make any alignment with the enemy of God, then we've placed ourselves in a very dangerous position, and the consequences will be our own fault. Choosing to 'just go with the flow' and live in comfortable ignorance and compromise, simply because everyone else is doing it, will make fools out of the people of God! The LORD holds us accountable, so consider the matter and ask Him to help you search your heart.

On a lighter note, if you search the scriptures, you'll find that the LORD has ordained certain celebrations and feasts for the people of God. These are the holidays and traditions we should be celebrating. It's time for the church to rise up, shake the filth of the world off of her garments, and walk in the truth and blessings of what God has intended for us.

The heart that is perfect toward the LORD will discern between good and evil and make no agreement with the ways of wickedness. It will not compromise what's right. A perfect heart will not provide a place or opportunity for idols, false gods or idolatrous practices to be exalted.

REMAINS PURE FROM SEXUAL SIN

The perfect heart will not corrupt itself with the idolatry of sexual sin. Earlier in our study, we read that before Solomon began to build the temple, King David prayed for him to have a perfect heart toward the LORD (1 Chronicles 29:19). However, Solomon had a lust for beautiful women. This lust led him into idolatry and turned his heart away from the LORD:

<u>1 Kings 11:1-4</u> But king Solomon loved many strange women, together with the daughter of Pharaoh, women of the Moabites, Ammonites, Edomites, Zidonians, and Hittites; ²Of the nations concerning which the LORD said unto the children of Israel, Ye shall not go in to them, neither shall they come in unto you: for surely they will turn away your heart after their gods: Solomon clave unto these in love. ³And he had seven hundred wives, princesses, and three hundred concubines: and his wives turned away his heart. ⁴For it came to pass, when Solomon was old, that his wives turned away his heart after other gods: and his heart was not perfect with the LORD his God, as was the heart of David his father.

Solomon loved many **strange** (H5237/H5235) women. A strange woman could be associated with a variety of characteristics. She would have been a woman who was most likely a *foreigner* (non-Jewish). She may have been considered to be *adulterous*, outlandish and/or *different* in the areas of faith and/or customs. Many times, there would be something strange about her that would somehow link her to *calamity*. This proved to be the case with Solomon.

Part 1 • *Loving God* with All Your Heart

King Solomon's lust for beautiful woman was so strong that He married 700 wives and had 300 concubines from six different heathen nations. He married and united with them for political advancement with the kings and nations surrounding him, as well as to satisfy his covetous fleshly desires. Solomon may have thought this would provide safety and security for Israel. But in reality, it opened the door for spiritual adultery, rebellion against the LORD and wickedness to advance throughout the land. Solomon allowed himself to be wooed by the womanly charms of his wives as he catered to their demands. His disobedience to the Word of God caused him to turn his heart away from the truth and wrongfully pursue false gods.

WHAT'S IN A NAME?
When Solomon's wives and concubines came into his household, they brought their heathen customs and idolatrous practices with them. To understand what these women brought into Israel through their covenants with Solomon, let's take a look at who their people and nations were. There is much to be learned about the influence, character and history of a nation from its name:

The Daughters of Pharaoh were from Egypt. To the Israelites, the nation of Egypt had been the place of severe slavery. The children of Abraham, Isaac and Jacob were in bondage for four hundred years, until they cried out, and God delivered them from the hand of Pharaoh. *Egypt (H4714/H4693/H4692/H6696)* is described as a *limiting* place of *besiegers*, fortified, *hemming in*, a place of *distress*, a stronghold; to *cramp* and *confine*, to be a hostile adversary, to assault, and to bind up. Egypt speaks of the ways of the world, as well as the bondage and servitude associated with it.

The **Ammonites** *(H5984/H5983/H5971/H6004)* and the **Moabites** *(H4125/H4124/H1)* were the *incestuous offspring of Lot* and his two daughters. The Moabites descended from Moab and the Ammonites from Ammon. **Moab** *(H4124)* means *of the mother's father*. **Ammon** *(H5983/H5971/H6004)* means *tribal (that is, inbred); a congregated unit of troops or attendants;* the root meaning of Ammon means to *overshadow by huddling together*. Elsewhere in scripture, it translates as to become dim or to hide. So the very names of the Moabites and Ammonites stems from a root of perversion, darkness and secrecy.

The **Edomites** *(H130/H123/H122/H119)* were the offspring of Esau, the twin brother of Jacob. His name means *red, ruddy, rosy* and the root meaning is *to show blood in the face — to flush*. Esau was a hunter and was consumed with his lust. He was so foolish that when he wanted a bowl of potage, he sold his birthright to his brother Jacob to satisfy his immediate hunger. He gave no real thought to the consequences of his rash actions. Esau also married heathen women, and his brother Jacob obtained Esau's birthright and blessing. Consequently, Esau bore anger toward Jacob for many years. Through the character issues of Esau, the Edomites represented selfishness, a lack of self-control, neglect of spiritual things and indifference for responsible leadership.

The **Zidonians** *(H6722/H6721/H6679)* were from Zidon (also known as Sidon), and the meaning of their name is to *catch* by *lying in wait*. Elsewhere in scripture, it is translated as: to chase, hunt and take provision. This could speak of predator-like behavior, hidden destruction and death.

The **Hittite** *(H2850/H2845/H2865)* people were *aboriginal Canaanites* known to cause *terror*. Their name means to *break down and prostrate by violence, confusion* and *fear*. Elsewhere in scripture, it translates as: to make afraid, beat down, discourage, cause dismay, scare and terrify. Obviously, these people demonstrated the characteristic of what we would call terrorists today.

So, looking at the characteristics of these six nations, it is clear that when Solomon married his beautiful heathen wives, he also married himself to lineages of bondage, slavery, distress, adversity, the overshadowing of incestuous relationships, irresponsibility, lust, being attentively sought as prey, and terribly evil extremist activity. Through sin and compromise his understanding

CHAPTER 5 • THE 'PERFECT HEART' WORSHIPPER

was darkened, and his lust became as a spiritual fog. He could no longer clearly discern between that which was right and that which was perverted.

These strange women used their feminine charms to lay their alluring snares and catch the heart of Solomon. He gave into their whims and they seduced him into spiritual adultery. They influenced Solomon to the point that he, irrationally, built high places for their false gods, and they took of his provisions for their lavish lifestyle as a prize for the hunt. Not considering the effects of such disobedience and outright betrayal against the LORD, Solomon lost sight of the fact that the LORD was to be his first love.

Because the king chose to yield to the idolatry of his wives, instead of staying true to his love for God, he would eventually be beaten down spiritually. He would suffer discouragement, dismay and despair as he allowed his heart to be drawn away from the God who had been so good to him and blessed him so abundantly. When Solomon took these women as his wives and concubines, he made a covenant and came into physical and spiritual union with them. This would be the eventual demise and downfall of his Kingdom.

Solomon's heart was not perfect; therefore, he did not fully follow after the LORD. He sought to please his wives more than he sought to please his God. Therefore, Solomon disobeyed the LORD and did *evil*

(H7451/H7489) in His sight. This means that he was literally, *spoiling* and *breaking to pieces* his intended destiny, *making it good for nothing*. He became immoral, wicked and wretched before the face of the LORD. His wives' gods became his gods, and he built high places of worship for Ashtoreth the goddess of the Zidonians, Milcom the abomination of the Ammonites, Chemosh the abomination of Moab, and Molech the abomination of Ammon (1 Kings 11:5-8).

The word **abomination** (H8251/H8262) is a strong word and is defined in the Hebrew as utterly *disgusting, filthy,* detestable, *idolatrous, loathsome, polluted* and abhorred. Because Solomon didn't stand up for truth and righteousness, he fell into lies and wickedness. He allowed his wives to practice their polluted worship as they burned incense, made sacrifices and performed their loathsome, disgusting and detestable acts to their demon-inspired gods.

When it came to women, Solomon simply coveted what was pleasing to his eyes. Thus, he entered into unholy covenants and married those who practiced evil. This is how Solomon was completely given over to compromise and became a contributor in the abominations committed against the LORD. As he sought to fulfill the lust of his flesh, he undeniably disregarded the commands and covenant of God.

The LORD was angry with King Solomon for his alliance with idolatry and had appeared to him twice and warned him concerning it. He had made it very clear to the King that he was not to worship or go after other gods. But Solomon would not hear, nor obey the commands of the LORD. For this, He took ten tribes from the kingdom of Solomon and gave them to Jeroboam. In due course, since he ignored the LORD, adversaries rose up against him.

When Solomon died, his son Rehoboam reigned in his stead. Even so, the fullness of Solomon's destiny, and the inheritance to his lineage, had been spoiled. His descendants' dignity and greatness had been stolen by lust and idolatry (1 Kings 11:9-13, 29-36, 43).

So what's in a name? Influence, history and character are all connected to names. Influence is the capacity or power to be a compelling force or to produce effects on the actions, behavior and opinions of others. We saw this in how Solomon's wives swayed him away from godliness. History records the past events connected to particular people groups, countries and periods of time. We saw the history of what Solomon's wives were exposed to before coming into his household. Character reflects the features and traits that form the individual nature of a person. Names can carry a greater impact than many might imagine.

Solomon's heathen wives had influential, historical and character trademarks that had been engraved into the fabric of who they were. Though beautiful, they were rebellious to the LORD. Therefore, every area of their lives was out of order. Because Solomon did not stand up for righteousness, he also fell into rebellion and disorder. Concerning the influence, history and character of his enemies, he must have ignored, underestimated and/or became extremely dulled in his discernment. The results were spiritually and morally devastating.

What can we learn from the life of Solomon? Well, it was a lust for beautiful women that deceived this king, who was once renowned for wisdom. So, no matter who you are, be aware of any personal appetites for sexual sin. Call it out for what it is — name it. You cannot repent for something you don't recognize. Submit that sin nature to the Lord, and ask Him to consume it with His Holy presence, filling you with all that is Him and nothing else. Continually, seek the Lord to live your life with a perfect heart toward Him.

Walk Faithfully: Mortify Your Members
Just as sexual sin leads to idolatry, idolatry leads to sexual sin. This is because there are spirits of lust and perversion associated with false worship. These spirits motivate people to offer up their bodies to whatever they have made to be their god. If we do not know the LORD (or if we allow our relationship with Him to be adulterated through self-worship, the worship of other gods, the worship of people or the worship of

CHAPTER 5 • THE 'PERFECT HEART' WORSHIPPER

things), it's only a matter of time before we find our physical bodies involved in illicit sexual behavior.

We live in a world where people are willing to worship almost anything, except the one true and living God. In the practice of these idolatrous belief systems, people offer up abominable sacrifices. Many times, children are the ones who suffer most in the midst of modern day idolatry.

Yes, in our present day and at the hands of their own parents, many children are undeniably neglected, abused or even killed. For instance, one of the most heinous crimes of idolatrous worship in our world today is abortion. In such cases, precious babies are put to death for the selfish sins of the parents (even in cases of rape, at least one of the parents have sinned). These babies are ripped from the womb, burned with saline solutions, or their brains are sucked from the back of their little heads at the time of their live birth. Moreover, their dead little bodies are harvested for organs and tissues and then sold at exorbitant prices! These are abominable acts; they are filthy and wicked before the LORD. These precious, vulnerable babies are sacrificed to devils on the altars of lust, convenience, fear, shame, pride, selfishness, poverty, hatred, secret sin and the love of money.

Those who commit, endorse or agree to the act of murderous abortion have set themselves up as false gods. They presume to declare when life should be given and when it should be taken. If such a person does not repent of their wickedness, they will face the eternal judgment of God.

As the people of God, we're not to become entangled in the things of this world — the lust of the eye, the lust of the flesh and the pride of life (1 John 2:16). Rather, as born again believers who have risen with Christ, we're to seek and set our affections on those things which are above, and not on the things of the earth (Colossians 3:1-3). We're to lift our sights to focus on the spiritual things of God, that we would not be ensnared by the things of the flesh. Lust and ungodly associations can ruin lives, especially for the man or woman of God.

Remember, in this portion of the book, we're dealing with ungodly compromise, lust and sexual sin as formidable acts of idolatry. In today's modern and corrupt society, most people do not equate such behaviors as sinful or idolatrous. Unfortunately, this is true even in the Church! Let's make it plain. Whoredom is rampant not only among the people of world, but also among many who call themselves believers! Why are men and women who say they love Jesus taking their clothes off and climbing in bed with one another without first being committed to one another through the sacred covenant of marriage? Why are they selling their bodies and souls for 15 minutes of sensual pleasure? It's because they're in bondage! They love the addictive pleasure of their sin more than they love the LORD, and they're not obeying the Word of God pertaining to such things. These sinful, illegitimate behaviors and lusts are to be put to death according to:

***Colossians 3:5** Mortify therefore your members which are upon the earth; fornication, uncleanness, inordinate affection, evil concupiscence, and covetousness, which is idolatry:*

In this one verse, we see the mention of five sins beginning with fornication and ending with idolatry. We'll look at each one in the order they're listed as well as a possible scenario of how these things may operate collectively. At the same time, this is not a set order, it's just to demonstrate how these sins can layer and overlap.

Fornication** (G4202/G4203/G4204/G4205/G4097)* is translated from the Greek word ***porneia (porno, pornographic and pornography are also derived from this word). The term fornication includes all forms of *harlotry, adultery, incest, indulgence in unlawful lusts* with the same sex (homosexuality and lesbianism), whoredom, bestiality *and prostitution.* Fornication also includes debauchery — addictive and excessive indulgence in sensual, self-focused pleasures. One final definition of fornication is *idolater.* This relates to all those who participate in any illicit sexual act outside of a one man, one woman marriage relationship.

Part 1 • *Loving God* with All Your Heart

Those who commit fornication have wrongfully offered their bodies and souls to someone (or something) other than God. This is a form of idolatrous worship. By biblical definition, we see that sexual sin and idolatry are linked together.

Since sexual sin is idolatry, it opens a spiritual portal for devils to take control of human passions. Thus, fornication leads to **uncleanness (G167/G169)**, which is defined as physical and moral *impurity* and *lewd*ness motivated by *demonic* activity. Fornication and uncleanness, coupled together and under the evil influence of perversion, can lead to **inordinate affection (G3806/G3958)**, which causes those involved *to experience a usually painful sensation or impression through improper, immoderate, excessive, unreasonable or unrestrained conduct and feelings.* In other words, there is a loss of rational self-control — physically and mentally — because the demonically controlled passions of lust have taken over.

Once things are out of control, **evil concupiscence (G1939/G1937/G1909/G2372/G2380)** causes a *longing* in the heart to fulfill its lustful desires for that which is forbidden. It's motivated by a depraved, fiercely wicked and injurious obsession that rushes to be satisfied. Next is **covetousness (G4124/G4123)** which is defined as eagerly *holding* to and *desiring more* than one is rightly entitled to, resulting in *extortion fraudulency* and *greediness*. In context, Colossians

3:5 teaches that fornication, uncleanness, inordinate affection, evil concupiscence and covetousness are all forms of idolatry.

Idolatry (G1495/G1497/G1491/G2999) is defined as *image-worship,* referring to the worship of a form, an appearance, fashion, shape and/or sight. Idolatry implies *the worship of a heathen god* and it is sensual. Image worship involves what the eye sees, the hand reaches for, the nose smells, the ears hear, the mind allows, the heart desires and the body responds to. The object of idolatrous worship could be oneself, other people, things and/or demonic spirits. However, all idolatry is rooted in lust and deception. Fraudulent behavior (a failure to respect healthy and moral boundaries) is motivated by selfishness, which will cause one to lust after and take (or give) what was never rightly intended.

Illicit sexual sin includes every form of sexual activity committed outside the boundaries of intimate marital love between one biological man and one biological woman. All other sexual acts outside of God's set order are criminal offenses of lust, and they will create a vicious cycle of destruction for those who are caught up in its snares of death. The Apostle Paul commanded all believers in Colossian 3:5 to **mortify** *(G3499/G3498)* your **members** *(G3196).* This means to *deaden* and *subdue* the *limbs* or *parts of the body* that would cause you to fall into the sins of fornication, uncleanness, inordinate affection, evil concupiscence, covetousness and idolatry. It's far better to put sin to death and, thus, live in purity and freedom, than to let sin live and, as a result, die mentally, emotionally, spiritually and physically from the sorrowful consequences of forbidden perversions and the desecration of God's holy order!

Referring back to Solomon and his relationships with his heathen wives, if he had set his affections on things above instead of the things of the earth, he would not have been driven by lust. Then, he would not have worshiped false gods; he would not have forsaken the LORD; and he would not have suffered God's judgment. The life lessons of Solomon's moral and spiritual failures have much to offer to those who want to avoid the corruption and abortion of their destinies.

Unfortunately, moral failures seem to be a part of the normally abnormal cultural climates in which so many choose to live. Sexual perversion and misconduct are running rampant and covetousness and greediness seem to be the order of the day. Nevertheless, those who follow Christ are to live by a higher kingdom standard.

For those who say they belong to Christ: your body, soul and spirit are not your own; they belong to the LORD. We do not have the right to give any part of ourselves to another person, unless it's in a relationship which is in line with God's Word and would have His approval. In other words, the covenant of a godly marriage is the only avenue by which we can wholly give ourselves to another. Let us be reminded that there is a moral code of ethics, which every follower of Christ is to live by:

***Ephesians 5:1-6** Be ye therefore followers of God, as dear children; ²And walk in love, as Christ also hath loved us, and hath given himself for us an offering and a sacrifice to God for a sweetsmelling savour. ³But fornication, and all uncleanness, or covetousness, let it not be once named among you, as becometh saints; ⁴Neither filthiness, nor foolish talking, nor jesting, which are not convenient: but rather giving of thanks. ⁵For this ye know, that no whoremonger, nor unclean person, nor covetous man, who is an idolater, hath any inheritance in the kingdom of Christ and of God. ⁶Let no man deceive you with vain words: for because of these things cometh the wrath of God upon the children of disobedience.*

Notice that in this portion of scripture, we're either the children of God or we're the children of disobedience. We cannot be both. We must make the choice as to which we will serve. The Word of God is very clear; there are certain things in which the people of God are not to participate. The whoremongers, the morally and spiritually unclean, the covetous and idolaters will have no inheritance in the LORD. Those who refuse to follow the LORD will forfeit what would have been their eternal blessing and reward. Instead, they will experience the wrath of God. Don't be self-deceived; the LORD will not compromise, co-operate or negotiate with sin, but He will uphold the righteous standards and judgments of His Word.

We must understand that we have a responsibility to do what's right in the sight of the LORD. We're not to live as the servants of sin; we've been bought with a price — purchased and redeemed by the blood of Christ. Therefore, we do not have the legal or moral right to belong to ourselves. We are His, and we're to glorify Him in our bodies and in our spirits (1 Corinthians 6:19-20, 7:23). As followers of Christ and the children of God, we're to dedicate our bodies to the LORD and present ourselves to Him for service:

Romans 12:1 *I beseech you therefore, brethren, by the mercies of God, that ye present your bodies a living sacrifice, holy, acceptable unto God, which is your reasonable service.*

Learn from Solomon's failures. Offer yourself — your body, soul and spirit — wholly and completely to the LORD. Bless Him with the gift of who He has created you to be. Keep yourself holy and pure from all wrong relationships, covetousness, spiritual adultery and idolatry. And, most importantly, present the gift of a perfect heart — filled with pure love and faithfulness — to the LORD, for He alone is worthy.

SUMMARY OF LOVING GOD WITH ALL YOUR HEART

In Chapter 1, we learned the importance of the greatest commandment — to love the LORD our God with all our hearts, all our souls, all our minds and all our strength. We explored the richness of seeking and serving the LORD, as well as the importance of obeying His Word. Before we can truly love God, we must choose to make Him our LORD by believing in His Son and putting our trust in Him concerning all of life. When we do this, we enter into a submitted, intimate and personal love relationship. This is not an arrangement of mere duty; we are motivated by love. As we learn to love the LORD, we'll also learn to love our neighbors as ourselves.

In Chapter 2, we discussed religion versus relationship. In the process, we considered the blessing that comes with personal repentance, obeying the Word of the LORD and mentoring spiritual babes. Indeed, if we truly love the LORD, our lifestyle will reflect that truth.

In Chapter 3, in relation to heart attitudes and idolatry, we learned through the examples of royalty what we should and should not do. King Saul and his daughter Michal taught us the folly of ridiculing the righteous. However, King David modeled a proper response to criticism when we passionately worship the LORD. To love, honor and worship the LORD is our divine purpose; disobedience (prideful stubbornness, rebellion, iniquity, witchcraft, idolatry, bitterness, etc.) will derail us.

In Chapter 4, we saw the importance of loving the LORD with our whole, complete heart. True worshippers withhold nothing from the LORD. Whether in private or in the company of others, their worship is full and authentic. Whatever the circumstance or atmosphere, their love is refreshingly constant. As a 'whole heart' worshipper continually pursues their King, they earnestly seek to understand His ways and reflect His character in their lives.

In Chapter 5, we learned the character traits and benefits of having a perfect heart before the LORD. Perfect hearted believers walk in truth and do what's right according to God's Word. They're an army of kingdom citizens, who refuse to serve sin or give place to the devil through the idolatry of self-worship. They know how to keep rank and behave in a perfect way, without compromise. Their hearts are overwhelmed with love for the LORD, and they offer their entire being as a living, holy sacrifice to Him. As a result, they can see the strength of the LORD, receive favor and long life, reject trouble and remain pure. They are able to accomplish all of these things, because they are empowered of the Holy Spirit, who enables them. As true believers surrender every aspect of their lives to Him, they allow the LORD to perfect their hearts.

May you truly love the LORD with all your heart!!!

Part 2
Loving God with All Your Soul

∽ CHAPTER 6 ∾

THE SOUL DEFINED, THE BREATH OF GOD

Now that we understand what it means to love the LORD with all our hearts, let's look at the next portion of Matthew 22:37 where we are commanded to "***love the LORD thy God <u>with all thy soul</u>***." The *soul* (G5590/G5594) is defined as *breath*, and by implication, the *spirit* of mankind. In fact, we see the correlation between the breath of life and the soul of man in the creation story:

<u>Genesis 2:7</u> *And the LORD God formed man of the dust of the ground and breathed into his nostrils the breath of life and man became a living soul.*

We can understand 7 things from this scripture:
- God formed man.
- Apart from God mankind would not exist.
- There is no such thing as a self-made man.
- Our breath comes from God.
- The breath of God is our life source.

- His life fills our soul.
- If that breath is taken away, then our physical life will cease to exist on this earth.

Genesis 2:7 reveals how powerless we are to even exist, let alone live, without the presence and breath of God operating in our lives. Without the release of God's creative power, there is no life. Lest we think more highly of ourselves than we ought to, we must remember that, in the beginning, we were nothing more than dirt that was transformed into a beautiful creation by the hand of a glorious God.

The LORD God **formed** (H3335/H3334) man of the dust of the ground. This means He *pressed, squeezed* and *molded* the man *into shape, as a potter* would create and shape a clay vessel for his specific purpose. After the LORD formed His masterpiece of the man, He breathed into his nostrils — literally blowing into the man and inflating him with the life of God.

God's breath transformed the dust of the earth into a living, breathing, first fruit of humanity. It was from this first breath of life that all of mankind would proceed. On the inside of Adam was a multitude, a company, a congregation of people that would impact eternity for either good or evil.

Because our breath came from God, He is the original source of life by which we are sustained. Every single moment of our lives, we're dependent upon Him to maintain our existence. When that God-breathed breath of life ceases to inflate our lungs, then we will encounter physical death and find our place in eternity (Genesis 6:17; 7:15, 22; Psalm 104:29; Hebrews 9:26).

According to Job 12:10 the LORD holds the soul of every living thing and the breath of all mankind. Even as Job went through his great trials, he acknowledged that it was the Spirit of God who caused his breath to remain in him (Job 27:3). Job also declared that the breath of the Almighty gave him life when he was created (Job 33:4). He certainly recognized the vulnerability of all mankind, when he declared that if the LORD sets His heart upon man and decides to gather or take away His spirit and His breath from man, then all flesh would die and return to the dust (Job 34:14).

So what's the point? It's simply this; the life of our soul comes from the breath of God. Therefore, neither our breath, nor our life belongs to us; they belong to God. Our breath and life are given to us on loan. For this reason, we're to use this precious gift of having a God-breathed living soul, to express our love to the LORD in a way that brings Him joy.

HAVE BREATH? PRAISE THE LORD!!

__Psalm 150:6__ Let everything that hath breath praise the LORD. Praise ye the LORD.

Part 2 • *Loving God* with All Your Soul

This verse features God's ordained purpose of our breath — to praise the LORD. It's not a suggestion to praise the LORD, it's a command! Let's examine Psalm 150:6:

The English definition for the word *let* means: to allow or permit, to grant occupancy, to cause or make to happen. It also means to involve, to release, to free, to reveal one's true feelings and to enlarge. So, anytime we *let* something happen, it is not by accident. It's an intentional event, based on our personal decisions.

In the Hebrew, the word **everything** *(H3605/H3634)* translates as: *the whole*; *all, any and every;* to make *complete*. Elsewhere in scripture, this word is translated as: altogether, whosoever, whatsoever, howsoever and to make perfect. Basically, nothing is excluded from this command to praise the LORD.

The word **breath** *(H5397/H5395)* is defined as a *puff* of *wind*, a *vital breath*, a *divine inspiration*. Therefore, our breath is the force of God's life within us. In addition, within the breath of our praise, we carry the wind of divine inspiration. Essentially, we release God's very breath back to Him and into the earth realm when we praise Him.

As we consider these definitions, when the Word of God says, **"Let everything that has breath praise the LORD..."** it's speaking to whoever, whatever and the entirety of every living thing. That is, anything which has been created and has a vital breath. All breathing creation — every part of it — is to praise the LORD perfectly and completely, in whatever manner and ability He has ordained for it/them to do so.

Exactly how does the LORD desire to be praised? Well, in Psalm 150:6, the Hebrew word for **praise** *(H1984)* is **hâlal**. It's defined as being *clear in sound, but usually in color; to shine; make a show; boast, rave; be clamorously foolish* (to praise vigorously and without forethought) and *to celebrate*. So, individually and as a collective group of worshippers, we're to cry out with persistent and clamorously foolish praise to our God! Our praise is to be spontaneous and energetic; it can be released anytime and anywhere, because it's always appropriate to praise the LORD! According to Psalm 150:6, everything that has life is commanded to make (create) glorious praise of the LORD and to let it shine forth, without reservation or hesitation, wherever and however possible.

Why would God command us to praise Him this way? Because there is power in praise! Whether on a personal or corporate level, our praise lifts up the name of the LORD, tells of His mighty acts, and frees us from bondage. It becomes an assault weapon against the spiritual darkness of demonic activity, and it releases God's judgment against our enemies (Psalms 106:2, 145:4, 149: 1-9, 150:2). As we lift up and exalt the name of the LORD, He fights for us. As we testify of the greatness of the LORD, our praise brings expectancy, deliverance and joy to our souls. There are powerful, practical benefits of praise.

Now, let's consider the impact of Genesis 2:7 and Psalm 150:6 a little further. The Heavenly Father breathed the breath of life into mankind (Adam). As a result, man became alive to the purposes of God. Therefore, as the human offspring of Adam (and Eve) and the spiritual offspring of God — through faith in Christ — our ordained and primary purpose is to exhibit the life of God. We're to willingly and obediently fulfill His will and purposes in the earth. Everything else is secondary.

However, if we're to enter into this type of life, including vivacious praise and adoration of the LORD, we must press past ourselves. We must rise above and triumph over our fears, inabilities, struggles, pride, insecurities and even our unscriptural religious traditions and mindsets. Only then, will we experience the freedom of praising the LORD with sweet abandonment. Only then, will our expressions of praise and worship release the priceless, rich treasures of love that we hold in our hearts for the LORD.

Through the God-breathed life force that dwells within us, our words, actions and way of life should demonstrate the truth and power of God. As holy vessels of the LORD, we're to use our God-given breath in declarations and songs of praise that release the authority of God's Word and the life it carries, into the earthly and spiritual realms. As we do, we can expect to see victory and the manifest glory of the LORD. This is the gift He desires to receive from His people. Let everything that has breath praise the LORD!

CHAPTER 7
SEVEN MANIFESTATIONS OF THE SOUL

We have already discussed how the living soul of man receives its life from the breath of God (Genesis 2:7). Another quality of the soul is that, while it is a separate and distinct part of man, it is also still intricately woven into the physical being of man. As mentioned before, it is the realm in which the thoughts of the mind, the will and the emotions operate. So, when manifested, the secrets of the soul become the physical evidence or demonstration of that which is otherwise hidden within. One's morality (or lack of it) will be revealed, based on the condition of the soul. In this chapter, we will study seven manifestations of the healthy soul.

1 — THE REVIVED HEART & SOUL
In the beginning, God created mankind in His image and after His own likeness (Genesis 1:26-27). Yet, because Adam and Eve sinned against the LORD and disobeyed His commandment (to not eat from the tree of the knowledge of good and evil), every person born (throughout all generations) has been born with a sinful nature. The heart and soul of man turned from the LORD and became abnormal and perverse through the effects of sin and rebellion. Apart from the help and mercy of the LORD, man was without hope, destined to self-destruct and on a one-way path

to hell. Thankfully, it was not the LORD'S desire to leave us in that condition. Though man rebelled against the LORD, God has provided what's needed to restore the hearts of mankind to His original intent, through the spiritual circumcision of our hearts.

<u>Deuteronomy 30:6</u> And the LORD thy God will circumcise thine heart, and the heart of thy seed, to love the LORD thy God with all thine heart, and with all thy soul, that thou mayest live.

God's ultimate purpose for all He does is that we might know Him, love Him and live. But, if we're to experience life as He intended, we must allow the LORD to sever everything in our nature that is not like Him. This requires that our hearts be circumcised. To *circumcise (H4135)* the heart is to *curtail, cut* off and *destroy* anything that would keep the people of God apart from Him. This is necessary because separation from God equals death. When the LORD circumcises our hearts, He's examining and removing all the sinful, hindering, rebellious things that have been hidden deep inside of us. He's eradicating that which would cause death and destruction to operate in our lives (Colossians 2:4-15). As He cuts away the spiritual cancer of sin and deception, His life flows in and through us — like a healing balm — empowering us to live a life of righteousness and truth.

According to the last portion of Deuteronomy 30:6, if we allow the LORD to have His way in the circumcision of our hearts, and if we choose to love Him with our whole heart and soul, then we will live. This word *live* (H2416/H2421) means that we are *revived;* raised up and brought back from the dead. We are resurrected into new life by the power of God. He makes us *strong, fresh* and *alive.* He promises to nourish, preserve, save, recover, repair, restore and bring us into a place of wholeness in Him. This is the reward of choosing to love God with all our heart and soul.

2 — THE CLEAVING SOUL

As the nation of Israel (the people of God) were coming out of the wilderness and taking possession of the promise land, their leader (Joshua) was faithful to remind them to keep their priorities straight:

<u>Joshua 22:5</u> But take diligent heed to do the commandment and the law, which Moses the servant of the LORD charged you, to love the LORD your God, and to walk in all his ways, and to keep his commandments, and to cleave unto him, and to serve him with all your heart and with all your soul (also Deuteronomy 11:22, 13:4).

To *cleave* (H1692) unto the LORD is an aggressive action of *impinging* one's self upon Him by *clinging, adhering* and sticking to Him. This denotes a decision to *catch, pursue* and *follow hard after* the living God, with the intention of being joined to and continuing to abide with Him. This decision to cleave is motivated by our desire to be with the LORD and to have a true knowledge of Him. Cleaving is not a casual event, but rather an extremely intentional, intimately passionate expression of love and relationship.

God desires that we become one with Him. He demonstrated this concept through the intimate relationship between a husband and wife. After He created man, the LORD said it was not good for man to be alone. For this reason, He created the woman as a helpmeet for the man (Genesis 2:18). When God presented this amazingly gorgeous, tailor-made creation to Adam, he declared:

Genesis 2:23-24 *This is now bone of my bones, and flesh of my flesh: she shall be called Woman, because she was taken out of Man.* ²⁴*Therefore shall a man leave his father and his mother, and shall cleave unto his wife: and they shall be one flesh.*

Adam saw beauty in this feminine being who the LORD created for Him, and he desired to *cleave* (H1692) to her. This means Adam intimately *pursued* her, *caught* her, *clung* to her, *followed close* behind her, joined himself to her and chose to abide with her. He desired to know her and be known; to love her and be loved; to experience her and give himself to her. He wanted to become one with her.

Likewise, the lovers of God refuse to be denied His presence; they seek to become one with Him in the joy of spiritual oneness. Notice that the word 'cleave' in Joshua 22:5 has the same reference number *(H1692)* as the word 'cleave' in Genesis 2:24. Accordingly, just as Adam clave to Eve, those who choose to 'cleave' to the LORD, will fervently *follow after* and *pursue* Him, desiring to intimately dwell with Him.

Joshua also exhorted the people to serve the LORD with all their hearts and all their souls. To *serve (H5647)* means to be a *working* worshipper who is about the Father's business; co-laboring, *tilling,* sowing and harvesting souls in the earth for the Kingdom of Heaven. As we cleave to the LORD, learn His ways and love Him, serving becomes the natural expression of our everlasting adoration of Him.

3 — THE BOASTING SOUL

To boast in someone or something gives evidence to the fact that we have great confidence in that person or thing. When we boast in the LORD, we're declaring the superior qualities of His character and nature, as well as the wondrous works He has done, is doing and will yet do in our lives. In fact, when we boast in the LORD, our praise becomes an influential, faith-filled testimony and the heralding of our own deliverance. David makes the connection between the power of praise, the boasting soul and deliverance in the following verse:

Part 2 • Loving God with All Your Soul

Psalm 34:1-4 *I will bless the LORD at all times: his praise shall continually be in my mouth. ²My soul shall make her boast in the LORD; the humble shall hear thereof and be glad. ³O magnify the LORD with me, and let us exalt his name together. ⁴I sought the LORD, and he heard me, and delivered me from all my fears.*

Psalm 34 was written in regards to some of the struggles that David faced in the wilderness, as he fled from the sword of King Saul. Did you know that the name **David** (H1732/H1730) means *loving, to love, to boil;* and it implies *a love-token, lover* and *friend?* The definition of his name is also translated: well beloved. Of all these, I think the most intriguing definition is *to boil.* For something to boil it must come in contact with fire or extreme heat, which agitates the level of stability, thereby causing activated motion. In the changing circumstances of life, fiery trials may come, but the LORD uses these events to force the hidden things in our lives to the surface. It's in the trials of life that the hidden places and the secret things of the heart and soul are revealed.

From a young age, David was called by God and anointed to be King over Israel (1 Samuel 16:1, 13; Psalm 89:20). However, his kingship training would come through the difficulties and fiery trials he endured. As King Saul pursued him in the wilderness with murderous intent, the LORD used these trials to test and prove David's

CHAPTER 7 • SEVEN MANIFESTATIONS OF THE SOUL

character. Every experience prepared and matured him for the greatness of his destiny.

As David fought through his physical, mental and spiritual battles, the areas of weakness and the inconsistencies in his life were revealed. As he realized his vulnerability and cried out to the LORD, an intimate relationship was being firmly established. Within that relationship, the LORD was also building foundations of trust, obedience, humility, strength and stability into David, thereby equipping him for leadership. David had the heart of a worshipper and he was tenaciously determined to pursue and know the heart of his God. Regardless of what he had to endure, he was resolute and unwavering in his desire to fulfill the divine will of the LORD (Acts 13:12).

In Psalm 34:1, David declared that he would **bless** *(H1288)* the LORD at all times. This meant he would *kneel* before the LORD and *bless God as an act of adoration*. He would continually give thanks to Him through triumphant songs of **praise** *(H8416/H1984)*. The melodious hymns that flowed from David's lips commended, magnified, glorified and celebrated the greatness of the LORD. Regardless of situations and circumstances, David remembered that the LORD was his source of help and strength (Psalms 27:1, 121:2).

In Psalm 34:2, David goes on to say, *"...my soul shall make her boast in the LORD..."* This word **soul** *(H5315/H5314)* refers to the *life*, *vitality* and *refreshing* that God *breathes* into us. The breath of God has been given to us, so that we might use it to **boast** *(H1984)* of His superior qualities, glory, power and honor. This word 'boast' also comes from the Hebrew root word **hâlal**, which if you recall, means being *clear in sound, but usually in color; to shine; make a show; boast, rave; be clamorously foolish* (to praise vigorously and without forethought), and *to celebrate*. So, when we boast in the LORD for all He's done, our expression becomes an extravagantly elaborate, highly vocal expression of magnificent praise, shining forth to the glory of God.

Manifests Hope, Encouragement & Unity
Our boastful praise also affects other people. We see the impact of this in the latter portion of Psalm 34:2, *"...**The humble shall hear thereof and be glad**..."* In this verse the **humble** *(H6041/H6031)* refers to the poor or those who have been *depressed*, afflicted and beaten down in life. Yet, when they hear the boastful praises of God's people, it can offer them refreshing hope and encouragement. Praise is powerful and extremely contagious. When released through willing lips, it can bring freedom, healing and deliverance to the downcast or wounded soul. Enthusiastic praise blends faith and courage together and challenges us and others to believe and trust in the LORD.

In Psalm 34:3, David further extends the invitation to *"... **magnify the LORD with me and let us exalt His** *name together."* To *magnify (H1431)* the LORD is to make Him *large in body, mind, estate or honor* — to exalt His excellence and promote His exceeding greatness. However, if we fail to magnify the LORD, our thoughts toward Him can become small and faithless. Weak or diminished faith tends to disregard the supernatural aspects of God as Creator and Master of all things. If this happens, we cannot see the LORD for who He truly is, because we've created a false god that matches the feeble limitations of our own understanding and inabilities. We cannot see the magnificence of the LORD through a self-focused mindset that is filled with fears, doubts and unbelief. If we're to see the LORD as magnificent, full of power, glory, beauty, honor and superb splendor, we must activate our faith by learning to trust in His Word and the holy, righteous character of His name.

In Romans 10:17, scripture says that faith comes by hearing, and hearing by the Word of God. Therefore, if we're to magnify the LORD, we must meditate on the truth of His Word, apply it to our faith and boldly proclaim His promises over the situations of our lives. The revelation of God's Word empowers us to see and know the strength of His greatness, beyond what our current circumstances may seem to dictate.

To *exalt (H7311)* the *name (H8034)* of the LORD is *to raise* or heave *high*, extol and promote the *definite, conspicuous*, precise and clearly defined *position*, honor, authority, character, status and infamous renown of the LORD. To magnify and exalt the LORD together, speaks of the people of God coming into a place of unity and oneness for the purpose of lifting Him up. Therefore, David was encouraging the people to harmoniously declare and emphasize the great *appellation of individuality* of Almighty God — to recognize that there's no one like Him and no name greater than His!!

Manifests Faith over Fear

When we choose to bless the LORD with our continual praise, boast of His greatness, magnify Him and exalt His name, He will hear and **deliver** *(H5337)* us. This means He will *snatch away*, strip, spoil and rid us from all forms of **fear** *(H4035/H4032/H4033/H1481)* — the hostile terror which would seek to find a *temporary abode or permanent residence* within us. When the LORD delivers us, He defends, preserves, rescues, saves, brings recovery and causes us to break away from the source of our fears. Let this truth sink deep into your soul and spirit; when we magnify and bless the LORD, fear is ousted! It can have no dwelling place in us or power over us, when we praise and worship the LORD. The glorious presence of God drives away all fear, because it cannot abide where He has dominion.

We must realize that fear is an enemy, and we cannot afford to tolerate it. When fear is given a place of preeminence, it becomes like a spiritual and mental paralysis. Any unchecked fear can dominate and hinder spiritual development, torment the mind, block one's full potential and steal destiny. Tormenting fear and distress are evidence of demonic activity in a besieged soul. Remember, God has not given us a spirit of fear, but of power, love and a sound mind (2 Timothy 1:7). Therefore, we need to understand that fear is an opposing force to the power and love of God. If fear is allowed to gain control of the thoughts, the mind can lose its soundness and slip into a state of negative reasoning and temporary insanity.

Many times, fears are rooted in a lack of faith and trust concerning the 'what ifs' of life. This includes, but is not limited to, the concerns and the unknown events of the future; personal inabilities and insecurities; past failures; emotional wounds of the soul; unhealthy relationships, rejection and the critical opinions and words of others. If we're to be a kingdom people of divine purpose and destiny, we cannot concern ourselves with the fearful 'what ifs' of life. Rather, we must allow our faith to rise up, as we take courage in the LORD'S ability. We must believe that our God will be faithful to see us through every challenge we may face.

Fear is the opposite of faith. Therefore, where there is fear, faith cannot operate; and where there is faith, fear cannot operate. Faith is the substance of things hoped for, the evidence of things not seen (Hebrews 11:1). We know, according to Romans 10:17 that faith comes by hearing, and hearing by the Word of God. For this reason, it's accurate to say that hearing, understanding and applying God's Word to our lives becomes the substance of our faith. By definition, the **substance** (G5287/G5259/G2476) of faith is the underlying *support, assurance* and *confidence* that *establishes*, fortifies and *builds up* our spiritual foundation; thereby, strengthening us to *stand* strong in the LORD. Our faith in God's Word becomes the *essence* of hope, which encourages us to expect and anticipate the good plans the LORD has for us (Jeremiah 29:11). Uninhibited faith, based on the Word of God, stirs the spirit of the believer to see beyond the limitations of the natural realm and into the supernatural provision of the LORD.

Often, in the midst of praise and worship, the LORD will speak His desires into the spirit of those who pursue Him. As worshippers, we must be willing to follow Him into that place of destiny and purpose. As we walk in fellowship and agreement with Him, we will be successful, because God never fails! By faith, we take possession of all the LORD has intended for us; fulfill our divine destiny and reach our full potential in Him. Remember, God ordains our purpose and He'll be in the midst of it, fulfilling all things.

Saint of God, regardless of what's going on in your life, I challenge you to bless the LORD at all times. Let His praise be in your mouth continually. Let your soul boast in the LORD, as you magnify and exalt His name. Let your faith arise victoriously and know that the LORD delivers you from all your fears.

4 — THE JOYFUL SOUL

The possessor of the joyful soul demonstrates delight and gladness through the expressed manifestations of one's physical actions, speech and countenance. The joyful soul is triumphantly lighthearted and optimistically contagious, as it positively influences and ministers hope to others. Its source of delight and contentment is found in the LORD:

***Psalm 35:9** My soul shall be joyful in the LORD; it shall rejoice in his salvation.*

In the context of this verse, to be *joyful (H1523)* in the **LORD** *(H3068/H1961)* means to be in a state, position or condition of *rejoicing* in the *eternally self-existing* presence of *Jehovah*. The expression of this rejoicing is to *spin about under the influence of* a joyfully persistent, *violent emotion*. A joyful soul can rarely be contained, and there is always a physical manifestation or movement linked to its unrestrained joy.

The joyful dance of the soul demonstrates a willing enthusiasm to chase, follow after, pursue and accompany the LORD in the journey of life, which He has prepared. The how, when, where or why of the journey does not matter, because the joy filled soul expectantly embraces the existence of God's Spirit within. It experiences and awaits the fully manifest reality of His salvation, goodness, mercy, provision and promises all along the way.

In Psalm 35:9, the word ***salvation*** (H3444/H3467) is the Hebrew word ***yshû'âh*** which is defined as *something* that has been *saved, deliverance, aid, victory* and *prosperity*. It's also translated as health, help, salvation, save, saving (health) and welfare. It comes from the root word ***yâsha',*** which means to be open, wide and free; that is, (by implication) to be safe: to free or succor. ***Yâsha'*** also translates in scripture as avenging, defend, deliver, deliverer, help, preserve, rescue, be safe, bring (having) salvation, savior and get victory. The LORD alone provides our salvation through His great name!

<u>Acts 4:12</u> Neither is there salvation in any other; for there is none other name under heaven given among men, whereby we must be saved.

Jesus is our salvation. His name means salvation. Therefore, He is our deliverer, our preservation, our healer, our helper, our defender and our avenger. He does more than just save us from Hell. Through His victory over sin, death, hell and the grave, He brings us into (and He becomes) our place of *safety, freedom, victory, prosperity* and *aid*/welfare. When we understand our spiritual inheritance and the wealth of blessing contained in our salvation through Christ, rejoicing and spinning about in triumphant victory should be a natural response to the amazing grace of God.

MANIFESTS CHRIST — SALVATION & RIGHTEOUSNESS
In preparation of the coming wedding day, the LORD is graciously calling His Church to yield to Him and become the pure, spotless lover He has always intended her to be. As lovers of Christ, we're to joyfully put on the spiritual garments He has provided. He covers us in the beauty and holiness of His righteousness and salvation. As the Bride of Christ, we are to rejoice greatly in our beloved King!

***Isaiah 61:10** I will greatly rejoice in the LORD, my soul shall be joyful in my God; for he hath clothed me with the garments of salvation, he hath covered me with the robe of righteousness, as a bridegroom decketh himself with ornaments, and as a bride adorneth herself with her jewels.*

Whenever we declare the phrase, "I will..." this indicates that we've made a conscious decision and are determined to carry out correlating actions. The 'will' and condition of our soul is the prime motivator behind our "I will..." and/or our "I will not..." declarations. Therefore, our soul plays a major role in determining our direction in life, as well as our personal successes and/or failures. Based on the level of our soul's submission to the LORD, the 'will' also indicates our moral, mental, emotional and spiritual condition. To declare *"I will greatly rejoice in the LORD..."* and then joyfully demonstrate it as an expression of truth and sincerity in our lives, is a pretty good indicator that the soul is in good spiritual condition.

To make the decision to rejoice *greatly (H7797)* means to do so with strong, *bright, cheerful,* striking, noteworthy enthusiasm. This type of rejoicing is not just a passing thought or a glib, ho-hum expression of meaningless words. It's an intentional demonstration of immense delight in the LORD. It's an exultant reveling, a glorious appearance of exceedingly great elation and jubilance. This type of rejoicing positively affects our emotions, physical expressions and circumstances. To greatly rejoice in the LORD is to find our ultimate satisfaction and triumph in Him.

In Isaiah 61:10 (as in Psalm 35:9) the word *joyful (H1523)* means *to spin about under the influence of* a joyfully persistent, *violent emotion.* Joyfulness and freedom in the LORD should be characteristics in the lifestyles of His worshippers. When we come to a saving faith in Christ, our filthy, old rags of self-righteousness, death and destruction are cast aside. They're replaced with His garments of *salvation (H3468/H3467).* He wraps us in His *deliverance, liberty, prosperity* and *safety.* We're covered in the **righteousness** *(H6666/H6663), justice, moral virtue* *and prosperity* of Christ. Notice, by the definitions of salvation and righteousness, we have a double portion of prosperity! In Christ, we have everything we need. Just for your information, the English definition of *prosperity* is defined as *a successful, flourishing or thriving condition; prosperous circumstances, especially in financial respects; good fortune.* Salvation covers every area of our lives — spiritually, physically, mentally, emotionally and financially! This should cause us to express carefree exuberance and freedom, as we rejoice in the goodness of our God!

Every true believer is covered in salvation and the righteousness of Christ. Therefore, when the Father in Heaven looks upon us, we are accepted. When He sees us, He sees Jesus — our heavenly Bridegroom. When the Father sees the heavenly Bridegroom, He also sees the Bride within Him.

Just as we've received the spiritual garments He has placed upon us, it's perfectly fitting that we would also acquire the character and nature of Christ Jesus. As He was led by the Spirit of God, we're to be led by the Spirit of God. As He submitted to the Father in Heaven, we're to submit to the Father in Heaven. As He is holy, we're to be holy. As He did what was right, we're to do what is right. As the chaste Bride who is prepared for her Bridegroom, we're to be a reflection of Christ — full of virtue and purity.

Part 2 • *Loving God* with All Your Soul

Immoral behavior and wickedness are to be a thing of the past. As we celebrate the LORD, we're to walk with Him in unity and oneness of spirit. When was the last time you entered into the presence of the LORD with a liberating dance of great joy? When was the last time you found yourself spinning around in praise and passionately loving Him? Perhaps you should take a moment right now to show your appreciation for all He's done for you.

5 — THE HOPEFUL SOUL

In Psalm 42, the soul of King David was panting and thirsting with desire for the LORD, longing to see Him and be in His presence. In the midst of tears and the reproach of his enemies, David's soul was cast down, humbled and sinking into depression. Yet, in his time of despair, he remembered the beauty of being in the presence of the LORD and hearing the voice of joyful praise in the house of God (Psalm 42:1-4). Therefore, He encouraged his soul with the following words:

***Psalm 42:5** Why art thou cast down, O my soul? and why art thou disquieted in me? hope thou in God: for I shall yet praise him for the <u>help of his countenance</u>.*

Sometimes, in the midst of difficulty, we need to verbally remind ourselves of the goodness of the LORD and all He has done for us. David was a man who pursued the heart of God, yet, he still found himself in a great battle. He acknowledged that his soul was *cast down* (H7817). He felt the physical, mental and emotional effects of his condition. David allowed the reproach of his enemies to cause his soul to *sink low* and become *disquieted* (H1993). This means that within his soul, he *roared* with *great sounds* of *clamorous commotion*. His thoughts were in a *tumult of war* and *mourning*.

In the midst of his battle, David declared that he was determined to *praise* (H3034/H3027) the LORD. This expression of praise translates as the Hebrew word, *yâdấh*, which means to hold out an *open* and *extended hand* in *reverence* and *worship*. David lifted his hands to the LORD, even when his soul was in a state of distress, grief and lamentation. As he praised the LORD in the midst of his trials, David expected to find his *help* (H3444/H3467), *deliverance*, salvation and *victory* in the *countenance* (H6440/H6437) — the *face*, favor, acceptance, honor and presence — of the LORD. In due course, as David's soul sought the LORD, he moved from a position of seeking the help of the LORD'S countenance (in verse 5), to realizing that God was the *health* (H3444/H3467) of his own countenance in:

<u>Psalm 42:11</u> Why art thou cast down, O my soul? and why art thou disquieted within me? hope thou in God: for I shall yet praise him, who is the <u>health of my countenance</u>, and my God.

Knowing that his help was only found in God, David declared *"...for I shall yet praise Him..."* This word

yet *(H5750/H5749)* is defined as *continuance, again, repeatedly, still and more.* It also means that David chose to *protest* the disquieted condition of his soul. Through *excessive reiteration,* he chose to earnestly *testify* of the goodness of the LORD, even in the midst of his struggles. David found ***hope*** *(H3176)* — the ability to patiently *wait* and trust in the LORD — as he determined to *yet* praise Him. In so doing, he knew his God would restore his soul and the health of his countenance.

Let's also look more closely at the phrase, "*...the health of my countenance...*" The word ***health*** *(H3444/H3467)* translates as the Hebrew word ***yshu' ah*** *(yesh-oo'-aw)* which means something *saved, deliverance, aid, victory* and *prosperity.* It comes from the primitive root word, ***yasha*** *(yaw-shah')* which means to *be open, wide* or *free,* that is (by implication), to *be safe*; to *free* or *succor* (to bring help, relief and assistance). Elsewhere in scripture, it also translates as: to avenge, defend, rescue and preserve, as well as, salvation, deliverer and savior. In detail, this phrase is important, because it reveals that health represents more than just the general condition of the physical body; it also encompasses the soundness and vigor of one's entire being.

Many times, the condition of one's soul is revealed in the expressions of the countenance, which reflects the state of one's mental, emotional, physical and/or spiritual health. If any of these areas are out of alignment with the plan of God, there can be a negative manifestation of the soul. However, the soul that yields to the Word and will of the LORD also knows great freedom, joy and peace in Him, regardless of external circumstances. Therefore, our countenance, as well as our physical actions and the words of our mouths, become the tangible evidence of the well-being of our souls.

Worship and praise had become David's lifestyle and lifeline to God, even during the hard times. As he stilled his troubled soul in the presence of the LORD, he began to experience his physical transformation. The damaging stresses of David's life were replaced with the help, comfort and peace of the LORD. Through intimate worship and praise, David received spiritual and physical restoration, *deliverance, aid, victory, prosperity* and the saving health of his God.

Obviously, something happened between Psalm 42:5 and 42:11. There was a process to David's restoration. First, in his time of trouble, he sought the countenance, the face, and the presence of the LORD for his help. Then, he lifted his hands in **praise** *(H3034/H3027)*, with thanksgiving, and offered his *reverence* and *worship* to the LORD. Faithfully, the LORD responded to David's praise, and His help became the health of David's countenance. A supernatural transformation manifested.

Perhaps you've noticed that the Strong's Hebrew reference numbers for **help** *(H3444/H3467)* in Psalm 42:5 and **health** *(H3444/H3467)* in Psalm 42:11 have the same Hebrew reference numbers. The first reference number translates in the Hebrew as *yᵉshuʿáh (H3444)*. In the English language, *yᵉshuʿáh* translates as the name of **Jesus**. Christ Jesus is our Savior, our help, the health of our countenance and He delivers us from all oppression of the enemy.

Our hope in the LORD is motivation to praise Him and to trust that all is well. He embraces every situation of our lives and pours forth the help, healing and wholeness we need. Thereby, establishing us in His original intent and purpose of intimately knowing Him and experiencing His character, nature, splendor and glory in the earth. As we praise the LORD, He transforms us in the midst of our struggles. His magnificent power and presence envelopes our circumstances and brings peace.

6 — THE SATISFIED SOUL

The **satisfied** *(H7646)* soul is a contented, healthy soul that has *enough* joy within to meet its needs. It is *sufficed* and has no lack. It finds its *full satisfaction* in the LORD and will not be able to contain its praise.

<u>**Psalm 63:5-6**</u> *My soul shall be satisfied as with marrow and fatness; and my mouth shall praise thee with joyful lips: ⁶When I remember thee upon my bed, and meditate on thee in the night watches.*

In verse 6, to **remember** *(H2142)* the LORD means to *recognize* and *mark* Him as worthy of *mention*. It can also mean to mentally recount and record His goodness. When we're mindful of what the LORD has done, our praise is continually directed toward Him. We're aware of His power and presence, and we give attentive heed to Him, no matter the circumstance.

To **meditate** *(H1897)* in the night **watches** *(H821/ H8104)* is to *ponder*, study and *murmur*. It also means to engage in thought, contemplate and reflect on the LORD (His Word, His faithfulness, His character and His mighty acts) in the time of darkness. When we lay on our beds at night, we're to focus on the wonder of our God, including all the marvelous things He has done for us and the truth of His Word.

Even if we're going through a dark season in our lives (and we're unable to clearly discern what the LORD is doing), we can still know that He is *protecting*, *guarding* and *attending to* us. Indeed, in the midst of trial, our soul can be satisfied and we can express our contentment with stable emotions, sound thoughts and godly decisions. As we praise the LORD for His goodness, we allow Him to *hedge us about* in a place of preservation and safety.

MANIFESTS WHOLENESS, HEALTH & INTEGRITY
In Psalm 63:5, the satisfaction and vitality of the soul are also linked in description with the "***marrow and***

fatness" of the bones. Marrow is the flexible tissue on the inside of the bones. There are two types of marrow — red (productive) and yellow (supportive) — and both contain many blood vessels and capillaries. The red marrow produces three main blood cells: red (oxygen carrying), white (to strengthen the immune system and fight sickness and disease) and platelets (for wound healing). The fatty, yellow marrow supports the microenvironment, which facilitates and stimulates the work of the red marrow. When the red, white and platelet blood cells are mature, they're released from the marrow into circulating blood; thereby, providing strength and protection, health and healing, restoration and repair throughout the body. Thus, healthy marrow helps to nurture and maintain physical strength, through a strong defense against disease as well as the mending of the body.

The condition of the blood is directly affected by the bone marrow which, in turn, also affects the immune system. If the bone marrow is unhealthy it will produce weak and/or deformed blood cells. Thereby causing the body's oxygen, energy levels, immune system and healing ability to be compromised and diminished. An example of disease associated with deteriorating bone marrow and the production of deformed blood cells would be Leukemia, which is a cancer of the blood.

So what's the correlation between bone marrow and the satisfied soul? If the soul (which includes the mind, will and emotions) and spirit are healthy, the body will most likely be healthy. However, if the soul and spirit are in continuous turmoil and emotional upheaval, this could affect the health of the bone marrow which produces the blood cells that strengthen the immune system. If not properly dealt with, the sickness of the soul could cause the bones to dry up and the immune system to break down, thus compromising the body's overall health.

Most diseases have spiritual roots which originate within the deep places of the soul. Our thoughts and emotions can cause either healthy or destructive reactions to manifest in our physical bodies. In reference to the health and marrow of the bones, wrong thoughts, attitudes and emotions, such as shame and envy can cause rottenness and a drying up of the bones. Bitterness is, oftentimes, one of the hidden roots behind bone diseases (Proverbs 12:4, 14:30). The effects of shame, envy, bitterness, hatred, unforgiveness, pride, stubbornness and any other prolonged unhealthy emotion can literally eat a person alive from the inside out, and bring about a premature death. Yet, this does not have to happen. God's Word reveals that we have options according to:

Proverbs 17:22 *A merry heart doeth good like a medicine: but a broken spirit drieth up the bones.*

We can either choose to have a merry heart or a broken spirit. If we're broken, we don't need to stay

Part 2 • Loving God with All Your Soul

in that condition. We can seek the LORD for His healing and restoration in our lives. However, we must understand this: The extent to which we are willing to surrender our lives to the LORD (submit to and obey His Word) will greatly determine the impact and final outcome of our mental, emotional, spiritual and physical well-being.

In the context of Proverbs 17:22, the word **drieth** (H3001) means *to be ashamed, confused, disappointed* and *to dry up (as failing) or wither*; it's also translated as: to be confounded. Therefore, the spiritual roots of dry bones may be the result of condemnation and guilt related to shame, failure, scorning, disappointment, confusion and perplexity in a person's life. Perhaps they have been misunderstood, rejected, wrongly judged and criticized, abused or abandoned. Many times, those suffering from a broken spirit have experienced the effects of physical, emotional and mental wounds that have never been healed. The source of affliction may be self-induced or from an external source. Nevertheless, if the affected person does not release their pain to the LORD, it could cause not only their bones, but also their soul and spirit to dry up and wither away. Those with a broken spirit cannot function in a normal healthy manner, because the framework of their life is, literally, drying up from the inside out.

The opposite of a broken spirit is a merry heart! When the Word of God says a **merry** (H8056) heart doeth *good (H3190)* like a *medicine (H1456/H1455)* it's telling us that when we find the peace, understanding and wisdom of the LORD, all is *made well* and we're filled with *gleefulness* and rejoicing. When our heart is merry in the LORD, we *brighten up* and receive His protective and powerful *cure*, which prevents or *removes* the stinging pain, sorrows, disappointments and bitterness from past hurts and wounds. A gleeful heart receives the healing and blessing of the LORD. Thereby, maintaining or restoring joy, *beauty* and *soundness* to all that makes life seem *successful* and *right*. If we're to have a satisfied soul and a merry heart, we must obey the following scripture:

Ephesians 4:31 *Let all bitterness, and wrath, and anger, and clamour, and evil speaking, be put away from you, with all malice.*

Bitterness (G4088/G4089) is defined as *acridity*, which means to be extremely or sharply stinging or bitter; exceedingly caustic (cutting and sarcastic). Bitterness is *especially* defined as *poison, through the idea of* being overpoweringly *sharp (pungent)* and *piercing*. So, bitter people poison themselves with their own thoughts, words and actions. In addition, they lash out against others with the stinging, piercing bitterness that they so desperately cling to. Those who allow bitterness to reside within their souls will become imprisoned slaves to their chosen captivity.

When the root of **bitterness** is established, its emotional fruit will manifest as *wrath, anger, clamor, evil speaking* and *malice*. **Wrath** *(G2372)* means to *rush* with *fierceness, hard passion* and *indignation*. **Anger** *(G3709/G3713)* means to *reach out, covet* and *long for punishment* and *vengeance* against others. **Clamour** *(G2906/G2896)* is defined as *an outcry* (as in tumult, notification or grief); it also means to *croak* or *scream*, to *call* aloud (shriek, exclaim, entreat through crying out). **Evil speaking** *(G988)* refers to *vilification* (especially against God). It's also translated as blasphemy and railing. Those who spread rumors or make their thoughts known with the intent of causing hurt, hindrance or injury to others are speaking evil. **Malice** *(G2549/G2556)* is defined as *depravity*, active *malignity* or passive *trouble*. It's also translated as maliciousness, naughtiness and wickedness. Those who desire to love the LORD with all their soul must remove all these things from their lives. This cleansing must begin with the removal of the root of bitterness. Whatever is at the root becomes the primary source of trouble and defilement.

<u>**Hebrews 12:15**</u> *Looking diligently lest any man fail of the grace of God; lest any root of bitterness springing up trouble you, and thereby many be defiled.*

Bitterness of the soul pollutes every area of a person's life and hinders the grace of God from manifesting.

According to the Word of God, bitterness can cause weariness, as well as physical and emotional death (Job 10:1, 21:25). The sin of bitterness is also compared to wormwood, which signifies the painful experiences thru which a person clings to their resentful hostilities (Lamentations 3:15). Foolishness, greed, covetousness and a desire to control others are also manifestations of bitterness (Proverbs 17:25, Acts 8:18-24). A person's heart cannot be merry, nor their soul satisfied with marrow, if they're contaminated with the consequences of bitterness (Proverb 17:22, Psalm 63:5).

A bitter attitude is rooted in pride and self-justification. The proud, bitter person (who feels they've been violated, wounded or disappointed) tends to bear grudges against those who have offended them. Since their expectations weren't met, they feel entitled to judge others. Of course, the contamination of bitterness isn't worth the trouble it brings into a person's life or the pain it causes to others.

Cancer, arthritis, high blood pressure, heart disease and other auto immune diseases are, many times, directly connected to the sins of longstanding bitterness, anger, resentment, hatred and a failure to forgive others. These attitudes are sinful and destructive to those who embrace them. If not repented of and forsaken, the sins of the soul will become the demise of the body.

Anybody who's been hurt has had the opportunity to either become bitter or better through their experiences. Like any other emotion or attitude, bitterness is a choice.

Part 2 • *Loving God* with All Your Soul

If you want to go through life without meaningful relationships, suffer from sin-based diseases, die before your time and have a miserable life, just go ahead and keep your bitterness. Hold it close, nurture it, feed it and it will destroy you! The choice is yours, but you must know this: The bitter soul will never be satisfied.

Humility, repentance and forgiveness are required, if a person is to be set free from bitterness. Pride and offences must be cast aside. A willing submission and drawing near to the LORD will, in time, heal all pain, sorrows and disappointments (James 4:7-8, 10). He will bring deliverance and work all things together for good (Romans 8:28). God is a God of restoration, but we must live according to His Word. Remember, God resists the proud, but He gives grace to the humble (James 4:6).

MANIFESTS WHOLENESS, HEALTH & PROSPERITY

Referring again to Psalm 63:5, the soul is *"...satisfied as with marrow and fatness..."* This implies that the satisfied soul is nourished, productive, restorative and fat! In this context, **Fatness** (H1880/H1878) speaks of *anointing, abundance,* no lack and more than enough. To have an abundance of marrow is to have a wealth of health. The *satisfied* soul finds its fulfillment, healing and prosperity in the abundance of God's promises, as we see in:

3 John 1:2 *Beloved, I wish above all things that thou mayest prosper and be in health, even as they soul prospereth.*

CHAPTER 7 • SEVEN MANIFESTATIONS OF THE SOUL

The LORD desires for people to be prosperous and healthy. To **prosper** *(G2137)* and be in **health** *(G5198/ G5199/G837)* means *to be helped on the road* to achievement and to succeed in business affairs. Figuratively, it also refers to being mentally, emotionally, physically and spiritually *sound* and *whole*; thereby, causing the spirit, soul and body to flourish through the personal application of *true* biblical *doctrine* in one's life. As we prosper in the truth of God's Word, we also grow and mature spiritually. As the spirit continually feeds and matures on the Word of God, the soul also comes into alignment with God's plans and purposes. When the spirit and soul operate according to God's principles, this helps facilitate healing and wholeness, not only to the physical body, but to our entire well-being.

The LORD created us to flourish in Him. Each follower of Christ will, to some degree, impact the Body of Christ as a whole. The 'body' (whether physical or spiritual) has been endowed with purpose through the breath and life of God. Therefore, the healthy soul finds its true satisfaction in nothing less than God Himself. Wholeness, health and prosperity are the by-products of the completely satisfied soul.

The good measure of a healthy soul can be gauged by one's joy level, as well as one's spoken words. When the soul is satisfied and full of the life of God, it *shines* forth, *boasting* in the LORD and *celebrating* Him with

Part 2 • *Loving God* with All Your Soul

praise *(H1984)* and great glory. Regardless of life's circumstances, the soul that finds its pleasure in the LORD will live triumphantly and overflow with joy.

When we love the LORD with all our soul, He becomes the health, strength and light of our lives (Psalm 18:28, 27:1; Isaiah 60:1; Ephesians 5:8). Since He fills us with His Spirit and teaches us to flow in His anointing, all we need is found in Jesus. When we have Him, we have the fullness of abundant life, and our soul is satisfied (Psalm 23:5; Isaiah 61:1; John 10:10, 14:10).

HEALTH STARTS IN THE HEART

In relation to the satisfaction of the soul being compared to the fatness and marrow of bones (according to Psalm 63:5), we must also understand that the souls condition reflects what's going on in the inner sanctuary of the heart. If the heart is right toward God, then the body and soul will be right as well. The Word of God provides instructions for a dynamic health plan. It gives the advice we need to keep our bones and marrow strong, as well as how to live a long and happy life:

***Proverbs 3:1-8** My son, forget not my law; but let thine heart keep my commandments: ²For length of days, and long life, and peace, shall they add to thee. ³Let not mercy and truth forsake thee: bind them about thy neck; write them upon the table of thine heart: ⁴So shalt thou find favour and good understanding in the sight of God and man. ⁵Trust* *in the LORD with all thine heart; and lean not unto thine own understanding. ⁶In all thy ways acknowledge him, and he shall direct thy paths. ⁷Be not wise in thine own eyes: fear the LORD, and depart from evil. ⁸It shall be health to thy navel, and marrow to thy bones.*

In this portion of scripture, we see that the LORD wants us to be mindful of His words and hold them close in our hearts. The promises of God's Word motivate us and stir our desire to obey Him, as an act of love. The reward of this heartfelt love and obedience is blessing, increase, long life and peace.

There is great wisdom in Proverbs 3:1-2. In verse 2, the word **peace** *(H7965/H7999)* means being *complete* and having *health, prosperity* and *safety*. Elsewhere in scripture, it also translates as: favor, rest, wholeness and restoration. Many people are looking for peace, and God has shown us where to find its prescription. Peace, as well as long life, is found in knowing the LORD and obeying His Word.

In Proverbs 3:3, the LORD commands, *"Let not mercy and truth forsake thee: bind them about thy neck; write them upon the table of thine heart."* Mercy *(H2617/H2616)* is defined and translated as *kindness, beauty,* favor, good deeds and reproofs, which we come to know while walking in devout *piety towards God*. **Truth** *(H571/H539)* is defined as the *faithfulness; stability* and *verity established* in God's Word. The Lord extends His mercy and truth to us and we're to receive them as treasured possessions, and apply them to our lives.

We're not to allow mercy and truth to *forsake* (H5800) us. We're not to *loosen* or *relinquish* them. They're to be inscribed, celebrated and enclosed within our hearts. Mercy and truth are traits that should be operating in all those who say they love, serve and obey the LORD.

To *bind* (H7194) mercy and truth about the *neck* (H1621/H1641) means to *knit, tie, confine, love and make a league*. This speaks of making a covenant. Figuratively, it means to *ruminate* — chew on, meditate, muse, continue to ponder and savor the mercy and truth of God. As we do, we'll begin to understand that the LORD is *trustworthy* and *faithful*; He brings *stability* and assurance to our lives. We're to allow the Word of God to be written upon every area of our lives, including our hearts, minds, emotions and desires. God's mercy and *truth* should always be in our thoughts and at the center of our lives — enclosed, knit and tied into the very core of our being.

According to Proverbs 3:4, if we join ourselves to mercy and truth, the *favor* (H2580/H2603), *kindness* and *beauty* of the LORD is *bestowed* upon us. This means He will *graciously bend or stoop* down *to abide with* us and take pleasure in us. His abiding presence will direct us through His kindness, wisdom, intelligence, discretion, prudence and expert instruction; through Him we'll have good success.

Isn't it amazing that the God of all creation would actually bend down and delight Himself in us? In addition, this kind of favor means that the LORD Jesus will *implore (move to favor by petition)* the Heavenly Father on our behalf. Jesus demonstrates the amazing Father heart of God. It's His nature to teach us, intercede for us and dote over us. He desires to bless us in every area of life. Experiencing a successful life is to know and fulfill the fullness of God's perfect will. Experiencing God's perfect will is the fruit of delighting in Him.

Proverbs 3:5-6, reminds us that we are to trust in the LORD — not our own understanding, strength or ability. If we will learn to see things from the LORD's perspective, He will strengthen our areas of weakness and redeem our failures as opportunities for growth and maturity. Our former flaws and fiascos will become stepping stones to success in Him. We are to draw on His wisdom and allow Him to lead and teach us the lessons of life.

When we *acknowledge (H3045)* the LORD in all our *ways (H1870/H1869)*, we come to a place in our relationship with Him where we *observe* and discern how He operates in the large and small details of our lives. By acknowledging the LORD and following His *instruction*, we allow Him to lead us along a *road* or *course of life,* which will guide us into His ordained paths of righteousness. In so doing, we'll avoid the pitfalls and snares of the devil. By divine design, as we acknowledge the LORD, He **directs** *(H3474)* the events and experiences of our life journeys toward a *pleasant* place. He causes all things to flow into the *right* order and into perfect alignment with the will of God. This is when we experience the *prosperity* and blessing He has always intended for us.

In Proverbs 3:7, we're instructed to not be wise in our own eyes, but to fear the LORD and depart from evil. If we love and trust the LORD, we'll choose to honor, respect and reverently fear Him for who He is. We'll make lifestyle choices that will help us to decline and **depart** *(H5493)* from all involvement with **evil** *(H7451/H7489)*. To depart from evil is *to turn off*, revolt and rebel against those things which cause affliction, adversity, harm, misery, distress and wickedness. Therefore, we'll forsake all that's *physically*, *morally* and *socially* bad or displeasing to the LORD. Evil is a destructive force; it's *good for nothing*. It *spoils (literally by breaking to pieces)* everything it touches and influences. When we depart from evil, submit to the LORD and allow Him to take full control of our lives, He promises to give us the blessing of health:

<u>**Proverbs 3:8**</u> **It shall be health to thy navel and marrow to thy bones.**

Aside from Salvation, our greatest wealth is our health. This word **health** *(H7500/H7495)* means *a cure* and *to* *mend*. Elsewhere in scripture, it is also translated as: to heal, repair and thoroughly make whole. Therefore, when we remember the words of the LORD; embrace His mercy and truth; find His favor; trust in Him; acknowledge Him; depart from evil and fear Him, health, healing and wholeness are the result.

Proverbs 3:8 also speaks of health to our navel, but what does this mean? The ***navel (H8270/H8324)*** is another word for *the umbilical cord* (which connected us to our natural life source while we were in our mother's womb). Figuratively, the navel can also represent *the centre of strength*. Without that connection we would have died before we could have taken our first breath. Likewise, in a spiritual sense, we must be connected to the LORD if we're to receive our sustenance of life, health, healing, restoration and wholeness. He is the only one who can supply all that we need. If we are disconnected, there is no way for Him to feed His life into us. Jesus spoke of the need for this divine connection to Him in:

<u>**John 14:4-5**</u> ***Abide in me, and I in you. As the branch cannot bear fruit of itself, except it abide in the vine; no more can ye, except ye abide in me. ⁵I am the vine, ye are the branches: He that abideth in me, and I in him, the same bringeth forth much fruit: for without me ye can do nothing.***

Just as the umbilical cord connects an unborn baby with its mother to provide life and nutrition, we must be properly connected to the LORD. The natural umbilical connection provides what is needed for a baby to develop and grow strong enough to survive outside the womb. Likewise, the LORD is our lifeline. As we stay in unity with Him and grow in the things of God, He pours His life into us and gives us everything we need to survive in this world. In the areas of life which have died or suffered damaged, He's able to heal, strengthen, repair, rebuild, restore and resurrect. He is the master Creator; He knows how to give us new life and refresh our souls!

7 — THE REDEEMED SOUL

The redeemed heart and soul have been bought by the blood of Jesus. They are undergoing His process of total transformation, thereby, bringing change to the condition, nature and character of the heart and soul. These changes will be evidenced in the thoughts, words, actions and lifestyle of a believer. We see this in:

Psalm 19:14 **_Let the words of my mouth, and the meditation of my heart, be acceptable in thy sight, O LORD, my strength, and my redeemer._**

The term **words** (H561/H559) is defined in the Hebrew as *something said* or something answered. Elsewhere in the Bible, it is translated as: boasting, challenging, communing, promising, publishing and reporting. Our words are the direct results of our thinking; therefore, our thoughts are the seeds from which our spoken words germinate. Our thoughts and how we voice those thoughts will determine whether our spoken words will be acceptable to the LORD or not.

Meditation *(H1902/H1897)* is to make *a murmuring sound, a musical notation* or a *solemn* sound, as we *ponder* in thought. Murmured words may express pleasure, anger or any other emotion or feeling. Jesus said, "*...for out of the abundance of the heart the mouth speaketh*" (Matthew 12:24). What we meditate upon in our hearts, will eventually come out of our mouths, and it will reflect the focus of our mental ponderings, whether they be good or evil.

A right heart filled with right thoughts will release right words. Those right words create a fountain of life that brings great *pleasure* and *delight* to the LORD. This is what it means for our words to be *acceptable (H7522/H7521)* in His sight. Our thoughts and words are to be a melodious symphony in harmonious agreement with God's Word.

Most specifically, our words and lifestyle are to reflect the knowledge that our debt of sin has been paid and fully *satisfied* by Christ; He has redeemed us from all the curse of the Law. By the blood of Jesus and thru His righteousness and grace, we're saved from the penalty of sin, hell, death and the grave. We're redeemed by what Christ has done on our behalf, not by our own works or self-righteousness. If the meditations of our hearts and the words of our mouths exhibit this knowledge, then every utterance will be as a sweet savor before the LORD.

Overall, Psalm 19:14 is a manifestation or expression of David's desire to be pleasing and acceptable to the LORD. David knew he had to make the LORD his top priority in life, because He didn't want to fall into sin or allow it to have dominion over him (Psalm 19:13). Therefore, he purposed to bring the thoughts of his heart and the words of his mouth into proper alignment with the Word of God.

Through experience, David learned how the LORD was his **strength** *(H6697/H6696)* — his *rock* and *refuge* of fortified safety. In turn, his words of testimony revealed the fruit of his experience. David knew he could run into the presence of the LORD and be hidden in the safe *confines* of the secret place of the Most High God. He could dwell under the shadow of the Almighty, in the safety of His covenant promises (Psalm 91:1, 4). In this place, David did not fear the distresses and assaults of the enemy of his soul. He understood that in the midst of all his trials, his God was his faithful avenger and deliverer. He also recognized and acknowledged the LORD as his **redeemer** *(H1350)* — his *next of kin,* who would ransom, *buy back* and care for his soul and all that was rightly his.

David belonged to the LORD and he knew His secret place of intimacy and worship. Therefore, despite his circumstances, the condition of his heart and the words of his mouth reflected the understanding, truth and wisdom of that cherished relationship (Psalm 49:3).

Likewise, we must realize that, no matter how much the devil may rage against the people of God (with all his taunts and torments), satan still has no power against the saint of God who runs into the presence and mercy of their redeeming King. David knew the power of his God to redeem his soul, not only in life, but also in death:

<u>Psalm 49:15</u> But God will redeem my soul from the power of the grave: for he shall receive me. Selah

Though David spoke these words concerning his own soul, they were also prophetic words concerning the resurrection of Christ from the dead. When David wrote this verse, redemption was a thing of the future; nobody could be redeemed by the blood of Christ until His blood was shed upon the cross of Calvary. But once the atoning work of Christ was complete, it became available for all who would receive it. All who follow Christ are redeemed from the power of the grave!

In this verse, **redeem** *(H6299)* is defined as *to sever, ransom, release* and *preserve.* Basically, it means to deliver by any means and rescue the soul from the **power** *(H3027)* of the grave. This power of the grave indicates the authoritative custody, dominion, pain, terror, state and *means* by which **hell** *(H7585/H7592)* seeks to *demand* and press charges against us for our sins. Jesus — the ransomed Lamb of God — died in our place, completely freeing us from all the penalty of sin. Though He died, the grave could not retain the sinless Christ in its grasp. He ascended to the Father, as the spotless Lamb of God who carried away the sins of world, on the behalf of mankind. Death could not hold Him, and it cannot hold those who are called by His name. Just as Christ rose from the dead, those who are in Christ have been severed from the power of death; they've risen with Him and sit in heavenly places (Ephesians 1:3, 1:20, 2:6; 1 Corinthians 15:53-57). Hallelujah! We can rejoice! The power of the grave has been rendered powerless and has been completely cut off from the redeemed soul! Therefore, we can declare with David:

Psalm 71:23 *My lips shall greatly rejoice when I sing unto thee; and my soul, which thou hast redeemed.*

The redemption of our souls is the greatest cause for rejoicing. To **rejoice** *(H7442)* in song is to make music and cry out with celebrating praise and *shouts of joy* and triumph. Let's be clear; this is not simply a concert of hymns. The type of rejoicing described here means *to creak or emit a stridulous sound*, which is a harsh, shrill or grating sound. This is raucous commemoration of what the LORD has done for and in us. In this way, the **lips** become the delivery system of the treasured events of the soul. If our soul is redeemed, we are to make it known:

Psalm 107:2 *Let the redeemed of the LORD say so, whom he hath redeemed from the hand of the enemy.*

In this verse, to be redeemed from the hand of the *enemy (H6862/H6887)* is to be released by ransom from the means, power and direction of an adversarial *opponent*, whose intent is to shut us into *cramped, tight places* of *trouble*, affliction, tribulation, distress, sorrow, anguish, torment, oppression and vexation of the soul. Thereby, pressing us into *narrow* thinking, causing our vision to be limited, and hindering us from moving forward into our destiny.

In addition, this word *enemy (H6862)* is also defined as *a pebble (as in H6864)*, which is *a stone, pressed hard or to a point*; this implies *a knife*. Furthermore, the reference number describing the word 'pebble' *(H6864)* is from *(H6696)* which also means *to cramp* or *confine* in an enclosing or *hostile* manner. Two lessons we can learn from these definitions are:

1) The enemy's main objective is to steal, kill and destroy, but he may masquerade in a cloaked disguise that would seem less threatening to his potential victim. While he intends to pierce through our lives with fiery darts (as with a knife), we may wrongly view him as only a confining or distressing opponent, aimed at simply making us uncomfortable and unproductive. We must realize that the enemy of our souls is out to destroy our very lives, not just our lifestyle. It is Christ's sacrifice that has ransomed us from the piercing knife and destruction of the enemy (John 10:10; Ephesians 6:6).

2) When the Lord provides a confined place (Psalm 19:14; 91:1, 4), it's a place of provision, strength and safety. On the contrary, if we allow the enemy to force us into a confined place, it will be a place of deception, harm and hostility. Again, the enemy of our souls always has a wicked counterfeit to what the LORD has created. It's imperative that we purpose in our hearts to encourage ourselves and one another to seek the face of God and openly declare His truth. In so doing, we'll not fall into the intended schemes of the devil.

After all, when we're reaching out to the hands that were pierced and bloodied on our behalf, the hand of the enemy cannot restrain us. Praise the Lord! It's in Christ that we find our salvation and total transformation. As the redeemed, we live in the favor of God, rejoicing and proclaiming His goodness as we're changed into His likeness.

Is your soul redeemed?

Are you rejoicing in your deliverance?

Are you telling others how they can be redeemed?

CHAPTER 8

THE THIRSTY SOUL

God revealed so much to me concerning this eighth manifestation of the soul, it warrants its own chapter. A healthy soul will thirst for, crave and diligently seek the refreshing presence of the LORD. It will intimately drink of the river of life that flows from the throne of God (Revelation 22:1). Jesus Christ said that He was the giver of living water, and that whosoever would drink of Him would find eternal life and would never thirst again (John 4:10, 14). We must drink of Christ — the Word of God made flesh — if we're to have life in our souls; only then, will we be truly satisfied. As you read and ponder the conditions and characteristics of the thirsty soul, I challenge you to allow the LORD to satiate your entire being with His unending and everlasting waters of eternal life.

When you think of someone with a thirsty soul, which biblical person comes to mind? My first thought is of King David — a passionate worshipper. The LORD said of Him, *"...I have found David, the son of Jesse, a man after mine own heart, which shall fulfill all my will"* (Acts 13:22). When the scripture says that David was a man *after* (G2596) God's own heart, this indicates that he passionately desired to touch and be joined to the heart of his God, whom he cherished.

Part 2 • *Loving God* with All Your Soul

David wrote of how his soul thirsted for (and pursued after) God with mighty *intensity:*

Psalm 42:1-2 *As the hart panteth after the water brooks, so panteth my soul after thee, O God. ²My soul thirsteth for God, for the living God: when shall I come and appear before God?*

MANIFESTS A DEEP DESIRE

When David described how his soul **panteth** *(H6165),* he was saying that he *longed* for God with an earnest and strong desire. He craved to be refreshed by the LORD, as he sought to drink in His presence. In an effort to help satisfy his spiritual thirst, David made it a priority to seek the LORD early as indicated in:

Psalm 63:1-4 *O God, thou art my God; early will I seek thee: my soul thirsteth for thee, my flesh longeth for thee in a dry and thirsty land, where no water is; ²To see thy power and thy glory, so as I have seen thee in the sanctuary. ³Because thy lovingkindness is better than life, my lips shall praise thee. ⁴Thus will I bless thee while I live: I will lift up my hands in thy name.*

When David said, "...*early will I seek (H7836) thee...*" it meant that he was up at the *dawn* of the morning, *earnestly searching* for and *painstakingly* pursuing after the LORD. He had to satisfy the longing — the deep yearning and passion — he had for his God, and it was God alone who could satisfy David's diligent spiritual thirst. David knew that his God was his lifeline; without Him, David's life would have been a barren desert of failure, destruction and corruption. He was thirsting to see the **power** *(H5797/H5810)*, *strength, force, security, majesty* and *praise* of His God. David wanted to experience the *weight* of rich **glory** *(H3519/ H3513)*, *copious splendor* and the honor of being in the sacred place, in the midst of God's holiness. To be wholly consecrated before the LORD was his greatest desire.

David understood the **loving kindness** *(H2617)* of the LORD, since it had operated in abundance within his life. He had come to know the *beauty* (favor and mercy), as well as the *reproofs* and correction of the LORD. These things were better than life itself, because David was experiencing the reality of his God. As he knelt in *adoration* before the LORD, he made a lifetime commitment to **bless** *(H1288)* Him. Offering up **praise** *(H7623)*, he commended the LORD with a *loud* voice and shouts of triumph. David yielded himself to the power of God, and he lifted his hands to acknowledge the position, honor, authority, character and infamous renown of His LORD and King. David also lifted up his hands in anticipation of experiencing the revealed glory of God. He knew that His God was the only one who could truly satisfy his longing.

***Psalm 143:6** I stretch forth my hands unto thee: my soul thirsteth after thee, as a thirsty land. Selah*

David, stretched apart his open hands to the LORD, trusting Him to meet and fulfill the longing of his soul. The beauty of the thirsty soul reaching out to the LORD is that He longs to pour out the living waters of life upon those who seek Him. If we, in earnest desire for the LORD, will lift our hands to Him, He will never allow our thirsty soul to die in the wilderness.

WATER IN THE WILDERNESS

The first time the word 'thirst' is mentioned in scripture occurs after the children of Israel came out of the land of Egypt. They were transitioning from slavery and bondage into freedom, and it was not a comfortable journey. They were in the wilderness of Sin (pronounced, Seen), complaining about the lack of water. They didn't realize that their thirst was just a challenge that would become the catalyst for a miracle. It would cause them to see the power and provision of the LORD supernaturally manifest on their behalf. Though they cried out with complaints and a lack of faith, the LORD knew exactly what He would do.

Exodus 17:1-6 *And all the congregation of the children of Israel journeyed from the wilderness of Sin, after their journeys, according to the commandment of the LORD, and pitched in Rephidim: and there was no water for the people to drink. ²Wherefore the people did chide with Moses, and said, Give us water that we may drink. And Moses said unto them, Why chide ye with me?*

wherefore do ye tempt the LORD? ³And the people thirsted there for water; and the people murmured against Moses, and said, Wherefore is this that thou hast brought us up out of Egypt, to kill us and our children and our cattle with thirst? ⁴And Moses cried unto the LORD, saying, What shall I do unto this people? they be almost ready to stone me. ⁵And the LORD said unto Moses, Go on before the people, and take with thee of the elders of Israel; and thy rod, wherewith thou smotest the river, take in thine hand, and go. ⁶Behold, I will stand before thee there upon the rock in Horeb; and thou shalt smite the rock, and there shall come water out of it, that the people may drink. And Moses did so in the sight of the elders of Israel.

As I was considering this text, I realized that the LORD led his people to a place of thirstiness. The scripture says they journeyed from the wilderness of **Sin** *(H5512)*, which was a *desert*, and pitched in Rephidim. The primitive root meaning of **Rephidim** *(H7508/H7507/H7502)* is defined as: to *spread* a bed; by implication, it means to *refresh* and comfort. The LORD had brought them to a place of rest, refreshing, and comfort, yet they didn't see it for what it was.

When the children of Israel left Egypt, they also left behind all that was familiar to them. The old way of life was a thing of the past, and the new way was yet to come. They were leaving the outskirts of their Egyptian bondage and moving forward in their journey to freedom. Their transition was difficult; they did not have effortless access to what they needed, and their faith was tested in their wilderness experience. Clearly, they were in a situation where only the LORD could meet their needs, and He would have to do it by miraculous, supernatural means.

As one might expect, while traveling through the desert, the people became extremely thirsty. They wanted and needed water, but they were unaware of any available water source. When they couldn't meet their own needs, they became frustrated. Instead of looking to God as their source, they began to **chide** *(H7378)* with Moses, demanding that he meet their needs. This means they had become contentious and started pleading and complaining, as they raised *controversy* and accusations against Moses. The people became obstinate in their murmurings against him and began to begrudge his leadership. Instead of trusting in the LORD'S provision, they falsely accused Moses of bringing them into the wilderness to kill them with thirst.

The people became so angry, they wanted to kill Moses. Now, how smart was that? Take out the anointed leader? Then what would they do? But isn't that the way carnally minded people think and respond sometimes? They can become so focused on themselves, what they want, when they want it, how they want it, why they want it and where they want it, that they can't see the bigger picture of what God is doing in their lives. The people's complaints did nothing to better or change their circumstances. The children of Israel could have accused Moses and whined all day long about their situation and not one drop of water would have manifested to quench their thirst.

LESSONS IN THE WILDERNESS
The wilderness of transition is where life lessons are taught and experienced. God isn't moved by complaints, doubts, fears, unbelief, lack or dire circumstances. God responds to faith. Without faith it's impossible to please Him (Hebrews 11:6). When we come to God, we must believe, first of all, that He is; He exists and is well able to help us in our time of need. Secondly, we must believe that, when we diligently seek Him, He will reward us. When we have faith and trust in the LORD; when we bring our petitions before Him, believing that He will hear and answer us, this causes the heart and hand of God to be moved on our behalf.

Moses was a humble man who believed and trusted in his God. It was through his intercession and faith, and not the complaints of the people, that the LORD met their need. God answered Moses and directed him to gather the elders of Israel together, to take up his rod and meet with Him upon the rock in Mount

Horeb. The name **Horeb** *(H2722/H2717)* is defined as a *desolate* place, being *parched through drought* and destruction. Remarkably, it was in this dry, decaying place, that the LORD would bring forth pure, refreshing, thirst quenching, life-giving, cleansing water from a rock. The word **rock** *(H6697/H6696)* is defined as *a cliff or boulder, a precipitous edge*, and figuratively, *a refuge.* Elsewhere in scripture, 'rock' is also translated as: mighty God, strength, etc. So, God chose to demonstrate His power as the miraculous provider of Israel by bringing forth water out of a rock. By doing so, He symbolically illustrated that He was a solid refuge for His people in the midst of desolation. God heard the cry of a faithful intercessor and He responded powerfully on behalf of His people.

This is such a marvelous picture of how God operates! He delivers us from bondage, takes us out of the old life of slavery and oppression and leads us into a new life of promise and blessing. Yet, during the course of transition, He brings us to a place in the wilderness — a place of need where we realize our utter dependence upon Him for our survival. When we see the LORD as our only life source, we begin to experience Him in a supernatural dimension.

Our life in the LORD is a tailor made adventure to prepare us for destiny. There will be times when we'll find ourselves living on the edge of the precipitous cliffs of life. As we seek God's face and cry out to

Him, He will lead us in new directions, callings, experiences and territories that are unfamiliar to us. This is usually a good indicator that the LORD is leading us into a new season of life. Yet, if we're to walk into our new seasons of destiny, and experience the fullness of blessing that He has for us, it's imperative that we allow the LORD to lead us out of our comfort zones.

We must be willing to venture into the unknown, if we're to experience a deeper, richer, relationship and a greater level of understanding with our God. We may have to leave behind everything that is familiar and comfortable. Indeed, it's in the uncomfortable places and in the transitions of life, that we experience the supernatural power of God working on our behalf.

As the children of Israel cried against Moses, and then Moses cried out to God, there was already a plan, but it was something far different than anything they had previously experienced. This redeemed nation of people would see God miraculously provide for them. He wanted them to have a deeper understanding of who He was and how much He loved them and desired to care for them. The LORD revealed His plan of supernatural provision as recorded in:

***Exodus 17:6** Behold, I will stand before thee there upon the rock in Horeb; and thou shalt smite the rock, and there shall come water out of it, that the people may drink. And Moses did so in the sight of the elders of Israel.*

God Himself was going to stand before Moses as he obeyed the command to 'smite' the rock. There was a partnership going on between them. God had the provision, but Moses had to cooperate to bring it forth. God could have smitten the rock, or spoken to it, or cracked it wide open and caused rivers of water to come forth. But the LORD was establishing Moses' leadership, as well as building up the faith of the people. Moses could not have performed the miracle without the LORD, and the LORD was not going to perform it without Moses. If Moses had heard the voice of the LORD and went to the rock, but refused to smite it as the LORD commanded, then the people would have remained thirsty, and some may have even died. It was through Moses' obedience to the Word of God, that the supernatural provision of God was released to the people.

CHRIST IN THE WILDERNESS

Let me pause to stress something that we must understand: When the LORD speaks and commands His people to do something, He's not making friendly chit chat. He means business. He always has a purpose and a specific plan of how that purpose is to be fulfilled. When the LORD speaks, it's our responsibility to be obedient to what He says.

When God told Moses to **smite** *(H5221)* the rock, this meant that Moses was *to strike* or beat the rock. This may sound crazy, but there was prophetic significance to the command. Both the Old and New Testaments refer to the LORD as a rock or stone; let's discuss the significance of this correlation.

In the Old Testament, the LORD is referred to as the rock of our salvation. He is our shield, our high tower, our refuge, our Savior, our deliverer and our strength in which we trust. He is referred to as the stone which the builders refused, yet He was the headstone of the corner (the standard for building all things), the tried stone, the precious cornerstone and a sure foundation (2 Samuel 22:3, 47; Psalms 18:2, 46, 62:7, 89:26, 95:1, 118:22; Isaiah 28:16). In the New Testament, Jesus is the stone which the builders rejected — the chief cornerstone, which set the foundation for the church — a stumbling stone, a rock of offense and a living stone (Mark 12:10; Luke 20:17-18; Acts 4:11; Romans 9:33; Ephesians 2:20-22; 1 Peter 2:4-8). Thus, the 'rock' in Mount Horeb was a picture of the coming Messiah, Jesus Christ.

Even as God told Moses to smite the rock, Christ (our rock) was struck and afflicted. He was wounded for our transgressions; He was bruised for our iniquities; the chastisement of our peace was upon Him; and by His stripes we were healed (Isaiah 53:5). It was through His beatings, stripes, fatal wounding and the blood that flowed from His body, that we could be cleansed of all sin.

His death made it possible for us to be worthy to partake of the living waters of eternal life. Mankind

Part 2 • *Loving God* with All Your Soul

must come to the Christ, the 'rock of salvation' to receive the blessings and provision of God and to enter into relationship with the heavenly Father. The waters of life, which freely flow from the merciful heart of God, are offered to all who will believe in Him — to all who are willing to come and drink of the 'rock' (Isaiah 44:3; John 4:10, 14).

Motivations & Expectations in the Wilderness

When the children of Israel were in the wilderness, they were desperate. They needed water to survive. But there was a process by which God would bring forth the miracle of provision.

The truth is: God is desirously looking for those who will respond to Him in faith. He will grant miracles and supernatural provision to those who are willing to follow and obey Him. The LORD knows exactly what He wants to do in and through our lives. If we want to see the power and glory of the LORD flow like water from the rock, we must allow Him to lead us into what we're to do, as well as how, when, why, where and with whom we're to do it.

If Moses had hit any other rock than the one God prescribed, there would have been no water; and Moses would have been in trouble with the LORD. Faith, trust, humility, a love for God and obedience are required, for the miraculous to be released. Just as the LORD proved Himself to be a strong refuge for Israel, He is still our strong refuge and our rock of salvation today. Only through trusting obedience will we be able to receive of Him and drink of the waters of life.

Periodically, we need to check the condition of our hearts and take inventory of our souls, to see if we're truly loving and trusting in the LORD (2 Corinthians 13:5). It's possible to want the blessing of God, without really desiring the God of the blessing. To seek deliverance from dire circumstances or uncomfortable situations, without thirsting for the presence of the LORD, is to lack understanding of the love relationship He desires with us. If we want what God has for us, but we're not willing to walk in love and obedience, then our attitude is selfish and ungodly, and the blessings will not come.

We may feel like we're facing overwhelming struggles in our own wilderness experiences of life. We may imagine that we're dying of thirst and not going to make it to the end of our spiritual journey. In wrestling with doubts and unbelief, we may fear that the LORD is not paying attention, moving fast enough on our behalf or responding to our needs, like we think He should. We may become angry with Him or those whom we expect to take care of us, in our time of desperation. It's in the tough situations of life, when we don't understand or we don't know what to do, that our faith is being tried and tested. When this happens, we must learn to see beyond our current circumstance, and reach out to the Father's heart. If not, our tendency will be to pass an unrighteous judgment against God, when in reality, we should be judging ourselves. When it comes right down to it, it doesn't really matter how we feel about things. What matters is that we continue to seek the LORD and listen to His solutions to the problems we face in life.

If we (in our limited, fleshly understanding) judge God to be unfaithful or untrustworthy, then a corrupt seed has been allowed to take root in our souls. If we allow this ignorant and carnal mindset to displace God from His rightful position upon the throne of our hearts, then the god of our self-will has taken over. Because the carnal self-will is not led by the Spirit of God and has departed from His wisdom, foolish behavior and wrong decisions are inevitable. Therefore, if we are determined to fulfill our own fleshly desires and work out our own solutions, in our own limited ability and understanding — without the counsel and direction of God's Word — then we will exhaust all our wisdom, strength and resources. The consequence of our actions will negatively affect us, as well as those around us; tragedy and/or failure will result.

Those who do not trust the LORD to be their protector and provider will tend to put their trust and unrealistic expectations upon family members, friends, leaders and those in governmental positions. When expectations are not met, they become angry or desperate and behave foolishly. We see this today, as nations rise up against government leaders in the midst of civil upheaval and natural or national disasters. They expect mere men to be able to fix the issues and problems that run rampant in the world today. But God never intended for us to fully depend on our own strength, ability, resources, human understanding or other people. He has designed life in such a way that, all things are held together in Him (Colossians 1:17). If we exile God from our existence, our lives will fall apart; we'll never experience life to the fullest, because God Himself is the fullness of life. It's time to get our priorities straight. We cannot drink from manmade cisterns that have been polluted with political agenda and false ideologies, and expect to be satisfied. We cannot place our expectations on man, for those things which only God can provide and fulfill.

What wilderness experiences are you facing today?

What transitions are taking place in your life?

Has God led you into a thirsty place?

Are you doing what God has required of you in the miracle working process?

Are you drinking from the 'rock of salvation' and allowing Him to meet your needs today?

RIVERS, FOUNTAINS, POOLS & SPRINGS – OH MY!
God loves all people and He created human beings with relationship in mind. He has always desired to

Part 2 • *Loving God* with All Your Soul

have intimate fellowship with mankind, but we must first choose to believe in Him. For those of us who do choose to believe, the Lord has various ways of communicating with us, ministering to us and refreshing us. He takes great delight in being our Heavenly Father and Provider. For example, He has great compassion for the poor and needy, and He promises to provide for those who will seek Him:

<u>**Isaiah 41:17-18**</u> *When the poor and needy seek water, and there is none, and their tongue faileth for thirst, I the LORD will hear them, I the God of Israel will not forsake them.* ¹⁸*I will open rivers in high places, and fountains in the midst of the valleys: I will make the wilderness a pool of water, and the dry land springs of water.*

So who exactly are the poor and needy? The **poor** *(H6041/H6031)* are those who have been *depressed in mind or circumstances*. They may have been humbled by being beaten and cast down, weakened, hurt, ravished, afflicted and placed or forced into a lower position through hardship. The **needy** *(H34/H14)* are those who are in *want*, especially in their *feelings* and emotions. They're destitute to the point of begging for what they need. They deeply yearn or *breathe after* (as if panting for) the satisfaction of their need with an acquiescent, submissive willingness. In desperation, they will do most anything to have their need met. All of us have been poor and/or needy at some point in our lives.

In Isaiah 41:17, to **seek** *(H1245)* means *to search out by any method*, but *specifically, through worship or prayer*; it also implies *to strive after*. This is what catches the heart of God and causes Him to **hear** *(H6030)* the petitions we bring before Him. As He hears and *responds* to a heart of worship, He gives close *attention* and takes *heed*, concerning the specific needs and concerns of the worshipper. Why does the LORD respond to worship and prayer? The answer is very simple: it takes faith and humility to come to Him in this way. In spite of what's going on, faith rises up and says, "LORD, I need you, I love you, I want you, and I'm going to follow you, praise you, worship you and obey you, no matter what!" This type of worshipper will experience the reward of their faith (Hebrews 11:6).

In Isaiah 41:17-20, the LORD says that when the poor and needy seek water, because their **tongue** *(H3956)* **faileth** *(H5405)* **for thirst**, He will be faithful to hear and answer them. This means, there may be times when the ability to (literally or figuratively) drink, eat or talk (i.e. get refreshment, nourishment or communicate) has failed, been *eliminated* or *dried up*. During those times, when we cry out to Him in worship and/or prayer, He will miraculously quench our spiritual and natural thirst. Not only will He supply and meet all our needs, but He will do it abundantly. After all, He is God and all things are possible with Him (Matthew 19:26; Mark 9:23, 10:27).

Whenever we feel poor and needy, it's good to know that the LORD is a covenant keeping God, and He promises to not *forsake (H5800)* us. He's absolutely committed to keep the promises of His Word. Therefore, He will never *permit* us to be *loosened* or *relinquished* from the power of His presence. He will never fail us, refuse us or leave us in a state of destitution. He is our refuge and strength — our very present help in the time of trouble (Psalm 46:1; Hebrews 13:5). He will supply for us, regardless of what part of life's journey we're currently experiencing.

For the thirsty soul, He promises to open rivers in the high places; fountains in the valleys; pools in the wilderness; and springs in the dry lands. The LORD willingly pours out the water of life to all who are thirsty for Him. It doesn't matter if we're in the high places, the low places, the desolate places or the dry places of life. His grace, mercy and provision are still available. In Isaiah 41:18, to *open (H6605)* these supernatural water sources, means that the LORD causes the flow of life giving water to be *loosed*, so it can flow and break forth upon us freely. As these flows of water are *opened wide*, we're refreshed in spirit, soul and body. These God ordained waters of cleansing and refreshing begin *to plough* through us and *carve* their path of blessing into the fibers of our existence. As the Spirit of God does this, He removes everything that's inadequate, unclean, unholy and useless. He replaces those things with His healing, restoration, strength, hope, life and a sense of purpose and vision. Those who are thirsty for the LORD will be satisfied.

Let's take a closer look at the beauty of the flowing waters of the LORD. As we look at these definitions, find a way to connect the meanings to your own life. Claim the joy of God's goodness and provision for yourself.

Rivers in the High Places

Rivers (H5102) are defined as *sparkling, cheerful,* radiantly *running streams*. The dancing waters have their own sheen and reflect their unique beauty and luster. Figuratively, rivers also mean *to assemble*; this can be seen as they flow together as one. A sparkling, shining river is clean and free of pollution and contaminates. It's a source of satisfying refreshment and brings cheer, comfort and revitalization to the one receiving its benefits. When the rivers of God flow into our lives, we are completely rejuvenated.

The **high** (H8205/H8192) places are prominent, well known, worn down, naked, exposed, bare places. They stick out visibly for all to see. We may go through experiences that cause us to feel worn down. We may have bare places that have been exposed for all to see.

Yet, the LORD promises that as we seek Him, worship Him and commune with Him in prayer, He'll cause His sparkling rivers of cheer to assemble into the bare (naked and exposed) places of our lives. That which was previously impoverished and lacking in the essentials of life will experience the flow of His blessing. Compassionately, the LORD will wash away all emptiness and shame related to such places in our lives.

FOUNTAINS IN THE VALLEYS

Fountains *(H4599/H5869)* refer to *springs* and fresh water wells. Figuratively, these fountains are *a source of satisfaction* and favor. The root word for fountains in the Hebrew is *'ayin* and it is defined as *an eye* (sight); by analogy, the fountain is *as the eye of the landscape.*

Valleys *(H1237/H1234)* are defined as *a split*, or *a wide level valley between mountains*. It comes from a root word which means *to cleave, to rend, break, rip or open.* A valley is a depression either between two higher elevations or at the base of a single higher elevation. A valley also symbolizes enclosed gloom, fear and death (Psalm 23:4). The LORD sees us when we're in the valley, and if we seek Him, He will refresh us with Himself.

If we're walking through the valleys of life, and we're tempted to fear, it's so wonderful to know that we can cleave to the LORD. His eye (His fountain) is upon the landscape of our lives, and He will cause His refreshing springs of favor and satisfaction to break forth all around us. The LORD is in the midst of any valley that we must pass through. Although we may feel like we're surrounded by insurmountable trials and mountains, the LORD will make the way. He'll cause us to break forth from the dark shadows into a place of safety and joy in His presence. The LORD is our fountain of life and light, and He allows us to drink of His pleasures (Psalm 36:8-9). He frees us from everything that would seek to depress, discourage or keep us from the vision and purpose that He has placed upon our lives.

STILL WATERS — POOLS IN THE WILDERNESS

The *wilderness (H4057/H1696)* is defined as *a pasture or desert* where livestock are *driven for the purpose of arranging* and caring for them, much like a shepherd would his sheep. When a shepherd is in the wilderness with his flock, he communicates with them; he *speaks* to them and calls them to follow him. He teaches them, ministers to them and prepares safe places for them (protecting them from ravenous wolves and other predators). A good shepherd makes the wilderness bearable.

In the same way, the wilderness of this world can be a wild, dangerous and harsh place. Yet the LORD, who is the Good Shepherd, brings us through our wilderness experiences unscathed, as He provides for all our needs. This is reflected in:

Part 2 • *Loving God* with All Your Soul

<u>Psalm 23:1-2</u> *The LORD is my shepherd; I shall not want. He maketh me to lie down in green pastures: he leadeth me beside still waters.*

The people of God are the sheep of His pasture. While He may lead us into the wilderness to learn of Him, He will also help us to find our rest in His presence. As we lie down in **green (H1877/H1876) pastures (H4999/H4998)** we experience a *pleasant* and *beautiful* place of habitation — much like *a home* — which is suitable for tender life *to sprout*, be nurtured, grow in maturity and become useful.

Jesus, the Shepherd and Bishop of our souls, fully intends for His sheep to partake of the water of His Word, and to trust and grow strong in Him, as well as follow after and imitate Him (1 Peter 2:25). As we do, He leads us by the **still (H4496/H4495/H4494/H5117)** waters — *a settled spot* or, figuratively, *a home*. In *an abode* of stillness, we're able to enjoy His *peace, consolation, comfort, rest and quiet*. It's in the tender, watchful presence of the LORD that all His lambs are fully satisfied, strengthened, refreshed and empowered to walk with and follow the leading of their protective shepherd.

SPRINGS IN THE DRY LAND

People and nations suffer droughts, because their natural sources of water flow have been interrupted or cut off. Likewise, people and nations also suffer the effects of spiritual droughts, because their source of living water from the Spirit of God has been interrupted or cut off. If land or a human soul is dry and left to its *arid*, neglected and withering condition, any life that was previously present, will fall into a state of great desolation and vanish away. The deception and darkness of sin causes souls and nations to wither and die. Our lives and our lands are in need of the cleansing refreshing waters of the LORD; He promises to water the dry lands of our lives if we will earnestly desire Him.

A ***dry*** *(H6723)* ***land*** *(H776)* is a location in the *earth* that has been *parched,* burnt or scorched. It has suffered the heat of the sun, lack of rain, extended drought, and barrenness. It's become *a desert*, a wilderness, or a lonely and solitary place. Dry land may also represent the earth at large, a specific country, a common field, a nation of people or an individual soul.

If we want the blessing of God to flow in our lives, we must humble ourselves, repent of our sins, seek His face and turn from our wicked ways. Only then, will God hear from heaven, forgive our sin and heal our land (2 Chronicles 6:26-27, 7:14). The LORD changes dry land into ***springs*** *(H4161/H3318)* of water by causing an emergence — *a going forth of water from a source* that did not previously exist. A land may be dry, but the LORD is able to open the earth to allow the waters to flow forth.

Part 2 • *Loving God* with All Your Soul

Likewise, there are springs of living water which the LORD desires to pour into those who seek Him. He desires that we would drink from the wells of salvation and partake of His protection, provision and deliverance, and that we would be satisfied and refreshed in Him (Isaiah 12:3, 32:2, 35:6-7, 58:11). But we must remember that the LORD pours into us, so we can be poured out for the benefit of others as well.

Remember, the LORD is faithful to pour Himself into the lives of those who are thirsty for Him. He causes hidden treasures of blessing to manifest, as He refreshes the souls of mankind. He teaches us His Word and pours His Spirit and blessing upon us and our children (Proverbs 1:23; Joel 2:28-29; Acts 2:17-18).

<u>Isaiah 44:3</u> *For I will pour water upon him that is thirsty, and floods upon the dry ground: I will pour my spirit upon thy seed, and my blessing upon thine offspring:*

Also in Isaiah, we see a beautiful culmination of the work of the LORD, foretelling the refreshing of His people through the covenant with Christ:

<u>Isaiah 49:8-10</u> *Thus saith the LORD, In an acceptable time have I heard thee, and in a day of salvation have I helped thee: and I will preserve thee, and give thee for a covenant of the people, to establish the earth, to cause to inherit the desolate heritages;* ⁹*That thou mayest say to the* *prisoners, Go forth; to them that are in darkness, show yourselves. They shall feed in the ways, and their pastures shall be in all high places. ¹⁰They shall not hunger nor thirst; neither shall the heat nor sun smite them: for he that hath mercy on them shall lead them, even by the springs of water shall he guide them.*

The LORD hears the cries of His people. He gives them His salvation, help, preservation, freedom and provision. They have an inheritance in Him, for He's a merciful, covenant keeping God. He delivers those who seek Him from the power of sin, as He mercifully leads them and feeds them in places of prominence. He quenches their thirst, while He satisfies and comforts them by the springs of water.

In verse 10, the **springs** *(H4002/H5042)* of water are defined as *fountains* that *gush forth*. Can you picture it? Even as the springs of the LORD are abundantly sent forth into the dry, parched places of our lives, we should break forth into joyful singing for the comfort and mercy He has so graciously extended to us (Isaiah 49:13)! All throughout scripture, we can see how the LORD wants to quench and fill the thirsty soul. The Anointed One, Jesus, also reminds us in:

<u>*John 7:37-39*</u> *...If any man thirst, let him come unto me, and drink. ³⁸He that believeth on me, as the scripture hath said, out of his belly shall flow rivers of living water. ³⁹(But this spake he of the*

Part 2 • *Loving God* with All Your Soul

Spirit, which they that believe on him should receive: for the Holy Ghost was not yet [given]; because that Jesus was not yet glorified.)

All who thirst for the LORD are invited to freely and joyfully come and receive His living waters from the well of salvation. He allows all who seek Him, to come to Him; He will turn no one away. Drink of Jesus and receive His Holy Spirit. All those who thirst after righteousness shall be filled with the waters of everlasting life and will never thirst again (Isaiah 12:3, 55:1; Matthew 5:6; John 4:14, 6:35).

Go ahead, drink in and spiritually absorb all of His goodness and mercy. Delight yourself in Him and all that He represents. Be filled with the liberating truth and grace of His Word and experience His precious promises and blessings. Soak up His life-giving substance, which He generously pours into your thirsty soul. Allow Him to saturate every fiber of your being with Himself. Allow that same life and power which the LORD pours into you, to flow out to others like pure, sparkling, refreshing rivers. Let others drink of His life in you. Remember, we can only give out what we have taken in.

Are you thirsty, parched and dry?

What are you drinking in?

What is flowing out of your life?

LIVING WATERS — ETERNAL & REFRESHING

Those who love the LORD will drink of His living water throughout all eternity. In the Book of Revelation, the Apostle John records seeing a great, innumerable multitude from all nations, kindreds, tongues and people, arrayed in white robes. They were before the throne of God in heaven, and they cried with a loud voice, *"Salvation to our God which sits upon the throne, and unto the Lamb"* (Revelation 7:9-10). This multitude of people was made up of those who came out of great tribulation. They worshipped with the angels and declared, *"Amen: Blessing, and glory, and wisdom, and thanksgiving, and honor, and power, and might, be unto our God forever and ever. Amen."* These saints washed their robes in the blood of the Lamb and they serve continually before the throne of God in His temple. God dwells among them, and they are eternally refreshed in Him (Revelation 7:11-15).

FOUNTAINS OF SUPPLY, SALVATION & HIS PRESENCE

The LORD meets every single need we have, both now and in eternity. There's no want or lack in the presence of the LORD. Regardless of what the people of God go through in this life, the LORD has a loving promise for those who faithfully worship and serve Him.

<u>Revelation 7:16-17</u> They shall hunger no more, neither thirst any more; neither shall the sun light on them, nor any heat. ¹⁷For the Lamb which is in the midst of the throne shall feed them, and shall

Part 2 • *Loving God* with All Your Soul

lead them unto <u>living fountains of waters</u>: and God shall wipe away all tears from their eyes.

To ***hunger*** *(G3983/G3993)* and thirst no more, means that those who stand and worship before the throne of God will no longer suffer by *toiling for daily subsistence* or *pining* after their basic needs. They will no longer be *famished* or *crave* that which was previously lacking. Every need is completely satisfied in the presence of the LORD. Jesus, the Lamb of God, ***feeds*** *(G4165/G4166)* and *tends* to His people like *a shepherd* and rules over them in loving authority as their heavenly Pastor. He ***leads*** *(G3594/G3595)* and *commands with official authority* as He guides and *teaches* those who joyfully trust in and partake of Him.

He abundantly offers the eternal supply of the fountains of life and every heavenly enjoyment, which is found in Him. This pleasure of heaven is available to all who will believe that the blood of Jesus — that river of spiritual life, which flowed out from the fountain of His body upon the cross — has fully cleansed them of all unrighteousness. For those who will believe and choose to trust in Christ Jesus as their LORD, Savior and King, there's no fear of punishment. He has taken the entire penalty for our sin upon Himself. Therefore, He is able to wipe away, erase and obliterate every tear related to the sin and failures of those who trust in Him. All suffering, sorrow, pain and death are wiped away (Revelation

21:4). In His presence, the sinful existence of our past is no longer; He makes all things new.

With all this being said, let me be very clear about something. Yes, there's coming a time when the people of God are going to be in the physical, literal, glorious, manifested fullness and presence of the LORD of glory. We will have the awesome, amazing and joyful exhilaration of seeing Him face to face! However, we need to understand that we have access to the Father in Heaven now, while we are still living on this earth. We may not, literally, see His beautiful face or the fullness of His glorious splendor in our earthly state of existence. Nevertheless, we can know His presence on a level that comforts us and takes away all our pain and sorrows. By faith, when we stand before the throne of God and just love on Him, He fills us to overflowing in the Spirit, and we are completely satisfied in Him.

THE LORD'S RIVER OF REFLECTION & LIGHT

In the final chapter of the New Testament, we read that the river of life flows in the New Jerusalem — the eternal city of God. It's called the river of life, because it originates from the eternal LORD God Almighty, the source of all life, the Lamb of God — Jesus Christ, the Righteous. Those who belong to Christ can freely drink of the life of God, now and throughout all eternity.

__Revelation 22:1-2, 17__ And he showed me __a pure river of water of life__, clear as crystal, proceeding *out of the throne of God and of the Lamb. ²In the midst of the street of it, and on either side of the river, was there the tree of life, which bare twelve manner of fruits, and yielded her fruit every month: and the leaves of the tree were for the healing of the nations . . . ¹⁷And the Spirit and the bride say, Come. And let him that heareth say, Come. And let him that is athirst come. And whosoever will, let him take the water of life freely.*

This river of life originates and proceeds out from the throne and presence of God. It represents the life, power and Word of God, flowing from Him to all the redeemed inhabitants of the eternal city of God. This is a **pure** *(G2513)* river, *clean* and as clear as crystal. These **crystal clear** *(G2986/G2985/G2989)* waters shine as a bright *lamp, radiant* and *magnificently* gorgeous. They are *sumptuous in appearance* — as a flaming torch, *brilliantly beaming.* In view of these definitions, the river of life shines with the pure magnificence of God's character and holiness. Thereby, reflecting His holy fire, radiant glory and vibrant unending life. The river is a combined visual of His beauty. He is the source of living water and, at the same time, our God is a consuming fire (John 4:14; Hebrews 12:29)!

In relation to the fire and light associated with the river of life, let's look at some scriptures that represent these aspects of God. Scripture records symbolic and literal manifestations of the LORD as He has interacted with man. In Genesis 15:17-18 the LORD is referred to as a smoking furnace and a burning lamp that passed between the pieces of Abram's sacrificial offering. God, in vessels of fire, came to seal a blood covenant with Abram and to promise a land to his forthcoming descendants. The smoking *furnace (H8574/H5216)* is defined as *a fire pot* that *glistened* as a *lamp* or *light*, it represented the presence of the LORD. Still, another related reference is found in:

Exodus 27:20 *And thou shalt command the children of Israel, that they bring thee pure oil olive beaten for the light, to cause the lamp to burn always.*

In the tabernacle of Moses, this lamp (also known as the golden candlestick) was placed on the table of showbread. It represented Christ (as the light of the world) and had seven golden, oil-fed candlesticks. In the Book of Isaiah, the seven golden candlesticks represent the seven aspects of God's Spirit — the spirit of the LORD, of wisdom, of understanding, of counsel, of might, of knowledge, and of the fear of the LORD (11:1-5). In the Book of Revelation, they represent the seven Spirits of God (which are before the throne) and the seven churches (1:4, 11-20; 3-4).

In regards to the candlestick in Revelation, the light and fire of God represent both Christ and His Church. By analogy, the oil of His presence and anointing in our lives causes us to shine forth with His fire and light. Christ allows His glory to be seen in His Church (John

Part 2 • *Loving God* with All Your Soul

17:22). He is the light of the world, and He has called His Church to also be the light of the world. We're to shine like a city on a hill that cannot be hid (Matthew 5:14; John 8l2). When the world sees the followers of Christ, they should see the essence of who He is in us. As a testimony of His eternal life which we possess within our being, we're to shine brightly. In the following scriptures, we see that the LORD, His Word, His salvation and His righteousness represent the light of God:

<u>2 Samuel 22:29</u> For thou art my lamp, O LORD: and the LORD will lighten my darkness.

To say the LORD is our **lamp** *(H5216/H5214/H5135)*, is to say that He *glistens* in our lives; He is *the burner* that *shines* with *fiery light*. Darkness cannot stay where light is present. The LORD will **lighten** *(H5050)* our **darkness** *(H2822/H2821) by causing misery, destruction, death* and the absence of light, to be overcome by His *glittering illumination*. The people of God should never be in spiritual darkness, because He has given us the light of His Word, according to:

<u>Psalm 119:105</u> Thy word is a lamp unto my feet, and a light unto my path.

In 2 Samuel 22:29, the LORD is our lamp. In Psalm 119:105, God's Word is a lamp that *glistens* and gives **light** *(H216/H215), glorious illumination* and *happiness* to the paths of life that He has ordained for us to travel.

In the next scripture, Zion's righteousness and salvation are to go forth as brightness and a burning lamp:

***Isaiah 62:1** For Zion's sake will I not hold my peace, and for Jerusalem's sake I will not rest, until the righteousness thereof go forth as brightness, and the salvation thereof as a lamp that burneth.*

Who or what is **Zion** *(H6726/H6725)*? Zion is a *mountain* of the LORD *in Jerusalem;* also known as the city of David, the joy of the whole earth and the place where the LORD dwells (Isaiah 2:3; 2 Samuel 5:7; Psalms 9:11, 48:2). Salvation, strength and the perfection of beauty shine out of Zion (Psalms 14:7, 20:2, 50:2).

In addition, while Zion is a place, it is also a nation of people. Zion is God's inheritance; He saves her as His purchased and redeemed congregation (Psalms 69:35, 74:2). Those who trust in the LORD shall be as mount Zion — immovable and abiding forever (Psalm 25:1). The God of Zion reigns forever, and the children of Zion are joyful in their King (Psalms 146:10, 149:2). Zion is redeemed with judgment and her converts with righteousness (Isaiah 1:27). Almighty God, the LORD of Hosts, has claimed Zion as His own people (Isaiah 51:15-16).

Those who are called by the name of the LORD are born in Zion, by the power of His Spirit, and they're established by God (Psalm 87:5). Symbolically, Zion represents the overcoming Church of the Living God and He dwells in the midst of her. By definition she is a *conspicuous monument* or *guiding pillar*. Regarding the church of Philadelphia, Jesus said:

Revelation 3:12 *Him that overcometh will I make a pillar in the temple of my God, and he shall go no more out: and I will write upon him the name of my God, and the name of the city of my God, which is new Jerusalem, which cometh down out of heaven from my God: and I will write upon him my new name.*

The New Jerusalem is the holy city of God, and Zion (the Church of God and the Bride of Christ) is the New Jerusalem. Like the river of God, she has the glory of God within her. Resembling a precious stone, clear as crystal, her light shines forth. She passionately stirs the fires of God within and beautifully illuminates all that is around her (Revelation 21:9-11). Zion shines forth as a monumental city on a hill for all to see. Her reflection is mirrored in the river of life, for it flows through the heart — the center and innermost part — of who she is.

Zion, the Bride of Christ, is completely dependent upon her God. She has entered into an everlasting love covenant with her beloved King. She has received His gift of salvation and drinks freely from the water of life. She walks in the light of God's Word and His holy fire burns within her. She is sealed by the Spirit of God and washed by the blood of the Lamb. In unity, the Spirit and the Bride bid all who will hear the Word of the LORD and all who are thirsty, to come, trust and believe in the LORD, as well as drink freely from the waters of eternal life (John 7:38; Revelation 22:17).

THE TREE OF LIFE, ETERNAL LIFE & THE BRIDE OF CHRIST
In Revelation 22:1, we focused on the river of life, its origin and characteristics, as well as how the Bride of Christ possesses its same qualities. This river is full of the life of God; therefore, wherever it flows it brings forth life. In Revelation 22:2, we also see that the tree of life is nourished by the river of God:

***Revelation 22:2** In the midst of the street of it, and on either side of the river [of God], was there the tree of life, which bare twelve manner of fruits, and yielded her fruit every month: and the leaves of the tree were for the healing of the nations...*

In the New Jerusalem, the river of God (which is the river of life) runs through the middle of the street, in the midst of the city. The tree of life is nourished by the river of life, and it seems to be the only fruit producing tree mentioned in the Book of Revelation. Yet, this tree bares 12 different types of fruit. It seems the LORD has placed a full scale garden into one tree of life. This example of God's fruitfulness and life is flourishing in the center, the heart, of the New Jerusalem.

Before mankind was physically created, God provided the original tree of life for man in the midst — the center,

Part 2 • *Loving God* with All Your Soul

the heart — of the Garden of Eden (Genesis 2:8-9, 3:22). It's interesting that, in the New Jerusalem, the tree of life is located in the midst of the city as well. In both accounts, God's fruitfulness is found in the center of what He has created. He desires for His life, His provision and His fruitfulness to be found in the center of our lives! In fact, He desires that we partake of what He has made available for us, throughout all eternity.

It was always God's intention that man would partake of the fruit of life and live forever. The Word of God tells us that whosoever finds the LORD, finds life and favor (Proverbs 8:35). Jesus, the Prince of life, said of Himself that He's the way, the truth and the life, and that whosoever believed on Him has eternal life (Acts 3:15; John 3:36, 14:6). When we recognize that Jesus is our life source, we can boldly proclaim:

<u>Galatians 2:20</u> *I am crucified with Christ: nevertheless I live; yet not I, but Christ liveth in me: and the life which I now live in the flesh I live by the faith of the Son of God, who loved me, and gave himself for me.*

Those who have the Son, have life (1 John 5:12). It's just that simple. I believe it would be safe to say that the river flowing from the throne represents the Father God. It also represents Jesus — the Word of God — for He came out from God and is the personification of the life of God (John 16:27).

In addition, I believe the tree of life represents the Bride of Christ. You see, in truth, everything in heaven and in the New Jerusalem represents Christ, for He is God. Furthermore, in Revelation 22:2, we read about how the tree of life *"...yielded 'her' fruit..."* This may seem confusing unless you understand that the Church (the spiritual Bride of Christ) is 'in' Him and, therefore, Jesus and the Church are one. In a marriage relationship, it's the bride that conceives and brings forth the life that her husband has sown into her. Likewise, the Bride of Christ is the carrier of God's seed, which is His Word. In the earth realm, the Bride of Christ bears and births forth the fruit of the will of God.

Again, the tree of life in the New Jerusalem bore twelve manner (or distinctions) of fruit. Twelve represents the number of government. Though I will not go into detail, we can see from the following Old Testament examples that the number 12 is directly related to nations, the ministry of the priesthood and the government of God. There were the twelve tribes of Israel, 12 rods of authority and 12 stones on the priests' breastplate (one for each of the heads of the 12 tribes). There were 12 cakes of bread on the table of shewbread, 12 chargers of silver, 12 silver bowls, and 12 spoons of gold used for service in the tabernacle of Moses. The prophet Elisha sacrificed 12 yoke of oxen to the LORD, when Elijah the prophet placed his prophetic mantle upon him.

Part 2 • *Loving God* with All Your Soul

In the New Testament, there is mention of 12 disciples, 12 apostles, 12 baskets of food, 12 thrones and 12 legions of angels. Jesus at 12 years of age, was questioning, talking with and astounding the Jewish religious leaders with His spiritual understanding. Also mentioned are the 12 patriarchs, the 12 tribes as well as 12 thousand from each of the 12 tribes of Israel. In the book of Revelation, there is mention of the woman in heaven (that is, the Church seated in the heavenly realm), clothed with the sun and the moon under her feet; upon her head she wore a crown with 12 stars. The woman travailed in birth and bore a son, who would rule the nations with a rod of iron; this son speaks of Christ. There is also mention of 12 gates made of 12 pearls in the New Jerusalem and they are guarded by 12 angels. I believe it's safe to say the number 12 clearly speaks of the God's governmental authority and rule in the Kingdom of God.

In the beginning, man first encountered the Kingdom of God in the Garden of Eden. God has always had a people — a remnant, who love and serve Him. The LORD is manifesting and bringing forth the truth of His Kingdom in the earth, and He's doing it through His people and His Word. Jesus commissioned His disciples (including all those who would come to put their faith and trust in Him) to preach the gospel of the Kingdom of God throughout the earth. He also gave them power over devils and to heal the sick, in His name. As they went forth preaching, the LORD went with them and confirmed the Word of God with signs following (Matthew 10:1-4, 7-8; Mark 16:15-20). What God started in the Garden of Eden is an eternal work and the good fruit of it will continue throughout eternity.

The Church of Jesus Christ is a living, breathing, fruit bearing organism. A tree void of life cannot bear fruit, but through the life of Christ, a healthy spiritual tree bears pleasing, sweet fruit because of the life operating in it. The fruit is a reflection of the root, which nourishes the tree. Christ taught that those who trust in Him would bear fruit, because they are connected to Him:

***John 15:4-5** Abide in me, and I in you. As the branch cannot bear fruit of itself, except it abide in the vine; no more can ye, except ye abide in me. ⁵I am the vine, ye are the branches: He that abideth in me, and I in him, the same bringeth forth much fruit: for without me ye can do nothing.*

Notice that the first word in this passage is *abide (G3306)*, which means *to stay (in a given place, state, relation or expectancy)*. Elsewhere in scripture, it is also translated as: to continue to dwell, be present, remain, stand and tarry. We're to abide in the life and presence of Christ, and He also abides in us.

In reference to Revelation 22:2, the **Fruit** *(G2590/G726)* of the tree of life is in its mature perfection. Its sweetness causes it to be *preferred* and *plucked*.

Part 2 • *Loving God* with All Your Soul

Consider the grape vine: the vine bears the branches, and the branches bear the fruit. Jesus said He is the vine and we are the branches. He's the life source and we're connected to Him; thereby, bearing the sweet fruit of that union.

We're able to abide in Christ, because He has delivered us. He has plucked us from the filthiness of this world and from the lies and snares of the devil. Christ has transplanted us into His fruitful vineyard (Isaiah 61:3). He pours His life into us, and we bear the fruit of who He is, in the Kingdom of God. Through salvation in Christ, we are preferred by God. He has called us out of darkness and into His marvelous light, to become His chosen generation, royal priesthood, holy nation and peculiar people (1 Peter 2:9).

THE LEAVES OF THE TREE & THE TAKING OF THE WATER
As we continue in Revelation 22:2, in reference to the tree of life, the verse tells us that "...***the leaves of the tree were for the healing of the nations...***" The ***leaves (G5444/G5443/G5453)*** of this tree are defined as *sprouts* and represent that which is *an offshoot, a race* or *clan,* which have been *germinated* by the LORD *to grow.* Does this sound like the leaves of the tree represent the Body of Christ? Evidently, these leaves — the offshoots, race and clan which the LORD has brought forth — are for the healing of the nations. But, if we're in eternity (in the presence of

the LORD, where no sickness dwells) why would there need to be healing? When Jesus returns for His Church, we will rise up to meet the LORD in the air. We will receive glorified bodies and there will be no more sickness (1 Corinthians 15:53-57). So why is healing needed? Healing is not needed in the heavenly realm; it's needed in the earthly realm!

This is another indicator of how the LORD desires for the realities of heaven to manifest in the earth. Let's remember the prayer of Jesus, *"...**thy kingdom come, thy will be done, <u>in earth as it is in heaven</u>**..."* (Matthew 6:10). Can you see Jesus as the tree of life? Can you see yourself as an offshoot of Him? As He releases healing to you, can you see yourself releasing healing to the nations? When the LORD brings forth **healing** *(G2322/G2323)* in the lives of His people, it's a total and thorough makeover! He effectively ministers to our brokenness and, ultimately, *cures* every physical, mental, emotional and spiritual sickness and disease (Psalm 147:3; Jeremiah 17:14; Hosea 14:4; Luke 4:18; 1 Peter 2:24; Revelation 22:2).

We are a living tree rooted in Christ! In Psalm 1:1-3, the godly man (or woman) is blessed and prosperous. The righteous are like a tree planted by the rivers of water, bringing forth fruit in their season and their leaves do not wither. The righteous delight and meditate in the law of God. The primitive root meaning of the word **law** *(H8451/H3384)* means to *flow as water.* Figuratively, it means *to point out* or *teach.* As we receive and drink in the living water of God's Word, we will bear much fruit. We become as trees of life drinking from Jesus, the Word and water of life. The LORD is so gracious and merciful. He has extended the invitation for us — all of us — to come and drink freely of the water of life.

<u>Revelation 22:17</u> And the Spirit and the bride say, Come. And let him that heareth say, Come. And let him that is athirst come. And whosoever will, let him take the water of life freely.

This beautiful invitation is a call from heaven to all people, from every tongue, nation, race, clan, kindred and tribe. All who are thirsty are encouraged to come and freely **take** *(G2902/G2904)* of the waters of life for themselves. This is a summons from the LORD for every human soul *to use strength* to *seize or retain* the gracious gift of eternal life. Salvation and eternal life are free, because of Christ's sacrifice; they just need to be received with *vigor.* Come and drink from the well of salvation; the Spirit and the Bride are calling you!

Are you thirsty?

Are you ready to drink?

Does your soul pant for the LORD,
as the deer pants for the water brook?

SUMMARY OF LOVING GOD WITH ALL YOUR SOUL

In Chapter 6, the soul is defined as *breath*, and by implication, the *spirit* of mankind. God formed man of the dust of the earth and breathed the breath of life into his nostrils, and the man became a living soul. Our breath was birthed from His breath, and our soul is alive because of Him. Therefore, we must realize that our breath and soul are not our own. They originated with God and, therefore, belong to Him. This demonstrates our utter dependence on the LORD for our existence. Every breath should be used for His glory. Every utterance should be a testimony of praise. We are commanded to let everything that has breath praise the LORD (Psalm 150:6).

In Chapter 7, we learned seven manifestations of the soul — the revived soul, the cleaving soul, the boasting soul, the joyful soul, the hopeful soul, the satisfied soul and the redeemed soul. We examined what each of these manifestations of the soul looks like and the benefits of submitting our thoughts, feeling and emotions to the LORD. By allowing the Holy Spirit and the Word of God to reign over our souls, we remain healthy and free to love and praise the LORD.

In Chapter 8, we examined how the thirsty soul pants for and seeks after the LORD. It seeks water in the wilderness, when coming out of bondage or while transitioning from what was, toward what shall be. The LORD promises to provide rivers, fountains,

Part 2 • *Loving God* with All Your Soul

pools and springs for the poor and needy. He refreshes those who humble themselves before Him and nurtures them as a shepherd who cares for his sheep. He promises that all who are thirsty can come and drink of Him, and He will fill us to overflowing. Out of our bellies shall flow rivers of living water. The river of God flows from the throne, and that river represents Christ. Only in Him will our thirst be fully quenched and satisfied. As we drink of Him, we truly experience His life and bear much fruit.

Beloved, we're created in the image and likeness of Holy God. He has seen fit to breathe life into us, so that we might live. May your soul manifest the evidence of His goodness toward you, and may you drink of Him. He is so very worthy of our adoration. Therefore, let your soul rise up to love, bless and praise the LORD.

Part 3
Loving God with All Your Mind

❧ CHAPTER 9 ❧
THE BATTLE FOR THE MIND

As we continue our study on loving God, we'll now focus on the importance of loving the LORD with *"all thy mind."* We'll be examining many scriptures related to the mind, its influence and how our thought processes apply to loving and serving the LORD as He has commanded us. This is crucial, because the mind is where battles take place, decisions are made and victories are first won or lost. How we deal with conflicts in the mind, will determine how we respond to the LORD, and how we respond to the LORD will determine how we deal with the conflicts of the mind. It's quite a cycle. First, let's be reminded of our key scriptures:

<u>Matthew 22:37</u> Thou shalt love the Lord thy God with all thy heart, and with all thy soul, and with all thy mind.

<u>Mark 12:30</u> And thou shalt love the Lord thy God with all thy heart, and with all thy soul, and with

Part 3 • *Loving God* with All Your Mind

all thy mind, and with all thy strength: this [is] the first commandment *(also see Luke 10:27).*

Loving the LORD with ***"all thy mind"*** can be difficult, especially if the enemy of our souls is seeking to mentally assault, accuse, discredit, disrupt or tempt us. Have you ever been in a situation where someone has really hurt or upset you? Perhaps they used their words to cut right through your heart and soul. Afterwards, have you ever had that one-sided conversation where you talk to that non-present, careless person? Does the conversation persistently circulate over and over in your mind to the point of distraction? In response, do you battle with thoughts of unworthiness, inability, failure, fear, anger, bitterness or some other unhealthy emotion? Well, you're not alone, and there's help for the troubled mind. Trust in this truth: If we will hear, believe, meditate on, submit to and declare God's Word in every situation, we can live in victory (James 1:22, 4:7; Philippians 4:8).

If there's a battle going on in your mind, it's because the enemy has erected (or is trying to erect) a stronghold. He's looking for a place to set up his fortress of lies, torments and bondage, and he's seeking your permission to begin his building program! However, the LORD has given us mighty weapons to thwart the devil's evil plans.

The human mind does not belong to the devil, but that doesn't mean he won't try to steal it. If the devil is making a wicked playground out of your mind, the first thing you need to do is regain control of your mental faculties. Through the authority of God's Word, begin a spiritual cleanup campaign of the mind. Realize who the enemy is, deal with him and stop his assault against you! If you are a born-again follower of Christ, the LORD has given you the authority to do so. Allow God's truth to pull down all demonic strongholds, imaginations and thoughts that are contrary to the Word of God.

<u>2 Corinthians 10:3-5</u> For though we walk in the flesh, we do not war after the flesh: ⁴(For the weapons of our warfare are not carnal, but mighty through God to the pulling down of strong holds;) ⁵Casting down imaginations, and every high thing that exalteth itself against the knowledge of God, and bringing into captivity every thought to the obedience of Christ;

A holy warrior mentality is required if we're to overcome the demonic assaults on the mind. Those who know and use their authority in Christ will have victory. Spiritual warfare must be very decisive and proactive. Based on the previous scripture passage, we have four aggressive strategies that we must employ if we're to send the enemy running for cover:

- Walk
- War
- Cast down
- Bring into captivity

Part 3 • *Loving God* with All Your Mind

WALK

First, we must understand what it means to **walk** (G4043/G4012/G3961) in the flesh. In this context, **walk** means *to tread all around, as proof of ability;* figuratively, it means to *live, deport oneself, follow as a companion* or *be occupied with.* We are flesh and blood and must deal with our human nature, as well as the moral and physical passions and frailties of our humanness.

The flesh nature operates in a carnal mindset, which opposes the Word of God and the mind of Christ. This is why it's so important to realize that, although we live in the flesh, we cannot operate in the carnal mindset. We're not to be occupied with (or be a companion of) the corruption of the flesh nature. Rather, we're to walk and live in agreement with the Word of God. Therefore, we must repent of all sin, and forgive those who have offended us. In this way, we close off all spiritual and mental doors of entry. The devil and the flesh nature cannot operate in our lives, if we do not give them permission to do so.

Though we walk in the flesh, physically, we are to be spiritually led by the Spirit of God. This means we're to follow His leading. Learning to walk with the LORD is a process that involves movement. He leads, we follow. He desires to guide us on a journey that will take us from one level of understanding to another in Him. We cannot walk with God and physically, mentally, emotionally or spiritually stay where we were before. As we choose to submit ourselves to the Word and will of God, He directs us into the next step of our Kingdom purpose. As we follow Him, He gives us the power to tread down all the devises of the enemy.

***Luke 10:19** Behold, I give unto you power to tread on serpents and scorpions, and over all the power of the enemy: and nothing shall by any means hurt you.*

This is one of my favorite scriptures and I declare it quite often, just to remind the enemy of his impotence. I will go into a deeper study of Luke 10:19, in Chapter 11. For now, simply know that Jesus has given us power over the devil and we're not to put up with his foolishness. He is a defeated foe and we're to remind him of it continually! We are in a war that has already been won. We have the victory through Christ, but, we must continue to occupy the territory, lest the enemy forget his 'powerless, trampled under our feet' position.

War

Secondly, according to 2 Corinthians 10:3-5, we must understand that though we walk in the flesh, we do not *war* after the flesh. In the natural, to *war* (G4754) *is to serve in a military campaign* and *contend* with the enemy. To *war* also means *to execute the apostolate* (the office of an apostle, as a sent one) *with its arduous duties and functions.* In this sense, the role of a soldier is similar to that of an Apostle.

Part 3 • *Loving God* with All Your Mind

Apostles are kingdom warriors sent into difficult and strenuous situations of spiritual warfare. They're equipped, qualified and required to fulfill their duties and functions with great strength and vigor of spirit, soul and body. The apostolic ministry has a vital role in contending with the *carnal inclinations* of those in the church, who call themselves by the name of the LORD.

If we're to overcome the fleshly, carnal nature, we can't trust or lean to our own limited understanding. We must submit ourselves, as soldiers, to the authority of the LORD. He is our chief military Commander. We must *contend with* and *overcome* our *carnal inclinations,* by obeying His commands. As we *serve* and *execute* the *military campaigns* of the Kingdom of God, the LORD of Hosts will fight for us and give us great victories.

The true Church — the Bride of Christ — is a warrior in the earth. She is a many-membered army, who is tender hearted toward her Savior, but fiercely militant against His enemy. She is led by the Spirit of God and receives her marching orders through His Word. She lifts up her voice in the wilderness of this world, declaring, decreeing and demonstrating the truth and power of God. (Romans 12:4-5, 15; 1 Corinthians 12:12-14, 20).

Strategically, every member in the Body of Christ has been positioned by the LORD and given specific gifts, talents and abilities, to fulfill their kingdom purposes. The people of God are to discern the true believers in Christ, and come into unity with those of like mind and spirit. We're to stand together in Christ, as a spiritual army on a heavenly mission; we're to see each other as comrades in arms, corporately moving forward in victorious triumph. As each member functions in divine order, the power of God is released, and evil is overcome with good (Romans 12:1-21).

God has equipped us with weapons of warfare that are ***mighty (G1415/G1410), powerful, capable*** and strong. These weapons empower us *to be able* to make things which seem impossible, *possible* through Him. These weapons are for the purpose of gaining victory in the spiritual realm first, so that the will of God is free to manifest in the natural realm. These spiritual armaments have nothing to do with (nor do they originate in) the unregenerate flesh nature, human strength or reasoning. They are not used for the purpose of fulfilling the lust of the flesh or our own temporal agendas. Rather, they're to have a violent impact against the spiritual darkness of this world. The weapons of our warfare are designed to give us power over the enemy, as well as set the captives free and usher them into the eternal Kingdom of God!

The power of these spiritual weapons comes directly from the LORD God Almighty. The only way we can tap into this power is to be in Him. We can only be in God by being in Christ. Through the power of God in Christ, we become a conduit of power against the strongholds and activities of the enemy.

Though satan is defeated, he still tries to steal (what doesn't belong to him) from mankind. If the devil can deceive people into thinking he has power over them, then his lies will become their sad reality. But God has equipped His people to oppose the influence of the enemy and detach him from his fictitious authority. Standing in the righteousness of Christ and the armor of God, we're to give the devil no advantage. We're to resist him, steadfastly in the faith. (For more on weapons of warfare and how to defeat the schemes of the enemy, see Ephesians 4:27, 6:10-18; James 4:7; 1 Peter 5:8-9).

CAST DOWN

Thirdly, we use our spiritual weapons to *violently **cast down** (G2507/G138)*, lower, demolish and destroy all the ***imaginations** (G3053/G3049), reasoning* and *conceit* of the enemy. We refuse to listen to his accusatory criticisms and condemnation against us. We reject his assaults of shame and blame for the things of our past, which have been forgiven. We cast down every thought that's not in harmony with the Word of God.

As believers in Christ, we must make a stand. We must refuse to allow negative or sinful mental images to be played out in our minds. We can't tolerate demonically inspired, internal conversations or distractions. These things are designed by satan to take us away from the truth of who we are in Christ. We're to adamantly reject the idea of relinquishing what the LORD has promised us through His Word. Such a stand requires determined faith, a strong spiritual mindset and Holy Ghost boldness. In so doing, we will retain possession of our peace and God given inheritance!

In Christ, we have the power (through prayer and the authoritative application of His Word) to cast down every **high thing** *(G5313/G5312/G5311)*. This includes all psychological *barriers*, and things that have been *elevated* above (or exalted against) the knowledge of God. Anything lifted up and exalted above the name of Jesus or the Word of God is a lie and must be dealt with seriously. It's fictitious, misplaced and out of order; therefore, it must be cast aside. We're to provide no place of preeminence or *dignity to* such things. They must fall down in obedience to Christ and submit to the power of His name.

If our thoughts are contrary to God's Word, then we've failed to feed upon the Word of God adequately, and we've allowed the enemy to set up camp in our minds. If given opportunity, satan will sow his seeds of fear, doubt, unbelief, discontentment, lying deceptions and accusations. These seeds will then release poison and death into the mind and thought processes. If we do not take these mental demons captive, then they will become a device of satan to lead us into sin, bondage and captivity.

This is not an option for the worshipper who chooses to love the LORD with their whole mind. Think on this: If we love the LORD with our 'whole' (entire, undivided, fully focused) mind, then our mind will be 'whole' (unbroken, undamaged and unimpaired). The 'whole' mind is intact, sound, healthy and fully functioning — mentally, emotionally, physically and spiritually — as God intended. The complete unity of a 'whole' mind that loves God gives no opportunity for satanic influence to enter.

Bring Into Captivity

Fourthly, we command that all lies, imaginations, strongholds and arguments that seek to rise up, must *submit* and *subordinate* to the will of God. We must make them *heed* and *conform* to **obedience (G5218/G5219)** and *compliance* with the *commanding, authoritative, royal rule* of Christ. The enemy can't find a place to operate in the mindset that is obedient to the LORD.

The mind can only be controlled by satan if, through ignorance and/or carnality, permission is given to him. If he can gain access, he will attempt to use the human mind as a birthing room to bring forth all the nastiness which he has conceived within himself. He wants to twist the mind through deception, distress, trouble, confusion and misunderstanding. His goal is to set up mental strongholds, so he can entangle, take over and enslave lives for his wicked purposes. A tangled mind isn't rational, nor is it free to worship and love God. This is why every thought must be brought into captivity to the obedience of Christ.

From the time of the Garden of Eden, satan has tried to infiltrate the mind of mankind, but remember, the good news: We are in a battle that Christ has already won! Think on this: If you have truly given your life to Christ, His overcoming power is resident within you. We have the power and authority, through the name of Jesus and the Word of God, to conquer every evil ploy. To maintain your personal victory, aggressive action is required. Don't allow destructive, renegade thoughts to run rampant. Don't tolerate imaginations that would hinder the plan of God for your life. Refuse to be taken as a prisoner of war. Reject and put to death every imagination of the devil. Learn to treasure and embrace every Word and promise of God. Remember, we're victors, not casualties. We're free in Christ! Embrace it, believe it and live it!!

GIRD UP YOUR SOBER MIND

If you've ever encountered an intoxicated alcoholic, you can easily discern that they're out of control. Through uncontrolled lust and a lack of self-discipline, they've guzzled themselves into a state of oblivion. Many times, they become emotional, irrational, forgetful, completely dysfunctional and irresponsible. Their equilibrium is thrown off, so they lose focus and all sense of proper balance. Their desire for alcohol consumes them, until they are incapacitated. Those who allow themselves to become intoxicated through alcohol (or any other form of unbridled substance abuse) have put their lives under the control of something other than God's Holy Spirit.

Part 3 • *Loving God* with All Your Mind

Any influence that seeks to control us (apart from the Spirit of God) has an abusive, demonic root. This would include physical, mental, emotional and spiritual cruelty inflicted upon oneself or through others. Such abuse could include (but is not limited to) toxic thoughts, false humility, continual foolishness, wrong relationships, self-deception, self-hatred, self-mutilation, illicit sexual relationships, perversion, false doctrine, manipulative control, witchcraft, etc. If a change of heart and direction are not chosen, then destruction is inevitable. The reality is that all thoughts and actions start as a mental seed conceived in the mind; depending on the seed and the condition of the mind, the manifested result will either be good or evil.

An intoxicated mind is polluted with impurity and has become poisonous. A poisoned mind is venomous, ill-intentioned, lethal, and wicked. This is not the mindset of those who declare themselves followers of Christ. On the contrary, those who love the LORD are sober minded:

<u>1 Peter 1:13-16</u> Wherefore gird up the loins of your mind, be sober, and hope to the end for the grace that is to be brought unto you at the revelation of Jesus Christ; ¹⁴As obedient children, not fashioning yourselves according to the former lusts in your ignorance: ¹⁵But as he which hath called you is holy, so be ye holy in all manner of conversation; ¹⁶Because it is written, Be ye holy; for I am holy. (Also see Titus 2:1-8.)

A *sober (G3525)* mind is one that abstains from *intoxication* and is *discrete* and *watchful*. Therefore, the one who possesses this mindset will be *temperate, subdued, prudent and judicious in their conduct*. They'll also be *serious, vigilant, alert and observant*. They'll not be *excessive or overindulgent*, because the sober mind operates in self-control. It's obedient to Christ and in agreement with the Word of God; it's not ignorant or naïve. Therefore, it can't be easily deceived or drawn into harmful or dangerous thought patterns.

In 1 Peter 1:13-15, mental sobriety, obedience and holiness are linked together. We cannot be **holy** *(G40), sacred; physically pure, morally blameless and ceremonially consecrated* without a sober mind and an obedient heart. Therefore, we also cannot have a sober mind and an obedient heart without holiness.

To *"***gird*** (G328/G303/G2224/G2218)* **up the loins** *(G3751)* **of your mind"** is to *bind about (especially, with a belt)* as if to tighten down, wrap or secure the *disposition, imaginations, understanding* and *internal, procreative power* of the *deep thoughts* of the mind. The mind can be a powerhouse for good or evil. Therefore, we must keep it continually girded up and securely wrapped in the truths of God's Word. His Word becomes *the beam or scales of balance* for our lives, providing stability in times of difficulty, turmoil or loss. Through being spiritually and mentally joined or coupled to His Word, we experience true strength, wisdom and peace to our spirits, souls and bodies.

HELP IN THE MIDST OF THE STORM

You may have heard the phrase, "Gird up the ship." We see an example of this in scripture, when the Apostle Paul had been taken prisoner and was on his way to Rome, to stand before Caesar. Paul, the Roman soldiers and some other prisoners were traveling by ship. During the course of travel, the ship was caught up in a tempestuous, stormy wind. As the raging waves of the sea billowed up and crashed down upon the ship, it seemed the storm would consume the vessel, as well as the lives of those onboard. The battered ship was so damaged, it was forced to land on the island of Clauda for repairs (Acts 27:14-16). Part of the repair process, was to undergird the ship with helps:

<u>Acts 27:17-20</u> Which when they had taken up, they used helps, undergirding the ship; and, fearing lest they should fall into the quicksands, struck sail, and so were driven. ¹⁸And we being exceedingly tossed with a tempest, the next day they lightened the ship; ¹⁹And the third day we cast out with our own hands the tackling of the ship. ²⁰And when neither sun nor stars in many days appeared, and no small tempest lay on us, all hope that we should be saved was then taken away.

CHAPTER 9 • THE BATTLE FOR THE MIND

The storm was raging, and the ship began to break and split apart. It was, literally, being beaten to pieces. At the same time there was the danger of the ship sinking in quicksand. Those onboard were in a horrible predicament. They were fighting severe elements and situations that were aggressively working against them. If they didn't come up with a solution, the circumstances would abruptly end their journey and possibly their lives. Undergirding the ship with helps was the only natural course of action to take.

Helps *(G998/G995/G994)* are defined as *ropes* or *chains*, which are used to help or *aid* in the pulling together of something. To secure or "undergird" a ship with helps is to wrap the vessel with cables across the keel, down the sides and around the deck, to keep it from coming apart. In the same way, when we face the storms of life and are tempted to fall apart mentally and emotionally, that's when we need to wrap our mind with the "helps" found in God's Word. Open your mouth and *shout* to Him for *help,* protection and deliverance in the midst of your tumultuous situation. As you apply the Word of God to your life, the LORD will help you pull your thoughts and life back together, and you'll find peace and stability in the midst of the storm (Psalm 107:6, 13, 23-30).

WHEN ALL SEEMS LOST
On the second day of the storm, they were still sailing, but the crew had to *lighten (G1546)* the ship.

This meant they had to unload burdensome weight through an *ejection* or *throwing overboard of the cargo*. In this way, the storm worn ship could pass through the troubled waters more easily.

Likewise, there will be times in life when we need to reassess what is truly valuable. As an act of survival, we may need to let some things go — even seemingly important things. It's okay; just toss them overboard! The tumultuous seas of adversity will be happy to receive them. Getting rid of the heavy burdens that would hold you back, will free you up to pass through the storms of life more quickly.

As the storm continued into the third day, the crew of the ship cast all the **tackling** *(G4631/G4632)* into the sea. This included all the spare fishing gear, *furniture, equipment*, goods and sails. After these useful things were tossed into the sea, those on board had nothing except a beat up ship and their lives.

For many days, the raging storm was so bad that the crew and passengers couldn't see anything, except the dark, lowering clouds and the violent torrents of rain swirling around them. Back in that day, there was no modern technology to help direct a ship in the midst of a storm. Instead, the crew would rely on the positioning of the stars, sun and moon to help guide them in the direction they needed to go. In this case, the clouds and rain caused them to lose their bearings; they had no idea which way they were going. The storm was relentless; it raged until all hope of survival was lost.

Even so, in the midst of this desperate situation, Paul received a Word from the LORD to "fear not." The LORD promised Paul that the journey would be completed and he would stand before Caesar. The LORD also promised that all those who stayed in the boat would be saved from the destruction of the storm (Acts 27:21-25).

I see two principles in this situation. First, when we're in the perfect will of God, nothing can defeat us. We will fulfill our Kingdom responsibilities in the LORD. Secondly, when we're in the will of God, we're able to affect the lives of those around us for good, and perhaps, even be used to help save their lives.

Sometimes, the trials in our own lives may be so severe, we feel like we've lost everything. We may doubt our ability to survive. Yet, as long as there is life and breath, there is hope. When we face the storms of life, that's not the time to let our mind go crazy with fear or to lose hope. It's not the time to let the quicksand pits of life suck us out of existence. It's a time to believe, trust and endure. Even when things are difficult, don't abandon the ship; help is on the way! The LORD will come to our rescue. He is faithful. He keeps His promises, and He never fails! Stand and face the winds of adversity, and watch God move on your behalf!

Part 3 • *Loving God* with All Your Mind

In the course of passing through the turbulent, swirling challenges of life, at times, the darkness and confusion may seem to dominate and threaten to overwhelm us. We may wonder, where's God in all of this? We may feel devastated, lost and tossed about. Yet, in the midst of our struggles (when all hope seems lost), the LORD will send His Word to burst forth like a shining light of deliverance on the shore of life. He will save us, as He provides hope, direction and a way of escape. Our God will send His words of comfort at just the right time — when we need them the most.

It's also important to remember that whatever the LORD speaks to us in our time of trouble is also meant to be an encouragement and hope for those around us. We never go through the storms of life solely for our own experience or benefit. We go through them to be able to reach out and minister to others. We're able to share with them what the LORD has taught us and how He has victoriously delivered us, in the midst of our struggles.

As we go through challenges in life, we need to pay close attention and carefully monitor what we allow to transpire within our thought processes. Whatever we allow to reside in our minds will eventually reproduce itself. From 1 Peter 1:13, we know that the *loins (G3751)* (or *hip)* of the mind is like a mental womb. It has the *procreative power* to reproduce the likeness of what has been sown into it. God's promises will cause our minds to become spiritually and mentally fertile and bring forth a harvest of truth, hope and great expectations. This is why it's so important to sow the promises of God's Word into our minds. Though our faith and confidence in the LORD and His Word will be tried, we know that everything He has promised, He will perform and, in this, we find our peace.

PUT YOUR ARMOR ON!

In our quest to love the LORD with all our minds, it's important that we remain strong in Him and continue to walk in victory. Through His Word, God has provided His specific instructions for every situation. He has given us supernatural ability, which is activated through faith and obedience, to follow the leading of His Holy Spirit. He has equipped every believer with spiritual armor to cover, protect and empower them. We're exhorted in:

***Ephesians 6:10-12** Finally, my brethren, be strong in the Lord, and in the power of his might. ¹¹Put on the whole armour of God, that ye may be able to stand against the wiles of the devil. ¹²For we wrestle not against flesh and blood, but against principalities, against powers, against the rulers of the darkness of this world, against spiritual wickedness in high places.*

So, spiritually, we're to be **strong** *(G1743/G1722/G1412)* in the LORD and in the **power** *(G2904)* of His **might** *(G2479)*. This means, through our position in Christ, we're *enabled* (given the power, competence, ability and authority) to *forcefully* and wholly commit ourselves to *vigorously* stand against and oppose the devil. Jesus has supernaturally *empowered* us with the capability to exercise dominion, authority and control over satan and all demonic forces.

Indeed, the armored, Spirit-led saints of God will not tolerate the devices of the enemy. Devilish hordes will find themselves and their activities cut down and placed under the feet of the true lovers of God (Luke 10:19). By the Spirit of God who dwells in us and works through us, we are destined to overcome all the divisive, disruptive schemes and wickedness of the devil. Therefore, the saints of God who know their position and authority in Christ and walk accordingly, are a dangerous threat to satan.

To stand against the wiles of the devil, the LORD has provided us with spiritual weapons of armor. Because these weapons of armor are of a spiritual nature, they must be used by a spiritual people, with a spiritual mindset. If we're to be victorious warriors for the Kingdom of God, we must bring ourselves into alignment with the Word of God, and walk in the truths and principles of His Kingdom. Only then, will we be able to war in the heavenly realms, and pull down principalities, powers, rulers of darkness and spiritual wickedness, which seek to rule in high places. We must also learn to effectively use each piece of armor for its specific purpose. Strategically, we have been given an armor that is impressively tactical. Let's take a quick look at the protections and functions of the seven pieces of the armor of God in:

Ephesians 6:13-18 Wherefore take unto you the whole armour of God, that ye may be able to withstand in the evil day, and having done all, to stand. ¹⁴Stand therefore, having your loins girt about with truth, and having on the breastplate of righteousness; ¹⁵And your feet shod with the preparation of the gospel of peace; ¹⁶Above all, taking the shield of faith, wherewith ye shall be able to quench all the fiery darts of the wicked. ¹⁷And take the helmet of salvation, and the sword of the Spirit, which is the word of God: ¹⁸Praying always with all prayer and supplication in the Spirit, and watching thereunto with all perseverance and supplication for all saints;

1

— BELT OF TRUTH —

First of all, as believers, we are to have our **"*loins girt about with truth.*"** As previously mentioned, the *loins (G3751) specifically* refer to *the hip* and the *procreative power* of the mind (1 Peter 1:13). So, in Ephesians 6:14, we see that our mind is to be girded about with truth. If we're meditating on God's Word, then the spirit and life within that Word will empower us to carry and birth, that which has been sown into us. Jesus said, *"It is the spirit that quickeneth; the flesh profiteth nothing: the words I speak unto you, they are spirit, and they are* life (John 6:63). The phrase **girt about** *(G4024) means to gird all around as to fasten on ones belt.* To *girt about with* **truth** *(G226/G227) means to be true in doctrine and profession; true (as in not concealing anything).*

We are to wrap ourselves in the true doctrines and professions of God's Word. His truth is the belt that holds all things together and keeps our lives in proper order. Therefore, we're to align every area of our lives with His truth, as we enjoy clean and transparent lives before Him. In so doing, we're empowered to walk in (as well as bring forth) His spiritual life. The seed of God's Word germinates in our spiritual womb (our spirit) and allows us to become fruitful and multiply in the Kingdom of God. Since truth brings forth life, it frees us from the power of death.

Truth also gives us sharp discernment and the ability to uncover, expose and get rid of anything that is not in alignment with the Word of God. For instance, satan is a liar and the father of lies; he cannot stay or abide in the presence of truth. Hence, truth defeats the enemy and causes him to flee.

Jesus said we shall know the truth and the truth shall make us free (John 8:32), and that He is the way, the truth and the life (John 14:6). Truth and life are inseparable. So when we girt up our loins with truth, we're wrapping ourselves in the secure, life giving promises, ability and protection of Jesus Christ and His Word.

2
— BREASTPLATE OF RIGHTEOUSNESS —

The **breastplate** *(G2382)* is described as a protective *corset* which covers *the chest* or *thorax* (area between the neck and the abdomen). Thus, it covers and protects the heart and other vital organs, which facilitate the major systems of the body. Spiritually, the breastplate of righteousness protects and guards our hearts from the judgment and condemnation of offenses. Through faith, our sins are washed away by the cleansing power of the blood of Christ. The enemy may try to plot against us with accusations of our past, present or future failures. However, the former filthiness of the flesh and all the guilt associated with it is no longer a part of who we are. We have put on Christ and, by so doing, we have also put on His righteousness.

Jesus Christ is our **Righteousness** *(G1343/G1342)* and our *justification* before God. When God declares that we are justified, innocent, holy and acceptable before Him, the enemy has no authority to say otherwise. However, it is our responsibility to put on the righteousness of Christ, as well as seek and abide in Him, in order to live and act in accordance with His character and nature. In so doing, the intents and effects of satan's hostile assaults will have no power against the saint of God. The enemy will never see the welcome mat laid out for him. There will be no place for him to construct his accusations. Thus, the devil is rendered powerless and ineffective against us.

Part 3 • *Loving God* with All Your Mind

Our righteous justification is based solely on the Heavenly Father's character and impartial *equity* towards us. This *equity* was established through the passion, and sacrificial death, resurrection and glorification of Christ. All who believe and trust in Christ through faith are declared *innocent, holy* and acceptable before the Father in Heaven, for we have put on the righteousness of Christ.

If you have invited the enemy into your life by not putting on your breastplate of righteousness or not living in accordance with the character and nature of Christ, then repent and get back into your spiritual armor! You cannot be running around spiritually naked! Remember, armor is designed to protect the one wearing it, but if you don't have your spiritual armor on, you're fair game for the devil. When you're living in obedience to the Word of God, the enemy cannot get a stronghold in your life. Therefore, regardless of your past, there is no condemnation to those in Christ Jesus, who walk not after the flesh, but after the Spirit (Romans 8:1).

3
— Gospel of Peace —

We are also commanded to have our **"feet shod (G5265) with the preparation of the gospel of peace."** Our feet symbolize how we walk out the events of our lives on a daily basis. As we shod our feet with the preparation of the gospel of peace, we're making the decision to prepare for life by spending time in the Word of God — tying, wrapping and *binding* it in and upon our lives. As we allow the Word of God to grow on the inside of us, we begin to reflect the truth and peace of God, which is operating within us.

In Ephesians 6:15, the word **peace** *(G1515)* is probably from a primary verb meaning *to join* and it implies *prosperity*. A verb is an action word; therefore God's peace joins us to prosperity. But peace and true prosperity are not attainable apart from Him. As we're joined to God and live and walk according to His gospel of peace, we are privileged to enjoy the LORD's triumphant victory. His victory includes His richness, magnificent splendor, quietness and rest. These pleasure filled delights of the Gospel belong to us, through our relationship with Jesus Christ. Joined to Christ, we're free to partake of the richness of who He is; this is true prosperity. To be joined to the Prince of Peace is to experience His magnificent blessing (Isaiah 9:6). Whenever we focus on and trust in Jesus Christ, the peace and prosperity of God (which passes all understanding) will keep, guard and protect our hearts and minds (Isaiah 26:3; Philippians 4:7).

As long as we're walking in peace, the enemy cannot gain control over us. His torment cannot operate in the presence of God's peace. This is why we can laugh in the devil's face, when he comes against us with his feeble attempts to rob us of our eternal joy.

Part 3 • *Loving God* with All Your Mind

4
— Shield of Faith —

In Ephesians 6:16, we're told that, above all, we're to be *"taking the shield of faith . . . to quench all the fiery darts of the wicked."* First of all, this informs us that we will be targeted by the wicked. So, don't be surprised when the enemy tries to shoot his venom your direction. Just raise you armored shield of faith and watch his fiery darts ricochet away from you.

Spiritual weapons do us no good, unless we use them. **Taking** *(G353/G303)* the shield of faith means to receive it and use it, perhaps by propping it up; it also implies doing so with *repetition, intensity, reversal,* etc. In addition, the **shield** *(G2375/G2374)* is defined as *a large, door-shaped shield.* It comes from a root or primary word which is defined as *a portal or entrance.* Did you get that? The shield of faith is a portal or entrance! This tells us that faith will take us to another place. Using the shield of faith effectively, literally, allows us to access another level of spiritual reality, where we have never been before.

Faith *(G4102)* is the willingness to act upon the *persuasion, moral conviction,* assurance and fidelity of the *truthfulness of God* and His Word. Genuine faith is displayed as believers give *credence* to God's Word and remain *constant in their profession* of His truth. Obviously, true faith is based on having confidence and *reliance upon Christ for salvation.* Our reliance upon Him frees us from the worry of how we're going to get through the struggles of life. Faith gives us the courage to step into another realm of growth and experience with the LORD.

We will face fiery darts from the enemy in both the spiritual and natural realms. *Fiery (G4448/G4442)* **darts** *(G956/G906)* represent *missiles, spears* and *arrows* released against us. They are *kindled* or *ignited* and crafted to be violently or intensely thrown, with the intention of striking a chosen victim like *lightening*. Fiery darts can simply be defined as anything meant to tear down and destroy a person's identity in Christ, as well as their self-worth and value. Remember the devil comes to steal, kill and destroy, but Jesus came that we might have life and that we might have it more abundantly (John 10:10). Lifting our shield of faith is a pivotal move to sustaining victory.

The word **wicked** *(G4190)* represents not only *the devil,* but also *sinners* who are *derelict, vicious, facinorous (atrociously wicked, heinous, undeniably sinful), morally culpable* and full of *mischief.* Clearly, these are people who devise hurtful and evil schemes, intending to negatively impact or influence others. In their maliciousness, they seek to bring destruction to the righteous. Their fiery darts may appear in the form of accusations, disapproval and blame for moral failures; or they may come in the form of *guilt,* wrongful criticism, condemnation, abuse, grievances, reproach, reprimands, *calamities, disease* and lewdness. The devil and his cohorts cannot cause damage to the one who is protected behind barrier of God's shield the faith.

In spiritual warfare, when the shield of faith is lifted up, we are actually lifting up Christ; He is our shield (Psalms 3:3, 28:7, 33:20, 115:9-11). He surrounds us with favor, and He gives grace, glory and good things to them that walk uprightly (Psalm 5:12, 84:11). We are destined to walk in the blessings of the LORD. Therefore, when the fiery darts of the wicked hit Christ — our shield — they don't have a chance. They are instantly **quenched** *(G4570)* and the attacks against us are completely *extinguished*. In the end, that which was meant to inflame, incite, harm or obliterate us, will only refine us and bring us closer to the LORD. The battle strategy of the enemy is destroyed, wiped out of existence, annihilated and brought to an end, because we trust in Christ who protects and covers us.

5
— HELMET OF SALVATION —

The **helmet** *(G4030/G4012/G2776)* is defined as a protective *encirclement of the head*. This piece of armor is used to completely cover and properly protect the head from being *seized* or *readily taken hold of*. Helmets are generally worn by those participating in dangerous occupations or events to protect their:
- eyes (vision & purpose)
- ears (hearing)

- nose (discernment)
- mouth (words)
- brain (mind, thoughts and reasoning)

The Helmet of *Salvation* *(G4992/G4991/G4990/ G4982)* isn't just something a follower of Christ possesses; it also reveals the powerful role of the person who makes it possible for us to receive that salvation. By definition, Christ Himself is our salvation, because He is our *defender, deliverer* and Savior. He is the one who *provides defense, rescues* and *saves* us. He *protects* and grants physical and moral *safety*. Elsewhere in scripture, salvation is also translated as: to heal, preserve, make whole and bring to a place of health. Christ provides all we need, because He is our salvation.

The helmet of salvation (as with the other pieces of armor) represents Christ and the work He's perfecting in our lives. For instance, the helmet is defined as a protective encirclement of the head. Who is 'head' of the Church? Jesus! When we put on the helmet of salvation, we are being protectively encircled by Him, and He is working all the aspects of His gift of salvation into every area of our lives!

EYES
Let's take this a little further. A natural helmet also provides protection for the eyes. We live in a world that takes pleasure in presenting all types of wicked, lustful, death-filled things before the eyes of those

who care to look. Yet, followers of Christ are not to be joined to such things. King David said it very well:

Psalm 101:3 *I will set no wicked thing before mine eyes: I hate the work of them that turn aside; it shall not cleave to me.*

Whatever we choose to look at is what we choose to visually join ourselves to. If we allow ourselves to be joined to any *wicked (H1100/H1097/H3276)* thing, then we've connected with that which is unprofitable, *worthless* and *destructive*. We're not to *cleave (H1692)*, *cling, adhere* to or *abide* with such things. Rather, we're to hate them and recognize them as an enemy to our spiritual well-being. Our personal choices will reveal whether we're walking in the light and truth of God or dwelling in darkness. Jesus said in:

Matthew 6:22-24 *The light of the body is the eye: if therefore thine eye be single, thy whole body shall be full of light.* [23]*But if thine eye be evil, thy whole body shall be full of darkness. If therefore the light that is in thee be darkness, how great is that darkness!* [24]*No man can serve two masters: for either he will hate the one, and love the other; or else he will hold to the one, and despise the other. Ye cannot serve God and mammon.*

Our eyes are the gateway to the soul. Whatever we take into our soul will, to some degree, have a physical, mental, emotional and spiritual effect on us.

It will either build us up in our faith or tear us down. We have a responsibility before the LORD to protect our eyes and our souls from willingly participating in wickedness and corruption. We need to realize that, if we choose to partake in wickedness with our eyes, it can interrupt or destroy our ability to fulfill the spiritual vision and destiny God has planned for us.

EARS
The helmet of salvation protects our ear gates from that which is contrary to God's truth. We're told throughout scripture to "hear the Word of the LORD." We must be willing to hear, receive and properly respond to the voice of the LORD. Jesus said in:

Matthew 7:24-27 Therefore whosoever heareth these sayings of mine, and doeth them, I will liken him unto a wise man, which built his house upon a rock: ²⁵And the rain descended, and the floods came, and the winds blew, and beat upon that house; and it fell not: for it was founded upon a rock. ²⁶And every one that heareth these sayings of mine, and doeth them not, shall be likened unto a foolish man, which built his house upon the sand: ²⁷And the rain descended, and the floods came, and the winds blew, and beat upon that house; and it fell: and great was the fall of it.

When we hear and respond properly to the Word of the LORD, we're operating in wisdom, establishing ourselves upon God's truth and the solid rock of our salvation. On the other hand, those who hear the words of the LORD and choose to disobey are living foolishly; they've built their lives upon the instability of the world and its ways. The world offers no safety from the storms of life. Therefore, calamity and destruction are inevitable. Thanks be to God that when we honor the LORD, His protection and blessing are upon us.

Since each person chooses whom and what they will listen to throughout their lives, they control their own destiny. In fact, the final condition of each person's life is proof or evidence of their choices. A life lived is testimony to who they did or did not follow. Those who consider the Word of God in their decision making processes, invite the intentions of the LORD to manifest.

Mouth

Moving right along, the mouth is also to be up under that helmet of salvation. If the mouth and the heart that controls it, are not submitted to the LORD, untold trouble can result. While speaking to the religious leaders of His day, Jesus revealed that the condition and motives of one's heart are exposed through the words that flow from one's mouth:

Matthew 12:34-37 O generation of vipers, how can ye, being evil, speak good things? for out of the abundance of the heart the mouth speaketh. ³⁵A good man out of the good treasure of the heart bringeth forth good things: and an evil man out of the evil treasure bringeth forth evil things. ³⁶*But I say unto you, That every idle word that men shall speak, they shall give account thereof in the day of judgment.* ³⁷*For by thy words thou shalt be justified, and by thy words thou shalt be condemned.*

The tongue, in its unbridled state, is an unruly evil; it's full of deadly poison. That which we meditate upon in our hearts will be made known through our lips. For this reason, both the heart and tongue need to be under the control of the Holy Spirit (James 3). As lovers of God, our tongues are to be filled with that which is pleasing to Him.

***Psalm 19:14** Let the words of my mouth, and the meditation of my heart, be acceptable in thy sight, O LORD, my strength, and my redeemer.*

The *meditation (H1902)* of the heart refers to the *murmuring* sound of its *machination* — the scheming of plots within. *Meditation* also refers to the sound like that of *musical notation,* probably similar to the *moder affettuoso* to indicate *solemnity of movement.* In other words, either the heart will meditate on its own scheming ways and create a sound of discord, or it will meditate on the affection and tenderness of the LORD and observe His ways. The heart that meditates on the LORD creates a song of love that is **acceptable** *(H7522/H7521)* and cultivates the fullness of *delight, desire, favor* and *good pleasure* in His sight.

Part 3 • *Loving God* with All Your Mind

The words of our mouths are for the purposes of God. He desires to use us mightily to proclaim His truth, righteousness, peace, healing, safety, rest, prosperity and deliverance. We are to proclaim these things, not just for ourselves, but for the benefit of others. Since the words of the LORD are spirit and life, they benefit the speaker and the hearer alike. As we submit our hearts to the Spirit of the LORD, He uses our mouths and tongues to glorify Himself.

6
— The Sword of the Spirit —

The **sword** *(G3162/G3163/G3164)* is defined as *a knife* and, figuratively, represents *disputing, controversy* and *war* as used in the execution of *judicial punishment*. The sword also speaks of fighting, striving and quarreling. In Ephesians 6:17, the Sword of the Spirit is identified as the Word of God. It is described as powerful, sharp, piercing and discerning in:

Hebrews 4:12 *For the word of God is quick, and powerful, and sharper than any twoedged sword, piercing even to the dividing asunder of soul and spirit, and of the joints and marrow, and is a discerner of the thoughts and intents of the heart.*

For the Word of God to be **quick** *(G2198)* and **powerful** *(G1756)* means that it is always efficient, effective, *living, active* and *operative*. It defines truth and God's eternal, uncompromised standard for life. And, it is the final governmental authority, powerfully ruling over and influencing all of creation.

The Word of God — the sword of the Spirit — is **sharper** *(G5114)* than any two-edged sword. A single, decisive strike from this weapon of war will slice and sever with **piercing** *(G1338/G1223/G2425)* precision. Thereby, *penetrating, reaching* all the way *through* to the other side, **dividing** *(G3311/G3307/G3313)*, *separating, disuniting* and differentiating with meticulous accuracy and discernment between what is and is not pleasing to the LORD. The Word of the LORD will accomplish that which it has been sent to do. It will **prosper** *(H6743)* — *push forward* — until it performs and brings to pass the perfect and complete conclusion which the LORD desires:

<u>Isaiah 55:11</u> So shall my word be that goeth forth out of my mouth: it shall not return unto me void, but it shall accomplish that which I please, and it shall prosper in the thing whereto I sent it.

Keep in mind that, though the sword of the Spirit has been given to us as a spiritual weapon, we do not wield it alone. According to scripture, a sharp two-edged sword goes out from the mouth of the LORD (Revelation 1:16)! He declares His Word and fights with the sword of His mouth against those who deceitfully infiltrate with their idolatrous ways and rise up against the Body of Christ (Revelation 2:12-16). With the sharp sword of His Word, the LORD smites the nations and executes righteous judgment upon them (Revelation 19:15).

God's Word provides the spiritual and moral code of ethics, by which all people, nations and cultures can live peaceably among themselves and with their Creator. We're to use the Word of God to present truth — first, to ourselves and then to others. Because God's inspired words are spirit and life, they are profitable for doctrine, for reproof, for correction and for instruction in righteousness (John 6:63, 2 Timothy 3:16-17).

If we're to be effective warriors, fighting for the Kingdom of God, we must do more than just hear the Word of God. We must receive it and obey it. Live it. His Word must be the foundation through which every word is spoken and every decision is executed.

7
— Prayer —

Prayer (G4335/G4336) is a form of *worship* that binds and knits our hearts together with the LORD. Worshipful prayer is an experience with the living God, whereby we see the nature of His loving kindness and embrace His goodness. It's a time of communion, whereby we recognize His magnificence and verbally declare our heartfelt love for Him.

Through prayer, we also demonstrate our trust in the LORD, as we bring our *supplications* and requests before Him. In addition, we receive the intimate revelation of who He's called us to be. Nevertheless, prayer is not self-centered. Rather, through perseverance and intercession, we also reach out on behalf of others. This two-way communication between God and man causes a spiritual shift, which brings supernatural change into the natural realm. The spiritual battles may rage, but in His intimate presence . . . tucked away under the shadow of His wing, we receive everything we need (Psalm 91). Therefore, we should take delight in the LORD, as we pray without ceasing and give thanks in all things (1 Thessalonians 5:17-18).

The mind is a battlefield. Either we'll destroy the works of the enemy, or he will seek to destroy us. Yet, the LORD has given us His authority and the armaments we need to be victorious (Luke 10:19). Every spiritual weapon and every piece of armor has the stamp of His Lordship upon it. We're commanded in Ephesians 6:13, to take on the whole armor of God that we may be able to stand in the evil day. The evil day is not off in the future, we're living in it now! Put your armor on! Put on the salvation, righteousness, truth and peace of God. Lift up the shield of faith and wield the sword of the Spirit. Find your safety in Christ, and boldly proclaim His Word in the earth. Don't ever allow the enemy to catch you spiritually naked and exposed! Rise up and be who the LORD has called you to be in Him!

Part 3 • *Loving God* with All Your Mind

Finally, remember to **stand** *(G2476)* against the enemy! We are not standing in your own strength. The LORD of Glory is standing with us. The LORD will never leave us, nor forsake us. He abides with us forever. He has bound Himself to us in an eternal covenant of love. He has given us everything He possesses. As we completely yield ourselves to the LORD, we will lack for nothing. Our God is all sufficient, and in Him we're victorious!

The LORD has empowered and appointed us to establish His kingdom in the earth. Therefore, we can go forth with a conquering mindset. The Kingdom of God is at hand. As believers, we just need to reach out by faith and receive it. He is the King of Glory, and He is strong and mighty in battle (Psalm 24:8)!

CHAPTER 10
THE SPIRITUAL MIND

The decisions we make over the course of a day (whether consciously or subconsciously) are continuous and innumerable. Whether on a momentary, daily, weekly, monthly or long term basis, every decision we make impacts our lives. In fact, the thoughts and activities taking place within our minds will determine whether we're functioning in a life or death mentality. Every thought and decision will bear fruit, so we have the opportunity to choose what we will bring forth in our lives:

<u>Romans 8:6</u> *For to be carnally minded is death; but to be spiritually minded is life and peace.*

The *carnal (G4561/G138)* mind is controlled by the fleshly *human nature* with all its implied *physical or moral frailties* and weaknesses, as well as its unbridled *passions*. It is motivated by lust, pride, selfish desires and forbidden appetites. It demands what it wants, just because it wants it! Righteousness and inner character are disregarded or shoved away into a dark corner or the deep recesses of the mind, as self-absorption and personal agendas rule and reign.

The carnal mind is in love with the things of the world. For this reason, when challenged, it will respond inappropriately to the Word of God. The carnally minded person may even feign a religious belief, but inwardly, there's a hateful, hostile, rebellious opposition to the things of God. This renegade mindset is disobedient to the Word of God and is not under the control of the Holy Spirit. Though few would admit it, such a mindset has come under the influence or control of satan and has become the enemy of God. For this reason, it can never please God (Romans 8:7; James 4:4). It's impossible to genuinely demonstrate one's love for the LORD, while at the same time, operating in a carnal mindset.

Comparatively, the **spiritually** *(G411/G4154)* minded person has a disposition that is focused on Christ. Such character allows the Holy Spirit to have preeminence in the realms of feelings (emotions), thoughts (mind), inclinations (will) and actions (obedience). The continual renewing of the mind through the Word of God is a joyful, habitual practice for the spiritual mind. It's always hungrily partaking of and thirstily drinking in, the truths of God. The spiritual mindset places the LORD God Almighty in the highest place of priority and at the center of everything. By doing so, it's strengthened with the life and power of God and has the ability to overcome the foolish ways of the flesh. With this, the LORD is well pleased.

Contrasting the two, while the carnal mind is self-focused, the spiritual mind is God-focused. The carnal mind strives to exist in the midst of lies, death and destruction. But the spiritual mind enjoys life and *peace (G1515)*, along with the blessings of *prosperity, rest and quietness in the LORD*. The spiritual and carnal mindsets have nothing in common; they are exact polar opposites. What type of mind do you possess? Your destiny is largely determined by your thoughts and corresponding actions. Therefore, ask yourself the following questions:

> Do I allow the Holy Spirit to have His way in my life, or do I demand my own destructive way?
>
> Do I want life and peace or death?
>
> Do I need to change my mindset?

THE RENEWED MIND

The truth is: Apart from Christ, the mind is driven by its unruly lusts and becomes polluted with wrong perceptions and vain imaginations. The spiritually unregenerate mind is overloaded and overflowing with pride, foolishness, idolatry, perversion, uncleanness, reprobation, unrighteousness and deceitfulness (Romans 1:21-32, 8:5-8). That's the bad news. The good news is this: The LORD knows that every human being needs a mental renovation (a renewing and transformation of the mind), and He knows exactly what's required to make it happen. We're instructed in:

<u>Romans 12:2</u> *And be not conformed to this world: but be ye transformed by the renewing of your*

Part 3 • *Loving God* with All Your Mind

mind, that ye may prove what is that good, and acceptable, and perfect, will of God.*

Those conforming to Christ are in compliance with His Word, and they refuse to be **conformed** *(G4964/G4862/G4976)* to this **world** *(G165).* They reject being *fashioned* after the same pattern as those who disregard Christ. There should be no *resemblance* of character between those who love the LORD and those who do not. The followers of Christ will choose to seek out *association* and *companionship* with like-minded believers.

We're not to allow ourselves to be twisted *together* or *brought* into *union* with the corrupt moral fiber of the *age.* We're not to possess the ways of the world as our own, nor process our thoughts by its faulty standards. The worldly mentality does not reflect the mind of God, and by default, rejects His perfect will for mankind.

To be **transformed** *(G3339/G3326/G3445)* is to, literally or figuratively, *be changed or transfigured by a* metamorphic *process, signifying an adjustment of parts in* one's *nature.* As followers of Christ, we can no longer live as we did prior to knowing Him. We are not that old creature. The life that was, no longer is; and the life that has come forth is brand new. As spiritual transformation takes place, the mind is renewed by the Word of God. Our character and nature are changed and our actions and outward appearance will also begin to take on noticeable changes. The outer man becomes the evidence of what's happening in the inner man.

Also, in Romans 12:2, *renewing (G342/G341/G303/ G2537)* the mind is a *renovation* that produces new freshness. This kind of renewal is also linked to *repetition, intensity and reversal*. This is not a single repair, temporary facelift or an easy revamp. In reality, it's a complete overhaul and remodel, which requires the undoing, stripping and removal of everything that's not in line with God's Master plan for our lives.

RENEWAL BRINGS TRANSFORMATION
Transformation radically affects the form, appearance, nature, character, direction and sometimes the position of that which is being renovated. For example, a person who trusts in Jesus Christ as their LORD and Savior cannot continue to live as they did prior to receiving salvation. They'll no longer desire to live a life of wickedness. Rather, they'll hunger and thirst for righteousness. Instead of going their own way, they'll begin to follow Christ. Instead of leaning to their own understanding, they'll seek the counsel of God. Instead of doing what everybody else is doing, they'll lift up a godly standard of behavior. If former friends reject Christ, then the follower of Jesus will find new friends of like faith. This spiritual transformation will clearly manifest in and through the natural thoughts, words and deeds of the believer.

Those who faithfully abide in the LORD will continue to be transformed throughout their entire lifetime. This process results in the total makeover of a human being. The new man in Christ is wholly recreated in righteousness and restored to a state of innocence and holiness. He is justified, purified and consecrated through his relationship with Christ. The new man takes on the character of the LORD; he's no longer the person he used to be. His motivations and actions have shifted from the corrupt nature, to Christ's likeness. Everything takes on a different look, feel and perspective, as we read in:

<u>2 Corinthians 5:17</u> Therefore if any man be in Christ, he is a new creature: old things are passed away; behold all things are become new.

If something is made new, either it never existed before and it has come into existence for the first time, or it's been returned to its original state of quality — completely restored and able to fulfill its original purpose. As believers in Christ, our primary purpose is to love and experience life with the God who created us. Once we've tasted the goodness of the LORD and the sweetness of eternal life, we'll no longer desire what this world or satan has to offer. We're exhorted in:

<u>Ephesians 4:22-24</u> That ye put off concerning the former conversation the old man, which is corrupt according to the deceitful lusts; ²³And be renewed in the spirit of your mind; ²⁴And that ye put on the new man, which after God is created in righteousness and true holiness.

If we're to put on the righteousness and holiness of God, we must first cast off the old way of life. There must be a separation. While casting off the old way of life and putting on the new, we are **renewed** *(G365/G303/G3501)* in the ***spirit*** *(G4151)* of our minds. We do this by allowing the Holy Spirit to *intensely* and *repeatedly reform, reverse,* renovate, *regenerate* and spiritually change our *rational soul* and *mental disposition.*

As mentioned, this renewal affects our state of mind, including our thoughts, intellect and understanding. Our feelings (emotions) and even the very nature of our being are brought into alignment with the teachings of Christ. When our lives are in alignment with Him, miraculous changes take place in every area of our existence. For example, we're set free from:

- all bondage of the world (Romans 6:16-23). Instead, we experience truth and freedom in Christ (Galatians 5:1; John 8:32).
- all unproductive guilt and failure (Romans 8:1-2). Instead, we receive righteousness and freedom from sin (Romans 6).
- all pride and self-exaltation (Proverbs 8:13, 13:10, 16:18; 1 John 2:16). Instead, we are free to serve the LORD with pure hearts & humility (Matthew 5:8; Philippians 2:3-11; 1 Peter 5:5).

RENEWAL BRINGS OBEDIENCE
The renewed mind of the believer is continually being refashioned through transformation. The evidence is

Part 3 • *Loving God* with All Your Mind

demonstrated through the believer's desire to live in truth, obey the LORD and exalt Him above all else. Motivated by love, they seek to become a genuine worshipper. Functioning in the grace of the new covenant, they're no longer concerned with or interested in the pretentious keeping of religious rules and facades. Spiritual transformation through Christ and renewal of the mind through His Word are to be the aspirations of every believer.

As the LORD becomes foremost in our thoughts, we'll take delight in doing what brings joy to His heart. After all, it is His eternal goodness, grace and love that motivate us to live and walk in righteousness. So, as an open display of our love and worship for Him, we choose to obey. Therefore, obedience is not difficult; it simply becomes an expression of our delight in Him.

The sweet weight of His glory causes us to desire more of Him. In turn, we're motivated to rid ourselves of everything that hinders us from knowing Him more intimately. It is only through true, loving worship that we enter into the joyful presence of the LORD. His pleasure and presence becomes our feast of great joy! This is the fruit of a renewed and transformed mind; it causes us to completely fall in love with Jesus.

> What are some of the greatest transformations the LORD has performed in you, so far?

Think On These Things

As saints of the living God, we have a responsibility to make discerning choices as to the thoughts we allow to reside in our minds. God is holy and commands us to be holy. Our holiness in not based on our own ability, but we're made holy through our relationship with Jesus Christ. By definition, a **holy** *(G40)* life is lived in a *sacred, physically pure, morally blameless and ceremonially consecrated* manner. For this reason, we must allow the Spirit of God to direct, correct and, when needed, rebuke our thoughts. We are kindly exhorted in God's Word concerning our thought patterns in:

***Philippians 4:8** Finally, brethren, whatsoever things are true, whatsoever things are honest, whatsoever things are just, whatsoever things are pure, whatsoever things are lovely, whatsoever things are of good report; if there be any virtue, and if there be any praise, think on these things.*

To **think** *(G3049/G3056)* means to *take an inventory* or *estimate*. This scripture tells us where to focus our thoughts. We're to think on and take inventory of those things which are true, honest, just, pure and lovely; also those things which reflect virtue, praise and a good report. Each person has a sacred obligation to protect their spirit, soul (mind, will and emotions) and body. To take an inventory, helps us determine if our hearts and minds are in the right place and focusing on the right things.

Part 3 • *Loving God* with All Your Mind

Whatever we think on will cause us to either 'muse,' be 'amused' or become 'bemused' by our thoughts. The English definition for the word 'muse' means to think or meditate. The definition for the word 'amuse' means to divert from serious thought thru deception, by first occupying the attention. The word 'bemuse' means to bewilder or confuse. Our thoughts are not to be diverted by distraction, nor are we to be deceived, bewildered or confused. The mere fact that it's possible to be amused with deception or bemused with confusion shows us the importance of taking an inventory of our minds.

We, as the people of God, are not to waste our time listening to, watching or thinking about ungodly things. If a person or issue needs prayer, then pray according to the Word of God, release it and stay focused on Kingdom business. Don't allow yourself to be distracted from the purposes of God. Now, let's briefly study the eight characteristics of the things we are to think on:

1

— TRUE —

Things that are **true** *(G227/G2990)* speak of that which is transparent, *concealing* or hiding nothing. For thoughts or people to be true, they must have pure motivations (without ulterior motives), and be rooted in the truth of the Word of God. If you find your attention pulled toward things or people that are not true, stop. Turn away and run toward truth!

Remember — Jesus Christ, who is the Word of God made flesh, is also the way, the truth and the life; therefore, think on Him (John 1:1, 14; 14:6).

2
— HONEST —

To think on things that are **Honest** *(G4586/G4576)* is to think on that which is *venerable, honorable and worthy of reverence and adoration*. Secrecy, deception and evasion will not be found in the midst of honesty. If you focus on that which is upright, sincere and straight forward, then you will find truth. Truth and honesty are married together; they cannot be separated. The scripture says that God is not a man that He should lie (Numbers 23:19). Therefore, pursue the LORD and all He represents, for He is the perfection of honesty.

3
— JUST —

Those things which are **just** *(G1342/G1349)* are *equitable* and self-evident, meaning they are obviously fair and clearly *right*. They represent the *principles, decisions and executions of justice* to punish, pass judgment or take reparation against injustice. Just people and things also represent *innocence, holiness and righteousness*. If you find your mind absorbed or angrily inflamed with the unfair injustices of the world, know that the LORD is the righteous Judge and He will deliver justice upon the wicked. In the meantime, ask the LORD to help you be an example of His moral decency and virtue. Remember, Jesus is

Part 3 • *Loving God* with All Your Mind

returning to set up His Kingdom and He will make all things just and right; therefore, think on Him. (Psalms 9:8, 96:13; 2 Timothy 4:8).

4
— PURE —

To think on what is **pure** *(G53/G40)* is to think on that which is *clean, innocent, modest, perfect* and *sacred (physically pure, morally blameless, and ceremonially consecrated)*. In character and lifestyle, the saints of God are to be as a pure and chaste virgin. We are espoused to Christ, and He is jealous over His Bride (2 Corinthians 11:2). Purity speaks of things that are spotless and wholesome. In this sense, it refers to the type of lives we're to be living as the Bride of Christ.

Impure thoughts, immoral lifestyles or toxic relationships are not included in our way of life. If you're involved with these things, repent and turn from them! Arrest every mental temptation and assault, and bring it into subjection to the Holy Spirit. Turn from that which is contaminated; ask the LORD for the wisdom and power to resist such things, as well as those who participate in them (James 1:5, 4:7). It is those who are pure in heart who are blessed; they shall see God (Matthew 5:8)

5
— LOVELY —

Those things which are **lovely** *(G4375/G4314/G5368)* are *friendly, acceptable* and superior. A lovely attitude expresses *affection* and a willingness to carry out one's duty as a matter of principle. It's extended from the heart, reflected in the *tenderness of a kiss*, and speaks of love between friends (John 13:34, 15:12, 17; Romans 12:10; Hebrews 13:1; 1 Peter 1:22; 2 Corinthians 13:12). If you do find yourself in the midst of unpleasant thoughts, situations or people, focus on what's lovely and rise above what's not. Learn to operate in the love of God at all times.

6
— GOOD REPORT —

To think on things of a **good report** *(G2163/G2095/G5345)*, is to meditate on that which is *well spoken of*, well done and *reputable*. A good report speaks of one's reputation, good deeds, devotion and faith in Jesus Christ, as well as the preaching of the Gospel. Such a report makes the bones fat, bringing forth good health and satisfaction. (Proverbs 15:30; Mark 16:15; Acts 6:3, 10:22, 22:12; Romans 10:14-18; 1 Timothy 3:7; Hebrews 11:1-2).

Ear tickling gossip, rumors and scandals are not what our thoughts or conversations should center upon; such chitchat is unfruitful and damaging. When invited or tempted to entertain such nonsense, remind yourself and/or others to think on the good things of the LORD. By doing so, you will exalt Jesus and disarm whatever the enemy intends to use for evil. The good report of God's Word changes circumstances, releases blessings and turns potential destruction into hope.

7
— Virtue —

Virtue *(G703/G730/G142)* speaks of manliness; being full of **virtue,** *valor, praise* and *excellence.* It also speaks of *strength* and the *ability to* lift, *take up, take away; expiate* and *remove sin.* Jesus is the greatest example of manly virtue and the embodiment of all it represents.

In fact, Jesus' virtue was so strong that, when He walked the earth, His presence drew sick people to Him; and as they reached out in faith, believing and touching the hem of His garment, His healing virtue made them completely whole (Luke 6:19; Mark 5:30). In every instance, godly virtue mixed with faith brought forth miracles. Certainly, the name of the LORD, His loving kindness, greatness and mighty acts are excellent (Psalms 8:1, 9, 148:13, 150:2).

Jesus walked in the power, life, knowledge, glory and virtue of God, and He has called us to do the same (John 14:12; 2 Peter 1:3, 5). If we can believe it, His virtue will empower us to preach the gospel, heal the sick, raise the dead and cast out devils. He did it when He walked on the earth, and He'll do it now.

Jesus is the same yesterday, today and forever. If you will allow Him, He'll manifest His virtue through you. (Matthew 10:8; Mark 5:30, 16:15-20; Luke 6:19, 8:46, 9:2, 10:1, 17-19; Hebrews 13:8; 2 Peter 1:3, 5-9).

8

— PRAISE —

Praise *(G1868/G1909/G134)* is expressed through joyful *stories* and victorious testimonies of what God has done. Praise gives *laudation* to the *commendable things* — His great and mighty acts, as well as the merciful goodness and loving kindness of the LORD. As we praise the LORD and proclaim all that He's done in our lives, we magnify His greatness in our understanding (Psalms 106:1-2, 145:9-12).

For those who operate in a biblical mindset of praise, they know the LORD always has a good report. We're not only to think on those things that are true, honest, just, pure, lovely, full of virtue and worthy of praise, but we're to know and trust that He is all those things and more to us. As we think on the report of the LORD, we're encouraged to love Him more and more, for He is ever faithful. Focus your thoughts on that which is hopeful, positive and successful in life. Praise the goodness of the LORD our God, and openly express it with great joy.

Chapter 11

The Fearlessly Sound Mind

Have you ever had a day when you felt you were about to go crazy and lose your mind? You know, when everything seems to have spun out of control? The pressure's on and fears try to take control of your thoughts? You're wondering if the issues of life are about to overwhelm you and carry you into a place of temporary insanity? Well, I have great news for you! God has not given us a spirit of insanity or a spirit of fear!! Take courage — help is on the way and deliverance is yours!

As believers, it's important to discern what truly belongs to us and what doesn't, but in the process of figuring this out, we also need to discern 'who' is trying to give us what! Ultimately, there are two sources trying to bring things into our lives — God and satan. God brings blessings and all that we need pertaining to life and godliness (2 Peter 1:3). On the other hand, satan brings wickedness, deception, destruction and death (John 8:44, 10:10). Many times, people ignorantly blame God for the things satan has done; we must have the wisdom to discern the difference.

Throughout this book, I keep repeating the importance of establishing the truths of God's Word in our lives. This is because we must understand that the Word of God is the will of God! If we know the Word, then we

Part 3 • Loving God with All Your Mind

know God's will for our lives. If we know God's will, then we have discernment to recognize and reject the counterfeit schemes of the devil. Anything that doesn't line up with the Word of God is a lie — a snare of the enemy. God's Word is absolutely necessary for survival and success!

THE SPIRIT OF FEAR

In relation to loving the LORD with all our minds, it's essential that the mind be filled with the peace of God. Spiritual discernment and wisdom are keys to obtaining and keeping our peace of mind intact. When our mental and spiritual peace is in position, then our thoughts are rational and we're able to make sound, godly decisions. Let's see how the LORD has set us free from the mental torments of fear and all that goes with it in:

<u>2 Timothy 1:7</u> For God hath not given us the spirit of fear; but of power, and of love, and of a sound mind.

The word **spirit** *(G4151/G4154)* is defined as *a current of air, breath (blast) or breeze*, as well as *the rational soul* (figuratively or by analogy). By implication, **spirit** is also defined as the *vital principle* (the force that animates and perpetuates living beings) and the *mental disposition*. Depending on the context of usage, it can also indicate an *angel, demon* or the *Holy Spirit*.

Though satan may try to blast intimidation and threats into our minds, God has not given us a spirit of fear.

Many times, fear is based on the speculations of what 'could happen' and not the reality of what's 'actually happening.' Our soul's emotional stability, mental disposition and choices aren't to be controlled by the fear tactics of the enemy.

Fear (G1167/G1169) is defined in the Greek as *dread (timidity)*, and it implies being *faithless*. Those who are fearful lack assurance, courage and bravery. This, in turn, causes them to be easily upset, fainthearted and cowardly. If thoughts of dread, apprehension, uneasiness, distrust, anxiety, concern, worry (and the emotions associated with these feelings) control us, then we are operating in faithlessness toward God. Whether we know it or not, we're considering Him to be unreliable, dishonest, disloyal and untrustworthy concerning the circumstances of our lives. In turn, this perspective creates an entrance for more fear to penetrate our minds; it becomes a vicious cycle of torment to the fearful soul.

God has a better plan than torment, fear and timidity for His people. Even so, before we can be freed, we must recognize these devilish assaults for what they are. We cannot accept the devil's thoughts, as if they're our own. We must see them as camouflaged packages of deception, containing 'false evidence appearing real' (F.E.A.R.). If the devil's mouth is moving, he's lying! It's not God's will for us to tolerate satan or any of his schemes, so quit listening to him! Instead, we're to rest in the fact that the LORD has wrapped us in His perfect covenant love, and He has higher purposes for us.

When it comes to thwarting God's plan for our lives, the devil likes to pull out his varieties of fear. Some of his favorite forms are the fear of failure, the fear of rejection, the fear of the unknown and the 'what-ifs' of life. These fears, through the use of vain imaginations and self-deception, become a tool of the enemy to steal opportunities and damage relationships, before they have time to be developed. These fears may manifest as timidity or shyness, but unadulterated fear is at the root. If not dealt with, fear and timidity will hinder, cripple or even destroy the ability of a person to fulfill their intended purpose and destiny.

Another way the enemy tries to attack is by bringing negative input from those who are closest to us. They may think they're trying to protect or instruct us, but their counsel may be misleading. If they're giving 'advice' that is not backed up by the principles of God's Word, then it must be cast aside.

Once we understand what the LORD wants to do in our lives, we cannot allow our thoughts to be controlled by what others may think, say or do against us. Don't allow those who are in disharmony with God's plan for your life to sow fear, doubt, unbelief or hindrances into your mind. This is just another tactic of the enemy to get you off your path of destiny.

The Spirit of Power, Love and a Sound Mind

According to 2 Timothy 1:7, God has given us the spirit of power, love and a sound mind, so that we are equipped to overcome the spirit of fear. God, our Creator, has poured His own attributes into us, so that we might release them into life's situations. If we can believe and act on His power and love, by choosing to think as He thinks, then fear will be a thing of the past.

The LORD has not given us a spirit of fear. Rather, He has given us His ***power*** *(G1411/G1410)*, in order to make it *possible* to function in His strength and valor. Jesus has already destroyed the works of the devil (1 John 3:8). Then, just to keep the devil in his place, Jesus gave His own followers power to, fearlessly, tread over all the power of the enemy. And, He boldly declared that nothing shall by any means hurt us (Luke 10:19). If we know this and act on it, then fear has no place wherein to build a stronghold. As we operate in God's authority, His *force (miraculous power)* is released through us to perform His mighty works in the earth.

Can you see the importance of allowing God's power to rise up in you and be released? It's not about the devil, and it's not about your own strength and ability. It's about the living God being alive inside of you and manifesting His might and power through you!

Even more, God doesn't stop by just giving us His power! He has also given us His unconditional ***love*** *(G26/G25)*. He sees us as His Beloved and celebrates

His relationship with us (Ephesians 1:3-9). He lavishly pours out the gift of His *affection* and *benevolence* upon us. Once we understand the power of the love of God, we will find our rest and peace in Him. His power and love working in and through us becomes the catalyst to overcome every onslaught of the enemy. Ask yourself these three questions:

Is there anything or anybody bigger, stronger, mightier, greater or more powerful than the LORD?

Is there anything too hard for Him?

Do you really understand His love for you?

Respectively, your answers should be: no, no and yes. If you answered any other way, then you have not yet discovered the true nature and heart of Father God. If you desire to fully know Him, you'll need to search your heart, and ask the Lord to reveal who or what you've exalted to a higher position in your life than Him.

Continuing with 2 Timothy 1:7, we see that along with power and love, God has also given us the spirit of a **sound mind** (G4995/G4994/G4998/G4982/G5424). This means that we have been given a spiritual gift to be teachable, sober and *disciplined*. Also, we're able to receive the *correction* and redirection of the LORD as needed. A sound mind is also a *safe mind* that's been *delivered*, *protected*, healed, preserved and made whole by the LORD. Therefore, it operates with *self-control*, discretion and *moderation* in regards to

CHAPTER 11 • THE FEARLESSLY SOUND MIND

its *opinions or passions*. This is the keeping power of the LORD. Even if our feelings, thoughts or decisions somehow get off course (in sin), the sound mind has the ability *to rein in or curb* that old nature, restoring a place of safety to our thoughts. This is evidence that salvation is at work in the believer's life.

A sound mind is a gift from the LORD. Therefore, insanity, craziness, reprobation, rebellion and perversion have no place in the thought life of the true worshipper. Such madness cannot operate within a sound mind. If an unhealthy or ungodly behavior pattern, thought or fear manifests in or through us (and is allowed to act out), then we have placed ourselves under the influence of a controlling force, other than the Spirit of God. This ungodly behavior should alert us to the fact that we need to seek the Lord and come back into alignment with His Word. Every one of us is a work in progress and that work is carried out over a lifetime. Remember, battles are won or lost based on what we believe in our minds! As we submit to the LORD, and allow His Word to renew our minds, we are freed from every device of the enemy, and we have victory over him.

GOD'S PERFECT LOVE
Now, there is a healthy fear of God and a healthy respect for laws, rules and authority that will keep us out of trouble, but the spirit of fear is different. The spirit of fear is a crippling, controlling, manipulating force that, if not dealt with, will cause a person to

make wrong life choices. A person under the influence of fear may also suffer from manifestations of excessive anxiety and worry; the need to control everybody and everything around them; irrational thought patterns and actions; panic attacks, sickness and disease. Whenever fear is manifesting, there's a lack of understanding concerning the love of God. We read in:

1 John 4:18 *There is no fear in love; but perfect love casteth out fear: because fear hath torment.*

According to this verse:

- There is no fear in love and no love in fear.
- There is no torment in love and no love in torment.
- Fear cannot operate, when there is perfect love; and love cannot be perfect, as long as there is fear.

Perfect (G5046/G5056) **love** (G26/G25) speaks of the *complete*, mature *affection* and *benevolence* that the LORD has for His people; He chooses to dote over us as an intimate lover. This kind of love is also defined as *a love feast*, representing a mutually reciprocating relationship of love. If we fully comprehend that the LORD is completely and unconditionally in love with us, as well as eternally committed to us, then there's no way we'll allow tormenting fears to overtake or control us. Instead, we'll rest in His faithfulness, knowing that He is taking care of all things pertaining to us.

God's love for us exhibits His trustworthiness and commitment. This brings an element of freedom into the relationship, which allows us to experience great joy and peace in Him. **Torment** *(G2851/G2849)*, on the other hand, is defined as *penal infliction* meant to *curtail* or, figuratively, *chastise* (for crimes and offenses). In other words: if you commit the crime, you do the time! The truth is: sin creates a reason to be fearful. There is a righteous and just punishment for our criminal offenses against God. Yet, for love's sake, He has also extended His great grace, favor and forgiveness toward us through Christ Jesus:

<u>**Romans 3:23-24**</u> *For all have sinned, and come short of the glory of God; ²⁴Being justified freely by his grace through the redemption that is in Christ Jesus:*

<u>**Romans 6:23**</u> *For the wages of sin is death; but the gift of God is eternal life through Jesus Christ our Lord.*

Jesus has taken the penalty and torment of our sin upon Himself. He suffered in our place and, in exchange, has given us the gift of eternal life. There is no love like the love of God. It is perfect, complete, unconditional, powerful and without torment. Never allow fear or failure from your past to control your present or your future. Reliving your failures is a death sentence to your destiny. Instead, receive the spirit of power, love and a sound mind (which the

Part 3 • *Loving God* with All Your Mind

LORD has already given to you), and love Him with every fiber of your being!

Don't Believe the Lies!

We overcome the spirit of fear and the lies associated with it, by submitting to the power, love and sound Word of the LORD and allowing His Holy Spirit to work in our lives (2 Timothy 1:7). We must learn to recognize the enemy's tactics and crush his sinister agendas in the spiritual realm. Only then, are we able to take authoritative dominion over wrong thoughts, and overthrow the fear filled demonic schemes of the devil. Every ungodly fear is attached to a lie. Therefore, fear cannot take hold of us, if we reject the lie behind it and embrace the truth of God's promises.

The First Lie

The first sin ever committed was based on mankind believing a lie. One lie, flowing from the lips of a satan-possessed serpent, caused man to doubt the integrity of his Creator. One lie, believed and embraced, created an entrance for fear and rebellion to besiege the soul of man. One lie, honored above the Word of God and acted upon, changed the course of human history.

The first lie released in the earth was spoken by satan to mankind. This first lie took place in a perfect paradise — the Garden of Eden. Adam and Eve were the first to believe the lie. Alas, they would not be the last. Before we consider the downfall of man and the infiltration of sin into the earth, let's briefly reconsider his creation;

***Genesis 2:7** And the LORD God formed man of the dust of the ground, and breathed into his nostrils the breath of life; and man became a living soul.*

The Creator of all things does everything with a purpose. After He formed the man, He intimately blew His own **breath** *(H5397/H5395)* of life, a *puff* of *wind,* into the soul of a lifeless clump of clay. Thereby, imparting a portion of His *vital breath* — with its life giving force, *divine inspiration* and spiritual *intellect* — into the soul of mankind. Thus, man became a living soul.

Think about it! Man was nothing but a lifeless pile of dirt, until God breathed his creative power and spiritual DNA into him. Consider this: Man was made from the dust of the earth. However, when God created man from that dust, there were no bones, muscles, blood vessels, organs, glands, cells, fibers or tissues resident in that dust. Yet, through the breath and supernatural power of God, all the inward parts, fluids and systems of Adam's body instantly manifested and began functioning. With one puff of life giving breath, God deposited His miraculous power into man and he became a living soul with a functioning body! How magnificent is the LORD?! Truly, mankind is fearfully and wonderfully made, and the works of the LORD are marvelous (Psalm 139:14).

In addition, if man received God's life, God's spiritual DNA and God's wholeness when he was created and received the breath of life, then there was no part of him that did not come directly from Father God. If this be the case, then how did man become fearful? Why did he believe the lies of satan? One thing is for sure: Fear and deception did not come from God! Now, let's look at the treachery of the fall of man:

Genesis 3:1-10 *Now the serpent was more subtle than any beast of the field which the LORD God had made. And he said unto the woman, Yea, hath God said, Ye shall not eat of every tree of the garden? ²And the woman said unto the serpent, We may eat of the fruit of the trees of the garden: ³But of the fruit of the tree which is in the midst of the garden, God hath said, Ye shall not eat of it, neither shall ye touch it, lest ye die. ⁴And the serpent said unto the woman, Ye shall not surely die: ⁵For God doth know that in the day ye eat thereof, then your eyes shall be opened, and ye shall be as gods, knowing good and evil. ⁶And when the woman saw that the tree was good for food, and that it was pleasant to the eyes, and a tree to be desired to make one wise, she took of the fruit thereof, and did eat, and gave also unto her husband with her; and he did eat. ⁷And the eyes of them both were opened, and they knew that they were naked; and they sewed fig leaves together, and made themselves aprons. ⁸And they heard the voice of the LORD God walking in the garden in the cool of the day: and Adam and his wife hid themselves from the presence of the*

Chapter 11 • The Fearlessly Sound Mind

LORD God amongst the trees of the garden. ⁹And the LORD God called unto Adam, and said unto him, Where art thou? ¹⁰And he said, I heard thy voice in the garden, and I was afraid because I was naked; and I hid myself.

This is the first time scripture records that mankind was **afraid** *(H3372)*. Adam and Eve had listened to the devil's lies, dishonored the LORD and failed to morally *revere* Him. They denied and defied His righteous character, His holiness, truth, justice, integrity and supreme authority. Through their alignment with satan, they chose to create their own rules and lifestyle standards, based on the lust of their flesh, instead of living in accordance with the Word of God. Adam and Eve became *frightened* after they disobeyed the LORD and realized the gravity of their sin.

The spiral into sin went like this:
- God commanded.
- Satan challenged.
- Man rationalized and rebelled.
- Sin, fear, shame & nakedness manifested.

As a result of sin, the glorious light and presence of God departed from Adam and Eve, and tormenting fear entered into their hearts and minds. Simultaneously, the process of death began in their spirit, soul and body; they felt separated from God and hid themselves in the garden. They were naked and ashamed, yet they blamed the serpent and one another for their sin. Regardless of their excuses, they faced the judgment of God, were put out of the Garden and remained separated from His presence (Genesis 3:11- 24).

The seed of sin was conceived from compromise with a lying tongue. Don't ever forget that the devil is a liar, and he hates mankind — always has and always will. We see the venom of a lying tongue in:

Proverbs 26:28 *A lying tongue hateth those that are afflicted by it; and a flattering mouth worketh ruin.*

Lying is a weapon of affliction that destructively shoots forth from the mouth of the wicked. In fact, it's a hate crime! Along with pride, murder, wickedness, mischief, discord and false accusations, it's one of the seven abominations the LORD despises (Proverbs 6:16-19). Our ears are to be closed to the lies of satan, and our mouths should never come into agreement with anything he says.

To understand why the devil hates man, you must dig into the Word of God to find His treasures of truth. Man was the crowning glory of creation, and God wanted intimacy with them. To this very day, the enemy still seeks to destroy that relationship. So, let's look at the details of the devil's deep disdain for man:

THE FATHER OF LIES

Before man was created, the devil (whose name was, originally, lucifer) was the anointed cherub that covered the holy mountain and the throne of God. He was fully clad with precious stones and had tabrets (tambourines) and pipes on the inside of him. He was the master musician — the worship leader — in heaven. He was perfect and beautiful in all his ways, until he lifted himself up in pride and declared that he would ascend above the clouds and be like the Most High. He stirred up rebellion in heaven and polluted the sanctuary. At that point, lucifer lost his position and was thrown out of the presence of God. Like lightening, he fell from heaven. He was eternally demoted to the lowest position in creation. This created being, who used to be the worship leader in heaven, became the devil and His name was changed from lucifer to satan (Isaiah 14:12-16; Ezekiel 28:11-19; Luke 10:18).

It's interesting that the name **lucifer** *(H1966/H1984)* means *the morning star,* and it comes from the root word **hálal** (in the sense of *brightness*). From earlier mention, you may remember that Hálal is a Hebrew word for 'praise' and one of its meanings is to be *clear in sound.* Hálal also means *to shine; make a show; boast, rave; be clamorously foolish* (to praise vigorously and without forethought), and *to celebrate.*

As I was contemplating this, the LORD revealed to me that lucifer was created to be an 'instrument of praise' before the throne of God. He was created to bring forth the music of heaven. Can you even imagine the sounds that would have reverberated from the pipes and tabrets that were on the inside of him? It had to be one of the most glorious sounds ever created. Though he was positioned in the midst of the presence of God, he was not satisfied. His lust caused him to want something that was never intended for him. The *iniquity (H5766/H5765)* and pride within him caused him to become *morally distorted, evil*, unrighteous, vicious and rebellious. He had forgotten his God assigned purpose.

Also, remember that lucifer's name signified *brightness*. He was created to shine in the glorious presence of the LORD. Yet, he rejected his assigned position. By attempting to reposition and exalt himself, he sought to usurp the position and authority of God. For this reason, lucifer was cast out of heaven and the presence of God. He was stripped of his ministry, his position, and he lost his anointing. Even though satan has fallen, he still has the ability to transform himself as a deceptive angel of light for his own wicked purposes (2 Corinthians 11:13-15).

There are powerful lessons in this for the people of God and, especially, those who are called and anointed for the (worship) ministry. We're to be instruments of praise before the throne of God. If we're to continue to dwell in His presence, we must be willing to stay in our ordained position, as we serve in a spirit of humility and honor to God. We're not to be caught up in our own beauty or ability. Nor are we to give any opportunity for pride, iniquity and self-exaltation to operate within us. Striving to make a name for ourselves and seeking our own glory is not to be our objective in life. Rather, we're to reflect and carry forth the truth of God's Word and the light of His glory within us. We're to lift up and exalt the name of Jesus, for all glory belongs to Him and Him alone!

Also, if lucifer/satan is to be any illustration, we can see that it's possible for those who are not (or are no longer) operating in the purity of their anointed calling, to hypocritically appear as though they are. All that glitters is not gold! One who is following their own ambitions (instead of the leading of the Holy Spirit) will pollute the call of God on their life. Believers need to be discerning and particular about whom they receive from in all areas of ministry.

Those in leadership (as well as in the congregation) are to guard the spiritual condition of their hearts. We need to do periodic heart checks with the LORD and let Him examine us. If our hearts are messed up, our worship and lifestyle will be messed up; if our hearts are right, our worship and lifestyle will be right. We need to compare everything, concerning our worship and lifestyle, to the standards of God's Word. This is the litmus test for all believers, and particularly, for those in ministry positions who bear the responsibility of leading the flock of God.

It's the pure heart that beckons the presence of God, including the manifest light of His glory. The Spirit of God dwells in those who belong to Him. Therefore, we carry the foundation of life and the light of God's glory within us. Jesus is the source of all light and life, and He's called us to be the light of the world. If we follow Him, we'll never walk in darkness (Matthew 5:14; John 8:12).

Does your life radiate God's truth?

MOTIVE FOR THE LIE

When God created mankind in His own image and likeness, man became the human evidence and expression of his Creator. I believe Adam and Eve were covered in the light and glory of God. They shone with His radiance and beauty and were given dominion to rule with God's authority over all the earth.

Because satan hates God, he can't stand the fact that man was created in the image and likeness of God. Every time satan looks at a human being, he sees the image of God, which reminds him of his own humiliation and demise. In jealous rage, satan despises the fact that he was never given the full authority or dominion he so rebelliously desired. For this reason, he has revolted against God and man. The ambition of satan is to mockingly defy God and destroy mankind.

Chapter 11 • The Fearlessly Sound Mind

In an effort to disconnect man from God, satan knew all he had to do was convince Adam and Eve to reject truth and embrace a lie. It would be a battle of the minds. He would concoct a lie against God, by subtly twisting the command of God (that they were not to eat from the tree of the knowledge of good and evil). If he was successful, satan would then lead Adam and Eve into sin and disobedience.

The devil began his tricky and tangled perversion by approaching the woman to ask her, *"Yea, hath God said, 'Ye shall not eat of every tree of the garden?"* At this point, satan had taken the direct command of God and twisted it into a question; thereby, implying that God was withholding something from them. The devil knew that, if Eve would take the bait, then she would give into temptation and irreversibly fall into death and destruction. Yet, the LORD had already commanded Adam and Eve concerning this in:

***Genesis 2:16-17** ...Of every tree of the garden thou mayest freely eat: ¹⁷But of the tree of the knowledge of good and evil, thou shalt not eat of it: for in the day that thou eatest thereof thou shalt surely die.*

So, God gave Adam and Eve great liberty to eat of EVERY tree in the garden EXCEPT one — the tree of the knowledge of good and evil. They had an unlimited supply of delicious food to eat. They could munch fruits from every other tree in the garden, including the tree of life. But the devil didn't focus on their freedom. Rather, he directed their attention to the one limitation that God had given them, and he began to twist the Word of God concerning it. Beware of this demonic tactic. It causes a person to focus on what they don't have instead of all the blessings they do have. This stirs up discontentment and lust for that which is forbidden and brings death.

Eve made a fatal mistake when she decided to converse with the devil in snakeskin. Eve knew better than to eat from the tree of the knowledge of good and evil, but somewhere along the way, she got the idea that if she merely touched the fruit of the tree, she would die (Genesis 3:3). However, God didn't say that; He said that, if they 'ate' it, they would die. So at some point, either Adam or Eve added to the Word of God. That's a no, no!!

When the devil heard Eve speak something other than the exact Word of God, he knew he had something to build on. Illusively, he drew her into his pit of deception by responding with an outright lie, **"Ye shall not surely die: For God doth know that in the day ye eat thereof, then your eyes shall be opened, and ye shall be as gods, knowing good and evil."** (Genesis 3:4-5). With this lie, the devil was challenging God's integrity and His Word, as well as Adam and Eve's identity.

Now, why would satan lie in this way? Remember, when lucifer rebelled in heaven, he proudly declared that he would 'be like the Most High?' You see, this was the heart of the issue; lucifer didn't get to be like the Most High, so he certainly wasn't happy about Adam and Eve being created in the image and likeness of the Most High. Jealousy tore at his rebellious pride. If he couldn't be exalted, he didn't want anybody else to be exalted above him. The devil sought to displace Adam and Eve from their positions of dominion and to pervert their nature.

The devil knew that, if he could deceptively draw man into a position of distrust, pride and rebellion against God, then he could lead them into the snares of sin. His desire was to bring man into disobedience, so he could strip them of their dominion and separate them from their intimate relationship with the Father. If he could pull it off, then satan would rule over them, instead of them ruling over him.

Make no mistake, the enemy is consumed with self-exaltation, and he wants dominion over you as well. Even today, the devil is watching to see whether you will honor God or give into lustful desires, so he can take you captive. Be alert to the enemy's devices, and know that the LORD has a greater plan in mind for you!

> Will you take the bait of a lie, or will you obey the Word of the LORD?
>
> Who will you choose to love and serve?

THE INFLUENCE AND EFFECTS OF THE LIE

Once Eve embraced the lie of satan, she began to doubt the integrity of God. She mentally questioned His truthfulness, as if He were holding out on her and Adam. At that point, Eve (under the influence of the lie) was mentally embracing the forbidden fruit. She rationalized that, even though she knew God had said, 'No!' the fruit would still be good for food. Well, all the fruit in the garden was good for food! Why was the fruit on that one forbidden tree so deliciously alluring? It was because Eve had embraced the lies of the enemy. She allowed her lustful desires to become her top priority, instead of heeding the Word of God. She entertained the devil's agenda, and yearned for that which was never intended for her.

Eve was lured by the devil's persuasive temptation, and she began to mentally rationalize why it would be okay for her to disobey the LORD. Her actions soon followed her deceived mindset. As her eyes beheld that which she desired, her hands seized that which was forbidden.

When Eve reached out, touched and plucked the fruit from the forbidden tree, but didn't physically die (as she erroneously thought she would), she was emboldened to continue in her disobedience. As lust persisted in her heart, she probably reasoned that since she touched the fruit and didn't die, then she could also eat it and not die. Eve had deceived herself into believing that she knew better than God. Her belief in a lie changed her life forever, as she fell into sin.

As she partook of the wonderfully succulent fruit, Eve enjoyed the pleasures of sin . . . for a moment. However, her sordid satisfaction would be short lived. Because Eve listened to the tempter, she became a temptress.

After she had eaten and fallen into sin, she then offered the pleasure of the forbidden fruit to her husband. Adam, as a son of God, should have stood against the ploys of the devil. He should have spoken truth to his wife and obeyed the LORD, but he didn't.

Apparently, Adam wrongfully reasoned that, if Eve could eat the fruit and not die, he could do the same. Once the lie had been planted and given room to germinate, lust and self-justification became the fertilizer to make it grow. In their disobedience, Adam and Eve had listened to satan. Ultimately, instead of honoring the Word of the LORD, they embraced their very enemy.

When Adam and Eve turned away from the author and finisher of their faith, their character took on the rebellion and wickedness of the enemy of God. They had allowed the devil to twist their thoughts, to the point of believing that God was deceiving them and withholding pleasure from them. They allowed the devil to distort and pervert their perspective of God. When the man and woman began to think like the devil, they began to act like him. Therefore, they figured they had the right to override God's instructions. Thus, in their deception, they blatantly rejected the Word of God. Their chosen deception made it selfishly acceptable for them to fulfill their own will, instead of the will of God.

In the process of being conned, Adam and Eve forgot their ordained purpose — to rule and have dominion over the earth. So, as an unexpected bonus with the package of sin and death, fear overrode their lives. When their sin caused the light of God's glory to depart from them, they found themselves naked, shamefully exposed and subject to the *dreadful* spirit of *fear*. This was evidence of their *faithlessness* and lack of trust in their Creator. In fact, through sin, Adam and Eve shifted the spiritual, mental and physical condition of all mankind.

Remember, when the devil came into the garden, he came subtly — with clever lying words (to pilfer the mind), devious accusations (to attack truth and character) and sly temptations (to deceive and devastate), all packaged up in charmingly smooth, slippery snakeskin. His mode of operation and main objectives are still the same today. Every chance he gets, the devil still seeks to use his hissing deceptions and whispered enchantments to steal, kill and destroy (John 10:10).

If the devil can steal the Word of God, then he can deceive; if he can deceive, then he can destroy. But, if we hold up the Word of God as the ultimate truth, and use it as the standard by which we make every decision, then we cannot be deceived. If we cannot be deceived, then the enemy cannot steal from us. If he can no longer deceive or steal from us (because we are submitted and obedient to God), then we are restored to our rightful position of dominion.

If we're walking in our God given authority and dominion through Christ, then we again have the power to rule over satan and his demonic hordes. We're not to tolerate the lies of the enemy. We're to rebuke him with the Word of God and cast him out, in Jesus' name!

Adam and Eve made a horribly wrong decision when they rejected the divine will of God for their lives. By doing so, they chose to submit to the will of satan. They should not have entertained his accusations against God or put up with his rebellion. When the devil started talking foolishness, they should've exercised dominion over him, silenced him and cast him out of the garden.

Unfortunately, Adam failed in his leadership and Eve encouraged her husband to sin against the LORD. The forbidden fruit of their disobedience cost them more than they could have possibly imagined. As a result, satan stole their dominion and they were separated from the presence of God. They lost their innocence, identity, purpose, power, security and responsibility. And, in the end, they both eventually died.

Part 3 • *Loving God* with All Your Mind

Even so, God's merciful grace is so amazing, and if we're willing, we can actually learn from the mistakes of others. Learn from Adam and Eve. Don't allow the devil to entice you with deception. Don't allow him to whisper his obscenities against God in your ears. Don't allow him so sow seeds of discontentment in your mind. Don't allow him to tempt you with the lust of your flesh. Instead, learn to walk in the fullness of your God given dominion. Obey the LORD, and use His Word to expose the lies of the devil. Put the enemy to flight, in Jesus' name.

Are you wrestling with fear in your life?

Do you have any areas in your life where fear or lusts are drawing you into temptation, compromise, deceived rationalization or sin?

Have you considered the consequences of your actions, if you choose to give into those temptations?

Do you understand that, if you give into sin, you are submitting to satan?

Have you considered that fear, lust and compromise are destiny killers?

Are you ready to throw that slithering devil out of your garden of life?

LOVE GOD & PUT THE DEVIL UNDER FOOT!

Have you ever been in church service during testimony time, when some dear ole saint gets up to tell about how the devil has been after them all week? They may even share how he has been beating them down and giving them all sorts of trouble. Well, when I hear such 'testimonies' it sounds like the devil is being glorified, and the dear ole saint has an impotent god. It would appear the dear ole saint and the devil have come into some sort of unholy alliance and both are out of position!

The devil is not supposed to be chasing after the people of God. He's not supposed to be beating us down and giving us trouble! No! No! No! The people of God are to be casting the devil out, in Jesus' name, and giving him so much trouble that he doesn't want to be anywhere near us. We must remember that Jesus has given us power over the enemy and we need to use it:

Luke 10:19 Behold, I give unto you power to tread on serpents and scorpions, and over all the power of the enemy: and nothing shall by any means hurt you.

If Jesus gave us this power over the enemy, then why is satan (or his demonic representatives) up in our face? That snake is supposed to be under our feet! When Jesus gave us His ***power*** *(G1849/G1832)*, He gifted us with His *competent ability* and *force* to overcome the devil. On behalf of heaven, we are empowered to operate in a *superhuman capacity* of authority on earth. Having such power is a privilege. The LORD has given us jurisdiction, with *delegated influence and power*, so that we may officiate as His *magistrates and rulers*. Jesus has called and ordained us to emulate and bring forth His righteousness and *freedom* in the earth. Part of our Kingdom assignment is to exercise dominion over the devil, in Jesus' name.

So, God has clearly given us His power, **to tread on serpents and scorpions, and over all the power of the enemy**, but what does that look like? Let's find out! It's good to ask this question; it's even better to know the answer.

Far too many Christians only skim the scriptures on a superficial level, barely absorbing the meaning of the text. Rarely taking the time to definitively explore and analyze the original roots and meanings of the words, they find themselves in a state of neglectful ignorance; thereby, limiting their depth of understanding and empowerment for personal application and life changing results. If people don't understand how to apply the Word of God to their lives, then it cannot help them.

It's like having a fire in the kitchen and not knowing how to use the fire extinguisher. A sudden, unexpected life event that could have been a momentary disruption becomes a major disaster — all because of a lack of knowledge and understanding. As believers in Christ, we're not to be ignorant. We need to study the Word of God in depth, and learn how to apply it to our lives. It could be the difference between blessing or ruin, life or death.

Luke 10:19 declares that believers in Christ have power to **tread** *(G3961/G3817)* on serpents, scorpions and every manifestation of the enemy. We're to (literally or figuratively) *trample* underfoot, every demonic force that gets in our *path*! As we walk out the plan of God for our lives, we're to take heavenly jurisdiction over every single place where the soles of our feet trod. We're to use God's authority to take territory from the devil and reclaim it for the Kingdom of God!

In addition, to tread upon the enemy also means that we've been empowered *to hit* him with *a single, stinging blow* — a knockout punch!! So don't let the devil get up in your face! Hit him hard and knock him out with the Word of God and the name of Jesus! Once he is laid out in the spiritual dust, violently trample him underfoot, because that is where he belongs! Whenever we operate in the power of God and deliver that knockout punch to the devil, he doesn't have a snowball's chance in hell to come against us! He is a defeated foe!

Let's define what **serpents** *(G3789)* represent, so it will be easier to discern their activity. Serpents, figuratively, represent the *sly, cunning and artfully malicious* methods of *satan*, as he watches (with *sharpness of vision)* and seeks to find a way to come against us. He may try to attack us through human beings, mental torments or wickedly inspired spiritual manifestations. Bearing in mind the characteristics and behavior patterns of serpents, their attacking approach could be very smooth and hard to decipher until they're ready to strike. Spiritual serpents can be anything positioned in the hidden places of darkness — lying in wait to wage a surprising and venomous attack when least expected.

Scorpions *(G4651/G4649/G4626)* also hide in hidden places, moving about in *concealed* secrecy. They cause pain by suddenly *piercing* their victims with *stinging* blows and, then, they *dig* into their victims' flesh to inflict more venomous torment. However, if the flesh nature has been 'crucified with Christ' (Galatians 2:20), then spiritual scorpions are unable to pierce it or cause damage.

In the spirit world, these 'serpents' and 'scorpions' are demonic forces who *peer about* as *sentries* or *scouts*, *scoping* out a target with an implied *goal*. They diligently search for:

- Dark, secret places in their victim's nature or moral fiber — where they can hide, multiply and manifest their nature.
- Weak places in their victim's life and body — where they can overcome them.

- Cracks in faulty character and breaches in areas of compromise — where they can stealthily slip in to cause destruction and pain.

Yet, these demonic forces cannot infiltrate believers unless they are permitted access. They cannot gain access, if we deliver a spiritual knockout punch of God's power upon them, in Jesus' name. Instead, of inflicting pain and misery in their intended victims, they'll be lying in the dust, pulverized under our feet!

Lastly in Luke 10:19, the *power (G1411/G1410)* of the *enemy (G2190)* refers to satan's *force* and *ability* to operate in what would appear to be *miraculous power*; as well as his 'enemy' character trait of *hatefulness*. He is *odious, actively hostile* and has an *adversarial* and rebellious nature, which he exhibits against God and man. The devil never has good intentions toward his victims. He doesn't give anything to anybody without expecting to take their soul into complete captivity, bondage and destruction. Please understand — the devil has no problem moving in miraculous deception, if it brings him the end result he desires. Deception is his area of mastery and his motives are always perverse!

If the devil cannot find a place to attach to our flesh nature; then, he has no power to harm us. By the power of Christ, we can shut down satan's attempts to operate in our lives and victimize us. Those in Christ should never take on a victim mentality. We have the power to overcome the enemy, because the LORD called us to be victors, not victims!

As we close out this particular chapter, let's consider those who deal treacherously against us. They may unjustly and falsely accuse us or say hurtful things about us. They may lash out in an offensive manner, seeking to cause us pain. In those moments, consider the source. If there's no truth to their assaults, or if they're bringing up past failures that have been repented of and forgiven, then they have just become a mouth piece for satan, the accuser of the brethren. They're being used to launch the devil's attack. When this happens, most people have no idea that they're being used as the devil's pawn. Realize who the real enemy is, and trample him underfoot as Jesus has empowered you to do.

So, when people don't act right, choose to return good for evil and learn to love them, in spite of their sin. Forgive them for any offenses caused, and pray for their salvation and deliverance. Also, promptly and directly, rebuke, bind up and cast the devil out, in Jesus' name. Above all else, continue loving the LORD as you grow into the fullness of your calling and destiny!

⊷ CHAPTER 12 ⊶

TRUSTING GOD & OVERCOMING FEAR

So many people, including Christians, battle with fear. Too many believers are tormented with the fear of the unknown, fear of the what-ifs, fear of failure, fear of death, fear of loss, fear of being inadequate, fear of _____ (you fill in the blank). In chapter 11, we studied "The Fearlessly Sound Mind" and learned that God has not given us a spirit of fear (2 Timothy 1:7). Even so, in times of uncertainty and unexpected events in life, fear may try to gain access and erect a stronghold. For this reason, I believe the topic warrants further study.

If we're not continually building up our faith through the Word of God, doubts can enter in and assail our minds. (Romans 10:17). As alluded to earlier: Where there is strong, solid faith, fear cannot dominate; where there is strong fear, faith cannot operate. Fear and faith are opposing forces.

FEAR VS. FAITH

If not arrested and properly dealt with according to the Word of God, unbridled fear from the enemy can develop into a form of mental terrorism and spiritual torment. Some of the side effects or manifestations of fear are: emotional instability (dismay, dread, anxiety, apprehension, distress, insecurity, panic, etc.), broken relationships and isolation, irrational thinking (lack of trust, indecision, procrastination, double-mindedness,

Part 3 • *Loving God* with All Your Mind

horror etc.). If this debilitating fear is left unrestrained, it can overwhelm a person to the point of causing mental incapacity and emotional paralysis, as well as physical sickness and disease. As a result, if we receive the fear that the enemy seeks to put upon us, it will become the killer of dreams and a thief of destiny. This was never the plan of God for mankind.

***Faith** (G4102)* is the will to act upon the *moral conviction, persuasion,* assurance and fidelity of the *truthfulness of God.* Genuine faith is displayed as believers give *credence* to God's Word and remain *constant in their profession* of His truth. Obviously, the foundation of true faith is established in having confidence and *reliance upon Christ for salvation.* Based on this definition from the Greek language, we cannot have true faith apart from God. Therefore, our level of faith is directly related to how we respond to the LORD and His Word.

At times, it's possible to have strong faith in some areas, yet be weak in other areas. When this happens, we may struggle with double-mindedness and fearfulness in our weaker areas (Mark 9:14-29). Remember, we can always ask God to increase our faith.

As already mentioned, fearfulness indicates that a person does not have a full understanding of God's tender and unconditional love for them. If we have faith and trust in the LORD, we know He loves us and has control of every aspect of our lives. If this is true, then we have no reason to fear.

People of active faith learn to see beyond their current circumstances and fears. They allow the truth of God's faithfulness to encourage them (pushing past hindering obstacles) into their destiny. When we trust the LORD, we can know that the Holy Spirit within is perfecting all that concerns us (Philippians 1:6, 1 Peter 5:10).

Let's look at a few biblical examples of people — just like us — who encountered things that could have paralyzed them with fear. Some faced the supernatural appearance of angels, while others supernaturally endured their circumstances with boldness and prayer. Nonetheless, they were able to see through the eyes of faith; they chose to believe God and rose above their fears.

As a result, the lives (faith and actions) of these biblical characters impacted both history and eternity. God used them to make His glory known. Let's allow Him to use us in the same way.

1
— MARY —
(LUKE 1:26-38)

Mary was a young, unmarried Jewish virgin who had a great call of God upon her life. She was created with purpose and had a divine destiny. When she chose to submit herself to the LORD (in order to become the mother of our Savior, Jesus Christ), Mary experienced the miraculous, supernatural power of God upon her physical body and her life. Let's see how she carried out this great responsibility.

Part 3 • *Loving God* with All Your Mind

GOD'S GRACE, FAVOR & HOLY GHOST POWER

Mary was most likely going about her daily activities when the angel Gabriel appeared and said, *"...**thou art highly favoured, the LORD is with thee**..."* I imagine she was quite stunned to see a heavenly being stand before her, with the glory of the LORD radiating from him. Then, Gabriel spoke to her again and said, *"**Fear not, Mary: for thou hast found favour with God.**"*

In fact, scripture tells us Mary was *troubled (G1298)*, completely *disturbed* and *agitated with alarm* at the stirring words of Gabriel. He announced the plan of God; she would conceive in her womb, bring forth a son and call His name Jesus. He would be great and would be called, the Son of the Highest. He would forever reign and His kingdom would have no end. There was just one unusual detail. Mary was a virgin; she'd had no sexual encounter with a man, so how could she possibly give birth to a child?

The angel, Gabriel, told Mary to *fear (G5399/G5401)* not. This indicates that, even in the midst of this great favor and blessing, she was *frightened*, *alarmed* and in *awe* or *reverence* at the appearance of the angel, as well as the declaration of such amazing news. In spite of Gabriel's alarming announcement, Mary submitted her heart and her life to the will of God.

For Mary to have a baby would have been natural, but for her to have a baby without intimacy with a man would have been either impossible or supernatural.

Although she'd never had a sexual relationship with anyone, she did enjoy a love relationship with her Creator, prior to her conception of Jesus. God knew Mary was a godly woman of integrity, and she could be trusted with the responsibility of this calling. So, He called her as a woman of destiny, to fulfill a kingdom purpose. Mary could never have made such a thing happen on her own. She was simply a willing handmaiden who said "yes" to her God. She faithfully submitted to Him and obtained His *favour (G5485/ G5463)*. Thus, she received the *grace* of His *divine influence upon her heart and its reflection in* her *life*. God's graciousness reassured her and made it possible for her to *calmly* and *cheerfully* receive the unique plan of God for her life with *happiness* and *gratitude*.

In turn, the Holy Ghost came upon her to **overshadow** *(G1982/G1019/G4639)* and *envelop* her in a *haze of brilliancy*. He *invested* the force of His **power** *(G1411)*, *influence and miraculous ability* within her. Distributing the seed of the Word of God into her womb, the Spirit of God caused her to supernaturally conceive that 'holy thing' destined to be born of her.

Everything God does is supernatural, even when the supernatural appears to be natural. He's operating behind the scenes, long before we see the physical manifestation of what He's doing. He'll maneuver situations and circumstance to do the impossible, just to exemplify that He is God and controls all things.

Now, the LORD had chosen to use Mary mightily, but first, she had to allow her faith to rise above her fears. She also had to be willing to accept, welcome and nurture the seed of God's Word in her womb. Day by day, Mary kept the Word of God — the Christ child — hidden in the secret parts of her being and near to her heart. She allowed Him to grow within her, and at the appointed time, she gave birth to the Son of God. She was supernaturally used to bring about the Messiah — the one who would go forth and change people, kingdoms and nations forever.

GOD'S CALL, OUR RESPONSE

Similar to Mary, followers of Christ will (or should) experience unique supernatural encounters and adventures in the LORD. He organizes life events specifically designed to carry us into our destinies. Our personal journeys to destiny are as unique as the destinies themselves. By the LORD's masterful design, we've been tailor-made to fulfill our purposes in Him.

Sometimes the LORD calls us into areas of ministry, regions and/or nations where we would've never dreamed of going. We may feel very uncomfortable and think the task is beyond our ability. He may require us to do something totally unexpected, in which we have no current training. In our natural understanding, such a call may seem inconceivable. Yet, we're still compelled to seek out and fulfill the purpose (and its insistent yearning) that our LORD has placed deep down in our spirits. If you experience such things, just know that in the Kingdom of God, this is nothing unusual; as a matter of fact, it's quite normal.

Although we may not understand how we're to get from point A to point B, God sees the end of a thing from the beginning. It's not up to us to figure out how to do what He's called us to do. It's up to us to trust the LORD and follow His lead in the journey. When God calls us, He does not expect us to make things happen on our own. He's going to walk with us, teach us and guide us in the way we're to go.

Be aware that, during these times when the LORD requires something out of the ordinary from us, there will always be those who won't understand. Those who lean to their own natural reasoning cannot comprehend the ways of God. Instead of seeing God's potential in you, they may be focused on your past faults and failures. For this reason, they fail to see the grace and favor the LORD has placed upon your life. They may distance themselves from you, as they scorn or ridicule the unusual call on your life. They may wonder, "What makes you so special that God would choose you?"

Ultimately, our goal is not to meet other people's personal expectations of whom or what they think we should be. Don't allow their lack of understanding to hinder you from moving forward into your ordained destiny. In reality, it doesn't matter what others think, it only matters what God thinks of us.

Part 3 • *Loving God* with All Your Mind

If you're to reach your full potential in Christ, you must leave your former faults and failures in the past, under the blood, where they belong. Likewise, don't limit God, based on your own abilities or weaknesses. Instead, recognize His ability. Give Him permission to do great and mighty things in and through you. As we allow the LORD to work in our lives, He will grace us with His supernatural ability, and we'll be able to fulfill our greatest potential and life purpose.

God knows all our human frailties and shortcomings. Yet, He loves us in spite of ourselves. He still extends His grace, mercy, forgiveness and favor toward us. He actually invites us to be used for His glory. If we can believe it, He will abundantly empower us to flow in the manifestation of His miraculous power. Let's look at who the LORD chooses to call:

<u>1 Corinthians 1:26-31</u> For ye see your calling, brethren, how that not many wise men after the flesh, not many mighty, not many noble, are called: ²⁷But God hath chosen the foolish things of the world to confound the wise; and God hath chosen the weak things of the world to confound the things which are mighty; ²⁸And base things of the world, and things which are despised, hath God chosen, yea, and things which are not, to bring to nought things that are: ²⁹That no flesh should glory in his presence. ³⁰But of him are ye in Christ Jesus, who of God is made unto us wisdom, and righteousness, and sanctification,

and redemption: ³¹That, according as it is written, He that glorieth, let him glory in the Lord.

God calls those who, in the eyes of the world, just don't have what it takes. Nevertheless, God doesn't merely look at where we are; He looks at where He's taking us. All He needs are those willing vessels who (even in the midst of their weakness and inability) will choose to say "yes" to Him. These are those who the LORD will use mightily. Our glory is not found in our own effort; our glory is found in the LORD.

As we learn trust and obedience, we'll begin to see the power of God operating in our lives as never before. By His Spirit and the truth of His Word, the LORD fully equips us for all that needs to be done. We must also realize that, when the LORD calls and equips us, He's already prepared the hearts of those to whom He will send us. As a result, others will receive from the anointing He has placed within us. Remember this — the awesome and miraculous does not happen within the human comfort zone!!

BE COURAGEOUS

As the LORD calls us to progress through each phase of our destiny journey, at times, we may feel like the LORD has released a heavenly (yet alarming!) revelation upon us. His call may upset our world and shatter our comfort zones all to pieces. In fact, it may be absolutely terrifying at first, and that's okay, but we can't invite the reality of the unknown to strike fear into our hearts

Part 3 • *Loving God* with All Your Mind

and minds. It's at these times we need to remember that nothing is unknown to the LORD. He knows exactly what He's doing, and He is faithful; we need not fear.

As we walk out our faith journey (even during moments of alarming revelation), we should always respond with transparency, reverence and courage to the desires of the LORD. For instance, we can honestly share our thoughts and concerns with Him, as we also confess and repent of any fears, doubts or unbelief. Have no façades with God (John 4:23-24). Always talk truthfully with Him, while recognizing and honoring that He is LORD and that you choose to submit to His will.

Moving forward in the plan of God requires courage. Courage doesn't mean we don't have fears; it means we see a purpose greater than ourselves that we must attain. So, having said this, I would encourage you to step out in faith. Whatever the LORD has told you to do, do it! If need be, just do it afraid. As you move forward, you will receive His grace and be reassured of His great love.

As we desperately and/or joyfully cling to the LORD, our faith will continue to grow. In everything He's called us to do, we'll see God's hand directing, arranging and protecting our lives. When we obediently step out in faith, the Lord miraculously moves in us, through us and on our behalf. As a result, joy floods into our lives and, one day, we'll look back and see how all fears have been overcome. Truly, we'll be amazed at how the miraculous faith and favor of God equips and covers us.

We cannot afford to give unhealthy fears a place in our lives. We cannot allow them to shut down our faith or stop the favor, blessing and miraculous, supernatural power of God from operating in or through us. We must decide if we're willing to love, trust, honor and reverence the LORD enough to allow Him to have His way. Do we have the courage to allow Him to lead us into the destiny He has planned for us? As we say "yes" to His will, only then, will His power be released in and through us. When this happens, we'll be changed forever! Faith versus fear — the choice is ours.

> When was the last time you allowed the LORD to plant and grow a seed of destiny on the inside of your spiritual womb?
>
> What is that 'holy thing' God wants to spiritually birth out of you?
>
> Are you willing to overcome the fears and all the 'what-if's' of life, to carry out God's plan for you?

2
— The Shepherds —
(Luke 2:4-20).

After Mary gave birth to Jesus, her firstborn son, she wrapped Him in swaddling clothes and laid Him in a

manger (G5336) — *a crib for fodder* or a trough typically used to feed livestock. This is symbolically significant, because when Jesus began His public ministry, He declared the good tidings that He was the bread of life, which came down from heaven. He also declared that He was the giver of living water (John 4:10, 7:38). He promised that all who hungered and thirsted after Him would be filled (John 6:35, 48, 50-51). Jesus Christ alone is the sustenance of all life.

After Jesus' miraculous birth had taken place, Gabriel (the angel of the LORD), appeared to shepherds in the field and told them of the birth of the Messiah. The first thing the angel said was, **"Fear not: for, behold, I bring you good tidings of great joy, which shall be unto all people. For unto you is born this day in the city of David a Savior, which is Christ the LORD. And this shall be a sign unto you: Ye shall find the babe wrapped in swaddling clothes, lying in a manger"** (Luke 2:11-12).

Notice that Gabriel's first words to the shepherds were, **"Fear not, for behold I bring you good tidings of great joy"** (Luke 2:10). Gabriel must be one awesome looking angel. If you remember, he also told Mary to **"Fear not..."** There must have been something gloriously fierce about his appearance. Yet, the shepherds were encouraged to not fear this heavenly visitor who came to bare "...***good tidings (G2097) of great (G3173) joy (G5479/G5463)...***" Gabriel greeted the shepherds with an *evangelistic announcement* of *good news* (*the gospel*) with *the greatest cheerfulness* and *calm delight*.

Can't you just see this scenario? These shepherds are minding their own business, on a quiet evening in the fields, just relaxing with their sheep. Then, all of a sudden, Gabriel is standing before them with the glory of the LORD shining and radiating out from him. He proclaims his evangelistic message to the shepherds, "The Messiah has been born!" Now that was a night like no other!! After this amazing angelic announcement, the heavens erupted with multitudes of praising angels saying, ***"Glory to God in the highest, and on earth peace, good will toward men"*** (Luke 2:14).

Heaven could not remain silent about the gift of salvation that had come to earth in the form of a babe. As the angels departed, the shepherds quickly went to Bethlehem to confirm the heavenly declaration. They found Mary, Joseph and the babe (who was wrapped in swaddling clothes, lying in a manger), just as the angel had said. Then, the shepherds went all about, praising and glorifying God as they proclaimed what they had seen and heard. All those who heard this miraculous story wondered and marveled, as they perceived the truth of what the shepherds told them.

DESIRE TO PARTICIPATE IN MIRACLES!
Mary (because of her relationship with God and her faith in His promises) became a willing vessel to fulfill the will of God in her life. By accepting the call of

God, she allowed the spoken and written Word of God to be conceived in her. In the fullness of time, Yeshua — Jesus, the only begotten Son of God, the Messiah, the Savior of the world and God incarnate — was born.

On that night, heaven and earth came together as the angels announced His birth to the shepherds. The shepherds believed this glorious report and sought after their Messiah. Once they saw His face and experienced His presence, they went forth as the first evangelistic team to publically proclaim the miraculous birth of their Messiah and King.

Why did God choose an unmarried virgin to carry forth His glorious seed in her womb? Why did God send proclaiming angels to make known the joyful news of heaven to a group of shepherds in the field? The answer is simple; He knew that Mary and the shepherds would receive the truth and embrace the will of God. He knew they would allow Him to use them to carry out heaven's mission in the earth. Their willingness qualified them to experience the supernatural power of God; respectively, birthing out and making known the plans and purposes of the Heavenly Father.

From the throne in heaven, the Father dispatched angels to carry forth His heavenly message to the hearts of mankind. Within this message was wrapped the gift of salvation and redemption for all peoples, tongues, nations and tribes. God's message of love and eternal life is still bringing forth a bountiful harvest of souls for His Kingdom.

But, what would have happened, if Mary had said "no" to God? What if the shepherds had been paralyzed with fear when the angels declared and praised the birth of Christ? What would have happened, if they kept this amazing news to themselves? Well, the answers are very simple. The LORD would have used someone else; Mary and the shepherds would have missed out on the tremendous joy and excitement of participating in the unveiled revelation of God in human flesh.

> When was the last time you allowed God to use you for His glorious purposes?
>
> When was the last time you sought to evangelize others for Christ?
>
> What fears do you need to overcome to be able to proclaim the message God has given to you?

3
— JAIRUS —
(LUKE 8:41-42, 49-56)

Fear is a killer, but faith releases resurrection life and power! There was a ruler of the synagogue by the name of Jairus. In desperation he came to Jesus, fell down at His feet and besought Him that He would heal his twelve year old daughter. This child was his only daughter, and she was dying. As Jesus and His disciples were on the way to Jairus' home, word came that his daughter had died. When Jesus heard the report, He said, *"Fear not: believe only, and she shall be made whole."* At that moment, Jairus had to make a decision to either believe or doubt the Word of the LORD. If he doubted, then fear and devastation would overtake him and his household. If he believed, then a supernatural miracle would take place. When Jesus arrived at the home of Jairus, he put all the unbelieving mockers and mourners out. Then, He took the child by the hand, commanded her to arise, and her spirit came back into her body. The child was resurrected from the dead and her parents were astonished!

Receive a Supernatural Infusion of Faith

When Jesus told Jairus *to* **Fear (G5399/G5401)** *not,* **believe (G4100/G4102/G3982)** *only and [his daughter would] be made whole,"* He was saying, "Don't be *frightened* or *alarmed;* have faith by *entrusting* me, the Anointed One, to act upon the *persuasion, moral conviction,* assurance and fidelity of the *truthfulness of God* and His Word. Give *credence* to God's Word and remain *constant in your profession* of His truth; *assent to my authority* and remain *reliant on me with inward certainty.* Come into agreement with me, and your daughter will be made **whole (G4982)**; for I will save, *deliver, protect,* heal and preserve her."

I believe that when Jesus spoke those words to Jairus, this father received a supernatural infusion of faith to believe and trust God for whatever was needed. This religious leader had a desperate need, and he chose to put his faith and trust in the LORD to meet that need. When you think about it, what other worthy option did he really have? If Jairus had given into fear, the final outcome would have been heart breaking. Fear would have given open access for death to retain his daughter; loss, sorrow and mourning would have been the end result. But, Jairus chose to believe God for the impossible, in spite of the circumstances. As a result, faith overcame fear and he saw the miraculous power of God released into the lifeless body of his young daughter, as she was raised from the dead. It's faith that motivates God. If we want to see the miraculous, we must believe that God is, and that He rewards those who diligently seek Him (Hebrews 11:6).

> What dreams, hopes or relationships seem to have died in your life?
>
> What's been lost that needs to be restored?
>
> What promises has the LORD given to you concerning these things?
>
> Do you have the faith to believe God for the impossible?

Part 3 • *Loving God* with All Your Mind

4
— AN ANGEL & TWO WOMEN —
(MATTHEW 28:1-8).

As we discuss the story of the angel and the two women found in Matthew 28:1-8, Jesus had already lived, fulfilled His mission of bringing the Kingdom of Heaven to earth, paid the penalty of death for all the sins of mankind and risen from the dead on the third day. An angel descended from heaven and there was a great earthquake. The angel rolled away the stone from the door of Jesus' tomb and perched himself upon it; his countenance was like lightening and his raiment white as snow.

The Roman soldiers had been commanded to securely guard the tomb. It was their responsibility to make sure the disciples wouldn't secretly steal Jesus' body, and then falsely claim that He rose from the dead. But the divine intervention of the angel terrified the soldiers; they shook and became paralyzed with fear, falling to the ground like dead men.

God does have a sense of humor, doesn't He? When the angel manifested after the resurrection of Christ, those soldiers couldn't guard that tomb or Jesus' body, even though their lives depended on it. All those big, strong, rough, armored soldiers were laid out in the dirt in fear! Isn't that comical? 'Dead' men were guarding the tomb of the 'living' God?

When the power of God manifested, the soldiers could do nothing to stop it. Their natural strength and ability vanished, like a vapor in the wind, as they fell to the ground in fear and powerlessness. When the power and glory of God manifested, and the revelation that Jesus truly had risen from the dead became obvious, no opposing force could stand against it.

Once the soldiers collected themselves from the dust, I'm sure they were horrified with the reality that the 'man' they had killed was someone or something much more than what they had bargained. Realizing the condemnation of their actions for putting Jesus to death, I'm sure they feared for their own lives. After all, if a man could raise Himself up from the dead, what chance did they have to stand against Him?

Similarly, when Mary Magdalene and the other Mary came to the tomb, they were also startled to see an angel perched upon the rolling stone door at the tomb. But the angel spoke to them and said, *"Fear not, for I know that you seek Jesus who was crucified. He is not here: for He is risen as He said. Come see the place where the LORD was laid."* When the women saw that Jesus wasn't there, the angel told them to go and tell His disciples that He had risen from the dead, and would meet them in Galilee. After the angel had spoken to them, the women ran quickly (probably with mixed emotions of fear and great joy) to tell the disciples what the angel of the LORD had said.

Part 3 • *Loving God* with All Your Mind

LOVE & RELATIONSHIP RISE ABOVE FEAR

The soldiers were at the tomb, because it was their assigned duty; the women were there because they were seeking Jesus. These were two different reasons — one out of duty, the other out of love. There were also two different responses once Jesus arose and the angel appeared. The soldiers were incapacitated by their fear, but the women received the Word of the LORD spoken to them by the angel. There were two different responses, because there were two different heart attitudes represented. While the soldiers were terrorized, the women received great joy and were empowered to run and declare the message of the resurrected LORD. The soldiers and the women dealt with the same event, but faith, love, the Word of God and relationship with the LORD made the difference for the women.

Likewise, we're to run joyfully to fulfill the Kingdom assignment that God has given to us. We're not to lie down in the dust of guilt, shame, condemnation, inabilities and insecurities, trembling in fear. Rather, we are to rise up, hear the Word of the LORD, and run the race that is set before us, in Jesus' name. We're to rise up with great joy, for the glory of the risen LORD is upon us! As we draw others to Christ with the truth of His Word, we are to let His glorious light shine (Hebrews 12:1; Isaiah 60:1-3)!

5
— Paul —

The Apostle Paul was an Ambassador for Christ and a Minister of the Gospel. He encountered many difficulties, beatings, bonds, shackles and imprisonment. His sufferings and perseverance encouraged believers in his day (and still do in this present day) to stand strong and speak boldly for the Kingdom of God:

Ephesians 6:19-20 *And many of the brethren in the Lord, waxing confident by my bonds, are much more bold (G1722/G3954) to speak the word without fear.* ²⁰*For which I am an ambassador in bonds: that therein I may speak boldly (G3955), as I ought to speak.*

Philippians 1:14 *And many of the brethren in the Lord, waxing confident by my bonds, are much more bold (G5111) to speak the word without fear.*

1 Thessalonians 2:2 *But even after that we had suffered before, and were shamefully entreated, as ye know, at Philippi, we were bold (G3955) in our God to speak unto you the gospel of God with much contention.*

There are 7 Greek words dealing with boldness in the New Testament. Generally, to be **bold** means to be *out-spoken (publicly frank or blunt); confident in spirit or demeanor, courageous* and it *implies assurance.* The bold believer is fearless, unhesitating, daring and takes risks for what they believe to be right and pleasing in the eyes of the LORD. Boldness empowers us to go beyond the normal limitations of conventional thoughts and actions. When we mix faith and boldness together, we're able to see the unseen. Our spiritual boldness chases away fear and releases us to imagine and believe that all things are possible with God.

Walk in Boldness with Our Helper

One of the most amazing revelations is to realize that the LORD is our Helper. We always have access to Him. And we have the right to freely and boldly come before His throne. We can call upon the LORD at all times. He's always willing to extend His aid and assistance to us in our time of need. He longs to grant us the healing, salvation, restoration and deliverance we so desperately need. We never need to feel lost or alone, because the LORD is always available to give us His instruction and direction — to help lead us through the journeys of life. Within Christ, we have everything we'll ever need. This knowledge brings peace, comfort and strength, as we run into the presence of our glorious King and face the challenges of life together with Him (Hebrews 13:6).

In the presence of the LORD, we have life, eternal pleasures and the fullness of joy (Psalm 16:11). Oh, what an amazing God we serve! Regardless of the struggles we face, our mind can be at peace, and our thoughts can rest upon His faithful goodness and mercy toward us.

6
— JESUS —

Jesus came to destroy the works of the devil and set the captives free. He paid the price for our sins and ransomed us through His death, so we could be redeemed from the power of sin, death, hell and the grave. Only by His sacrifice, are we able to receive the gift of salvation. After Jesus' death, He descended into the lower parts of the earth (known as Hades or hell). From this place of the dead, Jesus led captivity captive and stripped the keys of hell and death away from the devil. He swallowed up and overcame death in complete and utter victory. Therefore, the power and sting of death have been abolished, and they have no power over those who trust in Christ as their LORD and Savior (Luke 4:18; Romans 8:2; 1 Corinthians 15:54-57; Ephesians 4:7-10; 1 John 3:8; Revelation 1:18).

PRAY TO BE STRENGTHENED

Jesus possessed the perfect peace of God within Him to accomplish His earthly mission. Even so, there were times when He struggled with what was required of Him. For instance, before the Roman soldiers came to arrest Him in the Garden of Gethsemane, Jesus prayed:

<u>**Luke 22:42**</u> *...Father, if thou be willing, remove this cup from me: nevertheless not my will, but thine, be done.*

Part 3 • *Loving God* with All Your Mind

Jesus, God the Son, loved God the Father so much, that He was willing to suffer and endure anything necessary to fulfill the Father's will. Before the most trying time of His life on earth, this decision for total obedience drained Jesus of His strength. Scripture tells us that an angel from heaven appeared and strengthened Him (Luke 22:43). Even Jesus had to take His eyes off His earthly circumstances and see His heavenly purpose. In His human limitation, He had to be encouraged in the pursuit of His ordained destiny. The same is true for us. We know that Jesus suffered great mental anguish in that place of prayer:

Luke 22:44 *And being in an agony he prayed more earnestly: and his sweat was as it were great drops of blood falling down to the ground.*

The fact that Jesus was sweating great drops of blood tells us that He was under such extreme mental and physical stress, that it was causing the capillaries under the surface of His skin to burst, mixing with the sweat of His body and then falling to the ground. Even so, Jesus persevered and pressed in with fervent intensity. Pursuing the love of the Father, He was determined to diligently fulfill all His Father's will and purposes.

PRAY TO PERSEVERE

As the story progresses, one of Jesus' disciples (Judas Iscariot) betrayed Him with a kiss (Luke 22:47-48). That kiss was a mark of identification, so the soldiers would know who to arrest. That tender expression, which was meant to demonstrate love and affection, became a weapon of hatred, abuse and betrayal on the lips of a deceiver.

Sometimes, those we have shared close and intimate relationships with can turn and rend us. They may have taken what they wanted from us, and when they felt we were of no more value to them, they sought to destroy us. Jesus understands this type of treacherous behavior. He identifies with the pain of our emotional wounds. Yet, just as He continued to press on into the will of God and persevere, we must follow His example. If we're to obtain the full blessings of heaven upon our lives, we can't allow the wickedness of others to rob us of our spiritual inheritance or stop us from reaching our personal destinies.

After Jesus was arrested, Peter followed behind at a distance to the high priest's house. He sat down next to a fire with others that were gathered there. Peter was snuggling up to a warm fire in the camp of the enemy! Within about an hour, three different people recognized Peter as being one of Jesus' disciples and, all three times, Peter denied that he knew the LORD (Luke 22:54-62). Before the night was over, Jesus was completely forsaken — Judas betrayed Him, Peter denied Him, and the rest of His disciples were scattered (Matthew 26:31).

As true believers, it's important that we not position ourselves into situations where the enemy can get the advantage over us. When inquisition or persecutions arise, our faith needs to be strong enough to stand in the midst of the enemy's camp and persevere. If not, any fears, doubts or unbelief lurking inside of us, will come to the surface. This may cause us to behave cowardly, instead of being bold as we should. In turn, this can bring shame and condemnation upon us, as well as damage our testimony in the LORD.

If you've ever been betrayed or denied by someone close to you, you can understand the sorrow and pain this brings. You didn't ask for it, but it came anyway. When those you have trusted, suddenly cast you aside like they never knew you, the heartache can be overwhelming. Jesus understood that level of sorrow, and yet, He continued on with the plan of God for His life. We, too, must learn that there are times when we must stand alone. Frankly, we simply have to push beyond those who forsake us, and rest in the truth that God will never forsake us. The LORD will walk with us every step of the way — through every trial, disappointment and struggle — as we just keep moving forward with Him.

Pray to Endure & Obey

It wasn't enough that Jesus was betrayed, arrested, and denied, but He was also misjudged, falsely accused, beaten, abused and murdered. Yet, because He was so in love with the heavenly Father and so determined to obey His will, He was willing to lay aside His own struggles and endure suffering. He would sacrifice His own life, so that man and God could be restored to a proper relationship of love and fellowship. While the end result was the salvation of mankind and freedom from sin, Jesus paid a very painful price to obtain that gift for us. He was the only one qualified to redeem mankind, and He was willing to do whatever was required to make it happen. He did it out of love, and He did it for each one of us!

I want you to seriously consider this: Jesus came to earth to accomplish a mission for the Kingdom of God, and likewise, we have been born into this earth to complete a Kingdom mission. You have a special assignment, and nobody can do it quite like you. God has placed special gifts, talents, abilities, desires and experiences within you that qualify you to fulfill your calling. Don't allow anything to stop you. Look past the pain and disappointments. By faith, see the end of the matter from the beginning. Press forward to that reward, regardless of what may try to stop you. An attitude of perseverance honors the LORD and demonstrates a love and passion for Him that will not be denied. Love Him and move forward in Jesus' name!

Now we've examined the experiences of Mary, the shepherds, Jairus, the angel and the women at the tomb, Paul and Jesus. These are just a few examples of those who overcame their fears and struggles, as they sought to please the Heavenly Father. They had many difficulties, but overcame every obstacle to fulfill the purposes of God. They submitted their will

Part 3 • *Loving God* with All Your Mind

to the will of the Father, so that they might bring Him glory. They saw past their own discomfort and pressed toward the mark for the prize of the high calling of God (Philippians 3:14). So, what's the message? Love God — believe, persevere, hope and prevail by His grace and ability — no matter what!

SUMMARY OF LOVING GOD WITH ALL YOUR MIND

In Chapter 9, we learned that the battles we face always begin by a thought being planted in the mind. The thief, satan, desires to steal our peace, erect mental strongholds in our minds and turn our lives into his combative warzone. How we respond to the lies of the enemy, as well as the truth of God's Word will determine who gets the victory. We must remember that our battle is not with flesh and blood, but it is a spiritual conflict. Yet, the LORD has provided us with mighty spiritual weapons and the armor we need to defeat the enemy. The Church is to rise up as the sober, vigilant, holy, warrior Bride of Christ, fulfilling the will of her Beloved King in the earth.

In Chapter 10, we examined the spiritual mind verses the carnal mind. The spiritual mind is transformed, renewed, focused on the LORD and controlled by the Spirit and Word of God. The carnal mind is corrupt, self-focused and controlled by the unbridled passions of the flesh nature, thus creating an inroad for spiritual attack. We're commanded to renew our minds by the Word of God, that we would not be conformed to the ways of this world. Our mindset will either bring forth life or death. If we're to live in righteousness, true holiness and victory, we must forsake carnality and take on the mind of Christ.

In Chapter 11, we addressed the fact that God has not given us a spirit of fear. Rather, He has given us power, love and a sound mind. Fear has torment and is a tactic used by satan to try to cripple us — mentally, spiritually, emotionally and physically. It's a thief of destiny and a form of temporary insanity. Fearfulness also signifies one's faithlessness as well as a lack of trust in Christ and the authoritative power of God's Word. We can't operate in fear and faith at the same time; they are rooted in two different belief systems. We must decide who we're going to serve.

In Chapter 12, we explicitly exposed fear as a form of mental terrorism and spiritual torment, along with some of its side effects. Also, faith was defined and examined through the lives of biblical characters that faced challenging situations. Each one made choices based on their faith that changed the course of history. All those who trust the LORD, step out of their comfort zones and obey the Holy Spirit, will experience the miraculous power of God on their behalf.

Part 4
Loving God with all your Might & Strength

CHAPTER 13

ZEALOUS LOVE

Zealous love, joined with the Word of God, has fire in it. It's a love that can't be restrained or quenched, because it's centered in truth. It's a love that's passionately committed and has right priorities. It's a love that will never willingly seek to harm or disappoint the one on whom its affections are focused. The LORD Jesus Christ, for love's sake, laid down His life that He might receive a peculiar and zealous people, as we see in:

Titus 2:14 *Who gave himself for us, that he might redeem us from all iniquity, and purify unto himself a peculiar people, zealous of good works.*

A **peculiar** *(G4041)* people are a *special* people whom God has claimed as His *own*. They are *beyond* what is considered to be *usual*. They do not have the same customs or habits as other people. Their ways are outside the limits of what many would consider to be normal, because they go above and beyond the status quo of most people. These unusually peculiar people of God are zealous of good works.

To be **zealous** *(G2207/G2206)* is to be a *zealot* — one who demonstrates great ardor and *warmth of feelings for or against* someone or something. These feelings cause one to have intense devotion, passion and fervent eagerness, while earnestly desiring to fulfill one's primary focus and cause. To be zealous of **good** *(G2570)* **works** *(G2041) is to toil (as an effort or occupation)* at doing that which is *beautiful,* morally *good, valuable or virtuous.*

The zealots of the LORD have been redeemed from **iniquity** *(G458/G459), wickedness* and *unrighteousness.* They're no longer lawless. They no longer violate *or transgress* the laws of God through sinful, illegal activities that go against His Word.

The zealots of the LORD may be considered fanatical — motivated or characterized by extreme enthusiasm or zeal. This may reflect what some consider intolerant or radical behavior. Yet, if we're going to serve the LORD properly, we must be intolerant of sin, ungodly compromise and the deceptions of the enemy. We cannot concern ourselves with being 'politically correct' and non-offensive. We must speak the truth and become radical for the things of God. This is especially true, when drastic changes need to take place; root issues need to be dealt with; and proper lifestyle foundations need to be established and built.

For instance, if somebody is dying from drug abuse, they must stop taking drugs; cut off all relationships with their drug dealers; become accountable to those who can help free them from the ravages of addiction; and deal with the root cause. Otherwise, they will die prematurely, while in sin and defeat. Those caught up in adultery (or other sexual sins), must repent and stop participating in illicit relationships; seek godly counsel and, in many cases, deliverance. Otherwise, the self-destructive behaviors of immorality will eventually bring physical, mental, emotional and spiritual death to those involved in such lifestyles.

Those ensnared in the traps of satan must have a radical intervention. Wonder why? Consider this: If a poisonous snake gets in your house, do you feed it and make it comfortable? No!! You get rid of it, by whatever means necessary and as quickly as possible. The enemy isn't playing around, so when lives are in danger, there's no room for compromise. You must take drastic measures to get rid of the threatening menace, restore proper order and do what's right for all involved.

I'm of the persuasion that, if our zeal is for the Kingdom of God and we're operating in obedience to the Holy Spirit (being in unity with God's Word), then zealous fanaticism and intolerant radicalism is more than acceptable before the LORD. Zeal can become like a fire to stir up the people of God, as well as their gifts and callings for the purposes of His Kingdom. Godly zeal can also rout the disorderly conduct of anything or anyone who's not operating according to the Word of God. Those who zealously love the LORD will place their relationship with Him (and, thus, personal obedience to His Word) at the top of their priority list, as we see in:

<u>John 14:21</u> **He that hath my commandments, and keepeth them, he it is that loveth me: and he that loveth me shall be loved of my Father, and I will love him, and will manifest myself to him.**

<u>1 John 5:3</u> **For this is the love of God, that we keep his commandments and his commandments are not grievous.**

When the LORD is first priority in our lives, everything else comes after Him. No other human relationship is of greater importance. If we're to follow the LORD, even our family relationships must become secondary. Jesus said in:

<u>Matthew 10:37</u> **He that loveth father or mother more than me is not worthy of me: and he that loveth son or daughter more than me is not worthy of me.**

As a peculiar and zealous people for the LORD (based on Titus 2:14; John 14:21; 1 John 5:3 and Matthew 10:37), we will do good works and keep His commandments. We'll live differently from the people of the world. We'll enjoy an intimately mutual love relationship with the LORD, and He will manifest Himself to us. We will not find His commandments grievous, and we'll do whatever is necessary to fulfill His will for our lives. If need be, we will sacrifice family relationships to follow after the LORD. The zealots of the LORD will love and serve Him with everything they've got; after all, this is how we are clearly commanded to serve the LORD, according to:

<u>Deuteronomy 6:5</u> And thou shalt love the LORD thy God with all thine heart, and with all thy soul, and with all thy might.

To love the LORD with all our **might** *(H3966/H181)* is defined in the Hebrew as demonstrating *vehemence.* Doing something vehemently implies doing it *wholly* and *speedily.* Elsewhere in the Bible, this word is translated as diligently, especially, exceedingly, greatly, quickly and utterly. It also means to be zealous, ardent, strongly emotional, intense, energetic and passionate. Synonyms of the word vehement are fervent, earnest, burning and fiery. It actually depicts the action of *raking, turning* and *gathering embers together.* So, to love the LORD with all our might is to be as a firebrand, vehemently burning and hotly glowing for Him.

Part 4 • *Loving God* with all your Might & Strength

Mighty love happens when we zealously pursue the heart and presence of our King with the intention of bringing Him great pleasure. When our hearts, souls and minds are in active agreement with the Word of God, then loving Him with all our might is a naturally visible manifestation of the passion dwelling in our hearts. We are affectionately committed to Him, because He has become our most precious and treasured friend and the recipient of our ardently devoted love and passion. It's our delight to please Him and give Him access to all that we have and all that we are. We joyously give Him everything, holding nothing back. Are you ready to go to that place in your relationship with the LORD? Only the lovers of God who are willing to lay down their lives for Him and His cause, will experience Him on this level.

Loving God and being loved by Him, is the most tremendously exciting experience a human being can ever have. If we're willing to receive it, He will plant His eternal seed of love and truth on the inside of us, and we'll begin to grow in the grace and knowledge of who He is. Then, as the love and truth of God continue to work maturity in us, we'll begin to bear spiritual fruit on the inside; this will eventually manifest on the outside of us, for the entire world to see. Also, when our relationship with the LORD is nurtured and watered by the Word of God, our love for Him and others surges. The love we have for God originated with Him, and it's to be returned to Him with great joy.

FAN THE FLAME

This burning love for the LORD (and the evidence of His presence in our lives) should be so strong that devilish hordes shake in our presence. The very fact that we're the offspring of God should cause great unrest and agitation to the realms of spiritual wickedness. We should never allow the passionate fire blazing in our hearts to be extinguished.

When your heart is aflame for God, there may also be those who will think you've gone off the deep end and will seek to stir up trouble against you. They'll say you've become an extremist or a fanatic, or they'll insist you're out of balance, radical, over the top, etc. There may be people who will try to shut you up, put you down, cast you out and even show you to the door, because they don't understand and can't figure out the reasoning behind your passion. They may feel intimidated, jealous or angry over your relationship with the LORD. In their lack of spiritual understanding, they may misinterpret you, misjudge you, speak evil of you, shun you and criticize you. These experiences will only serve to strengthen you. If you do not allow yourself to become discouraged, your haters will become one of the greatest assets to building your faith, because their assaults will force you into a deeper relationship with the LORD.

Listen, I've been there! I know what I'm talking about. In fact, I have come to appreciate my haters, because

Part 4 • *Loving God* with all your Might & Strength

they have provoked me to push forward in my relationship and my greater destiny with the LORD. One thing I've learned is to not waste my time fretting over such people. They're stuck in their religious or rebellious mindsets and need to be set free and delivered. My advice is simply this: Love them, pray for them and keep on going. I've learned that the persistent worshipper always receives the blessing of the LORD, and the consistent scorner will be left to their own ignorance and the consequences thereof.

Another hindrance that may occur is the diminishing of our passionate fires. This can easily happen amidst the events and distractions of everyday life. That's when we need to run back into the intimate presence of the LORD, and allow Him to stir up those simmering love embers. By dwelling in the secret place with Him, we'll once again become flaming firebrands, burning brightly with ardent and enthusiastic love for Him. By remaining in God's presence, our spiritual and natural strength (as well as our joy) are restored.

DANCING MIGHTILY BEFORE THE LORD

King David was an ardent worshipper and his heart burned with love for his God; but there were times when he sinned against the LORD, and it cost him dearly. One example (as mentioned in chapter 5 of this book), is when David sent for Bathsheba, the wife of Uriah the Hittite. He committed adultery with her; had her husband killed in battle; and then, took her to be his own wife. As a result of David's sin, the first son born of David and Bathsheba's illicit relationship died, and the LORD allowed evil to rise up against David from his own house (2 Samuel 11-12).

Another instance when the wrath of the LORD was kindled against David was when he numbered all the fighting men of Israel and Judah, in order to measure the strength of his armies. Therefore, the LORD sent a destroying pestilence (plague) upon the land. Over the course of three days, seven thousand men died from Dan to Beersheba (2 Samuel 24).

From these two examples, we can see that David's sin caused a breach in his relationship with the LORD, and it affected thousands of other people. He was openly rebuked for adultery and murder and, at least, 7,002 men died as a result of David's sin. The impact of David's sin caused grief, sorrow and mourning to the multitudes of loved ones who lost their fathers, uncles, husbands, brothers and sons. This travesty also reached to the following generations, as women became widows, and those who died would never father anymore children.

There may be areas in your life where you have also sinned against the LORD. You may have given the devil an advantage and suffered loss because of it. As a result, you may feel like the presence of God (along with your peace, joy and confidence) has vanished from your life. However, if you will return to

Part 4 • *Loving God* with all your Might & Strength

the LORD (repent of your sin and ask forgiveness), reclaim the Word of God and allow the praises of God to — once again — become the delight of your heart, then His presence, as well as your peace, joy and confidence will be restored. Remember, Jesus said that the thief comes to steal, kill and destroy, but He has come to give us life and that we might have it more abundantly (John 10:10). Regardless of what you've been through, the mercy and blessing of God upon your life is reason to praise Him.

Despite David's shortcomings and all the damage he caused, he still had a heart after God. As he returned to the LORD in repentance and brokenness, he received forgiveness and restoration. King David — like the rest of us — wasn't perfect, but he understood the power of repentance and praise for victory; as a result, the LORD used him mightily.

One of King David's expressions of praise was to dance before the LORD with all his might, strength, capacity, power, force and valor! Through the mercy of God, David was (again and again) free to offer up his praise and worship. When it came to praise, David got down to business; he withheld nothing from the LORD.

For instance, in Jerusalem, David had prepared a place of worship and pitched a tent to receive the Ark of God. To avoid any previous fatal mishaps (2 Samuel 6: 1-8; 1 Chronicles 13), he also commanded that none were to carry the Ark of God except the Levites, because God had chosen them to carry His Ark and to minister before Him forever (1 Chronicles 15:1-15). Also, David told the chief of the Levites to appoint their priestly brethren as the singers and musicians, and they were to lift up the voice of joy before the LORD (1 Chronicles 15:16-24). While the Levitical singers and musicians ministered before the LORD and the Levites offered sacrifices, all Israel ascended to Jerusalem with jubilant shouting, the blowing of shofars, and the noise of cymbals, psalteries and harps playing. Musical praise exploded into the atmosphere. David, as a priestly king, was girded with a linen ephod and danced before the LORD (1 Chronicles 15:27, 29). With his celebratory praise, David led the priests and the people to the tabernacle, where the Ark of God found its temporary resting place.

The LORD used David to usher in the Ark and the presence of God, as well as restore worship in the midst of Israel. An act such as this was achieved after a grievous failure, only because an imperfect king had a heart for a perfect God. This triumphant return of the Ark brought great joy and much celebration to the people of God.

An Overcomer's Love
David developed an overcoming love for his God. He delighted greatly in the LORD's presence and was never ashamed to run into the secret place of the Most High. However, not everyone embraced his openly exuberant expressions of praise and worship.

Part 4 • *Loving God* with all your Might & Strength

In fact, David's own wife (Michal) was a foe in his own house. As previously mentioned in Chapter 3 of this book, you may remember the history of David and Michal. She brazenly came against him in public with accusations, criticism and contempt for his so-called "shameless" expressions of praise and adoration for the LORD. I will repeat some of the facts from that story here, but with a different emphasis. Now, let's focus on how David loved the LORD with all his might, specifically, through his expression of dance.

Michal was King David's first wife, and she was also the daughter of the former King Saul (who reigned over Israel before David became King). She had been given to David as a reward for battle, when he and his warriors slew 200 Philistines (1 Samuel 18:27). In the beginning of their marriage, Michal loved David; yet, somewhere along the way, she seemed to become embittered against him.

As David, the Ark of God and the vibrant procession of celebrating worshippers entered Jerusalem, Michal kept herself at a distance. For whatever reason, she did not enter into worship or the festive praise and joyous celebration of the LORD. Instead, she watched from a window and observed her husband, the King, sacrificing to the LORD. She saw that David was fully enthralled in his passionate displays of worship and praise, but her heart was not right:

CHAPTER 13 • ZEALOUS LOVE

> *<u>2 Samuel 6:13-16</u> And it was so, that when they that bare the ark of the LORD had gone six paces, he sacrificed oxen and fatlings. ¹⁴And David danced before the LORD with all his might; and David was girded with a linen ephod. ¹⁵So David and all the house of Israel brought up the ark of the LORD with shouting, and with the sound of the trumpet. ¹⁶And as the ark of the LORD came into the city of David, Michal, Saul's daughter, looked through a window, and saw king David leaping and dancing before the LORD; and she despised him in her heart.*

David brought his sacrifices and **danced** *(H3769)* **before** *(H6440/H6437)* the LORD with all his **might** *(H5797/H5810)*. This means he *whirled* in the presence of and *before the face* of the LORD, with all the *strength* and *force* of *praise* he could muster. David was **leaping** *(H6339/H6338)*, *springing* about and dancing before the LORD, *as if* his *limbs would separate* and fly apart. What a beautiful exhibition of great assurance, strength and boldness from this earthly king. David joyfully abandoned himself to his heavenly King, whom he loved fervently — even more than life itself.

As Michal watched the procession from her window, the scripture tells us that, in her heart, she *despised (H959)* David. This means that, from the center and depths of her being, she *disesteemed* him; she distained and scorned him, as if he were a vile person. In her attitude toward her husband, she was disgusted by his behavior. She saw his actions as distasteful and regarded him with contempt. She not only despised her husband in her heart, but she openly mocked him and sought to bring shame upon him. His fervent, heartfelt expressions of love toward the LORD had provoked her. We see her attitude, as well as David's rebuke and her consequences in:

<u>2 Samuel 6:20-23</u> *Then David returned to bless his household. And Michal the daughter of Saul came out to meet David, and said, How glorious was the king of Israel to day, who uncovered himself to day in the eyes of the handmaids of his servants, as one of the vain fellows shamelessly uncovereth himself!* ²¹*And David said unto Michal, It was before the LORD, which chose me before thy father, and before all his house, to appoint me ruler over the people of the LORD, over Israel: therefore will I play before the LORD.* ²²*And I will yet be more vile than thus, and will be base in mine own sight: and of the maidservants which thou hast spoken of, of them shall I be had in honour.* ²³*Therefore Michal the daughter of Saul had no child unto the day of her death.*

In the context of this scripture, when it says that Michal came out to *meet* (H7125/H7122) David, it implies that he *encountered* her as she came against him in a *hostile* manner. What Michal did not understand about her husband was that he was not concerned about what people thought of Him. Because of her attitude and accusations, they most likely, had a heated argument and, most certainly, a falling out.

David's wife accused him of being vain and shamelessly uncovering himself. These were very serious accusations. To accuse David of being **vain** *(H7386/H7324)* was to say that he was *worthless* and *empty* of anything of value, except to be cast out or exiled. To say that David was **shamelessly uncovered** *(H1540)* meant that he had brazenly *stripped* and *revealed* himself. She believed he was *disgraceful* in his appearance. On the contrary, to "uncover" also means to advertise and publish. Now, that is exactly what David did. He advertised his total abandonment and published his great love for God, in whom he was passionately and eternally enamored. Michal did not see things from the same perspective as David; this is why her words were so contemptible.

King David's only focus was to celebrate his God and the restoration of His presence, and he did so with every ounce of strength found within his being. David was not deterred by his wife's criticism. As a matter of fact, he told Michal that he would **play** *(H7832)*, and be more **vile** *(H7043)* and **base** *(H8217/H8213)* in his own sight before the LORD. In other words, David was going to *laugh* and take great *pleasure* in rejoicing before the LORD, even if it made him seem *small, easy* or *trifling* to others. If necessary, he would freely and willingly bring himself down to a state of total *humiliation*, so that he might lift up and exalt the LORD. David did not esteem what she or anybody else thought, said or did. Nothing could quench or stop the fire of David's pursuant love for the LORD God Almighty. He had made the decision to submit his entire heart, soul, mind and strength — every part and ounce of himself — to be tied up, bound and knit together with the heart of God.

AN OVERCOMER'S IDENTITY
In spite of Michal's criticism and accusations, David knew who he was in the LORD. As a godly leader, he understood his duty as an example, demonstrating the proper, *honorable* and excellent manner in which the people should serve the LORD. His life was to exhibit the importance of praise and worship, as well as the need to lift up the holy standard of God's Word. In so doing, a worshipping king and a praising people invited the power and presence of God into their midst. Those who know their God will not hold back their praise; and when God shows up, no enemy can stand against His people.

Indeed, David understood his specific responsibilities while leading and ruling over God's people. As a *ruler* (H5057/H5046) and King of Israel, David had the moral responsibility to seek God, as well as to lead and protect the people. In the domains he was to govern, King David was to be their *military commander*, as well as a *civil* and *religious* leader. Moreover, he was to occupy the frontline of both the natural and spiritual realms of battle. To *"occupy" the front* means to invade, or take possession and control of a place that was formerly under threat of (or in possession of) an enemy. It also means to bravely uncover, expose and *stand boldly in opposition* of an enemy, verbally denouncing Him and declaring his defeat. Likewise, in the plan of God, every believer is:

- <u>Ordained</u> to rule as a king and priest of the LORD.
- <u>Called</u> to fulfill a specific position in the Kingdom.
- <u>Appointed</u> to live a life of excellence and honor before the LORD.
- <u>Anointed</u> to declare the will of the Heavenly Father in the earth and to expose, denounce and overcome every opposing force that comes against the Word and will of God.
- <u>To rise up and rule</u> in unity with the King of Glory; exalting His holy name and His righteous cause.
- <u>To lift up the holy and righteous standard</u> of the LORD, not being dissuaded by those who come against them in hostility.

So what about those who come against us? Well, let's recall what happened to Michal, according to:

***2 Samuel 6:23** Therefore, Michal the daughter of Saul had no child unto the day of her death.*

Part 4 • *Loving God* with all your Might & Strength

In the Jewish culture, it was considered a disgrace for a married woman to have no children. Michal had dishonored God and disgraced her husband by speaking against his character, actions and worship. As a result, she was disgraced. Her womb would remain unfruitful and lifeless. There would be no babe to suckle at the breast and no child to bring her joy. Generationally, she also wouldn't be propagated. She was cut off from the blessing of being able to bring forth anything that was a reflection of her. No descendent from the lineage of Saul would ever sit upon the throne again. This was her consequence for having a wrong spirit toward the LORD and despising the worship of her kingly husband.

It's interesting that the name **Michal** *(H4324/H4323/H3201)* means a *rivulet* or a small *container, stream* or *brook*. It also means *to be able* to attain, endure, overcome or have power to prevail. Her name declared her intended destiny. She was meant to be a source of refreshing, comfort and life — like cool water in a parched land — but there was something wrong in Michal's heart. As a result, she refused to associate with or join herself to the worship of God, thus hindering her own destiny. If her heart had been right, she could have been a shining example of the living waters of life; she would have poured into others. Instead, her bitterness caused her to become spiritually and naturally barren.

In relation to your own attitudes, consider these questions: What is your response when you see someone expressing their love to the LORD in passionate praise and worship? Do they embarrass you? Do you join with them? Ignore them? Wish they would sit down and be quiet? Do you try to shut them down? Do you encourage them, or do you speak evil of them? Why do you think you respond the way you do? Are there any areas of bitterness or resentment toward God or others for which you need to confess and receive healing? Your answers will reveal your heart condition toward the LORD and the importance of worship.

REQUIREMENTS OF LOVE

All relationships must have proper, healthy boundaries, expectations and requirements; the same is true with our heavenly Father. He intimately loves and dotes over those who belong to Him. They're continually in His thoughts, because they're precious to Him (Psalm 139:17-18). He desires relationship with His people and asks for few things in return. The LORD is looking for those who choose to love Him, seek Him and obey Him.

In the Old Testament, the LORD had very specific requirements concerning His relationship with Israel. Today, the Jewish people are no longer under the laws of the old covenant, because when Jesus came, He instituted the new covenant. Upon His resurrection, this new covenant was fully enacted. Nevertheless, the following scripture gives us an understanding of the unchanging heart of God and His desire to have relationship with His people:

Part 4 • *Loving God* with all your Might & Strength

Deuteronomy 10:12 *And now, Israel, what doth the LORD thy God require of thee, but to fear the LORD thy God, to walk in all his ways, and to love him, and to serve the LORD thy God with all thy heart and with all thy soul,*

A "requirement" of God is what He has requested or demanded. In this verse, there are four requirements:
1. Fear the LORD your God
2. Walk in all His ways
3. Love Him
4. Serve Him

If you stop and think about it, a proper relationship with the LORD has a progression to it. First of all, there must be a holy reverence, respect and honor for who He is. Only then, will we be able to walk with Him. As we walk with Him, we learn of His ways and begin to love Him. As we love Him, we begin to serve and worship Him. Interestingly, as these requirements of the LORD are fulfilled, a greater desire to be with Him is nurtured.

To *fear (H3372)* the LORD is to *morally revere* Him. This means to honor, respect and be in awe of who He is. It also means to highly regard and reverence Him in such a way that we don't want to do anything that would go against His will. This is the duty of all mankind toward God, for He is most holy and worthy of such adoration.

The LORD also requires us to be holy, as He is holy (Leviticus 20:7, 1 Peter 1:15-16). Therefore, we must become His disciples, sit at his feet, and learn of His holy and righteousness ways. Respect, humility and a true willingness to be taught are necessary for such a relationship. When we honor and reverence the LORD as we should, we are changed; relationship develops; wisdom is transferred; and revelation comes, as He graces us with His presence and divine blessing.

Part of sitting at the feet of the LORD and drinking in His wisdom is to learn to **walk** *(H3212/H1980)* in all His **ways** *(H1870/H1869/H3212)*. We learn to walk in His ways by spending time with Him; pursuing and following after Him; listening to and conversing with Him; being ready to receive what He has to say to us; and growing in the knowledge of Him. Relationship with the LORD is developed in the secret place of His presence, as He teaches us how to *carry* out His ways. As we position ourselves accordingly, we learn that He can be trusted to direct us in the *course of life* for which we were purposefully created.

LOVE HAS A PURPOSE — LIFE!
Still in reference to Deuteronomy 10:12, the **ways** *(H1870/H1869)* of the LORD, figuratively, speak of a *course* of life or *mode* of action. It also refers to conversation, customs and the journeys of life. The primitive root word implies the idea of *stringing a bow (by treading on it in bending)*.

The LORD prepares us for our journey in life, like He would a bow and arrow for use. He bends, sharpens and equips us with His specific purposes in mind. At the appointed time, He reaches into His quiver and chooses the appropriate arrow for a particular task. He, as the Master Archer, places His arrow in the bow and releases it, propelling it to its intended target.

We all have a specific purpose and release time. Before we can be released into our purpose, we must have godly character; be spiritually prepared and able to follow His lead. We must also be fully submitted, allowing Him to use us and send us, as He sees fit. An arrow never has a say in the matter; it simply submits to the hand of the archer.

When our purpose in life has been revealed to us, and we see it being fulfilled, we experience a divine sense of satisfaction in the plan of God. This satisfaction motivates us to further share the LORD's goodness with others. As we reach out into the harvest fields of the nations, laboring and planting His words of truth into the hearts of men, eternal souls will be won for Christ.

We must understand that the Heavenly Father doesn't teach us His ways and bless us, just so we can feel good and be happy all by ourselves. He does it so we'll be inspired to be a blessing to others and share His great love with them. We all have a part to fulfill in the great commission. As we expand our vision for life beyond ourselves and share the sweetness of the LORD with others, He will use us to draw them into the Kingdom of God (Matthew 28:19-20; John 17:13)!

One way we get beyond ourselves is to get outside the four walls of the church and demonstrate the life of Christ publically. In relation to reaching out to the lost, I once heard an evangelist say, "Set yourself on fire and others will come to watch you burn!" If we possess the fire of God within our hearts, it's because we have spent time with the source of the flame! When we enter and abide in the rich presence of Almighty God, we are transformed by the consuming fire of His glory. As we allow ourselves to be consumed by Him, His fire becomes our fire. As His fire burns within us, we gleam with the reflection of Him. We decrease and He increases. Everything that's not like Him is set ablaze and devoured. Thus, the fire removes every hindrance and makes us one with Him. When we are consumed with the fire of God, others cannot help but notice the flame!

Also, if we're to be in fiery union with the LORD, we must be fully engaged with Him. To be engaged is to be busy, occupied, involved and betrothed with the intent of marriage. We are espoused to Christ as a pure, chaste virgin, and He has already paid the bride price (2 Corinthians 11:2). As our heavenly Bridegroom, He wants the entirety — every single part — of who we are. We will only find our joy fulfilled by being one with Christ.

So, what could possibly keep us from such joy? Well, if we're to love Him more than our own ambitions and desires, death to self is required. Without full capitulation, our association with the LORD becomes a dry, distant, ineffective and carnal religious activity. Though there may be a showy display with some form of godliness, if we are not fully submitted to His lordship, our religious rituals are just external façades of vanity. Such empty, prideful rituals demonstrate superficial actions, while our hearts are purposely withheld from the LORD. This behavior reveals a spiritual detachment that must be dealt with, before the guise of religion thoroughly deceives the uncommitted, casual or apathetic. We can't have a spiritual mindset, if we're filled with carnality (Romans 8:6). And we're not operating in integrity, if we're acting like someone or something that we're not. As individuals, we must make the choice to fully surrender to God.

Without compromise, our hearts must be willing to fully embrace the LORD. If we're to be fully engaged with the LORD, we must have a pure and holy mindset, a passionate heart and a will to serve Him. We must find our ultimate delight in Him!

As we delight ourselves in the LORD, He gives us the desires of our hearts, and He rejoices over us with joy and singing (Psalm 37:4; Zephaniah 3:17)! Should we not do the same towards Him? Give Him what He asks and leap for Him with joyful songs. He delights in us, as we delight in Him!

Mercifully, the LORD has committed His covenant love to us. When we see His goodness and the great and mighty things He's doing in our lives, it causes us to love Him even more. Being fully engaged and joyfully pouring out our lives and love for our King, causes our personal relationship with Him to become the most wonderful, awe-inspiring and life-changing experience a person can have. It's truly a privilege to be ushered into the beautiful, enrapturing presence of His deep, abiding and eternal love. Indeed, it is life everlasting! Oh, beloved ones, be zealous for the LORD!

Chapter 14

THE RIGHTEOUS MIGHT OF A KING

So, how does one fully surrender to the LORD? How does one hope to have zeal ignited or restored within them? Exactly what sacrifices might be required? For some specific insight and example, let's look at an earthly king who sought to honor the righteousness of God with all his might; and ask, "Would I have been willing to do the same?"

Scripture records the reign of King Josiah in 2 Kings 21-23. He was eight years old when he began to reign and he reigned for thirty-one years in Jerusalem. Josiah was a good and righteous king who pursued the heart of God and honored His Word. He walked in the ways of his forefather King David, yet he did not turn to the left or to the right, but he followed the LORD fully. King Josiah refused to compromise anything he knew was right in the eyes of the LORD (2 Kings 21:26, 22:1-2).

Prior to Josiah's reign, the people had turned their hearts from the truth of God's Word and wandered far from His presence. They polluted themselves with the worship of idols and allowed the house of the LORD to be misused. Consequently, it fell into a state of shameful neglect and disrepair. The condition of their 'place of worship' was a visible indicator of their spiritual 'heart condition.' Therefore, King Josiah ordered that all forms of idolatry be removed from the land, and he decreed that money be collected from the people to restore the house of the LORD.

Within the house of the LORD, the restoration process revealed that the polluted things of idolatry had been mingled with the holy things of God. In the purging process, Hilkiah (the high priest), found the book of the law, which had been neglected and hidden in shadows of obscure darkness. The recovery of God's Word had a profound impact on the nation; it would be used to set the house of the LORD and the hearts of the people back into proper order.

LEADING WELL

When King Josiah heard the Word of the LORD and understood the implications of it, he was exceedingly grieved and tore his clothes in anguish. He realized the extent of the people's disobedience and wickedness against the LORD. Their evil ways and the stubborn rebellion of their idolatrous hearts had alienated them from the LORD and brought corruption to the nation. The people's sin was unacceptable in the eyes of the LORD, and consequently, they were in danger of experiencing the wrath and judgment of God. It was time to make some drastic changes in the kingdom!

I want to make sure you understand what was going on in this scenario; as long as the people were in sin and rebellion against God, they were also in spiritual darkness. Through the worship of false gods, they had cast aside the light of God's truth. The Word of God was even physically concealed and hidden in obscure darkness. When man chooses the darkness of his own ways, he also chooses to reject the light of God's truth. So, what was rejected in the natural realm became hidden in the spiritual realm. However, when the hearts of godly leadership and the people began to repent and return to the LORD, the light of God's Word was again revealed.

As changes and restoration took place in the house of the LORD, Josiah knew that repentance, change and restoration also needed to take place in the hearts of the people. Therefore, he humbled himself before God and allowed the change to begin in his own heart and life first. As a godly leader should, he stepped up and led the people by his example. The King had a great tenderness toward the Word of God, and he wanted to please the LORD. Because of his repentant heart, the LORD decided to delay judgment upon the nation, until after Josiah's death (2 Kings 22).

There's much to be learned through King Josiah's example. For instance, the humility of godly leadership can delay the judgment of God upon a nation! God is righteous and holy. If nations are idolatrous and wicked, judgment will surely come; make no mistake about it. He cannot allow evil to go unchecked. But, if the men and women of God will rise up and declare the Word of the LORD, confess their sins and call their nations to

Part 4 • *Loving God* with all your Might & Strength

repentance, then He will respond with grace and favor. Even in the midst of a wicked and perverse generation (as in our current day), God will hear the cry of His people and extend His mercy (2 Chronicles 7:14).

This young king loved God, and he also loved his people. He was not content to just have his own life spared. He knew he could be a change agent and cause a shift in the nation, so he began to set things in order with the LORD and with the people.

The first thing King Josiah did was gather all the elders of Judah and Jerusalem, the priests, prophets and all the people. He called them to the house of the LORD. All were there, both great and small, and Josiah read the book of the covenant to them, so that they might hear the Word of the LORD. After Josiah read to the people, he made a covenant before the LORD. As the people stood in agreement, they promised to live by the words of God's covenant. The entire nation vowed to walk in His ways and obey Him with all their hearts and souls (2 Kings 23:1-3).

When it came to making things right with the LORD, King Josiah proactively took the lead. He didn't procrastinate or put his responsibilities off on anybody else. Instead, he was very wise and ruled with righteous diplomacy. For instance, he made sure the people understood what the LORD expected of them.

He knew that to accomplish the task before them, he had to educate and instruct the people. He also understood that the Word of God was the final authority. If the people would come in line with the truth of God, great things would be accomplished and everything would be set into proper order.

Temple Cleansing

Pertaining to the cleansing of the temple, King Josiah first addressed the spiritual leaders. He commanded that the high priest, as well as all the other priests and door keepers of the house of the LORD, work together. They were to bring everything out of the temple that had been used in the worship of the false god Baal. This included all items used for the worship of the groves and the idols of Asherah (Astarte, a Phoenician goddess), the sun god, the moon, the planets and all the host of heaven. The King commanded all those things to be burned outside the city of Jerusalem, in the fields and at the Kidron River. Furthermore, he removed all the idolatrous priests, whom the former kings of the nation ordained to burn incense in the high places of the cities of Judah and all around Jerusalem (2 Kings 23:4-6).

King Josiah's declaration to cleanse the house of the LORD began in the physical structure of brick and mortar and advanced from there. He understood the absolute necessity of cleansing all the filthiness of sin and idolatry from the house of the LORD, but he also knew the importance of cleansing such things from the heart and soul. Similarly, as believers in Christ, our bodies are the temple of the Holy Spirit — the sanctuary of the LORD — and He dwells within us. Therefore, we must allow nothing of a defiled or polluted nature to abide within us (1 Corinthians 3:16-17, 2 Corinthians 6:16). We are obligated to be pure vessels of honor for the LORD. Like Josiah, we need to be rid of all that is displeasing to the LORD.

If a nation is to return to the LORD, the spiritual leaders (and those who call themselves by the name of the LORD) must first get their own, individual lives in proper order. We can't condemn national leadership for their wickedness, if we ourselves are disobedient to the LORD. Repentance, revival and restoration must begin on a personal level, before it can manifest nationally.

Referring back to Josiah, he was really shaking things up in the kingdom, and that was only the beginning. He didn't stop with just cleaning idols out of the temple and getting the priests back in order. The King also tore down and overthrew the houses of the sodomites, which had positioned themselves next to the house of the LORD in the temple courtyard (2 Kings 23:7).

These **sodomites** (H6945/H6942) were *male prostitutes* who were *devoted* to *licentious idolatry* through the unrestrained, lewd and immoral sexual practices of homosexuality. The spiritual leadership of the nation had been so out-of-sync with the LORD, that these sodomites felt comfortable performing their unbridled acts of perversion in the house of God. What's wrong with this picture? How could the 'people of God' allow such wickedness to take place within the house of God?

It's no wonder the LORD was ready to let judgment fall upon the nation! Where were the righteous priests of the LORD? Where were the door keepers? To allow shameful and abominable perversion into the house of the LORD, demonstrated that the people had completely abandoned all that was right and holy. They had departed from the truth of God's Word and completely disregarded Him.

In addition to the leadership failing to uphold God's commands, the entire nation had seemingly forgotten their God. How is it that a society can move so far away from the truth of God, that they would allow such perversion to feel at home in (or be in such close proximity to) the house of the LORD? Even worse, how could a people who claimed to know God — a people who had been given the truth of God's Word and experienced His goodness — become so spiritually blind, that they would morally disintegrate to the point of accepting such vulgar behavior? Truly, they had forsaken the vision of who they were as a chosen people.

HAVE WE LET PERVERSION IN?
In the world we live in today, the idolatry of sexual perversion is running rampant as well! In parts of the

'religious realm' it's moved from the world straight to the pulpit! When the wickedness of the world moves into the house of the LORD and is shamelessly embraced by those in leadership, then they are in absolute rebellion against the LORD. They will surely be held accountable for their own sins, but they will also be liable for advocating and allowing others to continue in their sinful ways. Those who allow such idolatry in the house of the LORD have either never known the God they say they serve, or they have turned away from His Word, fallen into sin and failed in their Kingdom assignment.

The reality is that perversion has the opportunity to manifest in a person, church, organization, government or nation whenever they turn their heart and soul away from God. When deception is embraced and rebellion against the LORD is chosen, destruction and judgment are imminent. Does anybody remember Sodom and Gomorrah (Genesis 18:20-33, 19:1-29)? Think about it!

Religion versus True Christianity

At the start of this section, I used the term 'religious realm.' Religion (according to dictionary.com) is:

- a set of beliefs concerning the cause, nature, and purpose of the universe, especially when considered as the creation of a superhuman agency or agencies, usually involving devotional and ritual observances, and often containing a moral code governing the conduct of human affairs.

- a specific and fundamental set of beliefs and practices generally agreed upon by a number of persons or sects:
- the body of persons adhering to a particular set of beliefs and practices:
- the practice of religious beliefs; ritual observance of faith;
- something one believes in and follows devotedly; a point or matter of ethics or conscience:
- religious rites.

Did you notice that Jesus Christ is not mentioned in relation to any of the definitions of religion? There's a reason for this. The term 'religion' is very generic and it can be applied to any belief system. But, when a religion is devoid of Christ, all you have is deceptive ritual. Therefore, for clarity, I will define religion as:

- any belief system other than true — biblically based — Christianity.

Religion and true Christianity are at opposite ends of the spectrum; they are two completely different belief systems (also mentioned in Chapter 5). Religion is a manmade perversion of the truth and is demonic at its core. It's a thief that robs people of salvation, as well as the protection and powerful influence of God in their lives. Religion brings forth death and bondage to the spirit and soul of those who embrace it, thus keeping them from their divine destinies.

Part 4 • *Loving God* with all your Might & Strength

Let's be clear. Manmade religion cannot save the spirit and soul of man. Yet, within every religion, there are works-oriented systems by which followers are trying to be good enough (based on their own merits) to earn their salvation. You have those who believe the lie that there are many paths to God; or perhaps they believe that no matter what religious belief system they've chosen to adhere to, everybody is worshipping the same God, just by different names. Others believe their good works will earn them a ticket into heaven. Then, there are those who believe that everybody goes to heaven, regardless of how carelessly or wickedly they may have lived. All these beliefs are lies from hell and perpetrated by satan. Those caught in the snares of religion may have their beliefs, but they do not know the God who created them.

Therefore, based on their carnal nature and limited understanding, religious people create their own god. This is a god they can understand and control, because it's been birthed out of their own imagination. Thus, their god will never disagree with, instruct, correct or chasten them, because it represents their own ideals. These religious followers of 'the god of their own ideals' will then set up their own rules, rituals and lifestyle standards. But, most likely, these criteria will not be in agreement with the Word of God and are selfishly created to fulfill their own agendas. As a result, religion leads to the worship and self-exaltation of man.

To be enslaved in the bondage of religion places people in spiritually vulnerable and perilous positions. Many caught in the snares of religion may think they're doing just fine, but the presence of the living God is far from them. Since they do not know Christ or the truth of God's Word, they're unaware that their minds are being demonically influenced and manipulated.

Sadly, in an effort to appease their god and obtain a better eternal reward, some people have even committed suicide. They've made wrong decisions based on their erroneous view of God. The deception they believed and the truth they inherently rejected, contributed to their faulty perception of whom or what they considered their source of hope, redemption and salvation. They believed their works (and hence, their martyrdom) would give them a favorable place in eternity. Alas, these people discovered the truth too late; no one can earn eternal life. They either hadn't heard or understood, or simply rejected the truth that salvation is not based on what they do, but on what Christ has already done on their behalf. Serving false gods always leads to death and destruction.

Salvation and eternal life are gifts of God. They are freely given to all who will repent of their sins, and put their faith and hope in Jesus Christ (John 3:16-18, 6:40; Romans 6:22-23, 10:8-13; Ephesians 2:8-9). Those who reject Jesus Christ as the only means of salvation will

Part 4 • *Loving God* with all your Might & Strength

be separated from the loving presence of God. They will suffer the torments of a fiery hell for all eternity. This was never God's intention for mankind; but, when God's truth is rejected — by default — an eternity of misery, pain and anguish is chosen. Yet, Jesus said of Himself, *"I am the way, the truth and the life; no man cometh to the Father but by me."* Religion and false gods have never saved anybody. Jesus Christ is the only one who sacrificed Himself and was approved of the Father; He is the only way to salvation and eternal life. Whether or not you choose to accept this is completely up to you. (Matthew 25:41, 46; John 14:6; Acts 4:12, 10:43; 1 Timothy 2:5-6; Hebrews 2:3; 1 John 5:11-12).

True Christianity — which is the opposite of the world's religious systems and beliefs — consists of those who have forsaken their own ways and put their faith and trust in Jesus Christ, as their LORD and Savior. They have chosen to be involved in a holy, righteous, submitted, intimate, supernatural relationship with the one true and living God. Followers of Christ do not serve their own agendas, but seek to fulfill the will of the LORD. God's presence dwells among those who truly love and desire Him with all their heart, soul, mind and strength. And when the earthly life of a true Christian is over, they will spend eternity in the glorious peace and presence of the LORD.

True Christianity honors the Word of God. The fervent follower of Christ recognizes God's Word as the core tenets of their faith, the highest standard for living and the supreme law of governing authority in heaven and earth. They do not take the Word of God lightly, because through it, they have received the message of salvation. Therefore, God's Word is given the highest priority.

Let's also emphasize that 'true Christians' are NOT merely church goers! Now, don't misunderstand what I'm saying. We do want people to attend church, come to know and trust in Christ, and experience the beauty of salvation with all its wonderful benefits. However, just because someone sets their feet into a church building on a regular basis, does not make them a Christian. Nor does it grant them salvation or favor with God. Church attendance alone does not grant reward points to be used like a 'get out of jail free' card when they mess up. Let's get real! Rats can go to church, but that doesn't mean they're saved or serving the LORD. There's more to salvation than just stepping through church doors; true Christians step into Christ and live as He lived.

COMPROMISING? REPENT!
Perversion and the twisting of truth have always been tools and trappings of false religion; but it has various outlets. Aside from individuals, false religion is also implemented via the entertainment industry, including:

music, internet, news and social media, television, talk shows and obscene literature. In addition, this religious lie is found in many family relationships, educational institutions and business practices. It's seen in the streets, and it has even infiltrated the public offices and courts of nations. Indeed, perversion and the idolatrous worship of the will of man have, to some degree, infected every area of society.

Even some of God's people are guilty of shamefully compromising what they know to be right. They rarely open their bibles, but regularly open wide the gates of their eyes, ears, minds, hearts, bodies and souls to all sorts of wickedness. They view a steady diet of murder, adultery, foolishness, perversion, lustful desires and blasphemy against God, and they call it entertainment!! They participate in wrongful self-seeking relationships, fulfilling the unbridled desires of their flesh. They are rebellious to godly authority, and they have fallen into the world's slime pit of calling evil good and good evil (Isaiah 5:20). Church, it's time to wake up, repent and shake yourself from the wicked ways of the world!!

We must understand that sinful and compromising behaviors, attitudes and appetites indicate that a spiritual toxicity has taken place, and the temple of God has been polluted. This is spiritual adultery against the LORD. It will poison the spirit, snare the soul and divert the heart from the truth and presence of God. The LORD is not pleased when we take part of such things.

Do you call yourself a Christian? Do you say you're a follower of Christ, but at the same time you're living a double life of ungodly compromise or perversion? Are you involved in homosexuality, lesbianism or any other sexual deception or confusion? Have you opened yourself up to sedition, wickedness, idolatry, witchcraft, adultery, fornication or some other form of debauchery? Such lifestyles do not reflect the freedom or the work of God operating in you. Rather, they reveal the satanic deception, captivity and broken places in your life. If you call yourself a Christian, yet choose to continue as a slave to sin, then you are in rebellion against the LORD!

Know that the LORD yearns for you to break free of satan's bondage, but you must want the Living God more than your lifestyle. If you choose to live in loving obedience to the LORD, satan will no longer have control over your life, because he cannot remain where he is no longer received or embraced. Only when you're willing to fully lay down your life to the LORD, will you experience true freedom in Christ. You cannot have it your way and experience God's blessing at the same time. You must choose who you will serve. God will not come down to your substandard level of acceptability. You must come up to His standard of submission; obedience and holiness will follow.

So, if you know you've sinned against the LORD, and you're ready to repent and confess your sins to Him, now is the time to do so. If you want to be set free, healed and delivered, you must turn from your wicked ways. Renounce and remove every idol and unclean thing from your life. Meditate and feed on the Word of God. Ask the LORD to purge your heart and mind of all wickedness and unrighteousness (and everything associated with it). Let the power of the blood of Jesus cleanse you and restore you to your rightful place in Him. Become the holy, consecrated temple of God you're called to be. Fully give yourself to Him; serve Him; and let Him make you into the beautiful person He truly created you to be, in Jesus' name!

STAND STRONG!

As the ways of the world move further and further away from the truths of God, we're to stand strong for what's right. We can never bow to the demands of the wicked. We can never accept their agendas. We can never give our stamp of approval for their revolts against righteousness.

Remember, when people — even those who claim to know God — reject the truth of God, by default, they have chosen to believe and embrace the lies of satan. Once the lies are received, a demonic conception takes place in the soul. The thoughts, words and deeds that are birthed through that unholy union will, by their very nature, go against the Word and will of

God. As a result, those who conceive the lies of the enemy will build their lives on faulty foundations and will experience self-inflicted suffering. This is the fruit of embracing lies. If they continue in this path of rebellion and refuse to repent, the LORD will allow them to be turned over to a reprobate mind.

A reprobate mind occurs when people continually refuse to retain the knowledge of the true and living God in their minds. They shut Him out, so they can continue in their unrighteous, self-serving, rebellious ways. In effect, they set themselves up as false gods serving their own deluded, twisted and wicked agendas. They refuse to serve the LORD God Almighty, and they despise His righteous holiness. This reprobate lifestyle is nothing new. The Apostle Paul warns against it in:

Romans 1:18-32 *For the wrath of God is revealed from heaven against all ungodliness and unrighteousness of men, who hold the truth in unrighteousness; ¹⁹Because that which may be known of God is manifest in them; for God hath showed it unto them. ²⁰For the invisible things of him from the creation of the world are clearly seen, being understood by the things that are made, even his eternal power and Godhead; so that they are without excuse: ²¹Because that, when they knew God, they glorified him not as God, neither were thankful; but became vain in their imaginations, and their foolish heart was darkened. ²²Professing* themselves to be wise, they became fools, ²³And changed the glory of the uncorruptible God into an image made like to corruptible man, and to birds, and fourfooted beasts, and creeping things. ²⁴Wherefore God also gave them up to uncleanness through the lusts of their own hearts, to dishonour their own bodies between themselves: ²⁵Who changed the truth of God into a lie, and worshipped and served the creature more than the Creator, who is blessed for ever. Amen. ²⁶For this cause God gave them up unto vile affections: for even their women did change the natural use into that which is against nature: ²⁷And likewise also the men, leaving the natural use of the woman, burned in their lust one toward another; men with men working that which is unseemly, and receiving in themselves that recompense of their error which was meet. ²⁸And even as they did not like to retain God in their knowledge, God gave them over to a reprobate mind, to do those things which are not convenient; ²⁹Being filled with all unrighteousness, fornication, wickedness, covetousness, maliciousness; full of envy, murder, debate, deceit, malignity; whisperers, ³⁰Backbiters, haters of God, despiteful, proud, boasters, inventors of evil things, disobedient to parents ³¹Without understanding, covenant-breakers, without natural affection, implacable, unmerciful: ³²Who knowing the judgment of God, that they which commit such things are worthy of death, not

only do the same, but have pleasure in them that do them.

The scripture speaks very strongly concerning those who live a reprobate lifestyle. Nobody is originally born into reprobation. Its seed begins to grow in the hearts and minds of those who shun the knowledge of God. Because they reject and ignore the LORD and His Word, they set themselves on a path of self-deception, destined for destruction. They engage and take pleasure in unrepentant, persistent perversion, wickedness and rebellion against Him. Regardless of how the wicked try to justify or legalize their defiance against God and His righteous standard; no matter how they rationalize their sinful behavior; no matter how loud they shout that their twisted thoughts are to be accepted and embraced, the LORD does not accept the lifestyle of the reprobate. God will judge them according to their deeds.

Perversion is a falsification of truth. The LORD never created anybody to be homosexual, lesbian, bi-sexual, transgender, etc. Although ignorant men may accuse Him of such, the LORD does not create human beings to be slaves to sexual lust, fraudulent passions or perversion. To say they were born that way is a false accusation against God and an absolute lie from the pit of hell! The reasoning behind the accusation is that, if they blame God, then they feel they are justified in doing nothing to change their tendencies. In reality,

Part 4 • *Loving God* with all your Might & Strength

when men burn with lust for other men and women burn with lust for other women, they have departed from the truth and the original purposes of their Creator, God. Their lifestyles of sin become an abominable exhibition of their own stubborn insurrection against the LORD and mutinous revolt against His Word (Leviticus 20:13). This is unacceptable before the LORD.

We're to love the LORD our God with all our hearts, souls, minds and strength. Hence, we love what He loves, and we hate what He hates. God loves man and hates sin; He loves life and hates death; He loves holiness and hates wickedness; He loves purity and hates corruption; He loves freedom and hates bondage; He loves truth and hates lies. Conventional wisdom tells us not to hate, but the Word of the LORD declares otherwise. As much as we're commanded to love the LORD, we are also exhorted to resist and hate satan, as well as all of his works (Psalm 101:3, Psalm 119:104, 113, 128, 163, Psalm 139:21-22; Proverbs 6:16, 19, Proverbs 8:13; Ecclesiastes 3:8; Zachariah 8:17).

Agreeing with God's standard, we're to love and hate accordingly. As believers, we're to stand together in unity — with one mind and in one accord — with the LORD and one another (John 17:20-23). Together, we must boldly declare the gospel of Jesus Christ, for it is the power of God unto salvation to everyone who believes (Romans 1:16).

Protect the Helpless

As we continue with King Josiah, we see that after he'd dealt with the sodomites, he defiled and tore down all the high places of false worship. Included was the valley of Tophet, where helpless children were murdered as they were offered as human sacrifices to the false god Molech. These precious babes were meant to be a blessing to their parents. Instead, wickedness was stealing, killing and destroying them, so they became victims of idolatry. Josiah sought to stop the practice of child sacrifice and, thus, the shedding of innocent blood (Deuteronomy 19:10, 21:9).

Unfortunately, we see this same type of child sacrifice taking place in nations throughout the world today. In pagan religious practices, it's called child sacrifice; but in 'civilized' nations it's called abortion or merely a termination of pregnancy! Since it's referred to as a 'medical procedure,' it may appear to be more dignified and sterile, but the same murderous spirit is behind it. Truly, the main difference is that, in pagan societies, they wait for the baby to be born. In our 'advanced' society today, children are murdered in the womb, before they can even take their first breath. These murderous 'medical procedures' include: burning the precious babies with saline solution; ripping their limbs apart; sucking their brains from the back of their skulls after a live delivery or some other abominable method. Then, the abortionists take the mutilated, dead babies and sell their body parts for profit! On the perverted altars of a supposed pro-choice agenda, little babies are sacrificed to the idolatrous gods of lust, greed and the love of money, fear, ignorance, murder, inconvenience, unbelief, doubt, pride, hatred, shame, selfishness and irresponsibility.

Regardless of the reasons, abortion is an abomination and an altar to self-worship. Not only are these irreplaceable lives snuffed out by those who have no regard for the sanctity of life, but these dear children are murdered at the hands of those who should have loved them most. This is one of the most hateful and detrimental forms of idolatry. It's a form of rebellion that stems from the worship of self-will and a refusal to submit to the will of God. It reeks of its father, satan — the destroyer! The nation that intentionally permits abortion will be judged by God, and there will be no pardon (Deuteronomy 19:9-10; 2 Kings 21:16, 24:3-4; Jeremiah 2:32-34, 19:4-8).

THE NEXT PHASE OF CLEANSING

After hearing the Word of the LORD and repenting; dealing with the spiritual leadership; removing the sodomites, the idols of false gods and places of human sacrifice, King Josiah moved on to the next phase of spiritual cleansing. He took away the horses that were kept at the entrance of the house of the LORD. The pagans of the east (as well as the Greeks and Romans) worshipped and adored the sun. They also believed that the chariots of the sun were pulled by four horses. For this reason, the swiftness and versatility of the horse was revered. As part of their heathen practices, the sun worshippers mounted their horses every morning, supposedly to go meet the rising sun god. Some of the kings of Judah had also adopted this pagan ritual; this was why the horses had to be removed. The chariots used for this purpose were also burned (2 Samuel 23:8-11). Josiah refused to allow the representation of a false god to encroach upon the entrance of the house of the LORD. Without reservation, everything that was dedicated to idolatry was destroyed!

The purge of wickedness continued, as Josiah quickly rushed upon, overthrew, removed and destroyed the idolatrous altars, which had been used in sacrifice to the false god Baal. Josiah even removed the dust of the altars; he left no evidence of their former existence. These altars had been erected by the wicked Kings of Judah and King Manasseh. Their very creation and existence was rooted in an unrighteous rebellion against God. They were an abomination and, therefore, had to be completely destroyed.

Josiah was, literally, cleaning out the demonic nests and strongholds that the kings before him had erected. His heart was aflame with passion for his God. He was determined to faithfully and fearlessly rid the kingdom of all the filthiness of idolatry.

Part 4 • *Loving God* with all your Might & Strength

BREAKING DOWN CORRUPTION

Next, King Josiah dealt with the high places that were before (to the east of) Jerusalem. In Josiah's time, this location was known as the 'Mount of Corruption,' because of all the wicked practices of idolatry that took place there. Today, we know that same place as the Mount of Olives. In was in this location that the former King Solomon had built high places to the false gods of his 700 heathen wives and 300 concubines. Josiah was dealing with the idolatrous residue of King Solomon's rebellion and apostasy.

The LORD warned Solomon not to marry strange, foreign, idolatrous wives. Nevertheless, his lust for beautiful women caused the king to compromise his relationship with the LORD. He tolerated and supported their false gods and idolatrous practices. Solomon's rebellion against the LORD and his confederacy with wickedness, took Him on a downward spiral into sin and self-deception. Eventually, his own heart was turned away from the LORD, and he began to seek and pursue the heathen gods of his wives.

Solomon's compromise with idolatry, created a breach in his relationship with the LORD. Unlike the heart of his father, David, Solomon's heart was not **perfect** *(H8003/H7999)* toward the LORD. This means he was not *complete, friendly* or at peace with the LORD; neither was Solomon in a place of safety or right standing. Shamefully, the king's apostasy also plunged the nation of Israel deeper into sin and rebellion against the LORD (1 Kings 11; 2 Kings 23:12-13).

So, Josiah continued with his work. He broke down the idols and the high places of Ashtoreth, Chemosh and Milcom, which Solomon had erected for his wives. Then, Josiah took the bones of the idolatrous priests (who had disgracefully worshiped, served and burnt incense to false gods) and used them to defile and contaminate the high places.

BURNING UP CONVENIENCE

King Jeroboam also committed evil in the sight of the LORD. During his reign, he made two golden calves and placed them in the cities of Bethel and Dan. By encouraging the people to conveniently worship idols (instead of journeying to Jerusalem as God had commanded), He caused them to sin against the LORD.

Now think on this: How often do people, including God's people, choose to disobey the LORD simply because what He requires seems inconvenient, uncomfortable or takes extra effort? Furthermore, how often do we create our own religious systems, yet we're not in line with what the LORD has prescribed? If we set up our own belief ideologies apart from what the LORD desires, then we — like Jeroboam — have committed evil in the sight of the LORD.

Part 4 • *Loving God* with all your Might & Strength

To possess a determined passion to remove any idol from our lives, regardless of the reason for that idol, brings joy to the heart of the LORD. Such desire and action prove that we value the heart of the Lord above ourselves and the things of this world. With this in mind, whether it's for convenience, to pacify friends or family members or for any other reason, we must remove all rebellious ideologies from our hearts and minds.

King Josiah would not give place to any false deities. Therefore, he tore down the high place and the altar in Bethel that King Jeroboam had built. Then, Josiah took the bones out of the sepulchers in the mount and burned them upon the altar; thereby, polluting it (1 Kings 12:28-33, 13:2-3, 14:16, 15:30, 21:22). His actions fulfilled the prophetic word declared by the prophet:

<u>1 Kings 13:2</u> And he cried against the altar in the word of the LORD, and said, O altar, altar, thus saith the LORD; Behold, a child shall be born unto the house of David, Josiah by name; and upon thee shall he offer the priests of the high places that burn incense upon thee, and men's bones shall be burnt upon thee.

King Josiah was a man of great conviction, purpose and destiny. Before he was conceived in his mother's womb, God had prophetically called him to rule as King over the nation, to restore the house of the LORD and to root idolatry out of the land. Likewise,

CHAPTER 14 • THE RIGHTEOUS MIGHT OF A KING

before we were born, the LORD God Almighty called each of us to a mighty work in the Kingdom of God.

> Do you believe that? Are you ready to get into position to fulfill your ordained purpose?

As the king continued his campaign to rid the land of idolatry, he visited Samaria. The Samaritans were known for mixing the things of God with idolatrous practices, thus, provoking the anger of the LORD. Therefore, Josiah tore down all the houses, high places and altars that the kings of Israel had built in honor of others gods. He also killed all the priests (likely not Levites) that were serving idols upon the altars in the high places, and he burned their bones. Then, Josiah returned to Jerusalem (2 Kings 23:19-20).

RESTORING WORSHIP

It is noteworthy that King Josiah did not only root out idolatry; he also sought to restore a godly order of corporate worship. After extensive spiritual cleansing (concluded during his eighteenth year of reign), he commanded the people to hold the greatest Passover celebration since before the time of the Judges (2 Kings 23:21-23). You may ask, "Why would this be the greatest Passover feast (up to that day) since before the time of the Judges?" Well, during the time of the Judges, the people departed from the Word and wisdom of the LORD. Therefore, they did what was right in their own eyes, acting according to the desires of their flesh. This was the common sin of the people, which caused them

Part 4 • *Loving God* with all your Might & Strength

to spiritually and morally fall into a downward spiral of sin and compromise. So, since the time of the Judges, idolatry was rampant as the people served their self-will. By his example, when he taught the people to do what was right in the sight of the LORD, the king restored proper order to worship (Judges 17:6, 21:25).

Throughout his reign, King Josiah had zero tolerance for any abominations or occult activities. This included all forms of witchcraft, including fortunetellers, mediums, witches, wizards, sorcerers, those who conjured up and communicated with the dead and those who dealt with familiar spirits. King Josiah was determined to **put away** *(H1197), become brutish* and *kindle* or *consume* (i.e. burn with fire) all those who participated in such wickedness. Anytime the king discerned idols, images (family idols) or any form of false worship being used in the land of Judah or in Jerusalem, he sought to destroy it.

King Josiah's love toward the LORD and strong godly leadership caused a spiritual shift in the nation and delayed the coming judgment. Unquestionably, he served and worshipped the LORD with all his might. In fact, his zeal for righteousness highly motivated him to follow God's law, and he was well known for his obedient heart. As a result, up to that point in history, scripture records Josiah as being the greatest King who ever served the LORD:

Chapter 14 • The Righteous Might of a King

***2 Kings 23:25** And like unto him was there no king before him, that turned to the LORD with all his heart, and with all his soul, and with all his might, according to all the law of Moses; neither after him arose there any like him.*

After reigning in Jerusalem for thirty-one years, Josiah went out in battle against Pharaohnechoh (the King of Egypt) and was killed. After Josiah's death, the people anointed his son, Jehoahaz, to be king. He reigned in Jerusalem for 3 months and did what was evil in the sight of the LORD (2 Kings 23:29-32). Thereafter, the Pharaoh removed Jehoahaz from being king; instead, his brother, Eliakim (whose name became Jehoiakim), was given the throne. Just like his brother, Eliakim did what was evil in the sight of the LORD. Because Judah had forsaken the LORD, served other gods and shed innocent blood, they were brought under bondage and forced to pay tribute (2 Kings 22:16-17, 23:26-27, 24:2-4). In all of this, the LORD was faithful to fulfill His Word of coming judgment and keep His promise to Josiah that judgment would not come until after his death.

In his reign as king, Josiah did everything he could to right the wrongs in his own heart and nation. His uncompromised love for God became his motivation to fulfill his ordained destiny, which was prophesied before he was ever born. Josiah allowed nothing to stop him from fulfilling the will of the LORD. Through

Part 4 • *Loving God* with all your Might & Strength

His bold faithfulness, He raised a righteous standard in the land, and he pushed the judgment and wrath of God thirty-one years into the future. In the life of Josiah, we see a man who took a firm stand to love the LORD his God mightily — with all his heart, soul, mind and strength. It is my prayer that our nation would be blessed with rulers who would have a heart to set things right in the eyes of the LORD today!

It's important to understand that one righteous person (who fully loves and serves the LORD) can impact multitudes of people and change nations for all eternity. Could you be such a person? You may not be a national leader or someone who is well known, but you can still have a powerful impact on others. The LORD is looking for those whom He can raise up as world changers! Are you one of them? All you have to do is align yourself with the Word and will of the LORD, then stand up for what's right in His eyes.

> Are you willing to stand against the tide of evil that seeks to destroy your nation?
>
> Do you have any areas of compromise (idols) in your life that you need to repent of?
>
> Are you submitting to the Word of the LORD?
>
> Are there any high places within your mind that need to be surrendered to the LORD?

Do you have any hidden 'gods' or secret sins in your life that need to be exposed and destroyed?

Are there any wrong relationships that you need to break free from?

Are you willing to serve the LORD with all your might?

Are you standing strong?

SUMMARY OF LOVING GOD WITH ALL YOUR MIGHT AND STRENGTH

In Chapter 13, we studied the vehemence of zealous love. Its expression is a manifestation of the passionate spirit-driven heart and soul. Zealous love for the LORD is strenuous and wholly diligent in all matters pertaining to that relationship. It's a love that is ardent, pursuant, strong, intense, emotional, full of fiery energy and visible for all to see. This fervent burning love holds nothing back; it knows no boundaries and is fully willing to quickly do whatever is required to please the divine recipient of that love — Jesus Christ.

King David was an example of a zealous lover of God, as he danced before the Ark of the Covenant in Jerusalem. He was an enthusiastically ardent worshipper and he expressed himself openly for all to see. There was no shame in his extravagant exaltation and adoration of the LORD. Yet, his wife (Michal) ridiculed and despised her husband's actions.

In times of extremely zealous worship, there will be those who do not understand. But we're not worshipping for them; we're worshipping for our King. Therefore, it doesn't really matter what others think. We're to fervently pursue our God and express our love to Him, regardless of the opinions of others.

In Chapter 14, we took a glance into the life of King Josiah. This young King loved the LORD with all his

Part 4 • Loving God with all your Might & Strength

might and desired righteousness. He stood up for what was just and true in the eyes of the LORD. He also raised money to restore the house of the LORD, which had been neglected. As king, Josiah dealt with the spiritual leadership and removed idolatrous worship from the land. Moreover, he caused the people to hear the Word of God and called them to repentance. He wasn't concerned about being politically correct! He didn't mind what people thought of him. His only care was that things be made right between the LORD and His people. Josiah was a man of godly principle and an excellent example of loving the LORD with all his might.

Like Josiah, we're called to demonstrate and lift up the godly standards of the Word of God. To do this, we must remove all the idols from our hearts and fully repent of all wickedness. Then, we're to restore the things of God that have been neglected and call our nations to repentance. Above all, we must seek to love the LORD, acknowledging that He has a unique role for each of us in His Kingdom, so that we can fulfill our destiny in Him.

So far, our study has taken us on quite a journey with the LORD. We've looked rather extensively at what it means to love the LORD our God with all our hearts, souls and minds, as well as with all our might and strength. In Part 5 of our study, we'll look at what it means to love the LORD in all we do.

Part 5
Loving God in All You Do

∽ CHAPTER 15 ∾

LIVING LIFE IN CHRIST: WHAT'S IT LOOK LIKE?

To love the LORD in all we do, we must learn to operate in the mind of Christ concerning every area of our lives. In this way, we're consistently protected from unholy and hypocritical behavior, as well as an unrighteous representation of Christ. So what does the mind of Christ look like? How does it function? Well, as you might expect, God's Word gives us insight into the mind of Christ:

<u>Philippians 2:6-8</u> Who [Jesus], being in the form of God, thought it not robbery to be equal with God: ⁷But made himself of no reputation, and took upon him the form of a servant, and was made in the likeness of men: ⁸And being found in fashion as a man, he humbled himself, and became obedient unto death, even the death of the cross.

Part 5 • *Loving God* in All You Do

First of all, Jesus was in the **form** *(G3444/G3313)* of God, which translates in the Greek as *morphē*. This word is defined as a *section, allotment, division* or *share* transformed through an adjustment of *parts, shape* and *nature*. Therefore, Jesus **being** *(G5225/G5259/G756)* in the form of God manifested His *existence* as the Word of God made flesh, the Son of God and Son of man. In His earthly body, He represented and resembled the similarities, person and characteristic aspects of God, transformed into human flesh. In other words, He's both God and man.

Secondly, Jesus **thought** *(G2233/G71)* it not robbery to be **equal** *(G2470/G1492)* with God. This means that He knew who He was and saw Himself as fully equipped to *lead* and *command* with the same power and authority as the Father in Heaven. Jesus had all the wisdom and power of heaven at His disposal, and He wasn't afraid to use it!

Thirdly, even though Jesus knew His authority and magnificence, He humbled Himself and made Himself **of no reputation** *(G2758)*. He *emptied* Himself of His heavenly glory and all the accolades He deserved. He laid that part of His divine majesty and glory down. Instead, He **took** *(G2983)* upon Himself the **form** *(G3444)* of a **servant** *(G1401/G1210)*. This means He *adjusted* Himself to *take a hold* of the *shape, nature,* allotment and portion of being a servant — *a slave* in bonds. Christ, the King of Glory, positioned and *qualified* Himself to come under *subservience* and *subjection* to the Father in heaven. Such humility and servanthood reflects the mind of Christ.

HUMBLE SERVANTHOOD

Furthermore (according to Philippians 2:7-8), in order to fulfill His earthly assignment for the Kingdom of God, Jesus made Himself to be in the **likeness** *(G3667)* and **fashion** *(G4976)* of a man. Instead of reigning in all the fullness of His glorious existence and power, He subjected Himself to the confines of human flesh. He took on the physical *similarity (form & resemblance)* as well as the figurative *mode* and *condition* (emotions, external circumstances, limitations, etc.) of a natural man. This was quite an adjustment! It's evident that the manifestation of who Jesus was in Glory was different than the manifestation of who He was in His natural manhood.

Jesus had to take it down quite a few notches to get on the same level as man. He could only do this because He was willing to **humble** *(G5013/G5011)* Himself, even though He was God Almighty. Christ *depressed*, even *humiliated* Himself to the low *circumstances* and *disposition* of mankind, so He could reach out and minister to us.

Jesus' willingness to humble Himself (even to the point of suffering His own death upon the cross) was required in order to obediently fulfill the will of the Father. Have you personally met anyone (other than

Part 5 • *Loving God* in All You Do

Christ) who is determined to fulfill the will of the Heavenly Father, no matter what the cost? If you've had the privileged honor of knowing this type of person, then you've encountered someone who has the mind of Christ. Even if death is their final requirement, such passionate believers are willing to lay down everything they are and all they have, to complete their ordained assignments in the LORD.

What is your reputation?

Are you willing to lay aside your perceived reputation, so you can move forward in obedience and fulfill the call of God upon your life?

Are you willing to help ease the heavy burdens of those around you?

LABOR & REST

Obviously, while functioning in the mind of Christ is exemplified by a lifestyle of humble servanthood and sacrifice, it doesn't mean we're to have a religious, worker bee (works oriented) or churchy mentality. It's so easy to jump on the church bandwagon and get caught up doing all sorts of good works, without first seeking the will of the LORD concerning the matter. We're not to be running to and fro — to every Christian event. I'm not saying we're to be lazy in the things of God, but there should be prayerful consideration for all things.

CHAPTER 15 • LIVING LIFE IN CHRIST: WHAT'S IT LOOK LIKE?

Proper priorities and boundaries are keys to success in life and ministry. You may ask, "What does a successful life and ministry look like?" The answer is very simple. People who succeed in the Kingdom of God have decided, of their own accord, to submit themselves (in love and obedience) to the complete Lordship of Jesus Christ. They do so by living their lives according to the Word of God and following the leading of His Holy Spirit in all things, at all times. Ultimately, a successful life and ministry is the fruitful outcome of the lovers of God who choose to lay down their own agendas, in their service to the LORD.

I've seen church leaders who, through the continuous activities in their churches and elsewhere, have literally drained their people to the point of utter exhaustion. The people became so worn out, they couldn't function or even think properly. This is spiritual abuse and it's not of God. If we're to function in the mind and power of Christ, we must set proper boundaries in our lives.

Think about this: Jesus was the greatest servant that ever lived, yet He didn't run to the synagogue to get involved in busy work. Nor did He seek the Pharisees to find out what His Kingdom assignment was. Instead, He spent intimate time in prayer, seeking the will of the Father.

It's important that we take time to slow down and focus on the LORD. Every one of us needs to spend one-on-one time with Him. As we do so, He will lead us into what we are (and are not) to participate in. He will help us to find rest for our souls, as we see in:

Matthew 11:28-29 *Come unto me, all ye that labour and are heavy laden, and I will give you rest. ²⁹Take my yoke upon you, and learn of me; for I am meek and lowly in heart: and ye shall find rest unto your souls.*

When Jesus said *come (G1205)* unto me, He was extending an invitation to *come hither* and follow Him. He desires to minister to all those that *labour (G2872/G2873/G2875)* and are *heavy laden (G5412)*. This refers to those who *work hard* and *toil* to the point of suffering great physical and/or emotional *pain (weariness, fatigue, grief, mourning, lamentation,* etc.) resulting in a loss of strength. These servant hearted worshippers are *loaded up* and *overburdened with ceremony* (formal procedures of service) and/or *spiritual anxiety*. To these weary ones who come to Jesus, He promises *rest (G373/G303/G3973)*. This rest requires us *to stop* (refrain and *desist* from) carrying the heavy burdens and lay them down before the LORD. Jesus doesn't want us to be beaten down with the cares of life. Instead, He wants us to *lay back* and *repose* ourselves in the midst of His presence. He desires that we partake of His wisdom and counsel, finding our *refreshing* and strength in Him.

Jesus said, **"Take my yoke upon you and learn of me..."** The word *yoke (G2218)* means *to join*. It literally refers *to the beam of the balance, as connecting the scales.* To **take** *(G142)* the yoke means *to lift.* It implies to *take up* and, figuratively, to *raise (the voice)*. To **learn** *(G3129)* is to *acquire knowledge or skill by study; to receive instruction or experience; to become informed or acquainted with; to understand through exposure by example.* Jesus wants us to know the stability found only in Him. He's the yoke, the scale of balance, the standard of truth, and He's the physical manifestation of the Word of God. When we take His balanced yoke upon ourselves, we're joining ourselves to His stability. We're taking on the manifested Word of God, lifting Him up and raising our voice to declare His truth. He is our example of how we're to live. Each one of us must take up His yoke and become His disciple *(G3101)* — a *learner* who seeks to *understand.*

As we take Christ's yoke upon us, we come into proper balance with Him. He has sufficient strength to carry every burden and detail of life pertaining to us. Thus, we no longer operate in our own strength, wisdom, vision or purpose. He is our helper and our burden bearer. He takes that which we've toiled and labored under and replaces it with His rest. Therefore, we no longer carry the burdens of life by ourselves. No matter how heavy the burdens may be, if we'll just submit to His Word, He'll always bring the scales of life back into proper balance.

MEEKNESS & EXALTATION

As we continue our study of Matthew 11:28-29, we see that Jesus said of Himself, *"I am meek and lowly in heart..."* To be *meek (G4235/G4239)* is to be *gentle, humble* and *mild*. It also means to be patient, long suffering, docile, submissive and courteous. To be *lowly (G5011)* in *heart (G2588)* is to be *depressed* and *humiliated in circumstance or disposition*. In addition it means to be *humble* in *heart, thoughts* and *feelings,* and to be *of low degree (estate)*. Elsewhere in scripture, lowliness of heart refers to being brokenhearted. Meekness and lowliness were accurate descriptions of the Father's tender heart toward mankind. Likewise, as we follow Jesus' example, we'll take on His spiritual mindset to be strong, yet gentle. Meekness and lowliness are the gentle qualities the LORD desires for us to experience in Him and to adopt as our own.

For Jesus to touch the hearts of mankind and draw them into the Kingdom, He had to present Himself in a way that could be received. If Jesus had manifested in all His radiant glory and strength, the people would have been terrified. Jesus was (and is) the King of kings and LORD of lords. If anybody had the right to exalt Himself, it was Him. However, Jesus understood the bigger picture of His mission. Therefore, He chose to deal with mankind in a spirit of meekness and lowliness, so that we could receive, recognize and identify with the heart of the Heavenly Father.

Jesus came as a servant — meek, humble, lowly, and with no reputation. He was a love slave to the will of the Father. He honored the Father with His life and death. Still, we must emphasize that the beauty of Jesus' obedience was not only found in the fact that His life was used to redeem mankind, but that after the work was done, the Heavenly Father highly exalted Him:

<u>Philippians 2:9-11</u> Wherefore God also hath highly exalted him, and given him a name which is above every name: ¹⁰That at the name of Jesus every knee should bow, of things in heaven, and things in earth, and things under the earth; ¹¹And that every tongue should confess that Jesus Christ is Lord, to the glory of God the Father.

Exaltation comes through humility, obedience and a willingness to serve. Even though Jesus demonstrated by example, His disciples found it challenging to embrace and apply this principle to their lives. They vied for position, wanting to be recognized as the greatest in the Kingdom (Matthew 20:20-28; Mark 9:33-35). Jesus tells us the way to greatness in:

<u>Matthew 18:1-4</u> At the same time came the disciples unto Jesus, saying, Who is the greatest in the kingdom of heaven? ²And Jesus called a little child unto him, and set him in the midst of them, ³And said, Verily I say unto you, Except ye be converted, and become as little children, ye shall not enter

Part 5 • *Loving God* in All You Do

into the kingdom of heaven. ⁴*Whosoever therefore shall humble himself as this little child, the same is greatest in the kingdom of heaven.*

To be **converted** *(G4762)* means *to twist*; that is, *to turn* completely around or *reverse* your disposition. To **humble** *(G5013/G5011)* ourselves means to *depress* our self-preoccupied nature down to a lower position and willingly humble ourselves to the low *circumstances* and *disposition* of others. In this way, we're empowered to reach out and minister to them. This is not an attitude of unworthiness or false humility; rather, it demonstrates a heart of willing submission and honor to the will of the Father.

As a Little Child

Exactly what does it mean to humble one's self as a little child? To understand, we must first consider the characteristics of children. If children are under the care of loving and responsible parents, they have a simple, trusting purity of heart. Since their physical stature is small (low), they do not think of themselves as greater, bigger or more important than anybody else. They're not interested in exalted titles, authority or dominion. They're happy to just be loved, have a place to live, food to eat and clothes to wear. In these favorable conditions, they're free to dream of what they want to be when they grow up. They're also very trusting, and they rejoice in the simple pleasures of life. This is what childlike humility looks like.

In addition, since everything a child has is provided by somebody else, he/she has no personal legal rights to anything (other than to be properly cared for and loved). As children mature, they learn how to serve their families by taking on more tasks and responsibilities. Parents are to be their children's first teachers — training them in the ways of the LORD and teaching them, by example, how to submit to proper authorities (God, parents and other godly leaders) (Proverbs 22:6).

Now, let's compare these characteristics with the spiritual aspects of those little children who are welcomed into the Kingdom of Heaven. If we have the characteristic of childlike humility, we'll have a simple, trusting and pure heart before the LORD. We'll realize that everything we have has come from Him, and we know He loves and cares for us. We'll rejoice and be satisfied in the LORD, as we take great pleasure in His plans for us.

As we mature in our walk with the LORD, we'll allow Him to teach us His ways, as we faithfully fulfill the responsibilities He has entrusted to us. We'll learn to love and appreciate the family of God, and find ways to be a blessing to our brothers and sisters in Christ. We'll be connected to the heart of the Father and be so excited about what He's doing in our lives that we'll want to tell others about Him.

Accordingly, we will not allow ourselves to become puffed up with pride, nor will we seek positions or titles solely for our own personal gain. Rather, we'll live before the LORD with a heart of submission to His will. We must never forget that He's watching out for our best interest. Just as children seek to please their parents, our greatest goal in the Kingdom of God should be to bring pleasure to our King, our Father, and our LORD. This is the humble, childlike faith that brings greatness to those in the Kingdom.

STAYING IN POSITION

Let's also consider the fact that, even Jesus had to humble Himself as a little child, to fulfill the purposes of the Kingdom of God. First of all, from His heavenly throne, He made a decision to lay down His gloriously, high position of ruling all creation, to come to earth as the redeemer of mankind. Then, He had to condense Himself into the seed of the Word of God to manifest in human flesh as a tiny embryo in the womb. That, all by itself, is a mind boggling concept! Then, at the appointed time, Jesus experienced physical birth. He suckled at the breast of His mother and grew from being a baby, to a young child, to a young man.

By twelve years of age, Jesus was a young man so learned in the scriptures that He was questioning, teaching and astonishing the doctors (the advanced teachers of Jewish scripture) in the temple. Even though Jesus knew who He was and what He was about, the appointed time for Him to step into His full ministry had not yet come. Therefore, Jesus subjected Himself to his mother Mary and his adoptive father, Joseph. As He matured into manhood, He increased in wisdom, stature and favor with God and man (Luke 2:45-52).

Jesus was teaching in the temple at age twelve, but waited until He was 30 years of age to begin His public ministry. Likewise, we need to humble ourselves before the LORD and wait for His appointed timing. Even so, we may be tempted to become anxious to experience our personal destinies. We may be excited about our calling or the revelations we've received from the LORD, and consequently, we may be enticed to rush ahead of His timing. But, we need to allow Him to adequately prepare us for what's ahead. If we will trust the LORD, He will be faithful to raise us up when we are properly prepared.

Focus — Ministering to Others
While Jesus walked the earth, He taught His disciples how to achieve greatness in the Kingdom of God. It's not about personal rank, position or ability. Greatness is developed through the process of serving others.

__Matthew 20:20-28__ Then came to him the mother of Zebedee's children with her sons, worshipping him, and desiring a certain thing of him. [21]And he said unto her, What wilt thou? She saith unto him, Grant that these my two sons may sit, the one on thy right hand, and the other on the left, in thy kingdom. ²²But Jesus answered and said, Ye know not what ye ask. Are ye able to drink of the cup that I shall drink of, and to be baptized with the baptism that I am baptized with? They say unto him, We are able. ²³And he saith unto them, Ye shall drink indeed of my cup, and be baptized with the baptism that I am baptized with: but to sit on my right hand, and on my left, is not mine to give, but it shall be given to them for whom it is prepared of my Father. ²⁴And when the ten heard it, they were moved with indignation against the two brethren. ²⁵But Jesus called them unto him, and said, Ye know that the princes of the Gentiles exercise dominion over them, and they that are great exercise authority upon them. ²⁶But it shall not be so among you: but whosoever will be great among you, let him be your minister; ²⁷And whosoever will be chief among you, let him be your servant: ²⁸Even as the Son of man came not to be ministered unto, but to minister, and to give his life a ransom for many (also Luke 22:27).

The wife of Zebedee had no idea what she was really asking. She probably thought she was doing her two sons (James and John) a favor, by petitioning Jesus for their positions in His Kingdom. But isn't that the typical heart of a mother? Always wanting the 'very best' for her children? Always wanting them to succeed in life? From Jesus' response, we see that Kingdom position and authority do not come without a cost.

Chapter 15 • Living Life in Christ: What's it Look Like?

Testing, trials and struggles help build the character of those called to leadership. I believe Jesus perceived what this woman wanted before He asked her the question, "What wilt thou?" I also believe He knew the effect it would have upon His other disciples. Jesus knew that the words she was about to speak would uncover their personal hidden agendas.

Once this mother's desire was made known, it stirred up a hornet's nest of jealousy among the disciples. In reality, her request revealed their heart conditions, hidden motivations and underlying ambitions. As a result, they were moved with **indignation** *(G23/G43)* toward James and John. The disciples were so *grieved*; they became *greatly afflicted* and *sorely displeased*. They were so *bent* out of shape over it, that it caused them to *ache*. Even though they did not ask for it outright, the mother of James and John actually requested what all the disciples really desired for themselves.

By the response of the disciples, we see that they all felt like they were entitled to those coveted positions. Obviously, they were not happy that someone else might receive it. This is not the mind of Christ. Rather, it's a mentality that's looking for one's own personal benefits and the exaltation of self. Clearly, Jesus still had a lot of work to do in the hearts and lives of His disciples.

Jesus was the ultimate servant in the Kingdom. He came *teaching* the people the truth of how to love God and live right. He healed the sick, raised the dead, delivered those possessed of devils, worked miracles, fed the hungry and gave His life as a ransom for whosoever would believe. Jesus poured Himself out on the behalf of others and gave to those who could not repay. Jesus demonstrated kingdom ministry through serving others; this is what makes a person great in God's Kingdom.

Jesus, being the King of kings and LORD of lords, could have simply demanded that others lower themselves to serve Him, but He didn't. He did not come to earth to be *attended to*, or *waited upon*. Nor did He beckon His disciples to take care of His own personal needs, wants and/or desires. Indeed, Jesus said that He did not come to be **ministered** *(G1247/G1249)* to, but to minister. Likewise, we are also called to be ministering servants.

The followers of Jesus have been given His authority and dominion to fulfill the will of the Heavenly Father in the earth. However (even as the people, Priests, Kings and Ambassadors of God), our position alone cannot cause a lost heart to turn to the LORD. We must be willing to humbly pour out the life and love of God (which resides on the inside of us) to others. As we serve others in this way, they will see the power of God in demonstration. As God operates in and through us, He will draw the masses into His Kingdom. This is exactly what Jesus did, and we are to follow His example.

How do you see your position in the Kingdom?

THE MIND OF CHRIST IN YOU

If we're to minister in the power of Christ, we must operate with a mindset that is above our own understanding. In and of itself, our human thinking and reasoning is extremely limited. By submitting ourselves to the leading of God's Spirit, we can operate in the mind of Christ. Only if our minds are controlled by the Word of God, can His supernatural wisdom and guidance be free to manifest in our thought processes.

Have you ever encountered the supernatural experience of, naturally, knowing something in your mind, but at the same time (down in your spirit, in the core of your being), you know something else to be true about a situation or a person? In other words, the knowledge in your mind may be different than what's in your spirit. Even so, you know you must act on what is in your spirit, not what's in your mind. This is how the Spirit of the LORD often leads us.

If we're to follow the leading of God's Holy Spirit, we must cast aside the limitations of our own minds. I'm not talking about insanity, but putting aside our own human ways of doing things and bringing our thoughts into subjection to the LORD. Let me give an example:

Part 5 • *Loving God* in All You Do

Years ago, my son Joshua and I went on a mission trip to Mexico with Youth with a Mission (YWAM). In spite of the language barriers and our feeble attempts at using the Spanish language, the LORD moved supernaturally (in and through us) to lead people to Christ. Up to that point, this was one of the most amazing and life changing experiences we'd ever encountered. The LORD showed Himself strong, and afterwards, we were never the same. That trip, literally, changed the course of our lives and sent us in an entirely new direction.

Before returning to the United States, the director of that particular YWAM team extended an invitation for our family to attend their five and a half month Family Discipleship Training School. We would be trained in many aspects of ministry, service, evangelism, teamwork, biblical studies, projects, outreach events and, eventually, a mission trip to a foreign nation. Because of the intensity of its full-time training schedule, financial employment outside of school hours was not an option.

So, if the LORD led us to attend the school, we'd be required to leave everything behind and relocate 900 miles away to the rural town of Weyerhaeuser, Wisconsin. This meant our family would also need to trust and believe God for ten thousand dollars, to cover the costs of school and to maintain our household expenses back in Tennessee. In reality, we didn't have the ten thousand dollars. It made no sense (in our natural understanding) that we should embark upon such an adventure. Yet, the Spirit of God was relentlessly pulling on our hearts. Our family was to take a step of faith and trust Him in this exciting, new spiritual escapade. We knew it would be a supernatural plunge into destiny!

After the decision was made to obey the LORD, we aligned our actions with our faith, loaded up the truck and headed for Wisconsin. With only twenty-five hundred dollars in my purse, we set out on a journey of faith that would be life changing. We made a decision to believe that our God would supply our every need, according to His riches in glory (Matthew 6:25-34; Philippians 4:19). We knew the LORD was the only one who could take care of us; we couldn't do it on our own. We chose to put our trust in His faithfulness and believe that He would make the way for us, regardless of how impossible the circumstances appeared to be.

Over the five and a half months that followed, we saw the LORD bless us in so many ways. That's not to say that our faith didn't get wobbly at times — especially, when the bills came due and the money wasn't there. However, as we sought the LORD and laid our financial concerns before Him, He told us what to do in every situation. We expected Him to meet our needs, but we never knew exactly how He was going to do it. Money would arrive at what seemed to be the last

Part 5 • *Loving God* in All You Do

minute, but praise be to God, it arrived! In order to believe beyond our visible circumstances, He was teaching us to put our faith and trust in Him.

Many times, our needs were met by unexpected or unknown sources. For instance, one morning I was leaving our dorm room; I looked down and saw a one hundred dollar bill lying on the carpet. It had been anonymously slipped under the door during the night. We faced many financial struggles, but somehow, the LORD always came through for us.

During the last month of training, our foreign mission trip took us to the nation of Trinidad. We saw the LORD move mightily. Everywhere we went, people trusted Christ for salvation. We ministered in the power and anointing of God as never before. We knew the LORD was preparing us for greater things in the Kingdom. After the completion of our mission trip, we graduated from the school and went back home. Little did we know that our lives would never be the same!

Our experience with the LORD through YWAM rocked our world! It was the catapult the LORD used to project us into our ordained destinies. My son returned to YWAM for more training; after that, he spent three years as a missionary in Mexico. Since that time, I have also continued my involvement in missions, by ministering in a dozen different nations. Isn't the LORD marvelous!

Chapter 15 • Living Life in Christ: What's it Look Like?

This is just one example of how the mind of Christ, if given the chance, will operate within us. Remember, in our natural minds, it made no sense to leave everything behind and go to YWAM. Our natural circumstances were screaming that the money wasn't there. Instead of relying on our own understanding, we listened to the Holy Spirit. We allowed faith to arise, as we entered into an amazingly intimate journey with Him. As a result, our lives were gloriously transformed and eternal souls were saved. God's agenda is always so much bigger than our circumstance, ability or wallet. It takes faith to operate in the mind of Christ, but when we take that step, we enter into His supernatural realm of blessing and provision.

Be Like Christ

The LORD desires that we love as He loved, serve as He served, and minister as He ministered (Galatians 2:20; Matthew 23:11; Mark 10:45). We're to forbear with and forgive one another, even as Christ did for us (Colossians 3:13). We're to be one with Him, carrying out the will of the Father in the earth (John 17:20-23). If we are to accomplish this, we must obey:

<u>Philippians 2:5</u> *Let this mind be in you, which was also in Christ Jesus:*

To comprehend this verse, we must understand the phrase **'this mind.'** What type of mind was in Christ? The answer is found in the verses before and after. In Philippians 2:1-4, **'this mind'** refers to loving one

Part 5 • *Loving God* in All You Do

another and being in one accord. It's associated with comfort, fellowship of the Spirit, mercy, joy and lowliness (humble modesty) of mind. Basically, it's the type of mind that esteems others more than ourselves and watches out for their good.

So, while we're made in the image and likeness of God, we're also to have a servant's heart. We're not to promote our own name or reputation for our personal glory. Rather, we're to operate in humility and obedience to the will of the LORD. We're to lift up His great name, giving Him all the glory (Philippians 2:6-11).

God is working in and through our lives in a way that pleases Him. Therefore, we're to do all things without murmuring, grumbling and disputing. As sons of God, we're to be blameless and harmless, giving no viable reason for rebuke in our manner of living. In the midst of a crooked and perverse generation, we're to shine as lights of illumination, holding forth the Word of life to a dark and dying world (Philippians 2:12-16).

As believers and followers of Christ, we're to **let this mind** *(G5426/G5424)* — reigned in from the ways of the world and curbed by the Spirit of God — be alive and operate in us with spiritual understanding. According to the English definition, to **let** means we're to *grant the use of, allow, permit* and *assign* our mind to come into agreement with the mind of Christ. In this way, we can feel, think and understand as Jesus did when He walked the earth! He received direct instruction and wisdom from the Father. Within our spirits, we can also receive this same Heaven sent knowledge, which flows from the throne of God. In Him, we can know all things:

1 John 2:20 *But ye have an unction from the Holy One, and ye know all things.*

This **unction** *(G5545/G5548/G5530)* from the Holy Spirit of God is a *special endowment,* which *employs* and *consecrates* us for our service to the LORD. It *furnishes what is needed* to accomplish our Kingdom assignments. Unction is also defined as *an unguent or smearing* and implies to *rub with oil*; this suggests being anointed. We are anointed to know all things through the power of the Holy Spirit. Can you stretch your faith to believe that, because the LORD wants to be in such close fellowship with you, He will tell you exactly what you need to know through His Holy Spirit?

The English definition for the word 'unction' is also defined as an act of anointing (especially for a medical treatment or religious rite in the treating of sickness); something soothing or comforting. Unction is also defined as an excessive fervency, in manner and speaking; the shedding of divine or spiritual influence upon a person; an unguent – an ointment, salve, liquid or semi-liquid for application to wounds and sores. This is so awesome! By definition, the 'unction' of the Holy Spirit gives us what we need to be healed physically, mentally, emotionally and spiritually, as it equips us to minister before the LORD and to others.

Part 5 • *Loving God* in All You Do

This unction or anointing comes from the Holy One. In the Old Testament, we learn that the Holy One is the LORD God of Israel who dwelt between the cherubim (2 Kings 19:14-19). He's the LORD of hosts (Isaiah 5:24) and the One worthy of praise (Psalm 71:22). He's our Defense and our King (Psalm 89:18); our Counselor (Isaiah 5:19); the light of Israel — a flame (Isaiah 10:17) who dwells in the midst of Israel (Isaiah 12:6). He's the maker of mankind (Isaiah 17:7); the source of joy and rejoicing (Isaiah 29:19); the One who gives rest, salvation, quietness, confidence and strength (Isaiah 30:15). He's the LORD our Maker, Redeemer, Husband, the God of the whole earth, and He's from everlasting (Isaiah 31:1, 41:14, 47:4, 48:17, 49:7, 54:7; Habakkuk 1:12). In the New Testament, the LORD is the Holy Anointed One — the Savior, Jesus. He's the one who casts out devils (Mark 1:23-26; Luke 4:34); the incorruptible one (Acts 2:27, 13:35) and the Just one (Acts 3:14). The scriptures teach us that the Holy One who gives us the anointed unction to know all things, is both the Father and the Son (1 John 2:20).

Through the Holy Spirit, the power and anointing of the Father and Son are released into our lives. Through His revelation, we can know all things and understand the unseen things to come. We see an example of this with the Prophet Isaiah. Before the birth of Jesus Christ — the Messiah — this prophet was given unction to know of the specific anointing that would be upon Him:

Chapter 15 • Living Life in Christ: What's it Look Like?

<u>Isaiah 61:1-2</u> The Spirit of the Lord GOD is upon me; because the LORD hath anointed me to preach good tidings unto the meek; he hath sent me to bind up the brokenhearted, to proclaim liberty to the captives, and the opening of the prison to them that are bound; ²To proclaim the acceptable year of the LORD, and the day of vengeance of our God; to comfort all that mourn;

Scripture also records how Jesus fulfilled this prophecy:

<u>Luke 4:18-20</u> The Spirit of the Lord is upon me, because he hath anointed me to preach the gospel to the poor; he hath sent me to heal the brokenhearted, to preach deliverance to the captives, and recovering of sight to the blind, to set at liberty them that are bruised, ¹⁹To preach the acceptable year of the Lord. ²⁰And he closed the book, and he gave it again to the minister, and sat down. And the eyes of all them that were in the synagogue were fastened on him. And he began to say unto them, This day is this scripture fulfilled in your ears.

Jesus was and is anointed to preach the Word of God; heal the broken; declare deliverance and liberty to the captives; free those in bondage; work miracles and comfort all that mourn. Everything Jesus did was an extension of the anointing He carried. Therefore, every act of Christ fully demonstrated the Father's heart toward mankind.

Part 5 • *Loving God* in All You Do

Acts 10:38 *How God anointed Jesus of Nazareth with the Holy Ghost and with power: who went about doing good, and healing all that were oppressed of the devil; for God was with him.*

God (the Father) anointed Jesus Christ — the manifestation of God in the flesh — with His Holy Ghost. Thereby, furnishing Him with everything He needed while on the earth. Through the power of the *Holy (G40) Ghost (G4151/G4154)*, Jesus actually carried God's *sacred, pure* and *holy breath, rational soul* and *mental disposition* within His humanity. In every way, God was Christ's life source and Jesus Christ was the perfect demonstration of God's life. Everything He thought, said and did was in perfect agreement with the mind and heart of God.

Jesus — the likeness of God in man — was and is endowed with an *abundance* of *miraculous power, (G1411/G1410)* and the *ability* to perform *miracles*. He was and is the manifest appearance and expression of God's *strength, might* and *force*. He was born, anointed and led by the Spirit of Holy God.

Likewise, every true believer in Christ is born of God (1 John 3:9, 4:7, 5:1, 4, and 18). As redeemed human vessels, we also carry the anointing and power of God's Holy Spirit within us. We have the same Spirit living in us, as was made manifest in Christ!! Do you believe God would endow you with an abundance of miraculous power and the ability to perform miracles?

This is faith without limits, and it causes God's supernatural to become our normal; that which seemed impossible, becomes possible through Him.

Are you ready to trust God for greater things?

Are you ready to move in agreement with the supernatural 'unction' of the Holy One within you?

Are you willing to reach out and minister to those who need to receive from the LORD of glory?

Will you submit to the LORD and allow Him to release His anointing of miracle working power through you?

ABIDE IN HIM

Living by faith and flowing in God's anointing must be learned through experience. The LORD has given us His Holy Spirit to lead, guide and teach us (John 14: 16-17, 26). All we need to do is believe, receive His instructions, follow His lead and abide in Him:

1 John 2:27 But the anointing which ye have received of him abideth in you, and ye need not that any man teach you: but as the same anointing teacheth you of all things, and is truth, and is no lie, and even as it hath taught you, ye shall abide in him.

God has invested His anointing to abide in His people. For the anointing of God to '**abideth (G3306) in you**,' as the scripture says, means it *stays in a given place* through relationship, and creates a *state* of *expectancy*. God chooses to abide in us. Likewise, we choose to abide in Him. It's a mutually intimate relationship of faith, comfort, hope, anticipation and joy. Abide also translates as: to dwell, endure, be present, remain, stand and tarry for thine own.

As we align ourselves with the LORD and allow His Holy Spirit to instruct us in the ways of truth, we receive His wisdom. In this way, He equips us to function in the power of His anointing. Only those who dwell in Christ can receive His Spirit:

<u>*1 John 4:13*</u> *Hereby know we that we dwell in him, and he in us, because he hath given us of his Spirit.*

In John 2:27, we see the anointing *abideth* in us, and in 1 John 4:13, we see that we *dwell* in God. To **dwell** (G3306), has the same meaning as **abideth** *(G3306)* which, as already mentioned, means to *stay* or remain in Christ (and He in us). Again, this speaks of a continually enduring love relationship.

The Spirit of God intimately woos and pursues us, strengthening our covenant bond in Christ. He's our comforter and teacher. He guides us into all truth; brings the words of Jesus to our remembrance; speaks the Father's heart; and shows us things to come (John 14:26, 16:8, 13).

In summary, if we're to live our lives in Christ, we must be God-focused, not self-focused. We must lift up the name of Jesus and not ourselves. We're to exemplify a spirit of humility, meekness and voluntary servitude. With simple, trusting, childlike faith, we submit our will to the will of our Heavenly Father. Our primary goal is not to seek exalted positions in the Kingdom, but to pursue the God of the Kingdom, until His character and nature have fully become our own.

By bringing our thoughts into alignment with the solid truth of God's Word, Christ will establish His mind in us. Remember, Jesus Christ is the Word of God and His Word is eternally settled in Heaven (John 1:14; Psalm 119:89)! His Word is the final authority and the standard by which the Holy Spirit teaches us (John 16:7-15). Therefore, when He speaks, we're to respond with prompt and willing obedience.

If our thoughts aren't in agreement with the Word of God, then we've not put on the mind of Christ. It's that simple! We're not to entertain the wicked thoughts and faulty belief systems of the world. We must reject the philosophies, vain deceits and traditions of men that are in conflict with the holy, righteous ways of God (Colossians 2:6-8). Only when we are fully submitted to the LORD, will our hearts be able to cry out *"Father... not my will, but thine, be done"* (Luke 22:42); this is what living life in Christ looks like.

CHAPTER 16

LOVING GOD THROUGH SERVICE

Throughout this book we've considered what it means to love the LORD our God with our whole heart, soul and mind. This focus includes loving God with every choice we make and everything we do. Accordingly, we're going to look at the concept of loving God through serving Him.

A great man of faith, Dr. Norvel Hayes, taught me a valuable lesson. He said, "If you don't know how to do something, find somebody who does and sit at their feet and learn from them." That was some of the wisest counsel I have ever received; it has served me well over the years. One thing I know is, if we want true wisdom and understanding, we need to abide in the presence of the LORD and learn of Him.

If we're to learn how to serve well, we must look at the greatest servant who ever lived; Jesus was the most excellent of teachers. While ministering to His disciples, He demonstrated the heart of a servant. He did this through the menial task of washing their feet (John 13:1-16). Typically, this job would have been assigned to the house servants. Yet, Jesus, in all His greatness, stooped down as a humble servant and, one by one, began to wash the stinky, crusty feet of His disciples. The LORD of glory lowered Himself to an inferior position, as He ministered to and served the needs of

His disciples. Jesus brought physical cleansing, spiritual refreshing and teachable moments to His disciples, as a demonstration of ministry service:

John 13:14-16 *If I then, your Lord and Master, have washed your feet; ye also ought to wash one another's feet. ¹⁵For I have given you an example, that ye should do as I have done to you. ¹⁶Verily, verily, I say unto you, The servant is not greater than his lord; neither he that is sent greater than he that sent him.*

Jesus was **Master** *(G1320)* and **Lord** *(G2962)*, not only over His disciples, but over all creation. Yet, He took time to teach them how to become great leaders. He was their *Master, instructor and controller* — the one who regulated, directed and restrained them with *supreme authority*. Jesus had and has all knowledge and wisdom; by Him all things consist (Colossians 1:15-20). There is no one like Him or above Him. He is God, all by Himself! Who better to learn from?

Jesus' **example** *(G5262/G5263)* demonstrated the value and power of having a heart of servitude in ministry. Practically, His example was *an exhibit for imitation*. He illustrated through His actions the 'how to' of ministry service to His disciples, thereby, providing a pattern or method of instruction. Jesus' example was also a *warning*; He reminded His disciples that they were not greater than whomever they served. In the context of John 13:1-16, Jesus also admonished His disciples with gentle reproofs, godly counsel and spiritual leadership, all of which are important preparations for ministry. Jesus washed the feet of His twelve disciples and exhorted them to serve one another with the same humility He demonstrated. I wonder if any of His disciples stepped forward that night to wash the feet of their Master, LORD and King. Jesus taught a Kingdom principle and spiritual key to promotion in:

<u>Matthew 20:26-28</u> ...but whosoever will be great among you, let him be your minister; ²⁷And whosoever will be chief among you, let him be your servant; ²⁸Even as the Son of man came not to be ministered unto, but to minister, and to give his life a ransom for many.

The title of *minister (G1249)* is not defined as some pompous, dignified position of self-importance or lordship over others. Rather, it speaks first of service, as to *run* errands; to serve as an *attendant* or *waiter* of tables, or to perform some other menial duties. To *minister,* specifically means to serve as a Christian *teacher, pastor, deacon* or *deaconess.* Those who desire a position of chief importance in the Kingdom must first learn to be a *servant (G1401/G1210)* — one *in subjection or in a position of* subservience. Every good minister and/or servant is submissive to someone greater than themselves. Therefore, if you want to be an effective minister or influential leader, you must first learn how to serve others. Remember, Jesus said, "*...in as much as ye have done it unto one of the least of these my brethren, ye have done it unto me.'*" (Matthew 25:40) We're to minister to and serve others, in the same way we would minister to and serve the LORD!

When was the last time you participated in a foot washing service?

Are you willing to humble yourself and wash the feet of Jesus, by washing the feet of your brothers and sisters in Christ?

DOING GOOD TO OTHERS

Remember, when Jesus — our LORD and Master — was here on Earth, He was anointed with and completely submitted to the Holy Spirit. He went about doing good and healing all that were oppressed of the devil (Acts 10:38). He exhibited the power of an effective life. Likewise, God has empowered us to effectively overcome evil and do that which is good (Romans 12:21; Psalm 34:14). We're also commanded to do good to them that hate us, as well as to all men, and especially to those of the household of faith (Matthew 5:44; Galatians 6:10). If we want to see miraculous healings and people delivered and set free from the enemy; if we want to be a world changer and positively impact humanity, we must also learn to flow in the anointing of God's Spirit.

Jesus was anointed and consecrated to fulfill His earthly ministry. By the Spirit of God, He was fully furnished with all that was needed to reach the hearts of men. The mighty *power (G1410)* and force of God was encased in His morality. This powerful anointing made it *possible* for Jesus to perform miracles and good works (Acts 10:38).

In the course of study, I learned something interesting; in the Greek language 'doing good' works for others is equated to the work of a philanthropist. Such givers are wealthy and they have more than enough to meet their own needs. They're looking for opportunities to invest money, property, help and assistance into the lives of others. They're, especially, interested in the welfare and advancement of those in need.

As Jesus **went about** *(G1330/G1223)* **doing good**, *(G2109)* He was functioning as a philanthropist! He became the healing cure, wholeness and health to all who would trust and believe in Him. He was on a heavenly mission to bring restoration, redemption, deliverance, healing, help and salvation to a fallen world. Everywhere He *traversed* (or traveled), He was a benefactor of blessing, benevolence and *philanthropy* for the good of mankind. As the power of God was released in Word and deed, all who were **oppressed** *(G2616)* under the dominion of the devil were set free. The Holy Ghost empowered Jesus to do what He was called to do, and every need was abundantly met.

Part 5 • *Loving God* in All You Do

Those in Christ are also called to be philanthropists for the Kingdom of God. Can you wrap your mind around that? Would you be willing to be used of God in this way? Can you believe it for yourself? If you can see it, you can have it! If you can believe it, you can do it! Jesus was able to do 'good,' because He was obedient to the will of the Father; the power of God was operating through Him. Likewise, the LORD has invested His power into all those who are obedient to the will of the Father. Through His Spirit, He equips and furnishes everything that's needed to do good works.

What has He placed on the inside of you?

What are you doing with that investment?

Is your spirit in agreement with the mind of Christ?

Are you willing to allow Him to use you mightily, to set the captives free?

SUPPORTING AND ASSISTING OTHERS

Those who take on the mind of Christ will center their thoughts on the principles of the Kingdom of God, share them with others, and bring delight to the heart of God. Consequently, there will be a vertical and horizontal extension of love, reaching up to the Father and also reaching out to those who are struggling. Benevolence toward others is evidence that the Holy Spirit is working in and through our lives. We see an example of this concerning the Apostle Paul in:

Chapter 16 • Loving God through Service

***Acts 20:33-35** I have coveted no man's silver, or gold, or apparel. ³⁴Yea, ye yourselves know, that these hands have ministered unto my necessities, and to them that were with me. ³⁵I have showed you all things, how that so labouring ye ought to support the weak, and to remember the words of the Lord Jesus, how he said, It is more blessed to give than to receive.*

In this text, we see that Paul not only worked to take care of his own ministry needs, but he's also provided for those who ministered with him. It's always been my belief that the work of the ministry should be supported by those who receive from the ministry (1 Corinthians 9:9-14). Yet, most of the time, this has not been the case. I have, personally, invested large amounts of money to be able to go to other nations and preach the gospel of the kingdom. Most places where I've ministered would be considered third world or developing nations. Many times, those who received of the ministry either could not or would not give to support the work. Even so, the LORD always provided. Sometimes the funds would come in after I completed my mission assignment. But, many times, the LORD has required me to make financial sacrifices into the Kingdom of God to take care of the expenses of ministry. Either way, the work gets done and the bills get paid. It's all about loving the LORD enough to serve Him in the capacity to which we've been called, regardless of the cost.

Part 5 • *Loving God* in All You Do

Remember, obedience brings the blessing. If we look to man to meet our needs, we will be disappointed; but if we look to the LORD, He is always faithful!

If you think the work of ministry is full of glitz, glamour and personal glory, you'd better think again. Ministry is some of the most challenging, demanding work on the planet. Most people have no idea about the countless hours of personal study in the Word of God, the continual spiritual warfare waged through prayer, the personal struggles and the required willingness to die to self, as well as the great financial sacrifices that are required from those in ministry leadership. Yet, ministers willingly do it, so others can get their spiritual breakthrough. Ministry is never about the minister; it's about God using willing human vessels to release His love, mercy, truth and salvation to every soul who will receive it.

While ministry requires much personal sacrifice, at the same time, it can still be very rewarding and fulfilling. Personally, I have endured times of loneliness, weariness or frustration in ministry. At times, I've honestly wondered whether what I've done with my life has had a positive impact on others. During such moments, I've even questioned whether it was worth the sacrifice. When this has happened, the LORD has graciously and quickly sent somebody to me whose life He has changed through my ministry. By the power and anointing of God, a soul was touched and set free. The glorious rewards of that moment are eternal. To know and see how God has chosen me to set others free through the truth of His Word is inspiring, and it's an awesome privilege!

As a minister, such special moments in my life become spiritual catalysts. Certainly, these instances encourage me to continue pressing forward, against all odds, into the fullness of my God ordained destiny. Even so, my motivation to minister doesn't depend on these affirming testimonies. Mercifully, the primary focus of ministry is never about us. But, it's all about the greatness of our God and His Word!

In relation to Acts 20:35, let's look at the concept of *laboring (G2872/G2873)* to *support (G482)* the *weak (G770/G772)*. This is actually an act of sacrificial love. It means *to take hold of (in turn)*, as we work together to help support and comfort those who are *feeble*, diseased, impotent and without strength. By definition, it implies that we should be willing to work hard, even fatigue ourselves, as we assist others. At the same time, no one person should have to bear the burden alone to support those in need. It's to be a joint effort — ministering to and through the Body of Christ — as we bear one another's burdens.

Jesus said, *"It is more (G3122) blessed (G3107) to give (G1325) than to receive."* According to definition, the greater blessing lies in the fact that the LORD will cause the unselfish giver to experience the *greatest*

Part 5 • *Loving God* in All You Do

degree of joy — being *supremely* blessed, *fortunate, well off* and happy — because they're granted the power to bestow or bring forth blessings into the lives of others. This is how giving, as the Holy Spirit leads, affects both the giver and the receiver in unique ways.

Through the abundance of His blessings, God sanctions us to be an extension of His love — touching, changing and benefiting lives. It's amazing how our bountiful LORD empowers us to bless others! Furthermore, such Spirit led giving always has the anointing, purpose, destiny and the blessing of God attached to it!

Regardless of where you are in your Christian walk, you must realize that whether you're in the pulpit or the pew, every believer is called to ministry. Consequently, we must learn how to do it effectively. If this is to be accomplished in a way that pleases our Heavenly Father, we must do so through full, obedient surrender to His Holy Spirit in every area of our lives.

Who has the LORD called you to bless?

What measure of sacrifice are you willing to endure, in order to be a blessing?

CONSIDERATION OF OTHERS
As we serve the LORD and love others, it's important to understand that everybody is not at the same place in their walk with the LORD. There are new born baby believers, young believers, maturing believers,

carnal believers, weak believers, struggling believers and strong believers. There are believers who are stupendously free in the LORD, having victoriously overcome the enemy in many areas of their lives. Then, there are others who still need to let go of past failures, hurts, abuses, lies of the enemy, wrong thoughts, wrong actions and wrong doctrines. Regardless of where we are in our spiritual lives, we should all be growing in our relationship with the LORD; in this growth process, we need to extend patience and grace to one another.

We should never use our liberty in Christ to cause hurt or harm to others. Of course, this way of living is addressed in Scripture. Let's take a look at some areas that could cause needless contentions among our brothers and sisters in Christ.

FOOD PREFERENCES
When the New Testament Church was learning to operate under the grace of God, instead of under the law of the Old Testament, there were issues that needed to be dealt with during the transition (1 Corinthians 8). One issue concerned the eating of (what would be considered by Jewish law to be) unclean foods. This pertained mainly to non-kosher meats and food offered to idols. In Romans 14, the focus was on clean versus unclean meats. Basically, unclean meats were those which came from scavenger animals, which (by nature and design) ate dead and

Part 5 • *Loving God* in All You Do

decaying carcasses or other unhealthy things. This could include what I call land and water vacuums, such as shellfish (which clean the pollution from the waterways), catfish, carp, pigs, vultures, opossums, rats etc. You can read Romans 14 on your own, but let's go to the crux of the matter:

<u>Romans 14:15</u> But if thy brother be grieved with thy meat, now walkest thou not charitably. Destroy not him with thy meat, for whom Christ died.

Under the Old Testament law, there were many dietary rules outlining what the Hebrew people could and could not eat. However, as the Church was growing and going into all the world to preach the gospel, the believers would find themselves amongst those who did not know or honor the dietary laws of the Old Testament. Therefore, as they went into a new city or home, the LORD Jesus told His disciples to eat what was set before them (Luke 10:8). This gave the disciples liberty to just go with the flow and focus on the work of the Kingdom. They no longer had to consider what meat they were going to eat with their potatoes. Even so, the disciples were not to use this liberty to **grieve (G3076)** or cause *distress*, sadness, heaviness or sorrow to their brethren who chose not to eat that which was previously forbidden (Luke 10:1-8). Though a preference may be biblically acceptable in our minds, it does not give us the liberty to impose or force it upon others.

CHAPTER 16 • LOVING GOD THROUGH SERVICE

Here's a real life example of this teaching in action: In the nation of Trinidad, many consider opossum a delicacy. As a missionary, I have been offered this 'delicacy' a few times. Each time I've tried to eat it, there's been a strong communication between my nose, brain, tongue and stomach. My discerning nose has always been the first to let me know this exquisite dish is not for me. It kind of goes like this: My nose says, 'Oh! What is that stinking smell?! My brain is saying to my tongue, 'Oh, you're about to eat a RAT! You're not going to like the taste of this stuff!' My stomach is saying to my tongue, 'If you DARE to send that stuff down to me, I'm going to wretch and send it right back where it came from!!' Though I've genuinely tried a few times, I simply cannot manage to get opossum from my tongue to my stomach.

Hello?! I don't care how much of a delicacy it's considered to be; opossum is still a rat!! In my mind, opossum has unclean written all over it, and I cannot eat it. They are scavengers, and they eat dead stuff! I cannot stomach the thought of eating a creature that has such poor taste in its dietary choices. However, I have no problem, generously, sharing my portion of this 'delicacy' with somebody else. After all, it is better to give than receive, right? By the way, I feel the same way about crab, shellfish and most pork products. So, if I ever come to your nation, please show mercy to me and don't make me eat that stuff. Just give me some cooked plant life and fresh fruits to eat; I'll be very happy and content!!

Part 5 • *Loving God* in All You Do

So, when it comes to food preferences, we're to allow people the freedom to enjoy whatever the Holy Spirit gives them liberty to eat. We're not to criticize or judge them in the matter. However, I do want to say one more thing about eating habits. Our bodies are the temple of the Holy Spirit. This is the only body we will have, this side of glory. We have a responsibility before the LORD to take care of the fleshly tabernacle He has entrusted to us. Liberty in Christ does not give us the right to, abusively, put garbage into our bodies and ruin our health. Foolishly, too many people destroy their bodies and leave this earth before their time, because they allow the lust of their flesh to control their appetites. Please love God enough to make wise food choices, and take care of the gift of life and health He has given you.

ALL TO THE GLORY OF GOD

Our next scripture takes things a little further than just eating. It also addresses other areas of our personal preferences and activities. Ultimately, the Word emphasizes that we keep a godly focus:

<u>1 Corinthians 10:31-33</u> Whether therefore ye eat, or drink, or whatsoever ye do, do all to the glory of God. ³²Give none offence, neither to the Jews, nor to the Gentiles, nor to the church of God: ³³Even as I please all men in all things, not seeking mine own profit, but the profit of many, that they may be saved.

As believers in Christ, we've been given great freedom and liberty. Out of respect, we're not to use that liberty to sin or harm others. Rather, with the goal of glorifying God, we're to seek to **please** those we meet.

To **please** *(G700/G142)* others is to minister to them in a profitable way, so they can fully benefit from what we're saying or doing. We're to hold their attention and simultaneously *keep* them *in suspense* — wondering with anticipation of what's coming next. We should *seek* to *lift* their countenance and stir the excitement that Christ has fully atoned for our sins and completely washed them away. This type of ministry generates great joy and a fruitful harvest of souls for the Kingdom of God. Our ministry goal is to come to a place of spiritual unity with others, to help them advance in the things of God (Romans 15:1-2; 1 Corinthians 10:23-24). We aim to do this in an *agreeable*, yet biblically sound manner. We must be careful not to compromise what we know to be right, just to please people.

In 1 Corinthians 10:32, we're also exhorted to **give none offense** *(G677)* to the Jews, the Gentiles or to the church of God. While recognizing our responsibility, we should also understand that there will always be those who choose to be offended no matter what we say or how we say it. Through their self-focused bitterness of heart, deceptions, grudges they've held against others and their rebellion against God, they'll find any irrational reason in their own minds to take up offence with the ministry and the ministers of God. But here's the deal: If they want to be offended because we lift up the standard of God's Word, declare His will and refuse to compromise what's right, then so be it! The exhortation to "give none offense" indicates that a person's rejection of the truth of the gospel should never result from any immoral, ungodly, proud or arrogant display of words and/or actions on our part.

So, as with to 'please all men in all things,' to 'give none offense' does not mean we're to compromise with sin, immorality or rebellion against God, simply to keep people from getting upset with us. We should never be fearful or timid about speaking the truths of God. Rather, we must recognize that the LORD will give us wisdom and direction on how to minister in a faultless manner. He will never lead us into agreement with any form of sin. Ultimately, we must teach and exemplify the standard of God's Word, as the final authority and code of ethics for our lives. In this we cannot compromise.

People must realize that the grace of God and the forgiveness of sins are gifts from the LORD. They are freely available to all who put their faith and trust in Jesus Christ as their LORD and Savior. While we can't make people repent or give their hearts and lives to Christ, we must give them an opportunity to either choose life in Christ or their own destructive ways. The choice is theirs to make; they are free to determine their own eternal destiny. Each person must decide if they want what the LORD has to offer.

As followers of Christ, we have a responsibility to represent Him well. We represent or re-present Christ well, when we minister in love. To speak truth as the Holy Spirit leads, is to minister in the love of God. One way we can minister in love is to value people. At times a person's value may be difficult to see. In the eyes of the LORD, a person's worth is not marked by their actions, level of wealth or poverty, life circumstance, abilities or inabilities, potential or even how they view themselves. Their worth only depends on how the LORD sees them. Regardless of their sin, lifestyle, attitudes or whatever else may be unsavory about them, our declarations of truth should never aim to diminish the intrinsic worth or value that the LORD has determined for human life.

From the Lord's perspective, He sees every person through eyes of love. He deems them to be so worthy and valuable that He was willing to lay His life down on their behalf. He died in their place, so they could have eternal life and relationship with Him. We should love and value others, by seeing the worth in them that Christ died to redeem.

Jesus paid the same price for the very worst of sinners, as He did for those who seem to have lived morally clean lives. He is the only one who can deliver a soul from hell and give eternal life! The fact is, due to the sin nature that every person is born with, we were all guilty before God and on our way to hell.

As true believers (regardless of what we think we know or perceive about a person), we're to preach the uncompromised truth of His Word and eternal life, with love and compassion, so that anyone and everyone has an opportunity to freely hear and receive. If we do this, we'll not seek to (mentally, emotionally, physically or spiritually) wound them, nor will our delivery of the gospel be harsh or cause a stumbling block to those who hear our words (Romans 14:13). We're not to strike out against or beat people down in any way. Remember, our method of delivery can make the difference between someone accepting or rejecting the message of salvation. We should never do things in a way that would cause people to rightly blame, discredit, find fault with or view the ministry as disgraceful (2 Corinthians 6:3).

In all we do, we're to do it to the glory of God (1 Corinthians 10:31). The concept of **all** *(G3956)* we do denotes the entirety of our *whole* life. It refers to what we do, how we do it, why we do it, when we do it, where we do it and with whom we do it. All these factors matter, because they determine if what we're doing will, indeed, bring glory and honor to the LORD. The **glory** *(G1391/G1380)* of the LORD refers to His *reputation*, presence, dignity, honor, goodness and the fact that He is worthy of our praise and worship.

For these reasons, the LORD is worthy of our loving allegiance and adoration: He is righteous, merciful, holy and just; He is the personification of excellence and virtue, kindness and generosity; He is perfect in all His ways and in all He does. He is the LORD God Almighty! In all that we do, our lives should reflect what and who we believe our God to be. If we don't believe it, we won't live it. If we don't live it, we don't believe it! Actions and beliefs cannot be separated, because we'll always act based on whatever is truly resident in our hearts. Accordingly, as true believers we're to respect and highly esteem His position, as well as reverence Him and conduct ourselves in such a way that His presence and character rests upon us.

When we care about the things the LORD cares about, we'll also live in ways that bring Him glory. For instance, His greatest desire is for mankind to be reconciled to Him. When Jesus came to earth, He came preaching repentance, the Kingdom of Heaven and the way of salvation (Matthew 4:17). After He rose from the dead, Jesus commissioned all His followers to go into every nation, to preach the gospel of the Kingdom of God and make disciples of all men (Matthew 28:18-20). So, one of the greatest ways we can give glory to God is to obey His Word by preaching it to others.

The believers of today are the spiritual descendants of those who have heard and believed the Gospel in generations gone by. We're the spiritual fruit of those

Part 5 • *Loving God* in All You Do

who have believed before us. The spiritual mantle of past generations has been transferred to us, so that we may reach the world for Christ. Therefore, we have a responsibility to boldly stand up and be an uncompromising voice for Christ, so He can expand the Kingdom of God throughout the earth and change eternity for multitudes.

As followers of Christ, we cannot keep our faith to ourselves, because if we love the LORD, we'll also love those for whom He has died. As a demonstration of that love, we'll seek to bring the lost into salvation and liberty in Christ. We must reach out and share the love of God with others.

HEARTILY, IN THE NAME OF THE LORD
In all that we do, we're also to do it genuinely and enthusiastically, in the name of the LORD:

<u>Colossians 3:17,23</u> *And whatsoever ye do in word or deed, do all in the name of the Lord Jesus, giving thanks to God and the Father by him...* ²³*And whatsoever ye do, do it heartily, as to the Lord, and not unto men.*

To **do** *(G4160)* something means that we've agreed to **make** it happen, and we've chosen to become personally responsible for our actions. Before we speak a word, we've made a conscious decision of commitment to bring it forth. Every **word** *(G3056)* we let come out of our mouths has been motivated by our *thoughts* and is an exhibit of our *reasoning* and the contents of our hearts. Every *deed* (G2041) represents whatever we consider to be worthy of our *work, toil* and labor. Our words and deeds are to be spoken and carried out in the *name* (G3686) of the LORD Jesus. This means that everything we think, say and do demonstrates the *authority* and *character* of God operating in our lives. Before we release our words or carry out our actions, we're to be sure that they're in alignment with the LORD'S desires. Once we discern that the motivation behind our words and deeds originates with Him, we're at liberty to do whatever we do heartily.

To serve the LORD *heartily* (G1537/G5590) is to minister before Him with vigorous exuberance, *originating from* a fervent *spirit*. No matter what the task, we're to do it thoroughly, sincerely, honestly and whole-heartedly. Half-heartedness is unacceptable in the Kingdom of God. We are to test and judge ourselves by the light of God's Word. In all that we do, we're to be genuine — distinguishing right from wrong and choosing good over evil. Our primary goal is not to please men, but rather, we seek to please and honor the LORD. Those who serve Him heartily will serve Him with excellence.

People of excellent spirit and character in the LORD, do not function with a status quo mentality. They have a different mindset and they see a greater vision of what the LORD is doing. Therefore, they learn to function in two different realms — the natural (earthly) realm and the spiritual (heavenly) realm. They know the richness of God's awesome presence and sweet companionship; therefore, they have been ruined toward the ordinary. They are passionate lovers of God, and they refuse to settle for less. They choose the will of God first and foremost, and they have found their place of citizenship in God's Kingdom. Therefore, they deem the option of living the status quo lifestyle to be worthless, inappropriate and unsatisfying. These are the people of God, the passionate burning ones, who have something of worth to offer the world — real life in Christ!

When ministering to the world, it's imperative that we do it heartily. Why? Well, the people of the world are looking for help, healing, peace, restoration and wholeness. And they're looking for these solutions in a world gone crazy. Most people, if they've searched their hearts, already know they've sinned before a holy God and are in hell bound trouble. They may not know it, but what they're really searching for is to be truly satisfied in their spirits and souls. Perhaps unaware, they sense a need to know their origin and how to make things right; they're looking for their Creator and Savior. They're not looking to be judged or condemned. And they're, certainly, not looking for a dead, lifeless, ritualistic religion that offers no hope, joy or peace. People are seeking true passion and life!

Those seeking the truth need: salvation through faith in Jesus Christ, sound biblical teaching, and deliverance from the lies of satan. When they find the LORD and employ His benefits, they'll find everything they're searching for and more. Knowing Jesus is the only way they will know true satisfaction, contentment and freedom.

The people of the world need to see Jesus and the Spirit of God alive and well on earth, manifesting and reaching out to them, through His followers. As the disciples of Christ, we're to reach out to the lost, and present them with the truth we carry within us. Our faith in Christ and our corresponding actions are to exude the love of God and His goodness, mercy and faithfulness. Our lives should demonstrate the Word of God, including works far greater than even He performed (John 14:12). We're to be shining examples of the power of God to save, heal and deliver. When we lift up Christ and sincerely love and reach out to people, they will be drawn into the eternal Kingdom of God — not the worthless formalities of dead religion.

CHAPTER 17

LOVE GOD THROUGH SELF DENIAL

As believers, there are times when we're required to demonstrate our sacrificial love for the LORD. We do this by laying down our own desires, in order to fulfill His. When the LORD requires a sacrifice, He's looking to see if we will trust Him and submit in loving obedience. As we yield to the LORD and give Him what He desires, our sacrifice becomes an offering of worship, with a sweet smelling savor. On the other hand, if we withhold from the LORD, this demonstrates that our heart is not perfect toward Him, and we've not fully relinquished the lordship of our lives to Him. Whenever the LORD requires a sacrifice, there is always a divine purpose and hidden blessing attached to it.

We may not understand why the LORD would require certain sacrifices from us. We may feel the cost is too high. We may not be willing to give what is being required, but that is when we must take the challenge to trust in the goodness and sovereignty of the LORD. If He is truly LORD of our lives, then whatever He wants is considered our blessing to give. May there be some comfort in knowing that the LORD doesn't ask us for anything without, eventually, replacing it with something better and more abundant.

Part 5 • *Loving God* in All You Do

The Christian life is a walk of faith; it sees beyond what we can observe in the natural. If we, through faith, can grasp the intentions of God's heart and perceive how much He loves us, as well as how powerfully He wants to use us; if we can look beyond our current struggles or discomforts and see the bigger picture of what He's doing; if we can get beyond our focus on self and offer ourselves to Him as willing vessels; if we can overcome the carnal mind and learn to function in the mind of Christ, then He will empower us to fulfill the purposes for which we were created. Submission, obedience and trust are loving responses which are birthed from a pure and faithful heart. A faithful heart says, "Our God is worthy of whatever He requires of us."

NOT MY WILL . . .
Before Jesus was arrested and crucified, He prayed in the Garden of Gethsemane. He knew He was about to be taken prisoner, falsely accused, beaten, mocked and crucified. He understood the suffering He was about to endure. Yet, He saw beyond His struggles and demonstrated His submission, obedience, trust and love toward the Father (toward Himself) when He cried out in:

<u>Luke 22:42</u> ... Father, if thou be willing, remove this cup from me: nevertheless not my will, but thine, be done.

Although we've considered this scripture previously, let's revisit it from a slightly different angle. When Jesus asked the Father to *remove this cup (G4221)*, He was petitioning for another way to redeem man, other than *drinking in the wrath and judgment of God into the vessel* of His human body. We must understand this: Jesus was God in the flesh and He was getting ready to drink His own cup of wrath! His righteous judgment would be poured out upon His own body to redeem all mankind. Every drop of His powerful, holy, righteous blood would become the necessary purchase price to cleanse away all sin. His gift of salvation — complete with healing, deliverance and restoration to God — would deliver the human race from eternal death. Yet, in a moment of human weakness, He was asking the Father to release Him from the required method of redemption — the torture of crucifixion and the separation of death. The words of Jesus in Luke 22:42 demonstrate the vulnerability of His humanity and the vexation of His soul, as He sought to fulfill the Father's mandate of redemption.

You see, it wasn't just the physical suffering that Jesus would have to endure. He knew that, when His wrath and judgment were poured out upon sin (which Jesus was going to carry to the cross), there was going to be a disconnection from Himself as the Father. Jesus knew this separation was part of the requirement of redemption, but that knowledge didn't cause Him to disregard reality. His crucifixion would be physically, mentally, emotionally and spiritually excruciating. He would experience all the villainy of sin and bear the torturous pain of death, without hearing the voice of the Father or even sensing His presence. He would suffer the full judgment of death, hell and the grave, and He would do it alone.

The work of Jesus Christ was so important. If He didn't allow Himself to be separated from the presence of the Father — literally, separated from Himself — then mankind would be eternally lost and forever separated from their Creator. If Jesus didn't die in our place for the penalty of sin, then mankind would spend an eternity tormented in a living death. If Jesus didn't go into the heart of the earth, take back the keys of hell and death and set the captives free, then there would be no rescue from the eternal fires of hell. It was for the joy that was set before Him, that Jesus was able to endure the cross with all the shame, disgrace and disfigurement that went with it. Let's look at:

<u>Hebrews 12:1-3</u> *Wherefore seeing we also are compassed about with so great a cloud of witnesses, let us lay aside every weight, and the sin which doth so easily beset us, and let us run with patience the race that is set before us, ²Looking unto Jesus the author and finisher of our faith; who for the joy that was set before him endured the cross, despising the shame, and is set down at the right hand of the throne of God. ³For* *consider him that endured such contradiction of sinners against himself, lest ye be wearied and faint in your minds.*

Jesus could see all those who, down through the ages of time, would come to trust in Him and be reconciled to God through His sacrifice. He knew that His blood — and His blood alone — was the only ransom for the sins of mankind (Matthew 20:28). The atoning power of His blood would free every man, woman, boy and girl from the penalty of sin. It was this perspective and promise of redemption that gave Jesus the strength He needed to fulfill His earthly assignment.

Jesus chose to drink of the cup of death, so that we could live. Seeing the end result of His sacrifice (i.e. the fruit of His suffering) made all the difference. Hence, He was filled with the exceedingly great *joy (G5479)* — *that is, cheerfulness* and *calm delight* — which was set before Him as He faced the temporal torment, yet eternal reward of this redemptive death process. For this reason, in His hour of temptation, He was able to say, **"Not my will, but thine, be done."** Jesus chose to see things from the Father's perspective.

Jesus had to die to His own human will, to be able to fulfill the heavenly will of the Father. When Jesus declared, **"Not my will, but thine, be done,"** in His mind, He was already dead, buried and resurrected, and mankind was redeemed. It was just a matter of completing the work. This was the joy that was set before Him! Every blood bought, redeemed, born-again, Holy Spirit filled believer is part of the eternal Harvest of God. Through what Christ did, we are risen up from spiritual death, and we are seated in heavenly places in Him (Ephesians 2:4-9).

SUBMISSION EXEMPLIFIED

Without a doubt, Jesus pursued the will of the Father during a time of extreme difficulty and victoriously overcame all desires of the flesh. All true victories, whether large or small, require submission to the will of the Heavenly Father. There are times in life when we may be tempted to give up and quit. But, if we're to faithfully run the race that is set before us, we must learn to see the bigger picture. When we're tested, we must overcome our flesh and, like Jesus, learn to see beyond our current circumstance to the joy that is also set before us.

The faithful promises of God will encourage, inspire and embolden us to persevere toward the blessings that the LORD has ordained for us. In this way, we'll be able to endure and overcome the temporary struggles, disappointments, pains and sorrows of life. We cannot afford to allow weariness, tiredness or faintheartedness to rob us of our appointed destiny and blessing. In fact, we must realize that our trials and tribulations will not only strengthen and challenge our own faith; they will also fortify the faith of others who receive from our ministry. After all, we can't talk the talk, if we haven't walked the walk! Willing obedience empowers us to obtain the prize that is attached to our overcoming victory in Christ.

It's encouraging to know that, there are many believers who have already walked this Christian walk. We are not alone and have been provided with important illustrations for living life in Christ. In Hebrews 12:1, the great cloud of **witnesses** *(G3144)* is analogized in the Greek with a vast number of *martyrs* who give testimony to the justice of God through Christ. A martyr is one who suffers and is willing to lay down their life, if need be through death, for what they believe to be right. There are many faithful believers who have lived victoriously and gone before us. They encourage us to persevere and run the race that is set before us. Even so, they are not our primary example.

Jesus is our primary example of how we're to live a faith-filled, overcoming life. He is the **author** *(G747)*, captain, prince and *chief leader* of our faith. What He started in us, He will complete; because He is also the **finisher** *(G5047/G5046)* of our faith. He brings our faith to a *state of mental and moral completeness*. Our *character* will *labor* toward maturity as our faith grows to perfection in Him. Through Christ and the work of His Holy Spirit in our lives, we're conformed to His image and likeness. He is the Creator of our faith and, until we stand before Him, He will continue

Part 5 • *Loving God* in All You Do

to strengthen us in it. When we see Him face-to-face, the full reality of our faith will be authenticated. Then, we will see how He used everything we encountered, to bring us to greater faith in Him. Indeed, Jesus is the beginning, the end and the purpose of our faith.

While bearing His cross, Jesus patiently and painfully endured the beatings, suffering, shame and disgrace of the crucifixion, as well as the cruelty of men. In fact, during His years of ministry on earth (and yet still today), our LORD and Savior, endured **contradictions (G485/ G483/G474/G473/G3004)**, contrary attitudes, *disputes,* and *disobedient* actions from those who have *refused* to accept Him as their Messiah. The mission of Jesus was profound. He poured out His life for those who would love Him, as well as those who would hate Him. He offered the gift of salvation freely to all who would receive it, along with those who would reject it (1 Peter 3:18). He freely gave His life and every last drop of His blood, so that we could be free. Very few people would have (or could have) endured what Jesus did.

Moreover, no one could have accomplished what Jesus — the Christ — did. He conquered death, hell and the grave (Revelation 1:18)! Such overcoming faith doesn't just happen. First, regardless of difficult circumstances, a believer must make intentional decisions to be a victorious overcomer. Jesus **endured** *(G5278)* the cross and died in our place, because He made an intentional decision to do so. By humbly submitting

Himself *to stay under* the authority of the Heavenly Father, as He remained obedient, He also chose to *persevere*. With great *fortitude*, He was determined to accomplish the will and purposes of God. No man took His life from Him; He chose to lay it down as an act of loving obedience (John 10:18). With purposeful resolve, Jesus' life, death and resurrection changed the eternal course of history for all humanity.

Likewise, as individual believers, we must choose to love the LORD with all our heart, soul, mind and strength. No matter the cost or what's required, we must choose to submit in obedience to the LORD. Jesus had His race to run, and we have ours. Let's determine to have an obedient heart of love that always says, "Yes!" to the Father in Heaven.

Can you recall a time in your life when you had to say to the Father, "Not my will, but thine, be done."

What was the end result of your obedience?

SEE, HEAR, SPEAK & DO

In John 5:1-18, we find the story of an impotent man, waiting to be healed at the pool of Bethesda, on the Sabbath day. He had been crippled for 38 years. Apparently, it was believed that an angel would come to the pool at an appointed time and stir up the waters. Then, the first person to get into the pool, after the angel stirred up the waters, would be healed.

Part 5 • *Loving God* in All You Do

When Jesus saw the impotent man, He asked him if he wanted to be made healthy and whole.

Although the man desired to be healed, his initial response to Jesus was to reiterate what had happened in the past. He said that when he tried to step into the pool after the angel troubled the waters, someone else would always get in before him. Consequently, he believed that someone else's actions, as well as his own helplessness, hindered him from receiving his healing. It would seem that the man could only see where his life had been, but he lacked the understanding to change his situation. It was as if, because of his failed efforts and the interference of others, the man had resigned himself to the captivity of his disability and limitations. This broken specimen of humanity did not yet realize the power of God that was about to be released into his mortal body.

Even so, the persistence of this man to remain at the pool for so many years was an indicator that he had a measure of hope. He desired a supernatural miracle, but when he tried to obtain his healing according to his own understanding and strength (based on his own ability), he was unsuccessful. Unfortunately, this man's hope was misplaced. He trusted in what he could see — the appearance of the angel. He trusted in what he wanted to do — get into the pool after the waters were stirred. When his strength failed him, he couldn't see past his circumstances and, therefore, considered his miracle unattainable. Yet, Jesus in His compassion saw past all that. He met the man where he was — at the level of faith where he could believe. So, Jesus said, *"Rise, take up thy bed and walk."*

When Jesus said *rise (G1453)*, He was literally making a public proclamation. He was telling the man (and all those around him) to *waken*, to *rouse from sitting; move out of sleep, disease* and *death*; and to *collect his/their faculties*. Jesus was, figuratively and publicly, provoking the man (and anybody who would believe) to come out of his/their *inactivity, obscurity* and the *ruins* of his/their past life/lives. I believe that if faith had been prevalent, when Jesus said *"Rise..."* then every infirmed person could have received miraculous healing.

When Jesus told the impotent man to *take (G142)* up his bed and *walk (G4043/G4012/G3961/G3817)*, He was commanding the man *to tread all around as proof of* his *ability*. But He was also, figuratively, commanding the man to *lift up* and remove the anchor that had held him in that stationary position of inability for 38 years. This hindering anchor was a mental (as well as a physical) weight of disability. The man had to *deport* himself from the former mental and physical position of poverty and sickness, in order to start living in the complete ability and power of Christ, now operating in his body.

The crippled man became a living witness of God's power and ability. He became a walking testimony of faith,

Part 5 • *Loving God* in All You Do

able to completely *trample* the power of sickness and disease. He was no longer captive to what had held him in a lifetime of bondage. By obeying the Word of the LORD, his faith and correlating actions delivered a *single stinging blow* — a knockout punch — to that infirmity. Obedience, plus faith, equaled the miraculous!

Expect and Respond to Persecution
When Jesus healed the impotent man, the religious hackles of the Jews began to rise up. They became angry because it was against the Law of Moses to do work or carry burdens on the Sabbath day. Never mind the fact that Jesus had just preformed a life changing miracle! Never mind the fact that a man had been healed and set free from his lifelong bondage! The religious Jews were only concerned about guarding their traditions, rules and rituals. They were spiritually blind and couldn't see the compassionate heart of God, who stood before them, encased in the flesh of their rejected Messiah.

In response, Jesus told the religious leaders that He was doing the work of His Father. By saying this, He was equating Himself with God, and this enraged the Jews. They felt that He had committed blasphemy; they were angered to the point of wanting to kill Him. In their eyes, Jesus wasn't anointed by the Spirit of God to do miraculous healings; He was just an irreverent Sabbath breaker and worthy of death. They refused to see what was happening right before their eyes, because they were stuck in their religious traditions. In reality, Jesus was working in complete unity with the Father in Heaven, but because of their hardened hearts and their lack of spiritual understanding, they couldn't comprehend the truth of what was happening.

Just like this crippled man, there are people waiting for the release of God's healing, resurrection power to flow into their bodies, souls and spirits. The Father in heaven is looking for human vessels that are willing to connect the power of heaven to the needs of earth. But just as the Jews became enraged with Jesus for breaking their traditions, there will be some that will not understand the followers of Christ who walk in the power of God today.

Those who do not take kindly to the supernatural power of God may come against you, speak evil of you, persecute you, disown you and try to discredit you. They may falsely accuse you and even try to put you to death. These people are operating with the same hateful spirit that was prevalent back in Jesus' day. Therefore, you must understand that, if you're going to live a righteous, godly life and be a voice for the LORD, you will suffer persecution. It's part of our kingdom job description. We're warned about this in:

<u>2 Timothy 3:12</u> Yea, and all that will live godly in Christ Jesus shall suffer persecution.

Part 5 • *Loving God* in All You Do

Persecution *(G1377/G1169/G1249)* is the suffering of reverent and devout Christians. Sometimes, believers may even have to *flee*, due to being *pursued* by the ungodly that are opposed to worship and adoration of the LORD. Be that as it may, the persecuted can find comfort in:

<u>**Matthew 5:10-12**</u> *Blessed are they which are persecuted for righteousness' sake: for theirs is the kingdom of heaven. ¹¹Blessed are ye, when men shall revile you, and persecute you, and shall say all manner of evil against you falsely, for my sake. ¹²Rejoice, and be exceeding glad: for great is your reward in heaven: for so persecuted they the prophets which were before you.*

By respecting the Word of God above the traditions and words of men, believers in Christ (just like that crippled, impotent man) must be willing to rise up in trusting obedience. We must break free of any and all bondage that would keep us from the fullness of our destinies. We're to be strong in the LORD — operating in His power and ability as He sees fit.

We are the Priests and Ambassadors of the LORD, and we are appointed for such a time as this. People are looking for the reality of God, not the facades of religion. They're looking and waiting to see a version of Jesus with skin on. There are people in our generation that need what the LORD has deposited in us. We have what it takes to set them free, in Jesus' name. So rise up saints of God and walk! Go forth and deliver a stinging knockout punch to the devil and all that he represents.

Follow God's Direction

When Jesus physically ministered on the earth, everything He did was directed by the Father in Heaven. There were those who embraced the ministry of Christ, those who misunderstood it, those who rejected it and those who hated it. There were those who joyfully received Jesus as their Messiah, and there were those who detested Him and accused Him of working in partnership with the devil (Matthew 12:22-28). When Jesus healed the impotent man, the Jews sought to kill Him. When He declared Himself to be the Son of God, and thus equal to God, the Jews wanted to kill Him all the more, but Jesus would not be dissuaded (John 5:16-18). We read in:

<u>John 5:19</u> Then answered Jesus and said unto them, Verily, verily, I say unto you, The Son can do nothing of himself, but what he seeth the Father do: for what things soever he doeth, these also doeth the Son likewise.

There's a very important principle in this verse. Jesus never did anything without first consulting with the Father. He always had His spiritual eyes on the Father, and He only did what He saw the Father do. He allowed the Father to fulfill the will of Heaven, through His vessel of flesh in the earth. Jesus saw, and Jesus did. If He didn't see it, He didn't do it. Just as Jesus was dependent on the Father's direction and leadership, how much more should we be dependent on Him? Jesus not only did what He saw the Father do, but He also judged according to how the Father judged:

John 5:30 *I can of mine own self do nothing: as I hear, I judge: and my judgment is just; because I seek not mine own will, but the will of the Father which hath sent me.*

Even though Jesus was physically in the earth and the Father was in Heaven, Jesus and the Father were in such unity! When Jesus said, *"... as I hear, I judge..."* He wasn't talking about the local gossip. He was talking about what He heard coming from the heart of the Father in heaven. Jesus could hear the voice of the Father in His spirit.

You see, Jesus didn't come to earth with His own agendas. His focus was on pleasing the Father above all else. He came with no ulterior motives. He loved the Father so much that He was willing to lay down His own life and His own will. Jesus was (and is) the physical personification of God. His purpose was to fulfill the Father's perfect will in thought, word and deed. The perfect will of the Father was for Jesus to redeem mankind, so that none would be lost and all could receive everlasting life. In agreement and unity with the heart of the Father, Jesus was determined that all who desired to be reconciled to God, would have that opportunity.

He was single-minded in His resolve to fulfill the ordained purpose of the Father through His life (John 6:38-40).

Jesus spoke forth the decrees and promises of the Word of God. Thereby, sharing the mind and heart of God with the people and extending the Father's love and plan of reconciliation. As mankind responded to the message of eternal life, the Father's heart rejoiced. The unity between the heart of the Father and the obedience of Jesus was a demonstration of ardent, sacrificial love.

In review, Jesus saw and did all that the Father desired. He heard the commandments of the Father, spoke them forth and judged with righteous judgment. Jesus did not speak of Himself; He spoke concerning the things of the Father in Heaven, according to:

<u>John 12:49-50</u> For I have not spoken of myself; but the Father which sent me, He gave me a commandment, what I should say and what I should speak. ⁵⁰And I know that His commandment is life everlasting: whatsoever I speak therefore, even as the Father said unto me, so I speak.

As stated before, Jesus was the earthly personification of the Father in heaven — the embodiment of the life of God. As the words of life reverberated in His spirit, He revealed the heart of the Father, full of mercy and grace, toward all mankind. Jesus Christ, the Son of God — and no other — has the words and the gift of eternal life. They are found only in Him, because

Part 5 • *Loving God* in All You Do

there is no other name given under heaven whereby men must be saved. Salvation comes through Christ and Christ alone. He is the one and only true God from which eternal life flows. He is our life source. Therefore, those who have the Son, have life; those who have not the Son, do not have life (John 6:68, 17:3, 20:31; Acts 4:12; 1 John 2:25, 5:11-13, 20).

CHAPTER 18

THE RESTORATIVE VISION OF GOD

Jesus had an earthly, human lifespan of 33 years. He also had a kingdom mission to accomplish within that timeframe. Part of this mission was to reveal God's desire and vision to restore what has been lost.

We know that, as Jesus walked in perfect obedience and unity with the Heavenly Father, He was totally submitted Him. Jesus saw what the Father wanted Him to see; He heard what the Father wanted Him to hear; and He spoke what the Father wanted Him to speak. But He didn't stop there. Jesus also did the works that the Father wanted to do, according to:

John 9:4 *I must work the works of him that sent me, while it is day: the night cometh, when no man can work.*

Jesus was **sent** *(G3992)* from heaven to earth, to fulfill the works of Father God. Dispatched *on a temporary, but heavenly errand,* He came to *transmit* and *bestow* the works and proper order of God's kingdom in the earth. He conveyed this through practical experiences with mankind, as He taught, established and confirmed the ways of God by His works.

To **work** *(G2038) the* **works** *(G2014)* of God means that Jesus came *to toil* with an intended *effect.* He

Part 5 • *Loving God* in All You Do

actively *engaged* the Word of God and demonstrated the mighty acts of the Father. He fulfilled His *occupation* of *ministry* — His specific task, which had been assigned by the Father. Loving, submitted obedience was the mindset of Jesus and it's to be our mindset as well. Like Christ Jesus, we've also been dispatched by God to fulfill our ministry tasks and assignments for the Kingdom of Heaven.

In the context of John 9:4, Jesus was about to heal a man who was born blind. He spit on the ground and made clay of the spittle. Then He anointed the man's eyes with the clay and told him to go wash in the pool of Siloam. Obediently, the man went to the pool, washed and received his sight (John 9:1-7). Before this man encountered Jesus, he had no vision for his life, but the man's obedience released supernatural, restorative power into the deformed areas of his life.

However, not everybody was happy about this glorious manifestation of God's power to heal and deliver. As discussed in the previous chapter, in John 5:1-16, Jesus healed the man at the pool of Bethesda on the Sabbath day. Then, in the context of John 9:1-7, Jesus healed another man and, again, it was on the Sabbath day. This caused a religious uproar among some of the Pharisees. They claimed that Jesus could not be of God, because in their eyes, He had sinned against God by working on what was to be a day of rest. Others questioned how He could do such a miracle, if

He were a sinner? So, this miraculous work of restoring sight to the blind caused a division among the religious leaders (John 9:13-16).

These Pharisees completely missed the point. There was a man standing before them who was previously blind, and now, he could see. Did the work of God not bring great rest to this man's soul? He would never have to beg again; he could actually work to earn his own living. Was this not the hand of God's mercy extended to him? Ironically, after encountering Jesus, the blind man could see, but these Pharisees (who had seeing eyes) were completely blind to the reality and truth of the Messiah. Therefore, they rejected the miraculous works and power, which flowed through Him. They were more concerned about religious protocol, laws, rules and regulations, than with the power of God manifesting in their midst. Despite their religious, self-righteous ignorance, Jesus continued to do what He had been sent to do — fulfill the will of the Father.

The attitude of the Pharisees is a perfect picture of how a religious spirit operates. It is counterproductive to the Word and ways of God. While those who operate with such a spirit and mindset may, externally, observe the works of God, they'll never personally experience the power of God released in or through their own lives. Those who reject the things of God will never be able to possess them.

Part 5 • *Loving God* in All You Do

Always remember: When we allow the mind of Christ to operate in us, the LORD may have us say and do some things that others may not understand or appreciate. Because of the condition of their hearts or simply where their minds are, they may not be able to comprehend or support our actions. Even so, each of us must realize that we have been born with a God ordained purpose to accomplish.

As mentioned before, we cannot allow the opinions and opposition of others to hinder us from fulfilling our kingdom assignments. If we're to fulfill our destiny in Christ, we must love Him enough to press past all the mess the enemy tries to throw at us. Sometimes, in the process of fulfilling the work of God, we must 'toil' past the difficult places to accomplish the task He has set before us. As we tenaciously push forward in the midst of difficulty, we will begin to experience the mighty acts of God, as He works on our behalf. We must truly commit ourselves to the plans and purposes of God.

KNOW YOUR EARTHLY MINISTRY, BECOME HIS VESSEL

Jesus came to the final phase of His earthly ministry at 33 years of age. As He faced crucifixion, He experienced His most difficult assignment. In an act of great grace and mercy, Jesus — the innocent Lamb of God — died for the guilty, pathetic condition of mankind. Exemplifying John 9:4, while He hung on the cross and neared the completion of His earthly life, the ***day*** had passed, and the *night* had come. In the darkness of His last moments on the cross, Jesus said, *"...it is finished."* Then, He bowed His head and gave up the ghost (John 19:30). His work and toil had come to an end.

This is how Jesus — the light of the world — completed His earthly ministry (John 8:12, 9:5). Until the darkness of death came, He walked, talked and worked by the light of God's truth. Thankfully, His death was not the end of this glorious story (John 9:4). Just 3 days later, resurrection power overran and conquered all the power of death, hell and the grave. All mankind would be redeemed, if they would only believe.

Jesus Christ was our example of how we're to live this life. He taught us how to love God and man. As we take on the mind of Christ, we'll also take on His character. As we take on Christ's character, we are conformed to His image. As we're conformed to His image, we're entrusted with the miraculous power of God. As we're entrusted with His miraculous power, we become His vessels, thru whom He can manifest His mighty works. God, Himself, has called us to speak His truth and set the captives free in His name! Clearly, if you are to represent God well, you must:

- See what God wants you to see.
- Hear what God wants you to hear.
- Speak what God wants you to speak.
- Do what God wants you to do.

Part 5 • *Loving God* in All You Do

If you're the physical representation of God in the earth, as His Priest and Ambassador, you're ordained to stand before people and nations. Your calling is to boldly proclaim the truth of His Word, as well as fulfill His will in the earth. So, you have powerful purpose, precise direction, amazing grace and the favor of heaven working on your behalf. Fearlessly, go forth into your destiny, knowing that God is for you; nothing and nobody can, effectively, stop or stand against you (Psalm 27:1; Isaiah 54:17; Jeremiah 29:11-14; Luke 10:19).

When we truly know and love God, we'll want to tell others of His great goodness and mercy. We'll want to share the truth of His Word and invite others to experience the priceless gift of salvation, plus all that comes with it. We'll love what God loves and hate what God hates, and we'll desire Him above all things. Such is evidence of our love relationship with Him.

As we love the LORD, we realize who He is to us and who we are to Him. In the midst of our relating, we also realize that we're not only His beloved children, but we also find our healing, deliverance, protection, purpose, joy, destiny, peace, confidence, victory and success in Jesus Christ. How could we not want to share such amazing and wonderfully good news?

LOVERS OF GOD WALK IN LOVE
As believers seeing, hearing, speaking and doing the will of God, we must also walk in love toward others. Faith works by love, and love releases the power of

God to work (Galatians 5:6). Loving God and loving others keeps us in a spiritual safety check; we're not tempted to misuse or abuse what the LORD's entrusted to us. If we want the power of God to operate in our lives, then sacrificial love is the key that will turn on that power:

<u>Ephesians 5:1-2</u> Be ye therefore followers of God, as dear children; ²And walk in love, as Christ also hath loved us, and hath given himself for us an offering and a sacrifice to God for a sweetsmelling savour.

What do we see in this scripture about how we're to live? We see that we are to be **followers of God**. But what does this mean? First, let's state what it doesn't mean. There are many religious people who say they love, believe in, follow and obey God. Yet, their lives do not bear a true witness to their confessions, and their actions don't line up with the Word of God. Instead, they've rejected and cast aside the truth — the commands of God — and replaced it with the precepts and traditions of men. By doing so, they've exalted themselves as gods. Yet, they're no gods at all; Jesus called them hypocrites (Matthew 7:6-9)!! They're dead in their own deceptions, because they've disregarded and abandoned the Eternal, Holy LORD God Almighty — the one who created all things and breathed life into mortal man. Jesus summed it up best when he said, **"This people draweth nigh unto me with their mouth, and honoreth me with their lips; but their heart is far from me** (Matthew 15:8-9).

Part 5 • *Loving God* in All You Do

We're not to embrace the precepts of or pursue men's traditions. Rather, we're to live as followers of God! To be **followers** *(G3402/G3401)* of God means we're to *imitate* God. If you think about it, imitation is the greatest form of worship and adoration. Every human being will follow something or someone and will become like that which they love, adhere to and adore. In other words, we become like what we worship. The followers of God are to become like Him.

By design, human beings are created with a desire to follow. They will either follow God, or they will follow the false gods of this world. We see examples of false worship in today's popular culture and extreme celebrity adoration, as people imitate their favorite ideologies, public figures, movie stars, singers, musicians, etc. Herein lays the problem. If the person or thing being followed is ungodly, the followers are conforming themselves to someone or something they were never intended to be. Why would we want to be twisted, unholy, imitation copies of someone or something else, when God has created us to be His righteous, amazing, original masterpieces? As we are being perfected in Christ, we can't 'sell out' to any of the distorted, fleeting cultural ideals and perverted false gods of this world.

Mankind was created in God's image and likeness (Genesis 1:26). As imitators and followers of God, we understand that God is our Father, and we are His offspring — His dearly, beloved children. So, it isn't a strange thing that we would live and act in the same way as our Creator. It's His original intention! We're to be an awe-inspiring, glorious reflection of Him. As followers and imitators of God, we should willingly offer ourselves in sacrificial service to the LORD and to those He's called us to serve. We're to walk in love, demonstrating His affectionate benevolence.

In relation to giving sacrificially to others, God has entrusted us to be good stewards over the blessings that He has bestowed upon us. Therefore, we're to use godly discernment in our giving. Just because somebody makes a demand or feels they're entitled to our service or provision, doesn't mean we should just give it to them. Instead, we're to give as the Holy Spirit directs and the Word of God declares. If we're faithful to do this, all needs will be met and we'll reap a great harvest of blessing.

Remember, obedience brings the blessing. We know that we love others, when we are obeying the LORD; and when we obey the LORD, we are walking in love. As we walk in the love of Christ, we exhibit a sacrificial lifestyle of obedience to Him. This lifestyle becomes our sweet smelling fragrance of worship before the LORD.

Lovers of God Cease from Sin

As born-again, Holy Spirit empowered, overcoming believers with the mind of Christ, we're also to cease from sin!! There should be no fornication, adultery, perversion, lying, stealing, hatred, anger, bitterness, racism, jealousy, strife or any other flesh natured nastiness going on in our personal lives or in the Church of Jesus Christ. Jesus — our precious LORD and Savior — allowed His physical flesh to be ripped from His body on our behalf, so that we could be free from the lusts of our carnal, criminally rebellious, nature. God's Word is clear about this:

<u>1 Peter 4:1-2</u> Forasmuch then as Christ hath suffered for us in the flesh, arm yourselves likewise with the same mind: for he that hath suffered in the flesh hath ceased from sin; ²That he no longer should live the rest of his time in the flesh to the lusts of men, but to the will of God.

In every way, the agonizing pain and vexation that Christ **suffered** *(G3958)* was emotionally, mentally, physically and spiritually excruciating. Our Savior suffered as a consequence of our sin — our criminal acts against God. He paid the full, complete penalty for all the wrongs we've committed; He left nothing undone. The sacrifice of Christ is a finished work of redemption!

CRUCIFIED, RISEN & FILLED — VICTORY!

Jesus has broken the power of sin, and He was the only one qualified to do it. The human flesh that enshrouded the Lamb of God became the sacrificial offering for our sin, but the sin was not His own. In fact, all the wickedness of the past, present and future was laid upon Him.

God, the Father, judged Christ's fleshly offering and poured out His judgment and wrath upon it. The result was death to every part of His being. He, who was the fleshly manifestation of the just and righteous God, died for the unjust and unrighteous — you and me.

Yes, Jesus died in our place. Death touched Him, but could not retain Him. Three days later, by the power of the Spirit of God, He arose triumphantly from the dead (1 Peter 3:18). Jesus died as the sin offering, but rose again clothed in holiness, eternal righteousness, resurrection life and power. The shackles of sin, death, hell and the grave were shattered and left under the judgment of God. In exchange, freedom, deliverance, forgiveness and cleansing were made available to all those who would believe and trust in Him.

Even as Christ was crucified, every person who surrenders their life to Him is also crucified with Him (Galatians 2:20). When Jesus rose from the dead, all believers (past, present and future) rose with Him. He was the first born among many brethren, and we are the spiritual offspring of God; we have the seed of His Word sown into our hearts (Romans 8:29; Matthew 13:23; Acts 17:28-29).

When Jesus walked on this earth, He overcame all the temptations of sin, and when He died, He broke its power completely. He gave no opportunity for sin to operate in His life. Instead, He triumphed over it in victory. His victory is our victory!!

We're no longer slaves to sin. We've been freed from the power of the old flesh nature. Therefore, we're to no longer be controlled by the affections and lusts of that former lifestyle of death. Through the power of Christ, we choose to mortify and put to death all sinful habits, thoughts and actions that try to rise up within us (Colossians 3:3-5). Since we've taken on the nature of the new man and the works of Christ, we have ceased from the previous works — the nature of the old man — and choose to live and act accordingly.

In fact, as new creatures in Christ (i.e. brand new people, created in righteousness and true holiness), we're being renewed in the spirit of our minds (2 Corinthians 5:17; Ephesians 4:22-24; Colossians 3:10; Romans 6). We've been cleansed of all wickedness, and the life that we now live, we live by the faith of the Son of God, who loved us and gave Himself for us (Galatians 2:20). It's not about us; it's about Christ and what He did for us.

Think about this: If Jesus loved us so much to allow His body to be ripped and torn for us, is it asking too much for us to lay down the lusts of our flesh to fulfill the will of God? In all honesty, sometimes it's a struggle to do what we know is right. But, in reality, it's only a struggle when we want our own way instead of His. If we're to move in the power and anointing of God, we must allow our flesh nature to be crucified, stripped from us and put to death. We can't simultaneously have the mind of Christ and a fleshly, carnal mind filled with lust, stubbornness and rebellion. We're called to walk in our new life and triumph through Christ!

WE HAVE A COVENANT MIND

In Genesis 1:26-27, God created man (Adam and Eve) in His own image and likeness. Yet (in Genesis 3), they committed the first criminal act against God; they rebelled against His commandment to not eat the fruit of the tree of the knowledge of good and evil. They listened to the devil and took what was forbidden. As a result of their sin, they lost the light of God's glory in their lives, thereby, discovering their own nakedness for the first time.

Sin did not only strip mankind of the image, likeness and glory of God. It also separated them from their Creator. Since the time of the first sin, which was committed by our first parents, Adam and Eve, all mankind has been born with a sinful nature.

In the Old Testament, Israel (like Adam and Eve) failed to keep the commandments of God. Because of the sinful nature and rebellion that ruled their hearts, it was impossible for them to fully obey the commandments and, thus, the covenant of God. No matter how hard they tried to obey the law of God, if they offended in one point (mentally, emotionally, spiritually or physically), they were guilty of breaking all the law (James 2:10; Deuteronomy 27:26; Matthew 5:17-28; Galatians 3:10).

Part 5 • Loving God in All You Do

The law — the Old Testament covenant — was never meant to save mankind from their sins. Rather, it was a code of ethics meant to show us our desperate need for a Savior. Nobody can keep the law in their own human strength or religious self-righteousness. It was designed (through its impossibility to keep), to point mankind to Christ Jesus. He was (and is) the divine provision and solution for the sin problem, which is impossible for man to cure. Because man could never fully keep and fulfill the law of God, the LORD promised a new covenant to the house of Israel and Judah in:

Jeremiah 31:31-34 Behold, the days come, saith the LORD, that I will make a new covenant with the house of Israel, and with the house of Judah: ³²Not according to the covenant that I made with their fathers in the day that I took them by the hand to bring them out of the land of Egypt; which my covenant they brake, although I was an husband unto them, saith the LORD: ³³But this shall be the covenant that I will make with the house of Israel; After those days, saith the LORD, I will put my law in their inward parts, and write it in their hearts; and will be their God, and they shall be my people. ³⁴And they shall teach no more every man his neighbour, and every man his brother, saying, Know the LORD: for they shall all know me, from the least of them unto the greatest of them, saith the LORD: for I will forgive their iniquity, and I will remember their sin no more.

The New Testament also speaks of this new covenant. In Hebrews 8:1-7, Jesus is ordained and acknowledged as our high priest. He is set at the right hand of the throne of Majesty in Heaven. He is the minister of the sanctuary and the true tabernacle of God. As the Lamb of God, He's ordained to offer gifts. This is exactly what He did, when He offered His life and blood as a sin offering. Through His sacrifice, He settled all disputes and brought reconciliation between God and man. He is the mediator of a better covenant, established on better promises. These promises are available to all who believe and are called by His name. Hence, Jeremiah 31:31-34 is the foretold promise of its intended New Testament fulfillment in:

<u>Hebrews 8:7-13</u> *For if that first covenant had been faultless, then should no place have been sought for the second. ⁸For finding fault with them, he saith, Behold, the days come, saith the Lord, when I will make a new covenant with the house of Israel and with the house of Judah: ⁹Not according to the covenant that I made with their fathers in the day when I took them by the hand to lead them out of the land of Egypt; because they continued not in my covenant, and I regarded them not, saith the Lord. ¹⁰For this is the covenant that I will make with the house of Israel after*

Part 5 • *Loving God* in All You Do

those days, saith the Lord; I will put my laws into their mind, and write them in their hearts: and I will be to them a God, and they shall be to me a people: ¹¹*And they shall not teach every man his neighbour, and every man his brother, saying, Know the Lord: for all shall know me, from the least to the greatest.* ¹²*For I will be merciful to their unrighteousness, and their sins and their iniquities will I remember no more.* ¹³*In that he saith, A new covenant, he hath made the first old. Now that which decayeth and waxeth old is ready to vanish away.*

When the scripture says the first covenant was made **old** *(G3833/G3820)*, this means it has decayed and worn out. It's been declared *obsolete* (no longer used) or *antique*. It's become antiquated — continued from, resembling or adhering to the past. The law of the old covenant **waxeth old** *(G1095/G1094)*, which is defined as *senility* and *senescent*. In other words, it no longer functions in the strength it once had. Like a cell that's no longer able to divide and multiply, it's still alive, but incapable of bringing forth new life. The old covenant has become a thing of the past. Yet, it played a vital role in pointing us to faith, forgiveness and redemption, which is found only through Christ Jesus.

Those who have accepted Christ Jesus as their LORD and Savior have been delivered from the strength and curse of the law. After all, **Christ has redeemed us** *from the curse of the law, being made a curse for us: for it is written, Cursed is every one that hangeth on a tree: that the blessing of Abraham might come on the Gentiles through Jesus Christ; that we might receive the promise of the Spirit through faith* (Galatians 3:13). Jesus, through His finished work of atonement, has repealed the law and caused its penalty to disappear. It's been actively *disfigured*, destroyed and *consumed* by His sacrifice. In this manner, the old covenant has **vanished** *(G854/ G853/G852)*. The law of God is no longer written in stone; it's now written in the minds and hearts of His people. Though Israel has not fully come to recognize Christ as their Messiah, they will eventually see and understand the new covenant of God (Romans 11:26).

Jesus, in obedience to the Word and will of the Father, fulfilled all the law and the prophets; He brought us the new covenant. If we're living in Christ, we have also fulfilled all the law and the prophets through the law of love. The law of love is simply this: We love the LORD our God with all our heart, soul, mind and strength, and we love our neighbors as ourselves (Matthew 22:37-40; Romans 13:10). Of course, as mentioned so many times in this study, we cannot do this in our own power or outside of a relationship with the living God. The ability to fulfill His new covenant is the fruitful result of loving the LORD above all else.

Part 5 • *Loving God* in All You Do

A COVENANT OF LOVE
It's not hard to live the Christian life, if we understand the deep, abiding, committed covenant love that God has for us. If we can grasp the intensity of His eternal affection, we will fall passionately in love with Jesus. Our greatest joy and delight will be to love and serve Him. As we love and serve Him, we also love and serve others. That's the new covenant all wrapped up in one sweet bundle. So, the old covenant is passed away and the new covenant has come through Christ:

<u>Hebrews 10:8-17</u> Above when he said, Sacrifice and offering and burnt offerings and offering for sin thou wouldest not, neither hadst pleasure therein; which are offered by the law; ⁹Then said he, Lo, I (Jesus) come to do thy will, O God. He taketh away the first, that he may establish the second. ¹⁰By the which will we are sanctified through the offering of the body of Jesus Christ once for all. ¹¹And every priest standeth daily ministering and offering oftentimes the same sacrifices, which can never take away sins: ¹²But this man (Jesus), after he had offered one sacrifice for sins for ever, sat down on the right hand of God; ¹³From henceforth expecting till his enemies be made his footstool. ¹⁴For by one offering he hath perfected for ever them that are sanctified. ¹⁵Whereof the Holy Ghost also is a witness to us: for after that he had said before, ¹⁶This is the covenant that I will make with them after those

days, saith the Lord, I will put my laws into their hearts, and in their minds will I write them; ⁷And their sins and iniquities will I remember no more.
(also see Jeremiah 31:33-34; Romans 11:27)

The old covenant had its purpose, but our sins are no longer covered by the blood of bulls and goats or the ceremony of burnt offerings. Jesus Christ offered Himself and His blood, once and for all, as the final sacrifice to wash away all sin. It's through His righteousness that we are now sanctified and made clean. All who believe in this new covenant and follow after Jesus Christ are forgiven. The curse of sin has been stripped of its authority and washed away, by the power of the precious blood of Jesus!

In relation to God's covenant with His people, I love what Hebrews 10:17 says. God is not forgetful, but He has made a conscious decision to remove all memory of our *moral errors,* offenses, trespasses, failures and faults from His mind. Every *illegal* act, every form of *wickedness,* all unrighteousness and every *violation* or transgression of God's law, from Adam to the end of time, has been dealt with through the consecrated blood of Christ (Romans 5). Only those who refuse to be cleansed by His blood (by believing in Him) will suffer the consequences of their sin (Mark 3:29). Isn't it glorious that He declares how He will no longer remember our **sins** *(G266/G264)* or **iniquities** *(G458/G459)*?

Part 5 • *Loving God* in All You Do

In our spirits, we're to embrace the truth that God, the Father, has already judged the sins of mankind, by laying the full punishment and judgment for sin upon Jesus Christ, the sacrificial Lamb of God. Therefore, anyone who puts their faith and trust in the atoning work of Christ will never have to stand before God for the judgment of their sins. After all, their offenses against God no longer exist. From the moment we repent of our sin and turn to Christ for salvation, God has no further remembrance of our former wickedness. How amazing is that?!! We have been justified, made righteous and set free in Christ!

Through the great grace, mercy and forgiveness of God, there are no hidden skeletons in the closet and no lurking scandals to torment us. The LORD is not reserving the vilest sins of our past to hold over our heads. When Jesus poured out His blood for our cleansing, it was a complete work of forgiveness. This forgiveness is the greatest blessing, and it's called salvation by grace through Christ (Ephesians 2:5-8)! This is the glory of being in a new covenant relationship with the only true and living God. He has cleansed us so perfectly, there's not even a lingering residue of the stench of our former sins, but only the fragrance of worship!

In Hebrews 10:16, the LORD says, **"This is the covenant that I will make with them after those days, saith the LORD, I will put my law into their hearts, and** *in their minds will I write them."* Interestingly, the phrase *"put (G1325) my laws (G3551) in their hearts (G2588)"* has specific meaning. It means that the LORD is committed *to give*, bring forth and powerfully minister the *principles* of the *Gospel*, as He feeds His *prescriptive* word into the *middle* or center of our beings. This includes our *thoughts, feelings* and even the broken places in our hearts. Furthermore, for God to **write (G1924/G1909/G1125)** His laws into our **minds (G1271)** is to *physically* or *mentally inscribe* and *distribute* them into our *deep thoughts* as a *superimposition*. This allows every core *exercise* of our minds, and even our mental *disposition*, to be covered by the Word of the LORD. God desires to, intimately, write His covenant love letter on the inside of us as a treasure; what a gift!

God's new **covenant (G1242/G1303/G1223/G5087)** is His eternal *contract* or *will*. It's *the channel* through which He's chosen *to place* or *dispose* the new knowledge and understanding of our relationship with Him. It's also through this covenant that He has gifted us with His Holy Spirit. It's His Spirit and the transformational, resurrection power of God that gives us a new heart of tenderness toward Him, as well as a willing mind. Ultimately, it's through the new covenant that our now soft, pliable hearts and minds are able to receive wisdom and understanding from the LORD.

By God's grace, every true believer can obtain a covenant heart and mind. He always equips us with what's needed. In fact, by receiving the wondrous gifts of His grace and mercy upon our lives, we can also receive the deeper truths of His anointed Word. Those whose hearts and minds are in unity with the LORD, will experience a godly shift in their mental processes. This Holy Spirit-inspired shift causes our words, thoughts, feelings, imaginations, deeds and plans to move into another level of understanding, love and obedience to the LORD. As a result of this new level of relationship, the LORD ushers us into a divine, supernatural existence — dwelling in the glorious presence and revelation of God!

CHAPTER 19

LOVING GOD = LIVING BEYOND RELIGION

If a person is to love the LORD with all their heart, soul, mind, strength and might, they must get past a religious mindset. Unfortunately, many people have experienced religion, but have never known the true and living God on a personal level. The LORD never called us to be religious. He's called us (and made provision for us) to experience an intimate, eternal relationship with Him. Furthermore, the LORD is not impressed with (albeit sincere) functions and sacrifices, if we've not allowed Him to fully possess our hearts.

When I refer to a religious mindset, I'm referring to the status quo or expected norm for nominal worship, which has been determined by man. I'm referring to the practice of rituals void of personal relationship between the 'worshipper' and the one being worshipped. I'm talking about attending church services (whether it be once a week or twice a year), as though showing up in the church building is either doing God a favor or completing a kind of penance timecard. I'm talking about a mindset that entertains and is content with empty religious functions, which have no life in them.

As we begin the final chapter of our study, let's revisit one of our key verses in context. In this passage, we see that Jesus also ministered to the religious leaders of His day about the importance of love and right

Part 5 • *Loving God* in All You Do

relationships. There is much we can glean from this conversation in:

Mark 12:28-33 *And one of the scribes came, and having heard them [the Sadducees and Jesus] reasoning together, and perceiving that he [Jesus] had answered them well, asked him, Which is the first commandment of all?* [29]*And Jesus answered him, The first of all the commandments is, Hear, O Israel; The Lord our God is one Lord:* [30]*And thou shalt love the Lord thy God with all thy heart, and with all thy soul, and with all thy mind, and with all thy strength: this is the first commandment.* [31]*And the second is like, namely this, Thou shalt love thy neighbour as thyself. There is none other commandment greater than these.* [32]*And the scribe said unto him, Well, Master, thou hast said the truth: for there is one God; and there is none other but he:* [33]*And to love him with all the heart, and with all the understanding, and with all the soul, and with all the strength, and to love his neighbour as himself, is more than all whole burnt offerings and sacrifices.*

It's interesting that a scribe (who should have known the answer to his own question) was asking Jesus to tell him which commandment was the greatest. I find it hard to believe that a professionally trained scribe wouldn't have known the answer. To love the LORD with all one's heart, soul, mind and strength is, obviously, the greatest command in the entire Kingdom of God.

After all, if a person is ignorant of or refuses to obey this first command of God, they'll not be able to obey any of the other commands of God, nor will they be able to live in His Kingdom. Could it be possible that this scribe is an example of how a person can be involved in their religious activities and functions, yet still miss the whole point of truly loving God as their top priority?

When Jesus responded, He not only gave the scribe the first and greatest commandment, but He included the second greatest command as well. Why? Could it be that the scribe and the religious leaders were not loving the people or extending God's compassion and mercy to them? Love, or the lack of it, is reflected in how we honor or dishonor God and those He has created in His image and likeness. In truth, it's impossible to love God without extending that love to others. Love is the motivation behind every positive emotion and respectful action. It boils down to this: love God with everything in you; and love and treat your neighbor, as you would love and treat yourself. If people would just fulfill these two commands, our world would be a totally different place to live.

Instead, because of their rebellion against God, those who love the wickedness of sin have created a criminally laden world environment that is spinning out of control. If people would simply follow God's commands, there would be no theft, murders, adultery, fornication, perversion, covetousness, deception, war,

Part 5 • *Loving God* in All You Do

fighting, idolatry or selfishness. There would be no need for the military, police departments, jails, prisons, private investigators, lawyers, Judges, courts of law or death sentences. We would not need nuclear warheads, national defense or armies. We would not be tempted to politicize and legislate welfare, government mandated healthcare or high taxes. Instead, people would always respond to the needs of their family, friends and neighbors. We also would not need locked doors, home security systems, weapons of self-defense or guard dogs. All these things are the result of people not loving God or not loving and treating others, as they would want to be loved and treated. And let's be reminded that people can't love or fully obey God's commands without His Holy Spirit working within them. Just the same, a society will reap its rewards or destruction based on how its citizen's do or do not obey the Word of the LORD.

The Kingdom of God and the people of God operate in a different spirit than the world. They exhibit a higher, holy and God-inspired way of living. It goes beyond the rote rituals of religion and steps into the spiritual reality of living out the principles of God's Word in all we think, say and do. The very Spirit of God and His miraculous nature manifests in our lives, when we hear, receive and obey the LORD and His Word.

Jesus said in Mark 12:29, "... **Hear O Israel; the Lord our God is one Lord...**" Let's consider this verse.

To ***hear*** *(G191)* includes hearing *in various tenses*. Throughout the Greek scripture, this word is rendered as: *give audience* and allow a verbal message to *come to the ears; be noised* abroad or *reported, so* that it might be hearkened unto and given proper attention. In view of this, hearing is a conscious decision to engage the mind to *understand* what's being declared.

To absorb the sounds of words, but not receive or internalize them with a response, is the same as not hearing (and, thus, not receiving) what is being spoken. Listening demands a response! Concerning the Word of God, once it is heard and understood, there should be a response from the heart. Jesus wanted the people (including the religious leaders of his day and mankind throughout history) to actively hear, understand and respond to His Word. After all, He manifested in the earth as the Word of God made flesh (John1:1, 14). The Anointed One — Jesus Christ — desires for people to understand, internalize and respond to Him!

Still, how many times do people 'go to church' and hear the Word of God released into the atmosphere, but aren't truly attentive to what is taught? How often do people make an effort to review or study a lesson for themselves? When the Word of the LORD is released, we need to give it our full attention; take it into our spirit; and let it become a part of us. If we don't heed the Word of the LORD, we are dishonoring Him and missing out on the blessing of His covenant promises.

Part 5 • *Loving God* in All You Do

LIVING BEYOND SELF

When Jesus said in Mark 12:29, "*...**the Lord our God** (G2316) **is one Lord** (G2962)*" He wasn't being simple or redundant. He was saying that the God of Abraham, Isaac and Jacob is truly the only *supreme Divinity* and *magistrate;* He's to be respected as the *controller* of all things, because He has dominion, *supremacy and is the supreme* and ultimate *authority.* Without a doubt, He was saying that the LORD is the only God. As we have seen throughout this book and in scripture, Israel had a terrible history of idolatry. Jesus wanted them to understand; they were not to be chasing after false gods. Rather, they were to pursue, only, the one true God. This is still relevant for us today. There is one God – Yahweh – and we're to serve Him and Him alone.

I want to share a brief history on the origin of Israel. The natural nation of Israel is genetically related to the descendants of Jacob — who was the son of Isaac, who was the son of Abraham (who was the Father of the faith, because God made an eternal covenant with Him). Jacob's name meant 'heel catcher' and he had a conniving, shrewd nature. Through manipulation and deception, he obtained the birthright and blessing of his firstborn brother Esau. Esau was so angry about losing his birthright and blessing to Jacob's conniving ways, he wanted to kill him. So, Jacob fled from Esau's wrath (Genesis 25 & 27). Because of his character issues, Jacob endured many struggles, but eventually, the LORD gave him a new name; he was called Israel.

Isaac and Rebecca sent Jacob to the home of his mother's brother — his uncle Laban. Jacob remained with his uncle for twenty years and prosperously tended his flocks. In addition, Jacob married Laban's daughters (Leah and Rachel) and began to father what would, in time, become the twelve tribes of Israel (Genesis 28:1-2, Genesis 29-30).

Although Jacob was faithful to serve his father-in-law, Laban repeatedly cheated him out of his proper wages (Genesis 31:38). Contentions arose between the sons of Laban and Jacob. So, Jacob took his wives, children and flocks, and he left the household of Laban.

As Jacob's family was on their way to establish a home and life of their own, Jacob learned that his brother Esau was pursuing him with the intention of killing him. That night, Jacob divided his family; he left Leah with her children in one location and Rachel with her children in another. During the night, Jacob had a face-to-face encounter with the LORD and physically wrestled with Him all night long (Genesis 32). It's certainly interesting how it was Jacob's fear of Esau that provided the setting for a divine encounter.

As morning came, Jacob was still wrestling the angel; in fact, before he would release the angel, Jacob demanded a blessing from the LORD. When the angel saw that Jacob was prevailing against him, he touched the hollow of Jacob's thigh and his thigh went out of joint while they wrestled. Though the

Part 5 • *Loving God* in All You Do

angel's touch weakened Jacob's strength, he was still very persistent and determined to receive a blessing. Then, the angel of the LORD demanded that Jacob confess his name and his nature (as derived from his name). **Jacob** *(H3290/H6117) — the heel-catcher, the supplanter* — confessed and, in that moment, the angel of the LORD gave him the new name, Israel.

With this new name, God also gave Israel a new vision for his life. When we search out the meaning of the name **Israel** *(H3478/H8280/H410)*, we find something very interesting. **Israel** is defined as *he will rule as God* with power *to prevail* as a prince, by the *strength* and *might* of *Almighty* God. Just as Jacob (Israel) wrestled with God and received strength and authority to rule and prevail as a prince with God, even so, all who are called to kingdom leadership will also go through their time of wrestling and empowerment with the LORD. The wrestling takes place when we say we want Him, but we also want our own way. We may have wrestled all through the dark night season, trying to obtain what we felt we were entitled to receive. Yet, when the LORD puts his finger on our strength and brings us to a place of brokenness and weakness, then, we are ready to surrender and submit to His authority. Only then, are we ready to rule as heirs with God! Like Israel, when the LORD touches us, our nature and our purpose are changed forever.

Chapter 19 • Loving God = Living Beyond Religion

It's only when we step down from the throne of our life (and allow the LORD to take His rightful place), that we become qualified to receive what He has intended for us. Through humble submission, our ambitions and focus in life make a supernatural shift from the things of this world, to the things of God. As our desires begin to change, His vision for our lives becomes clearer. We leave behind the old life of seeking our own self-fulfillment, and we step into the new Spirit-led life of loving and experiencing God. We must come to a place of fully surrendering and submitting ourselves to Him, declaring from a truly dedicated heart and life, "Not my will, but thine be done!" In that moment, we catch the revelation and express the truth: There is a God who is greater and wiser than we are.

Submission brings us to a sweet place in the LORD. Once we realize He holds our lives in His hands and sees everything pertaining to us, from beginning to end, we experience His peace and joy in our lives. We see Him (and Him alone) as our source of wisdom, strength and strong support. He is our provider, and He cares for our every need. As we walk with Him, He ushers us into our divine purpose and gives us the desires of our hearts (since His desire has also become ours); this is a significant and sweet place, indeed.

Living in His Kingdom
Today, all followers of Christ are intricately tied into the lineage of Abraham, Isaac and Jacob; spiritually,

we are grafted in through faith. There's also still a natural lineage that flowed from Abraham to Isaac, then to Jacob and through the 12 tribes of Israel. In due time, Mary — the chosen mother of Jesus — would descend from the tribe of Judah. She would conceive of the Holy Ghost and bring forth Christ Jesus — the spiritual seed of God. He was the first born of many brethren. All who trust in Him for Salvation have become the offspring of God and the spiritual seed of Abraham. Therefore, all who would descend from Abraham's lineage (whether naturally or spiritually) are also called to a royal Kingdom lineage.

Just as there's a natural nation of Israel, there's also a spiritual Israel. Spiritual Israel is made up of all Jews and Gentiles who believe and put their trust and faith in Jesus Christ as their LORD and Savior. Remember, those who make up this spiritual nation are a chosen generation, a royal priesthood, a holy nation and a peculiar people. The people of God are called to be His Kings, Priests and Ambassadors in the Kingdom. We're to boldly proclaim the desire of our heavenly King in the earthly realms. Yet, we are seated in heavenly places, ruling and reigning with Christ. Our intended purpose is to rule as Almighty God (in compliance with His Word) and prevail by His power and might (1 Peter 2:9; Revelation 1:6, 5:10; Ephesians 1:3, 2:6, 3:10, 6:20; 2 Corinthians 5:20).

The LORD graciously walks with us in our earthly Kingdom purpose. By His Spirit, He empowers us to carry out the business of Kingdom government, administration, justice, protection, welfare and spiritual warfare over our homes, neighborhoods, cities, states, regions and nations of the earth. As we learn His ways, He entrusts us with more authority and responsibility.

The LORD has also given us mighty spiritual weapons. Through Him, we're able to abolish strong holds and cast down imaginations, as well as every high thing that exalts itself against the knowledge of God. We have the power to bring every one of our thoughts into obedience with Christ and into alignment with the Word and will of God for our lives. We victoriously prevail over and pull down all principalities, powers, rulers of darkness and spiritual wickedness in high places (Ephesians 6:12, 2 Corinthians 10:3-5).

Proportionally, the power of God is released based on our relationship with Him. In zealous love, we're to boldly, tenaciously and fervently fasten ourselves (along with all our hopes, dreams and desires) upon Him. When we love the LORD in this way, we will choose to lay our lives down for Him. As submitted lovers, laying down our lives for our Beloved King, we will experience His presence, His amazing grace and the impartation of His power working in and through our lives. As we truly love the LORD our God with our entire heart, soul, mind and strength, and love our neighbors as ourselves, we're qualified to experience the fullness of who He is.

SUMMARY OF LOVING GOD IN ALL YOU DO

In Chapter 15, we studied the mind (or mindset) of Christ — what it looks like from a spiritual perspective and how it functions. A person operating in the mind of Christ is operating in agreement with the Word of God and is led by the Spirit of God. They're confident in who they are in God's Kingdom and are content to humbly serve. They're not self-seeking and have no need to exalt their own reputation. Rather, they take on the yoke of Christ and find their rest in Him. As believers, we are commanded to have the mind of Christ and to abide in Him.

In Chapter 16, we learned the importance of loving God through serving Him and, thus, serving others. If we want true wisdom and understanding, we must abide in the presence of the LORD and learn of Him. Jesus was the greatest servant who ever lived, so He qualifies as the best role model. To be an effective minister, we must be willing to do the menial and mundane tasks, as well as serve in positions of spiritual leadership. Jesus demonstrated this when He washed His disciples feet, healed the sick, cast out devils, turned the water into wine, multiplied loaves and fish, gave encouraging words and prayed for His disciples.

Jesus went about continuously doing good works. The Greek definition for the phrase 'good works,' means to do the work of a philanthropist. Like Jesus, the Apostle Paul ministered among the weak. He took

Part 5 • *Loving God* in All You Do

care of his own needs, as well as those around Him. Jesus and Paul both did the work of a philanthropist, laboring to assist others. Also, whatever we do in word or deed, we're to do it heartily in the name of the LORD Jesus. We're called to be Kingdom builders and, like Jesus, we can only fulfill that role by serving well.

In Chapter 17, we learned that loving God through self-denial is to love Him sacrificially — laying down our desires to fulfill His. Each of us must patiently run the race that is set before us. When it seems that life is an endurance test, we must learn to see beyond our current circumstances to the joy that is also set before us. Like Jesus, we all need to come to the place of decision where we can say to the Father in Heaven, 'Not my will, but thine be done.' The process of surrender and obedience develops godly character and brings us into spiritual maturity.

In Chapter 18, we studied how the works of God bring forth restoration in our lives. Where there's no vision, sight is restored, and the crippled are healed, as they rise up and walk in the power of God. Though we serve a miracle working God, there will be those who will never accept Him. Their unbelief, hardness of heart and faithlessness cause the blessings of God to be withheld from them. For those who are willing to receive from and obey the LORD, they shall receive His blessings.

We also touched on the pharisaical spirit of religion, which seeks to destroy or discredit the works of God and His servants. Of course, if we are God's Priests and Ambassadors, we're not to have a hypocritical, pharisaical spirit. We're not to be legalistically tied up in trying to keep the impossible standards of the Old Testament. Christ has redeemed us from the curse of the Law. Empowered with His truth, we need not be swayed or dismayed by religion. Regardless of what others may think, say or do against us, each of us has an assignment from the LORD; and we have a limited timeframe in which we're to fulfill it.

Therefore, our joyful response is to wholeheartedly seek the LORD God Almighty, that we would be able to see, hear, speak and fulfill His will. The LORD has written His new covenant — His will — in the hearts and minds of those of us who love Him, and He has sealed us with His Holy Spirit, thereby, marking us as His own. As we fulfill His will, our lives become a sweet smelling savor of sacrificial worship — a gift offered up to our Beloved King and God, who is our source of unending truth, love, life and joy.

In Chapter 19, we discovered that loving God requires us to live beyond a religious, self-righteous, works-oriented mindset, leaving behind its dull, lifeless platitudes. We must do this, if we're to sustain a loving, life-filled relationship with our Creator. Religion, based on man's limited understanding and void of the

Part 5 • Loving God in All You Do

supernatural power of God, builds barriers that restrict our love relationships with God and man.

When the LORD Jesus Christ told us to love God and love our neighbor as ourselves, He was establishing the love focus of the Kingdom of God. As Kingdom people, we serve one LORD — the Supreme Authority and Divinity over all things. He has called us to be Kings, Priests and Ambassadors. In Christ, we are a people of love and destiny, and we are to impact the world around us!

In fact, as spiritual warriors and bridal lovers of the King, we're armed with spiritual weapons to rule over principalities, powers, rulers of darkness and spiritual wickedness in high places. We're ordained to take authority over all that is not like God. Using our authority and spiritual weapons should be a commonplace practice.

But, more importantly (and above all else), we are called of God to be a holy, living sacrifice. Being fully submitted, we're to lay down our lives before the LORD. This is the true purpose and evidence of Loving God: To fulfill His Word and His will, as surrendered lovers.

Loving God

❧ Final Words from the Apostle ☙

In closing, I hope that your journey through this book has both encouraged and challenged you to step into a deeper level of intimate love with the LORD. He is your heavenly Bridegroom and He loved you enough to die for you. His immeasurable, infinite, everlasting, undying and passionate love freely extends toward you. All you have to do is reach out, receive it, and give your life entirely to Him. Go from glory to glory!

I earnestly pray that you will lay aside every hindrance that would keep you from experiencing the fullness of His abundant grace, mercy and power from operating in your life. I exhort you to rise up and release yourself from everything that has tried to keep you bound in captivity. Shake off the shackles of living below your God-ordained calling and purpose.

Finally, as you continue through life, I trust that the teachings of this book will arise in your mind to inspire you and kindle your confidence to enter into greater faith and freedom. Beloved, embrace the truth that you can dwell in the power and presence of God every day of your life; let it become your reality. In fact, I dare you to discover the awesome beauty of our God and who He has called you to be, as you truly embrace worship as your personal lifestyle.

Apostle Linda Mahoney

www.ingramcontent.com/pod-product-compliance
Lightning Source LLC
Chambersburg PA
CBHW060358230426
43663CB00008B/1307